ROBOT GHOSTS
WIRED DREAMS

See page 261 for information on previously published material in this book.

Published by the University of Minnesota Press
111 Third Avenue South, Suite 290
Minneapolis, MN 55401-2520
http://www.upress.umn.edu

Library of Congress Cataloging-in-Publication Data

Robot ghosts and wired dreams : Japanese science fiction from origins to anime / Christopher Bolton, Istvan Csicsery-Ronay Jr., and Takayuki Tatsumi, editors.
    p.   cm.
  Includes index.
  ISBN: 978-0-8166-4973-0 (hc : alk. paper)
  ISBN-10: 0-8166-4973-1 (hc : alk. paper)
  ISBN: 978-0-8166-4974-7 (pb : alk. paper)
  ISBN-10: 0-8166-4974-X (pb : alk. paper)
  1. Science fiction, Japanese — History and criticism.   I. Bolton, Christopher.
  II. Csicsery-Ronay, Istvan, Jr.   III. Tatsumi, Takayuki, 1955–
  PL747.57.S3R63   2007
  895.6'30876209 — dc22   2007027032

Printed in the United States of America on acid-free paper

The University of Minnesota is an equal-opportunity educator and employer.

12   11   10   09   08   07   10   9   8   7   6   5   4   3   2   1

CONTENTS

Introduction. Robot Ghosts and Wired Dreams
Japanese Science Fiction from Origins to Anime

Christopher Bolton, Istvan Csicsery-Ronay Jr., and Takayuki Tatsumi

Since the end of World War II, Japanese science fiction has been as much a world cultural presence as U.S. science fiction was after World War I, and for many of the same reasons. But Japanese science fiction did not arrive on the world scene by way of prose literature. The translation of Japanese prose science fiction into English was extremely limited through the end of the twentieth century; the situation was somewhat better for languages like French and Russian, but by and large Japanese science fiction entered global culture through new media. Like the pulp magazines that made science fiction a shaping genre of twentieth-century popular culture, Japanese science fiction has been distributed throughout the world in the most popular new communications technologies — television, videocassettes, arcade games, personal computers, and game consoles. These new media, moreover, have usually been introduced as vehicles for science fiction–themed spectacles that reinforce their futuristic aura. The marriage of medium and techno-scientific mythmaking has allowed Japanese science fiction filmmakers, game designers, animators, and manga artists to operate under the radar of cultural control exerted by American and European entertainment monopolies, and to develop themes, stories, and effects that synthesize the attitudes of their primary constituency: global youth culture.

The producers of Japanese science fiction have always been familiar with their Western counterparts, and in new media they have often had an eye on Western markets. As a result, Japanese science fiction texts have frequently been double coded, evoking Japanese national concerns and popular myths while resonating strongly with foreign audiences. This has been true for many parts of North America and Europe, but we can consider the specific history of the United States as a representative (if not universal) case.

The breakthrough works of global Japanese science fiction were the *kaijū eiga* — the big monster movies produced by Japanese studios, beginning with *Gojira* in 1954. These were reinvented by American producers, renamed (*Gojira* became *Godzilla, King of the Monsters!*), and remixed to satisfy American tastes. In the United States, the Japanese monster film became the archetype for cheap, cheesy disaster movies because of the sort of cultural and technological interference patterns that still characterize the reception of Japanese science fiction in North America today. In many cases, the original films' anamorphic wide-screen photography, which lent images greater scale and depth when properly projected, was reduced for American showings to a smaller format; the original stereophonic soundtracks (among the most technically innovative and musically interesting in the medium at the time) were rerecorded and rearranged; and additional scenes with American actors, shot on different screen ratios, were added, along with woeful dubbing. The American versions inevitably stripped out the stories' popular mythological resonances, their evocation of Japanese theater, and the imaginary management of postwar collective emotions.[1]

Even so, Japanese monster films gained immense popularity in the 1960s and 1970s, through a medium they had not been made for: television. The films came cheap; U.S. stations bought them for programs targeting children and teenagers. For this audience, the films' relative innocence and intimacy provided a pleasure different from the techno-moralistic paranoia of cold war American science fiction. The monsters had names and legendary provenance, in contrast with the absolutely othered menaces of *The Thing* (1951), *Them!* (1954), and *It!* (1966). They were not reducible to simplistic moral dualisms.[2]

The *kaijū eiga*'s affection for monsters was paralleled by a love of robots, particularly in Japanese comics, or manga, and animation, or anime. Tezuka Osamu's Tetsuwan Atomu (Astro Boy) appeared on Japanese and American televisions in 1963 and was the first of many friendly Japanese robots that contrasted with the phobic images of dehumanization dominating Western science fiction.[3] Cute anime automatons vitalized the robotic toys that Japan exported in large quantities in the postwar years, which has led one scholar to claim that "the American consumption of toy robots may have more to do with the Japanese presence in science fiction than does their success in industrial robotics."[4] Affectionate ambivalence has extended to each new step in the process of imagining virtual creatures, from boy robots to the superrobots of the 1970s, the "real robots" of the 1980s, the cyborgs of the 1990s, and the virtual pocket creatures that currently dominate children's television programming in both Japan and the United States.

The rise of Japanese economic power in the 1970s and relative economic decline in the United States led to an ambivalent fascination with Japanese attitudes toward development — the synthesis of robotic industrialization, neofeudal corporate culture, and the enthusiastic acceptance of new communication and simulation technologies in daily life. As Japanese investment and market share leaped worldwide, the future appeared to be saturated with Japanese elements, a Western perception distilled in *Blade Runner*'s enormously influential image of a futuristic Los Angeles that resembled Tokyo. Ridley Scott's 1982 film was the forerunner of japonaiserie in cyberpunk novels like William Gibson's *Neuromancer* (1984) and *Idoru* (1996), which took an adrenalized dreamscape Japan as their model for the future. Although he had little firsthand knowledge of the Japanese context, Gibson understood the science-fictional ramifications of the restless mixing of fashions and personal technologies conveyed in the image of the *shinjinrui* — the "new human" Japanese youth culture of the time. These interests ranged from techno-mystical cults to the adulation of "virtual idols" like Date Kyōko, a computer-generated simulacrum of a singer treated by her fans as a living rock star.[5]

Cyberpunk, which was often derided by Western science fiction critics for being cartoonish, immediately appealed to a Japanese sensibility that had been nurtured on science fiction manga and Japanese animation. The results were texts that synthesized the main themes of both Japanese and Western postmodernist science fiction — the breakdown of ontological boundaries, pervasive virtualization, the political control of reality — as well as their artistic media. Ōtomo Katsuhiro's *Akira* (which had begun its 2,200-page manga serialization in 1982) was released as an anime film in 1988 and subsequently shown to great acclaim in art-house theaters worldwide. Together with Oshii Mamoru's *Ghost in the Shell* (1995), *Akira* represented a fusion of contemporary art — anime, manga, cinema, digital graphics, and cyberpunk narrative — with contemporary themes, addressed to a global audience. The effects of this new "global" Japanese science fiction continue to propagate, in products from *The Matrix* (whose creators avow their debt to anime and manga), to multicultural media-remixes like Sakaguchi Hironobu's digital cinema based on the *Final Fantasy* video games.[6]

With its command of commercial children's culture, much of it through science-fictional scenarios and toys, and its model of media mix and technological hypersociality, Japan remains both a model of techno-futuristic transformation of the real world and a source of its meaning-giving science fictions.[7]

For Western audiences, this dominance of Japanese visual science fiction has eclipsed the fact that Japan also has a vibrant tradition of prose science fiction. The present volume seeks to remedy that blind spot with a broad treatment of science fiction — one that reveals the prose tradition and links it with the anime boom to present a more-textured picture of science fiction than the one suggested by either medium alone.

The work collected here shows how anime uses fantastic contexts and innovative visual grammar to provocatively address issues of nationalism, gender, and language. But these conclusions immediately suggest other questions. What was the discourse of nationalism in postwar fantasy literature and film — the works that inspired the first generation of anime creators? How did Japanese authors address the notion of the mechanical body in the 1930s — a time when the Czech word *robot* was just entering the Japanese (and worldwide) vocabulary and still decades before anime's love affair with the cyborg? And from the 1980s onward, as *shōjo* comics and anime for and about young women conducted radical experiments in gender bending, what was being written by contemporary feminist science fiction authors, some of whom were also manga artists themselves? Or to reverse these questions, how did anime recast and reinvigorate science fiction's familiar concerns? These are some of the queries this book seeks to answer by tracing a broader history of Japanese science fiction from its origins to anime and beyond.

The book's first half deals with Japanese prose science fiction; the second, with animation. Taken together, they examine a wide range of texts — from the idiosyncratic interwar detective fiction of Yumeno Kyūsaku to the cross-culturally produced and marketed film and video game franchise *Final Fantasy*. In these critical chapters, Japan scholars and leading Japanese critics range over much of the history of Japanese science fiction — not just its incarnation in different media but its beginnings, development, and future directions; its major schools and authors; and its national origins and relationship to Western genres.

Prose Science Fiction in Japan

American prose science fiction took more than thirty years to reach the zenith of its classical development in the 1950s, and only then saw the rise of New Wave speculative fiction in the 1960s and cyberpunk authors like Gibson in the 1980s. Japanese prose science fiction developed in the sixties and ran through the great paradigm shifts between outer space, inner space, and cyberspace much more quickly. To critics and readers in Japan, therefore, science fiction seems to have evolved in the Eliotic sense, within a simultaneous order, with hard-core science fiction, speculative fiction, fantasy, and monster narratives like *Godzilla* enjoying a peaceful symbiosis. From its beginnings, Japanese science fiction has incorporated the various science fiction traditions synchronically rather than diachronically, producing an extraordinary range of *magna opera*.

To understand the ahistorical evolution of Japanese science fiction, we can begin by historicizing it in the conventional manner. But we find that from the beginning Japanese prose science fiction develops in complex communication with other cultures, other media, and other genres. Any outline of Japanese prose science fiction must recognize that its "origin" is not unitary and its borders are fractally complex.[8]

Many critics locate the precursor or embryonic prototype of Japanese science fiction in the "irregular detective fiction" of the 1930s, a genre treated in Miri Nakamura's essay on Yumeno. Nakamura gives us one of the first extended English readings of Yumeno's 1935 novel *Dogura magura* — a fantastic murder mystery with elements drawn from hard science, including recently imported Western psychology. Written before the translation of Western science fiction, its combination of logic and fantasy seems to satisfy the desire for an origin of this emerging genre. But, as Nakamura demonstrates, even this early work unfolds in unexpected directions: its identification as the beginning of Japanese science fiction is tied up with the text's contested relation with the foreign, specifically China. And Nakamura shows that the anxiety over bodily mechanization so central in cyberpunk is already present in Yumeno's work. Finally and most significantly for our metaphor of Japanese science fiction in embryo, Yumeno suggests that the entire story may ultimately be the dream of an unborn fetus. The work that seems to range so widely through fantasy, Western science, media, and disembodiment finally returns to the womb. This is a fitting caution for any effort to map origins and borders of Japanese science fiction.

Japanese science fiction as an organized movement begins roughly twenty-five years later, with the publication of the first successful fanzine, *Uchūjin* (1957–, Cosmic dust), and the first successful commercial magazine, Hayakawa Publishing's *SF Magajin* (1959–, *SF Magazine*), founded by Shibano Takumi and Fukushima Masami, respectively. Many of the first generation of Japanese science fiction writers were discovered in *Uchūjin*, then nurtured as professionals in *SF Magajin*.[9]

The transition from early speculative fantasy like Yumeno's to the beginnings of modern science fiction is covered in the second chapter by Thomas Schnellbächer. He traces the topos of the Pacific from the lost-world fantasies of Kayama Shigeru in the forties through early modern science fiction novels and film (Kayama wrote the scenario for *Godzilla*). In probing the geographic and geopolitical boundaries of Japanese science fiction, Schnellbächer describes the Pacific as an ambiguous space that both connects and separates Japan from its neighbors, a place where Japan's prewar colonial dreams are addressed (or resurrected) as its new global identity is defined. He shows that during the formative time for Japanese science fiction, the genre's boundaries are intimately connected with those of the state. The chapter concludes by discussing two apocalyptic novels by figures from this first generation, Abe Kōbō (1924–1993) and Komatsu Sakyō (1931–). Abe's *Dai yon kanpyōki* (1959, *Inter Ice Age 4*) and Komatsu's *Nihon chinbotsu* (1973, *Japan Sinks*) both question the notion of Japan's localized national identity by imagining disasters in which the Japanese islands are swallowed into the Pacific.

Abe was a key actor in the postwar avant-garde, and the literary experiment of *Inter Ice Age 4* was instrumental in helping launch science fiction as a genre in Japan. But, ironically, Abe saw the coalescence of genre conventions as inherently limiting, and he moved on to more radical prose forms himself, drawing a distinction between science fiction and the avant-garde and effectively crossing outside the borders of the genre he helped found. Komatsu, on the other hand, became one of the three great pillars in this first generation, along with Hoshi Shin'ichi (1926–1997) and Tsutsui Yasutaka (1934–). These three founding figures continue to exert tremendous influence today.[10] Komatsu authored a range of prose science fiction as rich and varied as his Western counterparts like Isaac Asimov or Arthur C. Clarke. Hoshi became known as the master of the short-short story and by 1982 had written more than a thousand of them, many only a page or two long. His "Bokko-chan" (1961) was one of the first works of Japanese science fiction translated into English when it appeared as "The Manmade Beauty" in the November 1978 issue of the *Magazine of Fantasy and Science Fiction*.

Tsutsui, a slapstick New Wave metafictionist, combines the sensibilities of Charles Darwin, Sigmund Freud, and the Marx Brothers. From the sixties through the nineties, his work and reputation have crossed from science fiction into mainstream literary fiction: one of his later novels, *Kyokō sendan* (1984, *Fantasy fleet*), describes a weird battle between a race of stationery products and a race of weasels, establishing his literary talent as comparable to the most experimental of Latin American magic realist writers. Tsutsui's transition came at a time when several mainstream literary writers like Murakami Haruki, Shōno Yoriko, and the Nobel laureate Ōe Kenzaburō were already successfully incorporating science fiction themes and content into their mainstream (*jun bungaku*) fiction, and the line between these two areas remains more fluid in Japan than in North America. Again, this might be regarded as a compressed or accelerated version of a similar transition in the West, but at this point it is not clear who is following whom: Ōe and Murakami's brands of fantasy, for example, have had a strong impact on writers outside Japan.

One of these transitional authors, Shōno, is discussed in more depth in chapter 3, Kotani Mari's detailed and wide-ranging survey of fantasy and science fiction by Japanese women writers from the 1970s through the 1990s. The chapter treats fiction by Shōno and other important writers like Kurimoto Kaoru and Arai Motoko (who is taken up again by Azuma Hiroki in the following chapter). Kotani focuses particularly on social and bodily transformation — from morphing heroines and half-human heroes to twisted utopias and a whole city that is sucked into the earth. She sees these metamorphoses as an ambivalent hallmark of Japanese women's science fiction, a signifier not only for women's power and adaptability but also for their perceived monstrosity and isolation. Furthermore, Kotani shows how these texts twist or transform generic elements from Western science fiction: all these women authors are influenced by recent Western science fiction movements like New Wave, cyberpunk, and slash fiction. But they have reinterpreted those subgenres and exploited Japan's particular situation in order to forge a new literature. We see that in the way their stories alter received elements — from the feminist utopia to the phallic swordsman — in order to construct a new space for women within the genre.

Azuma's chapter, "SF as Hamlet: Science Fiction and Philosophy," provides a synopsis and a new take on the history of science fiction traced in the preceding three chapters. Azuma is well known in Japan for his theorization of postmodernism that turns on an analysis of recent *otaku*, or fan culture, and here he compares different generations of science fiction and science fiction fans with different stages of modern and postmodern philosophy. For Azuma, just as nineteenth-century dreams of a unified philosophy gave way to fragmentation in the twentieth century, the space empires and idealistic visions of older science fiction have become untenable, even as they retain a nostalgic appeal. Azuma links this to the shift from first-generation authors like Komatsu to later figures like Arai, whose teenage debut, manga-like narrative style, and rock-star popularity seem to Azuma to mark the beginning of a new era for science fiction.

The first section closes with an essay by William O. Gardner on more recent work by Tsutsui, showing how the walls between media are collapsing almost as quickly as those between literary genres. Gardner compares Tsutsui's cessation of print publishing (following attempts to censor one of his stories) to the author's experiments with electronic publishing — specifically the online dialogue with readers he conducted during the serialization of his novel *Asa no Gasupaaru* (1991–92, *Gaspard of the Morning*). Gardner shows how Tsutsui directed the discourse surrounding his fiction — the censorship controversy and the online postings about *Gasupaaru* — in a series of literary performances that exploited the "feedback loops" between author and readers. By blurring the distinctions between author, reader, and text, Tsutsui's work reconsiders reality as a hyperfiction, everyday life as an effect of the political unconscious, and the boundary transgressor as the best survivor.

Japanese Science Fiction Animation

The volume's second half focuses on Japanese anime from the 1990s onward, concluding with chapters on anime's audience and the next generation of animation, the cinematic digital animation of *Final Fantasy*. As discussed above, many of the issues raised for prose science fiction in the first half — like nationalism, gender identity, and the mechanical body — are the same ones explored for anime in the second half, and virtually every chapter in both halves devotes attention to the negotiation between text and image: all the essays in Part I invoke the visual at some point (even the plot of *Dogura magura* will finally turn on a painting), while several writers in Part II regard anime as interesting precisely for the new light it casts on earlier media, including live-action film and prose.

Susan J. Napier's reading of 1990s anime takes its title, its theme, and its opening from Western prose science fiction — E. M. Forster's turn-of-the-twentieth-century fantasy "The Machine Stops." Expanding her influential work on anime's apocalyptic vision, Napier sees in all these works a crisis of individual identity in our increasingly (but unstably) mechanized society. At the same time she takes up the familiar theme of the mechanized body, Napier discusses how some anime arguably transform these narratives. The pat, hermetic plots of some early science fiction are turned on their heads by the open-ended stories of longer animated series, which are sometimes scripted almost improvisationally during the broadcast season and which often feature self-reflexive elements that pose questions about narrative itself. *Serial Experiments: Lain* (1998) is the apt title of one of these series. Its heroine, a young girl who delves into an online virtual reality called "the Wired," eventually comes to suspect that she is an entirely virtual being and that the "real" world outside "the Wired" is simply part of her dreams. Napier shows how *Lain* and *Shinseiki evangerion* (1995–96, *Neon Genesis Evangelion*) are able to threaten the narrative conventions and construction of the genre itself, turning the narrative in on itself in a way that suggests Tsutsui's metafictional experiments and the power of media technology to erase or remake the world.

In a slightly different view, the salient visual gap between anime and live action moves us toward a reconsideration of simulation itself. Both Christopher Bolton, in chapter 7, and Livia Monnet, in chapter 10, draw parallels between the mechanization or digitization of the body and the grammar of digital media. The films Bolton and Monnet discuss are struggling to rediscover an organic body or spirit in contemporary science fiction narratives about technology. Both chapters draw a parallel between this search for a ghostly remainder in the mechanical body and the ways that digital animation returns compulsively to the idioms of live-action cinema to recover something supposedly lost in the transition from cinema to digital media. Bolton looks at Oshii Mamoru's *Patlabor 2* (1993), where giant robot "mecha" and their human pilots become an image of humanity disappearing in the machine's embrace. Bolton sees the film as a critique of mediated experience, and particularly mediated vision, but he also asks how an animated film can attempt a critique of the digital media culture to which the film itself belongs. Bolton concludes that *Patlabor 2* uses specific visual tropes to simulate live-action cinema, in order to construct a stable ground from which digital mass media can be critiqued.

Monnet examines a similar issue in the photorealistic computer animation of Sakaguchi Hironobu's *Final Fantasy: The Spirits Within* (2001), the first feature film based on the canonical video game series. The role of gaming and computer rendering in Sakaguchi's film arguably represents a new paradigm in animation and science fiction, but Monnet sees the film as haunted by the spirits of earlier media, not unlike *Patlabor 2*. To *Final Fantasy*'s narrative about spirits that haunt humanity from within and among us, Monnet adds a narrative of her own, in which the animation is haunted by its own lack and is driven to recover or reproduce the animism and spiritualism that surrounded early cinema. For Monnet, what drives this desire is not only the problem that the computer-animated characters are not lifelike but the fact that the life and agency have been sucked out of the heroine in particular. What ultimately haunts *Final Fantasy* are the ghosts of the women who are mistreated by the film and by science fiction at large.

Sharalyn Orbaugh's chapter on anime cyborgs pairs with Monnet's for the ways it also relates gender issues to the mechanized or digitized body. In "Sex and the Single Cyborg: Japanese Popular Culture Experiments in

Subjectivity," Orbaugh examines the concepts of sex and singularity in the human-mechanical hybrids that populate *Ghost in the Shell* and *Neon Genesis Evangelion*. For Orbaugh, the aspect of the cyborg that challenges conventional notions of individuality and gender is not so much the possibility of mechanical (singular, asexual) duplication as the breakdown of the singular body and its boundaries. It is permeability, ingestion, and absorption that define Orbaugh's cyborg and challenge the "heterosexual matrix." This reconfiguration of bodily geography and reproductive roles also returns us to the theme of earlier chapters — the motherless but connected child or fetus that dreams up the outside world.

Discussions of anime and its popularity, including the way it crosses between high and low media, must eventually turn to the question of anime's reception and hence to the fans of science fiction, anime, and manga, who are referred to with the reclaimed pejorative *otaku*.[11] Some of the richest work on anime now centers on these fan cultures, and one of the best-known Japanese critics in this field is Saitō Tamaki, who gives an overview of his work in chapter 11. While *otaku* has been a label associated with aesthetic and social immaturity, and an unhealthy preference for mediated or virtual experience (particularly in the realm of sex), Saitō suggests that the simulated sexuality of the *otaku*'s textual encounters is an inevitable and, in one sense, productive response to the increasingly mediated society in which we live.

In various ways, all of these chapters (like the chapters in Part I) explore how Japanese science fiction and its subjects lack clear borders. Both cross time, space, and media. Given this, we might be tempted to define the boundaries of Japanese science fiction using language. Is Japanese science fiction simply science fiction produced by Japanese writers in Japanese? No — even before *Final Fantasy: The Spirits Within* (produced in English by a Japanese director), this distinction was too simple, as the remaining chapters show. Naoki Chiba and Hiroko Chiba have contributed a linguistic study of anime vocabulary adapted from English and other languages. Chiba and Chiba reveal the web of connotations these loanwords carry and the way they inflect the notion of the alien in anime. One example is the language sung and spoken by the computer-generated virtual idol singer Sharon Apple and her human "producer" Myung in *Macross Plus* (1994). Sharon is an analogue of Date Kyōko and Gibson's "idoru" Rei Tōei, the virtual, nationless Japanese pop star who is identified by the English word *idol*, imported into Japanese as *aidoru*, then back into Gibson's English as *idoru*. Chiba and Chiba trace a similar process in the language of *Macross Plus*, showing how the hybrid language of Sharon Apple's music projects a complex mix of foreignness and Japaneseness, as well as interiority and inorganicism.

Finally, Takayuki Tatsumi concludes the volume with a case study of the complexities involved in translating "Yawarakai tokei" (1968, "Soft Clocks"), Aramaki Yoshio's story of a surreal Mars ruled by a latter-day Dali, whose cyborg daughter, Vivi, is afflicted with anorexia. Dali and his daughter both ingest a powerful nanotechnology that absorbs their psychological imprint, and when they excrete or regurgitate it, it transforms the Martian landscape to mirror their dreams and surreal visions. Tatsumi discusses the story's gender politics, as well as the complex transformation it underwent as it was translated and then rewritten for American publication by the science fiction author Lewis Shiner. Like the chapters by Orbaugh and Chiba and Chiba, Tatsumi's parable suggests that it is ingestion and digestion (and sometimes regurgitation), rather than simple borrowing or translation, that often characterize relations between these languages and texts.

Science Fiction Criticism in Japan

The stages and movements above arose partly in response to debates and controversies in the realm of Japanese science fiction criticism. So, finally, it may be helpful to describe some of these Japanese critical movements and show how the essays in this volume fit within this critical history.[12] In the early stages between the 1960s and the 1970s, first-generation writers like Abe Kōbō and Fukushima Masami defined science fiction and defended it against the literary prejudices of mainstream writers and critics.[13] This period was characterized in part by efforts to define Japanese science fiction in a larger world context — for example, to locate Japanese science fiction between the United States and Soviet examples. Komatsu Sakyō questioned Soviet science fiction's socialist ideology and redefined science fiction as a field investigating the science of literature, while Ishikawa Takashi ferociously and controversially criticized the hard-core fascist aspects of Robert Heinlein's *Starship Troopers* (1959).[14] Schnellbächer's chapter addresses these issues head-on, with specific reference to Abe and Komatsu, and the prewar as well as the cold war context. Bolton's reading of *Patlabor 2* extends the discussion into the Gulf war era.

Komatsu and Heinlein would become the symbolic figures mirroring the tensions and borrowings with Western science fiction and Western politics: debates on these issues and these two authors continued into the early seventies and flared again in the eighties and nineties. In 1970, "Soft Clocks" author Aramaki Yoshio published a rereading of Heinlein that defended Japanese science fiction's originality, in response to Yamano Kōichi's criticisms of Japanese imitations of Anglo-American science fiction. But as Takayuki Tatsumi describes in the Afterword, Aramaki's and Yamano's visions of science fiction are not so different: they share a strong taste for psychoanalysis and surrealism, and a desire to reinvent the generic framework of science fiction.[15]

Elsewhere, Aramaki and critics like Shibano Takumi attempted to define or describe Japanese science fiction in the context of Western philosophy, Shibano with the idea of "collective reason," Aramaki by reviving Renaissance humanism.[16] Though writing later than Aramaki and Shibano, Azuma Hiroki and his chapter on science fiction and philosophy should be seen in the context of the same critical tradition.

While the early stages of Japanese science fiction criticism reveal a certain modernistic tendency to redefine science fiction in our civilization, the latter stages carry us into a postmodern literary cultural context in which the imagination of science fiction performs a crucial role. As early as 1975, Tsutsui Yasutaka embraced the impact of the New Wave writer J. G. Ballard and identified metafiction (*chōkyokō*) as the defining feature of the next generation of science fiction. This metafictional turn is touched on in the Afterword, while in chapter 5 Gardner describes the superevolution of this impulse in Tsutsui's more recent work.

The 1980s saw a preoccupation with cyberpunk, and the West's vision of Japan's technophilia fostered a "Japanoid" cultural consciousness even among the Japanese.[17] As gender and cultural studies inflected Japanese criticism into the nineties, critics pointed out the sexism and "techno-orientalism" of cyberpunk and related genres, but also identified the hopeful possibilities suggested by their bodily and cultural transformations. This is precisely the tension Orbaugh, Napier, and Chiba and Chiba identify in cyberpunk anime like *Akira* and *Ghost in the Shell*. Kotani traces the same ambivalence about bodily transformation through successive generations of feminism and women's science fiction.

With rising critical interest in anime and manga in the 1990s, there was also more academic attention to fan culture.[18] The year 1994 saw the establishment of a class on *otaku* culture at the University of Tokyo, taught in subsequent years by Okada Toshio, the self-proclaimed "Otaking" and ex-president of Gainax, the legendary studio that produced *Neon Genesis Evangelion*. Okada and others have argued that *otaku* constitute a new generation (in the more radical theories, a virtual new species) that has an entirely different relationship to media and information. Among the writers in this volume, Azuma, Saitō, and Kotani have all contributed significantly to this ongoing discussion. Azuma has traced the recent rise of "third generation *otaku* tribes" — *otaku* who take pleasure in consuming databases rather than stories. Chapter 4 includes a sketch of this shift and its implications for science fiction and philosophy. Saitō has examined male *otaku* sexuality by tracing their obsession with the figure of the "beautiful warrior girl" *(sentō bishō jo)*. Chapter 11 summarizes this work and takes it a step further by considering female *otaku* and the genre called *yaoi*, male-male love stories whose authors and readers are overwhelmingly women. Kotani has been a pioneer in the study of *yaoi* and "Otaqueen" culture since the 1990s. Her introduction to Saitō's essay gives an overview of *yaoi*, and in chapter 3 she situates this genre within the larger tradition of Japanese women's science fiction.[19]

The increasing popularity of anime and visual science fiction posed new challenges for prose. In 1996 the Seventeenth Japan Science Fiction Award went to the monster movie *Gamera 2* (1996), spurring claims that prose science fiction was dead or in decline.[20] Some have seen the rise of the visual as the death knell of print science fiction, while others, like Kotani, see anime, horror, and *kaijū eiga* as forces that are boosting the broader popularity of print science fiction. Some balance was restored the following year, when the eighteenth award was shared by *Neon Genesis Evangelion* and the mystery writer Miyabe Miyuki's alternate history *Gamōtei jiken* (1996, *Incident at the Gamō mansion*).[21]

The original monster Gamera debuted in Japan in 1965 and took only a year to reach America's shores. Returning to Japan thirty years later to menace prose science fiction, this creature also returns us to the issues raised at the outset of this Introduction. The debate triggered by *Gamera 2* could be seen as the Japanese local version of the global phenomenon discussed in the opening paragraphs. What is the future of Japanese science fiction — in Japan and in the world? The two-part division of this book is not intended to take sides in an argument about whether anime has or will overshadow prose science fiction, in or outside Japan. Each contributor has a distinct take on that question and addresses it to one degree or another, implicitly or explicitly. What we can say — and what the studies in this book show — is that just like the alternate histories and future visions of science fiction, good criticism casts its eye both backward and forward, and is always ready to be surprised by what it sees.

Notes

1. *Gojira*, dir. Honda Ishirō (1954); reedited and released in the United States in 1956 as *Godzilla, King of the Monsters!*; both versions are available on *Gojira/ Godzilla Deluxe Collector's Edition*, 2 DVDs (Classic Media, 2006); Ken Hollings, "Tokyo Must Be Destroyed: Dreams of Tall Buildings and Monsters, Images of Cities and Monuments," in *Digital Delirium*, ed. Arthur Kroker and Marilouise Kroker (New York: St. Martin's Press, 1997), 247. On the *Godzilla* soundtracks, see

also Shūhei Hosokawa, "Atomic Overtones and Primitive Undertones: Akira Ifukube's Sound Design for *Godzilla*," in *Off the Planet: Music, Sound, and Science Fiction Cinema*, ed. Philip Hayward (London: Libbey, 2004), 42–60.

2. Chon A. Noriega, "Godzilla and the Japanese Nightmare: When *Them!* Is U.S.," in *Hibakusha Cinema: Hiroshima, Nagasaki, and the Nuclear Image in Japanese Film*, ed. Mick Broderick (London: Kegan Paul International, 1996), 54–74. On the production history of *Gojira/Godzilla*, see Stuart Galbraith IV, *Japanese Science Fiction, Fantasy, and Horror Films: A Critical Analysis and Filmography of 103 Features Released in the United States, 1950–1992* (Jefferson, N.C.: McFarland, 1994), 7–14.

3. *Tetsuwan Atomu*, dir. Tezuka Osamu, TV series (1963); edited and broadcast in the United States as *Astro Boy* (1963); the U.S. version is re-created in *Astro Boy Ultra Collector's Edition*, 11-DVD box set (Right Stuff, 2006). The anime was based on a manga series by Tezuka that started publication in 1951: Tezuka Osamu, *Tetsuwan Atomu*, vols. 221–38 of *Tezuka Osamu manga zenshū* (Complete manga of Tezuka Osamu) (Tokyo: Kōdansha, 2000); translated as *Astro Boy*, 23 vols. (Milwaukie, Ore.: Dark Horse, 2002–4). Throughout this book Japanese names are given in Japanese order. In the body of the text, an exception is made for our Japanese contributors who work and publish extensively in the United States, Hiroko Chiba, Naoki Chiba, Miri Nakamura, and Takayuki Tatsumi. In citations, we preserve the author's name as it is given in the original publication: usually given name and surname for English publications and Japanese order for Japanese texts.

4. Joshua La Bare, "The Future: 'Wrapped . . . in That Mysterious Japanese Way,'" *Science Fiction Studies* 27 (2000): 26.

5. *Blade Runner*, dir. Ridley Scott, DVD (Warner, 1997); William Gibson, *Neuromancer* (New York: Ace, 1986); Gibson, *Idoru* (New York: Berkley, 1997); on Date Kyōko, see Robert Hamilton, "Virtual Idols and Digital Girls: Artifice and Sexuality in Anime, Kisekae and Kyoko Date," *Bad Subjects* 35 (November 1997), http://bad.eserver.org/issues/1997/35/hamilton.html (accessed May 28, 2006).

6. These works are cited in full in the individual chapters that treat them. In the case of franchises like *Akira*, *Ghost in the Shell*, and *Final Fantasy*, there are frequently multiple manga, films, television series, direct-to-video releases, and games within a series, all with similar or identical names. The citations in each chapter specify which parts of a series are being treated and give publication information for the corresponding subtitled tapes or DVDs distributed in the United States. But for the full range of titles belonging to a given series, as well as details like the Japanese broadcast history and production credits, see Jonathan Clements and Helen McCarthy, *The Anime Encyclopedia: A Guide to Japanese Animation since 1917* (Berkeley, Calif.: Stone Bridge, 2001). This edition covers most of the anime treated in this book.

7. On Japan's role in globalized commercial children's culture, see Anne Allison, "Portable Monsters and Commodity Cuteness: *Pokemon* as Japan's New Global Power," *Postcolonial Studies* 6 (2003): 381–95; Gary Cross and Gregory Smits, "Japan, the U.S., and the Globalization of Children's Consumer Culture," *Journal of Social History* 38 (2005): 873–90. On Japanese hypersociality and media mixing, see Mizuko Ito, "Technologies of the Childhood Imagination: Media Mixes, Hypersociality, and Recombinant Cultural Forms," *Items and Issues* 4, no. 4 (2003): 31–34, http://www.ssrc.org/programs/publications_editors/publications/items/online4-4/ito-childhood.pdf (accessed May 28, 2006).

8. For those interested in Japanese science fiction authors not covered in this volume, see Takayuki Tatsumi, "Generations and Controversies: An Overview of Japanese Science Fiction, 1957–1997," *Science Fiction Studies* 27 (2000): 105–14; Tatsumi, *Japanoido sengen: Gendai Nihon SF o yomu tame ni* (Manifesto for Japanoids: Reading Japanese science fiction) (Tokyo: Hayakawa, 1993). (On Japanese name order in citations, see note 3.)

9. Shibano Takumi, ed., *Chiri mo tsumoreba: Uchūjin 40 nenshi* (When the dust settled: Forty years of *Cosmic dust*) (Tokyo: Shuppan Bungeisha, 1997); Shibano Takumi, ed., *Uchūjin kessaku sen* (Selected works from *Cosmic dust*), 3 vols. (Tokyo: Kōdansha, 1977). The latter collection includes the work of fifty-eight major writers, professional or nonprofessional, mainly from the first and the second generations.

10. Hoshi is taken up briefly in the afterword but not discussed at length in this volume. For a description of Hoshi's work, see Robert Matthew, *Japanese Science Fiction: A View of a Changing Society* (London: Routledge, 1989).

11. Karl Taro Greenfeld's novelistic account of Japanese subcultures, *Speed Tribes*, contains a typical characterization: "The *otaku* came of age way back in the eighties with Paleolithic 186 computers and Neanderthal Atari Pac-Men as playmates. They were brought up on junk food and educated to memorize reams of contextless information in preparation for multiple-choice high school and college entrance examinations. They unwound with ultraviolent slasher comic books or equally violent computer games. And then they discovered that by interacting with computers instead of people, they could avoid Japanese society's dauntingly complex Confucian web of social obligations and loyalties. The result: a generation of Japanese youth too uptight to talk to a telephone operator but who can go hell-for-leather on the deck of a personal computer or workstation." But as the essays in this book show, both *otaku* and the theories about them have continued to evolve since these words were written (Karl Taro Greenfeld, *Speed Tribes: Days and Nights with Japan's Next Generation* [New York: HarperCollins, 1994], 174–75).

12. This outline follows the history of science fiction criticism in Tatsumi Takayuki, ed., *Nihon sf ronsōshi* (Science fiction controversies in Japan: 1957–1997) (Tokyo: Keisō Shobō, 2000). The critical essays that are summarized or referred to in passing below are collected in that volume and are not cited individually here.

13. In English, see Abe Kōbō, "Two Essays on Science Fiction," trans. Christopher Bolton and Thomas Schnellbächer, *Science Fiction Studies* 29 (2002): 340–50.

14. Robert Heinlein, *Starship Troopers* (New York: Ace, 1987).

15. In the eighties and nineties, critics like Kasai Kiyoshi and Nagase Tadashi turned back to Komatsu and Heinlein, and the associated issues of Western borrowing and political orientation. Kasai looked beyond Komatsu's post-Hegelian dialectics and deconstructed his own debt to Karl Marx to try to move beyond Komatsu's work. Nagase criticized the claustrophilic mental history of the Japanese science fiction community, praised the American cyberpunk chairman Bruce Sterling, and reconstructed Heinlein as the prophet of speculative fiction.

16. Shibano Takumi, "Collective Reason: A Proposal," trans. Xavier Bensky, introduced by Tatsumi Takayuki, *Science Fiction Studies* 29, no. 3 (2002): 351–63.

17. On the Japanoid, see Tatsumi Takayuki, *Japanoido sengen*; Takayuki Tatsumi, "The Japanese Reflection of Mirrorshades," in *Storming the Reality Studio*, ed. Larry McCaffery (Durham, N.C.: Duke University Press, 1991), 366–73; Tatsumi, "The Japanoid Manifesto: Toward a New Poetics of Invisible Culture," *Review of*

Contemporary Fiction 22, no. 2 (2002): 12–18. See also Yoshiko Shimada, "Afterword: Japanese Pop Culture and the Eradication of History," in *Consuming Bodies: Sex and Contemporary Japanese Art,* ed. Fran Lloyd (London: Reaktion Books, 2002), 186–92.

18. The term *otaku* is also associated with the military plastic models, replica guns, and combat games that became very popular in Japan in the mid-1990s because of the concurrent boom in virtual reality war novels. But the word *otaku* and its association with science fiction date from long before this. In the late 1960s, science fiction fans already used this second-person Japanese pronoun *otaku* in a peculiar way, to identify a person who owns rare books. Basically bookworms, the first and second generation of fans in Japan used this pronoun to greet one another by saying, "Do you have this or that book?" Tatsumi Takayuki reports hearing this term for the first time in 1970, when he paid his first visit to the fanzine editor Shibano Takumi. It was only much later, in 1984, that the cultural critic Nakamori Akio, ex-spokesperson of the "shinjinrui" (Generation X), named the whole strange tribe of science fiction fans "otaku."

19. Okada published his *Otakugaku nyūmon* (Introduction to otakuology) in 1996 (Tokyo: Shinchō OH! Bunko, 2000); Azuma Hiroki, *Dōbutsuka suru posutomodan* (Animalizing postmodernity) (Tokyo: Kōdansha, 2001); Kotani Mari, *Joseijō muishiki* (Techno-gynesis) (Tokyo: Keisō Shobō, 1994); Saitō Tamaki, *Sentō bishōjo no seishin bunseki* (Armored cuties: A psychoanalysis) (Tokyo: Ōta Shuppan, 2000). Since Saitō's book was published, the *otaku*'s deep obsession with these beautiful warrior girls has come to artistic fruition in a 2002 television anime titled *Saishū heiki kanojo* (She, the ultimate weapon) created by Takahashi Shin and directed by Kase Mitsuko. Whether it is an ultragirlish figurine or a simulationist war fighter, members of the *otaku* tribe keep chasing and translating the sign of whatever attracts them.

20. *Gamera 2: Region shūrai,* dir. Kaneko Shusuke; translated as *Gamera 2: Attack of the Legion,* DVD (ADV, 2003). The original Gamera movie was *Daikaijū Gamera* (1965); translated as *Gammera the Invincible* (Alpha Video, 2003). This controversy is referred to as the "trash sf" *(kuzu sf)* debate, from a March 1997 special issue of the magazine *Hon no zasshi* (Book journal) titled "Japanese sf, a Decade of Trash," The story was also picked up in the February 9, 1997, issue of the financial newspaper *Nikkei shinbun.*

21. Miyabe Miyuki, *Gamōtei jiken* (Incident at the Gamō mansion) (Tokyo: Mainichi Shinbunsha, 1996). The early twenty-first century has also seen other signs of a resurgence of science fiction in the Japanese print media: in 1999 Tokuma Publishing started the Japan Science Fiction Award for New Talent with an aim to discover new novelists, while in 2006 Hayakawa Publishing inaugurated the Japan Science Fiction Criticism Award to support new critics. On the prospects for more English translation of Japanese science fiction in the new millennium, see the Afterword.

PROSE SCIENCE FICTION

1. Horror and Machines in Prewar Japan

The Mechanical Uncanny in Yumeno Kyūsaku's *Dogura magura*

Miri Nakamura

Very slowly . . . slowly . . . all the machines in the factory, piled on top of one another, begin to awaken. Their steam spreads from one corner of the factory to another. They move faster and faster. . . . my eyes can no longer follow them, and illusions of steel swirl around me. . . . Cruel, dark groans fill the room. They have the power to entrap any great soul in a hallucination of fear and death in an instant. How many countless bodies have the machines torn apart? Their echoes mock the ghosts of female workers and children who were shredded and beaten by them.

    — Yumeno Kyūsaku, "Strange Dreams"

I promise you that if you read *Dogura magura* five times, it will give you a different feeling each time.

    — Yumeno Kyūsaku, quoted in Ishikawa Ichirō, "Wakare" (1936)

Images of machines were ubiquitous in the literary landscape of Taishō (1912–26) and early Shōwa (1926–89) Japan. Some writers praised the beauty of machines and others explored their darkness. Yumeno Kyūsaku (1889–1936), a detective fiction writer known for his bizarre narratives and avant-gardism, belonged to the latter category. He envisioned machines as fearful entities tearing apart human bodies, and he often invoked mechanical imagery to strike fear into the heart of the reader. This chapter focuses on the discourse of horror and the mode of the uncanny that govern one of Yumeno's last novels, *Dogura magura* (1935).[1]

Yumeno worked in Fukuoka as a journalist for the *Kyūshū nippō* newspaper before he delved into fiction. He was also a master of Noh theater and a Buddhist monk. Yumeno's father was Sugiyama Shigemaru, one of the leading figures of the protonationalist political group "The Society of the Black Sea" *(gen'yōsha)*, leading many scholars to focus on the nationalistic ideologies embedded in Yumeno's works.[2] From 1926 on, Yumeno published detective fiction and numerous short stories in the popular journal *Shin seinen* (New youth) and quickly became a representative writer of what was understood in Taishō and early Shōwa Japan as irregular detective fiction *(henkaku tantei shōsetsu)*, so called because it differed from the more objective and rational methods of regular detective fiction *(honkaku tantei shōsetsu)*. Because of its frequent scientific themes, this category of irregular detective fiction is now treated as the forerunner of contemporary Japanese science fiction.[3]

Yumeno's *Dogura magura* is representative of this early science fiction — a group of texts dealing with science and science fiction tropes before the introduction of the American science fiction genre in the 1950s. The novel's strange title, according to both critics and the text itself, means "trickery" in Nagasaki dialect.[4] Because of its enormous length — 1,500 pages in manuscript form — Yumeno published the novel from *Shōhakukan* with his own funds. It narrates a tale about a paranoid mental patient who is told by two psychologists, Masaki and Wakabayashi, that he may be a murderer named Kure Ichirō. The patient searches for his identity throughout the novel and in the end discovers that not only is he Ichirō, but he is also a fetus dreaming inside his mother's womb.

Dogura magura is valuable not only for its literary qualities but also for the considerable historical insight it provides on the development of the studies of psychoanalysis at Kyūshū Imperial University.[5] Sugiyama Kura, Yumeno's wife, noted his frequent trips to the university's psychology department to collect materials for the novel.[6] Kyūshū Imperial University, which also provides the novel's setting, was the center of the study of psychoanalysis in the 1920s, and, although psychology was at that time considered as little more than a form of popular science, scholars there were conducting extensive research on Sigmund Freud, Richard von Krafft-Ebing, and Otto Rank.[7] It is also well known that the protagonist Kure Ichirō was modeled after Kure Shūzō (1866–1932), Japan's foremost psychologist who introduced European methods of treatment to Japanese institutions on his return from Austria in 1901.[8] The novel's setting at a mental institution is also reminiscent of the 1920 film *Das Cabinet des Dr. Caligari (The Cabinet of Dr. Caligari*, released in 1921 in Japan), the German silent film that became a huge hit in Japan and influenced the writings of numerous authors, including Yumeno, who even wrote a story called *Dr. Inugami* (*Inugami hakase,* 1931).[9]

According to his diary, Yumeno spent approximately a decade on this novel: "I have written a draft of the psychological study *[seishin shinri gaku]*" — a study now understood to be an early version of *Dogura magura.*[10] Although Yumeno thought of this bizarre novel as the culmination of his literary career, it puzzled critics at the time of its publication and failed to receive any critical attention until after the end of World War II.[11] Since then, however, it has been praised by literary critics as Yumeno's magnum opus and, through its treatment of psychological themes, has even been regarded as an important contribution to child psychology and embryology.[12]

Critics have also praised the novel's exploration of the theme of "doubling" in the midst of Japan's golden "age of machines."[13] During this time, when the impact of mechanical reproduction was making itself felt in all aspects of Japanese life, Yumeno exploits scientific culture as an essential ingredient of his particular brand of horror. Though many critics have picked up on the notion of the mechanical age as an important theme in the text, none has explored the potential that this mode of reading holds. Most have focused instead on the novel's metafictional or fantastic aspects. Ōishi Masahiko, for example, observes that the doppelgänger and the doubling in *Dogura magura* reflect "the Tokyo that Yumeno feared and the mass production and consumption associated with that Tokyo." The cultural critic Tsurumi Shunsuke has gone so far as to read Ichirō as an "antirobot," one who searches for the human spirit lost in the mechanical age.[14] I generally agree with these critics that a critique of the mechanical age underlies the text. However, the text does not merely subvert the ideologies of the machine age. Ichirō is not simply an antirobot. The scene is much more complicated than this, for bodies in *Dogura magura* are imagined through metaphors of machines and portrayed as possessing certain machine-like qualities. In other words, the text constantly blurs the distinction between robots and humans, between the mechanical and the biological. It is precisely through this mechanization of the human body that Yumeno succeeds in producing his own discourse of fear in order to defamiliarize the age of machines in which he lived.

The theoretical model of the uncanny will prove to be useful in my analysis of *Dogura magura.* I begin by discussing the significance of machines in prewar Japan and how, for Yumeno, mechanical imageries came to be regarded with fear. I then develop the idea of "the mechanical uncanny" — the literary mode that blurs the line between what is perceived as natural and what is perceived as artificial.

The Mechanical Uncanny

Taishō and early Shōwa Japan saw a rapid development in technology and modern media. This period, often referred to as Japan's "age of machines" *(kikai jidai),* witnessed the birth of high consumerism and mass production, not to mention the introduction and the popularization of new media such as film, photography, and radio. The social effects that this new mechanical age brought about became the focus of numerous essays and literary works in prewar Japan.

Machines became a dominant image in the era's texts. In 1930 the critic Hirabayashi Hatsunosuke wrote:

> People of today, since they were born, have grown up seeing steamships, telegrams, telephones, moving pictures, and airplanes. For these contemporary people, these things represent the natural environment, just like trees growing on mountains and water occupying the oceans. These things are not considered to be strange at all.... The contemporary age is the age of machines, in contrast to the people at the turn of the century, who feared machines.[15]

At the same time, Marxist scholars like Itagaki Takao (1894–1966) explored the relationship between "machines" *(kikai)* and "art" *(geijutsu).* Envisioning a Marxist utopia, Itagaki claimed that "machines are ... a gift from God that promises the happiness of the proletariat."[16] With the translation of early Western science fiction like Karel Čapek's *R.U.R.* (1920), and the Japanese release of Fritz Lang's *Metropolis* in 1929, mechanical objects like robots and cogwheels became ubiquitous in literature. Japan saw a "robot boom" during which popular science magazines like *Kagaku gahō* (Illustrated magazine of science) and satirical writers like Mizushima Niou began to feature robots in their texts. The image of *jinzō ningen* (literally, "artificial humans") was popularized through works like Mizushima's "Jinzō ningen jidai" (1923, The age of artificial humans). These early Japanese "robots" were also not awkward tin men. Rather, they resembled what we might now identify as androids, with bodies indistinguishable from those of human beings (Figures 1.1 and 1.2).[17]

Machines and technology in prewar Japan, however, did not simply represent social progress; they also were associated with fear and degeneration. In the words of one scholar, prewar literature depicting machines was in "a constant flux between a utopian dream of machines on the one hand and a pessimistic nightmare of them on the other."[18] After the release of *Metropolis,* machines and robotic figures were inseparable from the image of "the proletariat" in the popular imagination. Numerous works of proletarian literature began depicting machines as threatening forces that brutally murder factory workers, and it is this type of fearful imagery

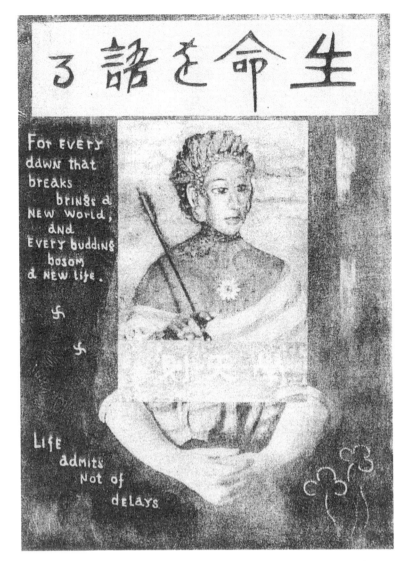

生命を語る

Figure 1.1. Japan produced its first robot in 1928. Created by the scientist Nishimura Makoto, the robot was named Gakutensoku and was exhibited throughout Japan. Nishimura put a great deal of effort into making the automaton appear humanlike: the robot not only could move its arms but also change facial expressions. What is interesting in regard to *Dogura magura* is that Nishimura also attempted to incorporate various ethnic features to create a hybrid appearance, which resembles the way Ichirō is described as a mixture of races in the novel. In prewar Japan, the human body was becoming an object that could be created from scratch, and Nishimura, like Yumeno, seems to embrace hybridity as an ideal aesthetic. Nishimura held a more "utopian" image of machines than Yumeno; for this reason, he tried to make the robot as "universal" as possible. For example, the cosmos flower on its chest is supposed to represent the cosmos and the world; the arrow he holds represents creation. For Nishimura, hybridity was a way to transcend racial boundaries, whereas Yumeno often emphasizes the borderline. The caption "Seimei o kataru" (Talking about life) refers to a chapter title in *Daichi no harawata* (Innards of the earth), from which this image is taken (Tokyo: Tōkō Shoin, 1930, p. 505).

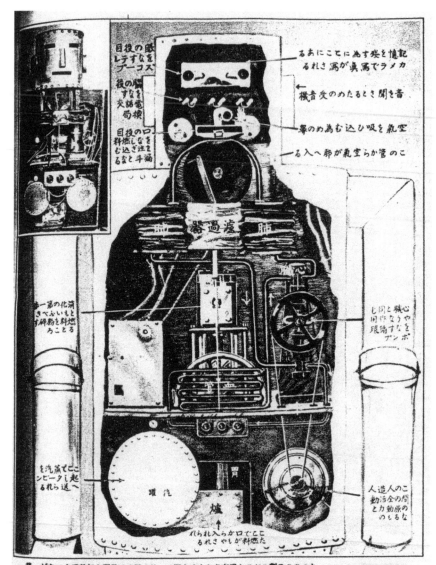

Figure 1.2. An example of the blurred line between the natural and the mechanical through the image of the artificial human, or *jinzō ningen*. The title for this image is "Robot with Physiological Organs." In prewar eugenic writings, the biological body was compared with a machine, and this image reveals how the human body came to be narrated through mechanical vocabulary and vice versa, transforming natural bodies into "statistical persons." This robot was exhibited in London and introduced to Japan in the science magazine *Kagaku gahō* in 1929 (vol. 12, no. 3, p. 328).

that was appropriated by the *Shin seinen* detective fiction writers like Edogawa Ranpo and Unno Jūza — the latter often referred to as "the father of Japanese sf" — not to mention Yumeno himself.[19] Although their works differ significantly from one another, these *Shin seinen* writers were all associated with the erotic-grotesque-nonsense *(ero guro nansensu)* movement, "the prewar, bourgeois cultural phenomenon that devoted itself to explorations of the deviant, the bizarre, and the ridiculous."[20] The erotic-grotesque-nonsense texts were targeted mainly at adolescents and were perceived as avant-garde and trendy. In other words, a huge consumer market for the bizarre was being established in prewar Japan, and this undoubtedly affected these popular writers' decision to depict a "nightmare of machines" rather than the "utopian dream."

For Yumeno, especially, it was imperative that the mode of fear, of the uncanny, be deployed in the detective fiction that is now regarded as early science fiction. Discussing the direction of future detective fiction, Yumeno declared:

> Humanity is like a small insect writhing at the bottom of scientific culture *[kagaku bunka]*. . . . Detective Fiction must be the ultimate popular literature *[taishūteki na yomimono]* that makes one fully taste the flavors of pleasure, intensity, and the gruesomeness that exposes this humanity through the mode of absolute fear *[zetsudai no kyōfu]*. It must make one shudder.[21]

Yumeno saw fear *(kyōfu)* as the ultimate mode of expression at the heart of popular fiction. This fear must capture the humanity "writhing at the bottom of scientific culture" and the disappearing human conscience threatened by science. This binary opposition between something human or biological and something scientific will appear again and again in his works, and what I refer to as "the mechanical uncanny" — a mode of fear that captures the invasion of the mechanical into the biological — was an important aspect of his writing.

Science, for Yumeno, is often translated into mechanical metaphors, such as the factory scene described in the epigraph, taken from his "Strange Dreams."[22] In his later works, mechanical metaphors are also applied to descriptions of human cognition. In the same year as the publication of *Dogura magura*, Yumeno declared in a letter to the writer Kōga Saburō:

> Science disregarded all things that were sacred, beautiful, and mysterious. . . . It investigated these mysteries to their cores and laughed at the fact that they were just calculations that can be reduced to electronic functions *[denshi no sayō]*. It thoroughly analyzed people's religious beliefs and declared that they were just egotistical expressions governed by $+/-/0$ [plus minus zero logic]. . . . Religion is a fraud. Art is self-centered. And love is nothing but a sex drive. It proclaimed this and was delighted.[23]

What Yumeno terms *science* is a force that reduces humans to mere numbers, turning them into "statistical persons" — bodies that can be converted into statistics and surveillance, into numbers and cases.[24] Similar to Yokomitsu Riichi's famous story conspicuously titled "Kikai" (1930, "Machine"), in *Dogura magura* there is no physical machinery (robots, factories, and so on); instead, the text deploys mechanical metaphors to capture the functioning of the human mind.[25] This equation of human cognition to machinery is already hinted at in "Strange Dreams," where the narrator shifts from scenes of factories to insane asylums, drawing a connection between physical mechanisms and psychological mechanisms, but Yumeno will further develop this idea through the mental institution of *Dogura magura,* where the protagonist becomes incapable of distinguishing between the mechanical and the biological within himself, finally becoming automaton-like.

Freud had already addressed fears about the mechanical in his renowned essay "The Uncanny" (1919). Quoting and criticizing Ernst Jentsch, who defined the uncanny as an effect that leaves "the reader in uncertainty whether a particular figure in the story is a human being or an automaton," Freud argues for a more complex model of the uncanny that takes into account psychological factors. Whereas for Jentsch an automaton represented the fear deriving from the uncertainty of whether something is human or mechanical, Freud reads the figure as a materialization of the protagonist's "feminine attitude towards his father in his infancy."[26] In other words, Freud takes figures such as automatons or doubles as representatives of the subject's infantile desires and fears and the return of these repressed desires. Although Freud's interpretation is oftentimes too restrictive, his own essay still builds on the paranoia toward machines epitomized by the figure of the automaton that has now become a representative object of the uncanny.

Although, as many parts of *Dogura magura* demonstrate, Yumeno was certainly influenced by Freudian psychoanalysis, Yumeno's mechanical uncanny is quite different from the Freudian uncanny. Yumeno's discourse of fear is strongly linked to his own sense of nationalism. In the same letter to Kōga, Yumeno defines science as a Western import that has destroyed "Japanese culture." In his nationalistic discourse, the supremacy of Western science in Japan was precisely what destroyed "all things that were sacred, beautiful, and mysterious" and created "mechanical puppets" like *Dogura magura*'s protagonist Ichirō.[27] Also falling into the broad category of science were two types of literature — Japanese naturalism and regular detective fiction, which were deemed more valuable than irregular detective fiction by literary critics, precisely because they were more rational and scientific.[28] For Yumeno, these works reinforced the dominance of

Western science in Japan, and his letter can be read as a nationalistic critique of Western influence on the Japanese literary and cultural milieu. In his texts, "Western science" becomes a dark force pitted against "Japanese culture."

The mechanical uncanny, therefore, is marked by a certain loss of both individual and national identity and a certain nostalgia for a pre-Westernized Japan. As I shall show, in *Dogura magura* Ichirō's identity — or national identity — becomes uncertain as a result of his mechanization. Yumeno plays with such Freudian themes as doppelgängers to portray this loss of identity. As Freud points out, an individual's uncertainty about self often manifests in the figure of doubles: "The subject identifies himself with someone else, so that he is in doubt as to which his self is, or substitutes the extraneous self for his own." In other words, there is "a doubling, dividing and interchanging of the self." Unlike in Freud's analysis, however, the double for Yumeno does not merely represent the manifestation of one's ego or an "uncanny harbinger of death."[29] Yumeno will add a twist to it by inscribing onto the double a completely different national identity. The uncanny will occur when Ichirō realizes that he is not a "pure Japanese," as he has previously assumed, and when he is "split" into two nationalities.

Moreover, the fusing of the mechanical and the biological applies strictly to the individual's own awareness of self, not to the individual's uncertainty about another mechanical object. That is, it is not that the characters are unsure if a robot is really a human; they are uncertain about whether they might themselves be mechanical, mere reproductions of other objects. The mechanical uncanny arises from this particular uncertainty that manifests itself in the psyche, this paranoia that points to the main questions in the novel as posed by Dr. Masaki: to what extent do people actually have control over their minds and bodies?[30] Can any human thought pattern, in the end, be reduced to a program, thus reducing humans to mere "statistical beings," similar to automatons?

Yumeno's conceptualization of human cognition as a machine is actually closer to the definition of the automaton given by systems theorists: a "self-organizing system" or a control mechanism that is "designed to follow automatically a predetermined sequence of operations or respond to encoded instructions," an object that represents the programmability of the human psyche. Automatons threaten "the metaphysical conception of the autonomous human subject, endowed with consciousness and free will."[31] It is not surprising, then, that *Dogura magura* has been described as a text that foreshadows the coming of cybernetics and biotechnology.[32] The mechanical uncanny occurs when Ichirō discovers the program underlying his own mind and realizes that he is under its control. It is a process by which something "non-human" is revealed within what was considered to be wholly human, and one's ideas about the natural and biological are disrupted by the existence of the programmatic within oneself.[33] The following section uses this metaphor of the automaton to explore the mechanical uncanny in the novel.

The Automata in *Dogura magura*

The subheading of *Dogura magura* — "a fantastic strange detective fiction" *(genma kaiki tantei shōsetsu)* — presents a fairly accurate description of the text. The strange story takes place in a mental institution at Kyūshū Imperial University and involves three main characters. Dr. Masaki and Dr. Wakabayashi are rival psychologists who work at the mental institution. The story is told in the first person by their patient, who has no recollection of his true identity. Throughout the novel, he searches for his identity, and he becomes understandably worried when he learns that he may be Kure Ichirō, a serial killer who has murdered both his own mother and fiancée. Ultimately, we discover that he is indeed Ichirō, but the novel's conclusion betrays the classic whodunit narrative. For, in the final scenes, Ichirō realizes that he is a fetus who has just dreamed the entire history presented in *Dogura magura*. Simply put, the unborn Ichirō has just had a long nightmare in his mother's womb.[34]

The bulk of *Dogura magura* is set up as a scientific experiment performed by Masaki and Wakabayashi. Their academic reputations depend on the success of their experiment, on whether Ichirō can remember his past. It is imperative for Masaki, especially, that Ichirō remember who he is, for that would validate all of Masaki's theories on human psychology. To help Ichirō remember his past, Wakabayashi hands him a collection of Masaki's writings that includes newspaper articles, eyewitness accounts of the two murders, a dissertation on the heredity of psychology, Buddhist sutras on insane asylums, and even a film about the experiment, that is, Ichirō himself.

Ichirō learns that Masaki was working toward a theory of "hereditary psychology" *(shinri iden),* which asserts that each cell in an individual's body possesses a memory bank of his or her ancestral past and that this memory can be recalled when a certain trigger *(anji)* is activated in the individual. If the ancestor were an insane serial killer, and if someone knew the trigger, then the individual could be used as a weapon. This is indeed, as Ichirō discovers, how the murders were committed. The trigger turns out to be a scroll depicting six decaying bodies of beautiful women, drawn by Ichirō's ancestor Go Seishū, a Chinese painter turned serial killer.[35] Masaki, it turns out, got hold of the scroll, fathered Ichirō, and framed Ichirō for the murder of his own wife Chiseko — Ichirō's mother — all in the name of science.

This complicated pastiche of texts — jumping back and forth between Ichirō's account and the "clues" given him — is held together by one main narrative: Ichirō's search for his true identity. Although Ichirō sees this as a personal endeavor, at the same time it becomes a crucial proof in support of Masaki's scientific theories. In his scholarship titled *The Ultimate Detective Fiction: The Brain Is Not the Site of Thought (Zettai tantei shōsetsu: Nōzui wa mono o kangaeru tokoro ni arazu)*, Masaki reconfigures the human body and goes so far as to say that human beings' reliance on the illusion of the brain as the center of the body lies at the root of various social ills:

> "The brain that thinks things" successfully effaced God from the human world and made human beings oppose the natural world. It began to construct a material culture for humans. The brain first thought up various weapons for humans and made it easier for people to kill each other. . . . It made various machines move about and turned the world into a smaller place. It invented a multitude of lights and expelled the sun, the moon, and the stars. It put human beings, the children of nature, into houses of steel and stone. It had them breathe gas and electricity and made their arteries solidify. It applied cosmetics of lead and dirt and made people amuse themselves with mechanical humans [*kikai ningen*]. (184)

Masaki's quote echoes Hirabayashi's comments on the age of machines. The brain is a world of material culture and technology, from which the "natural" world has been expelled. Once again, machines replace the biological and people become robots themselves, breathing artificial air and living under artificial light. Masaki tells a story of loss, where machines have effaced the natural world, and it becomes clear that his ultimate goal is to recover what was lost. As he never fails to remind Ichirō, if the experiment is successful and Ichiro remembers his past, then this natural world can be regained.

Evolutionist scholars like Tsurumi Shunsuke, therefore, have come to interpret the figure of Ichirō as an antirobot, as one who resists the dominance of the artificial and the mechanical:

> Artificiality may succeed in creating a cognition that is more complicated than the one life created. [In the future], there may be people with useless bodies who become loyal servants of intelligent robots and serve these artificial brains. . . . However, there will still be antirobot humans who would believe that they are living only to experience life itself. . . . I want to situate the protagonist of *Dogura magura* as one of these rebellious antirobots.[36]

It is true that Ichirō's search for his identity parallels Masaki's search for the lost natural world. However, what makes *Dogura magura* a disturbing text is that even when Ichirō remembers his past in the end, the natural world cannot be recovered. Ichirō becomes a mechanized being, and the natural and the mechanical in the text are not separate. As such, the existence of an antirobot is rendered impossible in the world of *Dogura magura*.

Even Masaki, a steadfast opponent of "artificiality" who tries to restore the line between the authentic and the artificial, cannot escape from the insidious vocabulary of the machine. He imagines the human body through mechanical metaphors and ultimately fuses the biological with the mechanical. In his dismissal of the brain as the site of thought and memory, Masaki describes the brain's operation as follows:

> Let us take a look inside this foolish, automatic, and reflexive phone company that we call the brain.... A large group of nerve cells, as you can see, turn themselves into phone lines, switches, codes, switchboards, relay stations, or antenna, vacuum tubes, dials, and coils. At the same time, they each have a certain sense of consciousness within themselves and separate themselves into specific specializations — one in charge of crying, one in charge of laughing, one that sees, one that hears, one that remembers, one that falls in love, etc. (225)

Masaki pictures the brain as an automatic system, where every organic cell becomes a mechanical object. These objects, however, still possess a certain consciousness and possess a specific human behavior (remembering, falling in love, and so on). Thus an organic substance can be divided into mechanical parts, and, at the same time, the mechanical parts can act in a human manner. The text of *Dogura magura* constantly fuses the biological mode of the body with descriptions of machines. "The natural" or the authentic aura is already a nonrecoverable entity in *Dogura magura*, just as auratic sounds have already disappeared, and thus it becomes more and more difficult for Ichirō to regain his complete identity. In fact, as the narrative progresses, the reader becomes more and more aware of the characters' mechanical aspects. Even elements normally understood to be specific to an individual — memories, family history, individual experience — are rendered in the text as mere repetition of events over which the individual has no control. Ichirō himself is a repetition of his ancestor, Go Seishū, the painter of the gruesome scroll. Every male member of this family line, when triggered by the painting, must kill women around them. In the words of Dr. Masaki, "They say that history repeats itself, but the human body [*nikutai*] and spirit [*seishin*] also advance by repeating themselves."[37] This strange evolutionary process, however, fails in *Dogura magura*. Ichirō, after all, is an insane murderer, hardly what one would call "evolutionary advancement." He is already programmed from the moment of his conception to follow and mimic the acts of those before him, even if the acts should be gruesome murders. The individual here is no longer autonomous in the sense of having a free will. He or she simply repeats the actions of his or her ancestors.

Repetition, in fact, plays a large role in the text, and it is here that we find a strong Freudian influence. In Freud's essay, the compulsion to repeat the same thing — "the repetition of the same features or character-traits or vicissitudes, of the same crimes, or even the same names through several consecutive generations" — is an uncanny phenomenon. Jacques Lacan later envisioned this compulsion as the "senseless functioning of a machine, the unconscious henceforth being identified with a cybernetic automaton." It is a recording of a narrative, which "by virtue of being recorded, enables the narrative to be repeated endlessly."[38] Ichirō's inheritance of the murderous genes and his ancestors' repetitive crimes certainly fall into this category, and even memory is reduced to a compulsive repetition in the novel. The narrative form adopts this repetition, as if to make the reader experience the Freudian uncanny. Toward the end the novel especially, each time Ichirō reaches a conclusion about the murders, his theory is undercut by a new clue. As he himself states, "My head is turning around and around in the same place … like an electric fan" (732). Memory here is a recorded program that cannot be overwritten, and the characters are thus trapped in their repetitive lives.

As the narrative advances, the realization that Ichirō's search for a coherent self will end in failure grows. This is confirmed by the fact that Ichirō himself becomes a replicable object. From the moment that he wakes up in cell number seven, Ichirō is haunted by images of himself. He looks at his reflection in the window, in a doorknob, and later, in a mirror, all the while trying "to recall some kind of memory by looking at the reflected face and figure" (4). The text becomes an investigation into Lacan's mirror stage — the moment when one's identity emerges and is confirmed by connecting individual consciousness to a specific, physical body. In Ichirō's case, however, this developmental stage ends in failure, and he cannot connect any memory or personal history to the reflections he sees.

These images of himself later take on the more concrete form of a doppelgänger. One of the more intense scenes in the novel occurs when Masaki forces Ichirō to face his doppelgänger. Masaki points to Ichirō's double standing outside the window, and Ichirō wonders: "That [person] and I … Kure Ichirō … and I … Which is Kure Ichirō?" (517). In classic narratives of the double, the double behaves almost like the protagonist's evil twin and threatens his or her existence. This is the case in "The Sandman" and "William Wilson," by E. T. A. Hoffman and Edgar Allan Poe, respectively, two writers Yumeno is often compared with. Here, however, Ichirō refuses to accept the fact that the doppelgänger is really a copy of himself, and he continues the search for his own identity. He convinces himself that it is the double who is the real murderer Kure Ichirō and that he himself is just an innocent look-alike. When this scene, like earlier "mirror stage" scenes, inevitably ends in Ichirō's failure to recognize his duplicated image, we begin to lose hope that he will remember anything about his past. Ichirō's dream in his womb, in his own words, is like a "frighteningly long serial film" where he is forced to watch a copy of himself performing gruesome acts of murder (218). He continues to insist on the distinction between himself and the replica until the very end. As the narrative progresses, other characters are also reduced to the status of reproductions and begin to lose their identities. Moyoko, Ichirō's fiancée and the only female character in the novel with a voice, turns up alive, but she, too, is just a reproduction of Go Seishū's wife. It also becomes evident that Wakabayashi and Masaki are in fact reproductions of one another. Masaki even proclaims at one point that he and Wakabayashi are the same. The novel's form, as if to correspond to this split self, is divided into two halves — the first half dominated by Wakabayashi and his theories and the latter half belonging to Masaki's experiment. Ultimately the two individuals are reduced to two symbols, M and W, inverse images of each other. No character in the entire novel possesses a stable, singular self. Every person is a reflection or a reproduction of another, as hinted at by Wakabayashi's first name — Kyōtarō, which literally means "mirror child." The text itself is duplicated, as Ichirō discovers a copy of *Dogura magura* on a table and experiences a strange sense of familiarity.[39]

The mechanical aspect of Ichirō is drawn out further by the fact that the text takes away his human side. Ichirō never regains his love for his fiancée, Moyoko, and is incapable of human relationships. Even though Moyoko calls out to Ichirō from the next room, she fails to evoke any emotion in Ichirō's heart:

> I [Ichirō] could not answer her call. No, I should not answer her call. I am someone who doesn't even know if she really is my wife. I can't even remember her face, even when I hear her deep, painful, and sincere screams. The only thing I can remember as part of my past's real memory is the sound of the clock "booooon" that I just heard. (10–11)

In the words of one literary historian, the characters in Yumeno's works "disintegrate as if their train of thought was burnt off, when discussing things like a woman's true feelings, or those things that cannot be converted into data."[40] Human relations hold no meaning for Ichirō, especially those with women. The only relation he can have with women is the one already programmed into him: he kills women to complete the scroll. Thus all we know about Ichirō's relationship with Moyoko or his mother and aunt must come from secondary sources (newspaper articles, Masaki's account, and so on), and although Ichirō's narrative consumes countless pages, he never discloses this type of information himself. He trusts the sound of the clock more than the voices of people, and it is highly significant that Yumeno chose the onomatopoeia of a clock for both the first and the last lines of the novel. Ichirō's mind, from beginning to end, is haunted by mechanical sounds, and although he can process these sounds and the information contained in articles, films, or the voices of his two doctors, he remains deaf to the cries of his former lover.

The epitome of Ichirō's mechanization process takes place, however, when Ichirō's body literally becomes a new weapon. Ichirō's recovery of his past signals the end of the experiment, but portends a grim future. It is clear from the text that if the experiment is successful, humans like Ichirō will be transformed into a new type of weapon. References to Ichirō as a weapon appear throughout the text. Wakabayashi expresses concerns about the experiment, knowing that its success will result in a weapon surpassing even "Nobel's dynamite, that which escalated all wars in the world" (36). Masaki, too, confirms the destructive potential of the experiment, stating that "if one is able to deploy this horrifying trigger mechanism . . . one would be able to perform crimes that not even the best detective could solve" (312). What Ichirō achieves in the end is not free will but a programmable body, the ultimate criminal tool. Yumeno will exploit this issue further in works such as "Rekōdo ningen" (1936, Record man), a story about Russian spies whose brains are replaced by tape recorders in order to capture every word uttered by the enemy.[41] In *Dogura magura*, however, the focus remains not on the application of the weapon but on its creation and its cognitive mechanisms.

Ichirō's search for his own identity ends in failure. The more he searches, the more he realizes that he is a reproduction of another and, as a result, the more he loses his claims to agency. Masaki's central question — "To what extent do people actually have control over their own body and mind?" — is answered at the very end (181). As the face of Go Seishū appears in front of Ichirō and laughs at him, Ichirō finally seems to give in to the fact that people have *no* control over their own minds. The novel's strange ending has traditionally been interpreted as Ichirō's realization that he is a fetus and his return to the infantile world. In actuality, however, the ending is quite ambiguous. Ichirō can still hear the cries of Moyoko from the hallway, as he imagines himself to be a fetus. In other words, Ichirō may not really be a fetus but may only be *imagining* himself as one. If we take the latter interpretation into account, we can read the ending as Ichirō's desperate attempt to return to the natural world and his ultimate failure to do so. Though the novel is centered on Ichirō's attempt to regain his subjectivity, in the end both he and the reader realize that the attempt is a futile one. Ichirō realizes that his fate has already been decided for him, that he is going to be a murderer like his ancestors. He cannot write his own experiences, as they are already written for him.

In the end, then, Ichirō, rather than being an antirobot, actually behaves quite like an inhuman "automaton" — a mechanized being that performs only those actions for which it has been programmed. His existence consists solely of a programmed past, and he is trapped in the nightmarish repetition of having to kill those around him over and over again. He is not even capable of human feelings and can only exhibit repetitive behavior. The oppositional binary of the biological and the mechanical is ultimately effaced, with the text able to envision human bodies only as another type of machine. Nowhere in the text do we find a coherent, purely "natural" subject.

The Uncanny Revisited

The uncanny can be located in several different places in the text. A textbook definition of the uncanny as "the return of the repressed" appears in *Dogura magura* in the form of the return of Ichirō's memory of his ancestors' crimes. The entire narrative is centered on the discovery of Ichirō's repressed memories of the murders, and when he actually remembers them, he realizes that he is living in a dream.

> Everything is a dream of a fetus.... I am still in my mother's womb and am suffering from this fearful "dream of a fetus." Booooon... the sound of the clock trailed from the end of the hallway. (736)

It is almost certain, given Yumeno's studies at Kyūshū Imperial University and his mention of Freud by name on several occasions in the novel, that Yumeno was aware of the Freudian psychoanalysis of dreams. The Freudian manner in which Ichirō's suppressed unconscious reemerges, and the "fearful" truth that comes to light, is thus not very surprising. The sound of the clock, toward the end, is yet another trigger mechanism; with each chime Ichirō recalls his "fearful memories" and sees dead faces from the past.

The mechanical uncanny, however, comes to the fore when the biological body is reconfigured as a mechanized one. As I have shown, Ichirō realizes that his search for his identity is futile, for he himself resembles an automaton. What is more, it is clear that the "authentic" that both he and Masaki are seeking can no longer be retrieved, for everyone around

Ichirō, including himself, is but a copy of another. The biological body, in the end, becomes a product of science, an object controlled only by the "mad scientist." In Yumeno's words:

> Countless scientists, the founders of modern civilization, were all fear-some bureaucrats who opposed God and morals.... The medicines and machines they created were all criminal weapons *[hanzai yōgu]* that undermined God and nature.[42]

This passage can be read as an abstract, of sorts, for the novel as a whole. Once Ichirō concludes that he can never be cured and that he is just a programmable "criminal weapon," he stops searching for the authentic self that never existed in the first place. As if to acknowledge his transformation into a mechanical object, Ichirō even goes as far as to describe himself as a "mechanical puppet" *(kikai ningyō)* (687), and in other parts of the narrative, we can also find Ichirō's movements being compared to mechanical objects like electric fans. The narrative "tricks" the reader into believing that the text is a detective novel about a man and his search for his true identity. It creates the expectation in the reader that there is, in fact, something like a coherent self. This expectation, however, seems to have been created only to be betrayed; in the end, order is not restored and in its place is the assertion that the artificial–authentic dichotomy never existed in the first place.

The mechanical uncanny emerges, then, the moment one realizes that what one considered to be a foreign other has appeared within oneself. In the case of Ichirō, it is the realization that he is an unnatural, mechanized being — the result of a destabilization of the artificial and the authentic. Furthermore, it is also the moment when he realizes that the man in the courtyard — whom he constantly refutes as himself — is indeed his double. Toward the very end of the novel, Ichirō discovers a newspaper clipping reporting several murders that took place at the mental institution on the day that he saw the double in the courtyard:

> Ichirō began to smile, and lifting again the bloody hoe, approached the two women who were standing there. He first cornered the girl who was dancing earlier and smashed her forehead. He then approached the older woman who was dressed like a queen and was calmly observing her surroundings. But when she yelled, "Insolent fool! Don't you know who I am?," Kure Ichirō was shocked and halted with his hoe in his hands. "Oh, you are Empress Yang Guifei," he shouted, and knelt upon the sand. (719)

Ichirō himself has no recollection of this event, but is completely frightened and bewildered at this discovery. What is defamiliarizing here is not only the murders he committed but the fact that Ichirō's double is inscribed as "Chinese" and that he bows to the reincarnation of the legendary Chinese empress Yang Guifei. Just a moment ago, however, arguing with Masaki, Ichirō had claimed: "What about academia? What about foreign scientists? I may be crazy, but I am Japanese. I know that I have inherited the blood of the Japanese race" (674). In other words, Ichirō the narrator believes strongly that he is of the "pure Japanese" race, but his doppelgänger is clearly marked as Chinese. There is obviously a strong nationalistic discourse at work here. The ease with which the novel distinguishes between what is "foreign" and what is "Japanese" is astounding. The text, after all, narrates a tale of a Chinese man killing Japanese women, and sciences like biology and mechanics are constantly marked as Western.[43] All the negative things in the novel, such as Ichirō's murderous genes and modern science, are conveniently situated in the foreign sphere.[44] In fact, there is something strangely "foreign" about Ichirō from the beginning. Ichirō's ancestral past, after all, narrates a Japanization of a Chinese man, who, we are told, was painting the morbid scroll as a patriotic gift for the Chinese emperor. This devotion to China that Ichirō exhibits is evident from the fact that all the women he murders are Japanese and that the one woman who can actually control him claims to be the reincarnation of Yang Guifei. This foreignness of Ichirō is drawn out by the fact that he is described by Dr. Masaki as a hybrid of myriad races, who has the skin color of "a white race," the inside of the nose resembling that of "a Mongol," a "Latin" facial structure, "Ainu-like" eyes, and a "Greek" nose. Masaki's descriptions echo the novel's discriminatory tone against the Chinese, when he declares that all of these nationalities existent in Ichirō have docile characteristics, except for one: "The brutal, cruel blood of the Continent [mainland China]," "the Mongolian genes hiding in the youth's nose" (320–21).

The uncanny in the novel, then, is linked to "a foreign threat" — a force epitomized by figures like monsters that threaten the individual's freedom and ultimately the nation as a whole.[45] However, whereas in a novel like *Dracula,* the threat is embodied by an outside force and the British conquer the monster in the end, in *Dogura magura,* Ichirō himself must realize that the monster lives within himself, that he himself is the foreign killer attacking his own nation. Not only must Ichirō realize that there is something unnatural and automatic within himself, he must also become aware that what controls his programmable body is precisely the foreign blood that flows within himself. This is precisely why someone like Ichirō is rendered as posing a threat. He is both Japanese and Chinese and threatens the distinction between the two nationalities. Even worse, he is a menace to his own country. It is not coincidental that Ichirō's realization that the man in the courtyard was indeed himself takes place right after he finds the newspaper article. Once he admits that the murderous Chinese doppelgänger was himself all along, the illusion that he is an innocent, "pure Japanese" citizen crumbles. The narrator Ichirō loses to his double. He becomes an object controlled by his Chinese blood, and he is traumatized by the fact that he himself is the foreign mechanism, the weapon programmed to kill the women of his country.

The mechanical uncanny in *Dogura magura* thus functions at two levels. First, as I have shown, Ichirō realizes that what he considers to be natural (like his memory) is actually mechanical and that he has something unnatural within himself and can never become the whole, coherent being he imagined himself to be. Second, this unnatural mechanical aspect is marked as foreign and disrupts the notion of pure race, undermining Ichirō's "Japaneseness." Although Ichirō tries to resist his foreignness, ultimately he fails to do so and becomes a "criminal weapon" controlled by foreign powers. Unlike typical detective fiction, in Yumeno's "irregular detective fiction" order is never restored, the monster is not conquered, and the mechanical uncanny remains triumphant.

Conclusion

Recent scholarship on the uncanny has come to explore its relationship to nationalism. Beginning with Freud and taken up again by Rosemary Jackson, the uncanny always connoted a certain discourse of fear associated with the foreign other, and this idea was taken further by scholars such as Homi Bhabha and Julia Kristeva as a way to discuss the heterogeneity and paranoia that exists within the borders of the nation.[46]

This chapter has explored just one aspect of how mechanical images appeared in prewar Japanese literature. It is remarkable how the fear of machines and artificiality overlap with the paranoia about the other that is clearly situated in imperial Japan. Although *Dogura magura* has become synonymous with Yumeno Kyūsaku's name itself, sociohistorical studies of the work have yet to be done. My point here was not that Yumeno was a strong nationalist or that he feared technology. Rather, I hoped to show how machines were a major trope of 1930s Japan as a metaphor that represented the human mind and body. The body continued to become mechanized and programmable in the following years of wartime Japan, as eugenicists and scientists carried on with their experiments and alterations on the body. Yumeno's novel can be read as a warning that cautions against these modifications, revealing the cruelty performed in the name of "science."

Notes

I would like to thank Mark Gibeau, James Reichert, the editors of the volume and of the University of Minnesota Press, and referees at *Science Fiction Studies* for their insightful comments and suggestions on this essay. I would also like to thank Jean-Pierre Dupuy for sharing with me his own theories on automatons and systems theory.

1. Yumeno Kyūsaku, *Dogura magura* (Tokyo: Chūsekisha, 1995). All quotations are taken from this edition of the text, and all translations are mine.

2. On nationalism in Yumeno, see, for example, Tsurumi Shunsuke, *Yumeno Kyūsaku: Meikyū no jūnin* (Yumeno Kyūsaku: The inhabitant of a labyrinth) (Tokyo: Riburopōto, 1989), 69–84; Junko Williams, "Visions and Narratives: Modernism in the Prose Works of Yoshiyuki Eisuke, Murayama Tomoyoshi, Yumeno Kyūsaku, and Okamoto Kanoko" (PhD diss., Ohio State University, 1998), 158–211.

3. For an excellent analysis of what was then considered "regular detective fiction" as opposed to what was "irregular" and "deviant," see James Reichert, "Deviance and Social Darwinism in Edogawa Ranpo's Erotic-Grotesque Thriller *Kotō no oni*," *Journal of Japanese Studies* 27 (2001): 113–41. On the connection between "irregular detective fiction" and "early science fiction," see Ishikawa Takashi, *SF no jidai* (The age of SF) (Tokyo: Kisō Tengaisha, 1977), 134; Robert Matthews, *Japanese Science Fiction: A View of a Changing Society* (London: Routledge, 1989), 13–38.

4. Williams, "Visions and Narratives," 190.

5. Oda Susumu cites *Dogura magura* as an important record of psychoanalytic studies at the university. Oda Susumu, "Seishin igaku no kenchi kara mita Nakamura Kokyō to *Hentai shinri*" (Nakamura Kokyō and *Perverse Psychology* observed from the point of view of psychiatry), in *Hentai shinri to Nakamura Kokyō: Taishō bunka e no shinshikaku* (*Perverse Psychology* and Nakamura Kokyō: Toward a new perspective on Taishō culture) (Tokyo: Fuji Shuppan, 2001), 17.

6. Sugiyama Kura, "*Dogura magura* shippitsuchū no omoide" (Remembrances of the days of writing *Dogura magura*), in *Yumeno Kyūsaku no sekai* (The world of Yumeno Kyūsaku), ed. Nishihara Kazumi (Tokyo: Chūsekisha, 1991), 112.

7. For background on psychoanalysis in Japan and on the role of Kyūshū Imperial University, see Taketomo Yasuhiko, "Cultural Adaptation of Psychoanalysis in Japan, 1912–52," *Social Research* 57 (1990): 951–91. Ōishi Masahiko also notes that psychology was a science that did not fit into Japan's modernization schema. Ōishi Masahiko, *Shin seinen no kyōwakoku* (The republic of shin seinen) (Tokyo: Suiseisha, 1992), 24.

8. Ōda Susumu makes this point in "Seishin igaku." For more information on Kure Shūzō, see Omata Waichirō, *Seishin byōin no kigen: Kindaihen* (The origins of mental institutions: The modern era) (Tokyo: Ōta Shuppan, 2000), 30–33.

9. Yumeno Kyūsaku, *Inugami hakase* (Dr. Inugami), vol. 6 of *Yumeno Kyūsaku zenshū* (Complete works of Yumeno Kyūsaku) (Tokyo: San'ichi Shobō, 1969). For more information on *Dr. Caligari* and its influences, see Okada Susumu et al., eds., *Gendai eiga jiten* (Dictionary of contemporary film) (Tokyo: Bijutsu Shuppansha, 1973), 209.

10. Nakajima Kawatarō, afterword to *Dogura magura,* 3.

11. For information about the 1930s reception of Yumeno's work, see the period essays compiled in the first section of Nishihara, *Yumeno Kyūsaku no sekai.*

12. For example, the embryologist Miki Shigeo discusses how *Dogura magura* invents the concept of "cell memory" *(saibō kioku),* meaning that each individual cell in the human body can contain certain memories. He builds on this theory and perceives the novel as a work that foreshadows today's biotechnology. Miki Shigeo, *Taiji no sekai* (The world of the fetus) (Tokyo: Chūō Kōronsha, 1983), especially the section on "the dream of the fetus" (143–51).

13. Hirabayashi Hatsunosuke, "Modanizumu no shakaiteki konkyo" (The social basis of modernism), in *Hirabayashi Hatsunosuke bungei hyōron zenshū* (Collected cultural criticism of Hirabayashi Hatsunosuke) (Tokyo: Bunsendō Shoten, 1975), 3:836–49.

14. Tsurumi, *Yumeno Kyūsaku,* 261; Ōishi, *Shin seinen,* 121. Ōishi unfortunately does not expand this observation into a developed thesis.

15. Hirabayashi, "Modanizumu no shakaiteki konkyo," 843–44.

16. Itagaki Takao, "Kikai to geijutsu to no kōryū" (The exchange between machines and art), in *Kikai no metoroporisu* (Machine metropolis), ed. Unno Hiroshi (Tokyo: Heibonsha, 1990), 452.

17. Mizushima Niou, "Jinzō ningen jidai" (The age of artificial humans), in Unno, *Kikai no metoroporisu,* 306–12. See also Yonezawa Yoshihiro, "Robotto būmu" (Robot boom), *Bessatsu taiyō: Ranpō no jidai – Shōwa ero guro nonsensu* (A special issue of *Taiyō*: The era of Edogawa Ranpō – Shōwa erotic grotesque nonsense), *Taiyō* 88 (Winter 1994): 52–53. The human qualities of robots at this time are remarked on in several essays in *Ninshin suru robotto: 1920 nendai no kagaku to gensō* (Robots that become pregnant: Science and the fantastic in the 1920s), ed. Yoshida Morio et al. (Tokyo: Shunpūsha, 2002). See especially Yoshida Morio's title essay (8–59), which discusses how the figure of Maria in *Metropolis* influenced the Japanese understanding of "robots."

18. Unno, *Kikai no metoroporisu,* 477.

19. Aramata Hiroshi, "Kikai e no shikōsei: Ranpō to puroretaria bungaku" (A taste for machines: Edogawa Ranpō and proletarian literature), in *Bessatsu taiyō: Ranpō no jidai – Shōwa ero guro nonsensu* (A special issue of *Taiyō*: The era of Edogawa Ranpō – Shōwa erotic grotesque nonsense), *Taiyō* 88 (Winter 1994): 30.

20. Reichert, "Deviance and Social Darwinism," 114.

21. Yumeno Kyūsaku, "Kōga Saburō-shi ni kotau" (A response to Mr. Kōga Saburō), in *Yumeno Kyūsaku zenshū* (Complete works of Yumeno Kyūsaku) (Tokyo: Chikuma shobō, 1992), 11:74. This oft-cited passage is one of the most famous quotations from Yumeno's essays. Edogawa Ranpō, for example, quotes it in his obituary for Yumeno and uses it to show Yumeno's flexibility toward the term *detective fiction.* Edogawa Ranpō, "Yumeno Kyūsakun shi to sono sakuhin" (Mr. Yumeno Kyūsaku and his works), in Nishihara, *Yumeno Kyūsaku no sekai,* 31–42. See also Tsurumi, *Yumeno Kyūsaku,* 235.

22. Yumeno Kyūsaku, "Kaimu" (Strange dreams), in *Yumeno Kyūsaku,* vol. 3 of *Nihon gensō bungaku shūsei* (Anthology of Japanese fantastic literature), ed. Horikiri Naoto (Tokyo: Kokusho Kankōkai, 1991), 94–119.

23. Yumeno, "Kōga Saburō-shi ni kotau," 73.

24. This terminology is taken from Mark Seltzer, *Bodies and Machines* (New York: Routledge, 1992), 91–118.

25. Yokomitsu Riichi, "Kikai," in *Yokomitsu Riichi zenshū* (Tokyo: Kawade shoten, 1955–56), 3:359–77; translated by Edward Seidensticker as "Machine," in *Modern Japanese Stories* (Rutland, Vt.: Tuttle, 1962), 223–44.

26. Sigmund Freud, "The Uncanny," in *The Standard Edition of the Complete Psychological Works of Sigmund Freud,* ed. and trans. James Strachey (London: Hogarth, 1955), 17:227, 232.

27. Yumeno, "Kōga Saburō-shi ni kotau."

28. See, for example, Yumeno's 1935 essay on the future of detective fiction and his critique of its "regular" form, "Tantei shōsetsu no shinshimei" (The new mission for detective fiction), in *Yumeno Kyūsaku zenshū* (Complete works of Yumeno Kyūsaku) (Tokyo: Chikuma shobō, 1992), 11:60–68.

29. Freud, "Uncanny," 234, 235.

30. Yumeno, *Dogura magura,* 181.

31. Jean-Pierre Dupuy, "The Autonomy of Social Reality: On the Contribution of Systems Theory to the Theory of Society," in *Evolution, Order, and Complexity,* ed. Elias L. Khalil and Kenneth E. Boulding (London: Routledge, 1996), 62. For an interesting analysis of Freud's automaton and its relationship to modern communication machines, see Christopher Johnson, "Ambient Technologies, Uncanny Signs," *Oxford Literary Review* 21 (1999): 117–34.

32. Tsurumi Shunsuke describes the text as "foreshadowing cybernetics" (*Yumeno Kyūsaku,* 259); and, as mentioned earlier, Miki Shigeo *(Taiji no sekai)* describes it as a text presaging the coming of biotechnology.

33. Dupuy, "Autonomy of Social Reality," 69.

34. Although it is beyond the scope of this chapter to discuss the role of the female bodies in *Dogura magura,* I believe that if any human body in 1930s Japan could be described as "mechanical," it was the female body, specifically in the context of the reproductive organs. Ishimoto Shizue, the famous activist of the birth control movement, for example, remarked in her autobiography — coincidentally published the same year as *Dogura magura* — that the women in Japan were "automatons afraid of their own shadows." Katō Shizue [Baroness Shizue Ishimoto], *Facing Two Ways: The Story of My Life* (Stanford, Calif.: Stanford University Press, 1984), 273. What underlies this statement is the eugenics movement that dominated prewar Japan's scientific discourse and that promoted the idea that female bodies must be manipulated through scientific methods in order to produce "healthy" offspring, untainted by physical and mental diseases. Female bodies in prewar Japan were becoming what Seltzer might call "statistical persons" (*Bodies and Machines,* 91–118).

35. Scrolls depicting decaying female bodies were a form of Buddhist art called *kusōzu* (painting of the nine stages of a decaying corpse), produced in Japan from the thirteenth through the nineteenth centuries. Viewers were encouraged to contemplate on the nine stages of a decaying corpse *(kusōkan)* as a way to learn about the defilement of a decaying human body and liberate themselves from worldly, sexual desires. Yumeno, being a priest at one point in his life, often draws from Buddhist traditions. Although the text does not treat the scroll as a Buddhist *kusōzu* per se, to the educated Japanese audience, this would have been evident. Also, it is interesting that the scroll connects the male heirs in the Kure family and their repeated murderous behavior. Yumeno seems to be playing with the idea of karmic cycle *(rinne),* and the idea of repeated behavior could also be attributed to the sins and the actions of Ichirō's ancestors. For more information and analysis of *kusōzu,* see Fusae Kanda, "Behind the Sensationalism: Images of a Decaying Corpse in Japanese Buddhist Art," *Art Bulletin* 87 (2005): 24–49.

36. Tsurumi, *Yumeno Kyūsaku,* 261.

37. Ibid., 572.

38. Freud, "Uncanny," 234. On Lacan, see Jean-Pierre Dupuy, *Mechanization of the Mind*, trans. M. B. DeBevoise (Princeton, N.J.: Princeton University Press, 2000), 19. On recording, see Friedrich Kittler, "Dracula's Legacy," in *Literature, Media, Information Systems* (Amsterdam: Overseas Publishers Association, 1997), especially 51–52.

39. Although this chapter focuses on the psychoanalytic–mechanical notion of repetitive behavior, it is worth noting that eugenics and the scientific advancement of race and the human body play a huge role in this as well. As Sari Kawana has noted, *Dogura magura* is a story about mad scientists performing experiments on their insane patients, a popular theme in interwar Japan, and the two scientists in the story are informed by popular contemporary notions of science and eugenics. For example, Dr. Wakabayashi often discusses Ichirō's insanity in terms of "passed down memory," claiming madness to be a hereditary disease that lies in Ichirō's ancestry. Also, Ichirō's face is described as a hybrid of races, which refers to the popular eugenic debate that racial hybridity (as opposed to racial purity) could improve the Japanese blood/race. Sari Kawana, "Mad Scientists and Their Prey: Bioethics, Murder, and Fiction in Interwar Japan," *Journal of Japanese Studies* 31 (2005): 89–120. For an interesting discussion of this debate and the idea of blood and eugenics in 1930s Japan, see Jennifer Robertson, "Japan's First Cyborg? Miss Nippon, Eugenics, and Wartime Technologies of Beauty, Body, and Blood," *Body and Society* 7 (2001): 1–34. Robertson describes how altered, cyborgian female bodies were becoming the target of eugenic ideals. For general background on the eugenics movement in Japan, see Suzuki Zenji, *Nihon no yūseigaku* (Eugenics in Japan) (Tokyo: Sankyō Shuppan, 1983); Sabine Frühstück, *Colonizing Sex: Sexology and Social Control in Modern Japan* (Berkeley: University of California Press, 2003).

40. Waki Akiko, "Yumeno Kyūsaku: Ishiki no jigoku no yūrei" (Yumeno Kyūsaku: The ghost in the hell of consciousness), in Nishihara, *Yumeno Kyūsaku no sekai*, 399.

41. Yumeno Kyūsaku, "Rekōdo ningen" (Record man), in *Yumeno Kyūsaku zenshū* (Complete works of Yumeno Kyūsaku) (Tokyo: Chikuma Shobō, 1992), 10:249–68.

42. Yumeno, "Kōga Saburō-shi ni kotau," 73.

43. This reflects Yumeno's own criticism that science was a Western import that came to dominate Japan. See Williams, "Visions and Narratives," 202.

44. Matsuyama Shigeo has also offered a similar reading of *Dogura magura* where he situates the text against the anti-Korean and anti-Chinese sentiment that was proliferating in wartime Japan. He cites specific incidents from this period that Yumeno was informed by, including the massacre of the Koreans during the Kantō Earthquake of 1923. It is significant that Yumeno claims to have begun writing the novel around the time of the earthquake, and Matsuyama sees the text as a production of the author's witnessing of the Japanese citizens' blind "madness" and cruelty against its foreign nationals. Matsuyama Shigeo, *Gunshū: Kikai no naka no nanmin* (Crowds: Refugees among machines) (Tokyo: Yomiuri Shinbunsha, 1996), 219–39.

45. Franco Moretti, "Dialectic of Fear," trans. Susan Fischer, David Forgacs, and David Miller, in *Signs Taken for Wonders: Essays in the Sociology of Literary Forms* (London: Verso, 1997), 93.

46. Anthony Vidler has a wonderful summary of recent scholarship on the uncanny in his introduction to *The Architectural Uncanny.* Rosemary Jackson talks about the uncanny and discusses how the fantastic shifts its shape according to what society considers as an other. Homi Bhabha uses the uncanny to capture the effacing borders between ethnic groups that exist within the nation, and Julia Kristeva ties the uncanny to a certain xenophobia. Anthony Vidler, *The Architectural Uncanny: Essays in the Modern Unhomely* (Cambridge, Mass.: MIT Press, 1999); Rosemary Jackson, *Fantasy: The Literature of Subversion* (London: Routledge, 1981), 61–67; Homi K. Bhabha, "DissemiNation: Time, Narrative, and the Margins of the Modern Nation," in *Nation and Narration* (London: Routledge, 1990), 319–20; and Julia Kristeva, *Strangers to Ourselves* (New York: Columbia University Press, 1994).

2. Has the Empire Sunk Yet?
The Pacific in Japanese Science Fiction

Thomas Schnellbächer

The sea as a narrative space pervades the genealogy of science fiction, from fantastic voyages in the *Odyssey* tradition to the adventure stories of the nineteenth century. But the oceans ceased to be the great unknown around the time of science fiction's immediate precursors in scientific romance. In hard science fiction, the oceans were long ago pre-empted by interstellar space, more recently by cyberspace. It is interesting, therefore, that in Japanese science fiction after 1945, a number of major works focus on the ocean surrounding Japan. In fact, from 1945 through the mid-1970s, the Pacific Ocean acquired the status of a Japanese science fiction topos. This is not simply a consequence of Japan's being an island nation: the ocean does not figure prominently in British science fiction; nor does the ocean retain any special status in Japanese science fiction today. The object of this chapter is to pinpoint the issues with which this topos was associated and to inquire into what its history reveals about the science fiction discourses of its time.[1]

In brief, my argument is that the ocean figures in works that are in some way associated with Japanese national identity, specifically with pre-1945 Japanese imperialism and the idea of Japan as a Pacific sea power. In some of these works, the ocean is also connected with mythic, archetypal nature, but this is a contingent ingredient. Modern Japan's geopolitical situation is the element most essential to the discourse in question.

From the sixteenth century on, Japan's military regents practiced a policy of isolationism, but toward the middle of the nineteenth century, pressure on Japan mounted to open its ports to international trade. This was eventually forced by a naval show of strength by the United States in 1853 and 1854. Shortly after this, a coup d'état in Japan was followed by the establishment of a European-type imperial monarchy (the Meiji Restoration of 1868), which was in turn part of an aggressive modernization program. The Imperial Navy played an important part in these changes and was viewed, no doubt rightly, as a guarantor of Japan's national autonomy in an age of imperialist expansion.

At the same time, Japan soon became a regional colonial power in its own right, and fantastic adventure stories played their part in spreading the colonial ideology. In Yano Ryūkei's novel *Ukishiro monogatari* (1890, *The Tale of the Floating Fortress*), for instance, a group of Japanese South Seas adventurers takes possession of a British warship and sets off to explore Africa. Yano was influenced by Jules Verne, whose works were immensely popular in Japan during the 1880s. There is no question that Verne's *Twenty-Thousand Leagues under the Sea* (1870) was a particularly important influence on all the works to be discussed here. However, the themes of Japanese identity and autonomy are even more prominent. Hence, while many of the narratives I discuss draw on well-known precursors (both Western and Japanese), there are significant variations. My discussion, for instance, features several idealistic renegade submarine commanders reminiscent of Verne's Captain Nemo. Yet all are patriots and naval officers — a far cry from Nemo's anarchism. Such telling variations suggest why it is possible to talk about a specifically Japanese science-fictional topos here.

The group of texts to be discussed includes internationally well-known works in various narrative media. In the film *Gojira* (1954; extensively revised for the U.S. market as *Godzilla, King of Monsters!*), the monster emerges from the Pacific, giving occasion for allusions to lost Japanese territories and Japanese technical expertise "misdirected" into war. Less popular but equally important is the first Japanese science fiction novel, *Dai yon kanpyōki* (1959, *Inter Ice Age 4*) by the avant-garde writer Abe Kōbō (1924–1993), which features a submarine genetic-engineering project. At the end of the period to be discussed stands the cult manga and anime series *Uchū senkan Yamato* (1974–83, *Space Battleship Yamato,* also known as *Star Blazers*), in which the legendary Japanese battleship Yamato, sunk in 1945, is salvaged in the twenty-second century and sent on an intergalactic mission to save the earth (Figure 2.1). Finally, Komatsu Sakyō's (1931–) novel *Nihon chinbotsu* (1973, *Japan Sinks*) was a major best seller whose popularity extended well beyond a science fiction readership; along with the Abe work, it is one of the few Japanese science fiction novels to be translated into a significant number of European languages.[2]

First, however, I discuss two lost-world romances published in 1947 and 1948 that were the debut publications of the mystery writer Kayama

Figure 2.1. Promotional poster for the laser disc release of the films in the *Uchū senkan Yamato (Star Blazers)* series, 1990. The series begins with the raising of the World War II battleship *Yamato,* which is converted to a space-going vessel.

Shigeru (1909–1975). These novels introduced into fantastic literature the characteristic postwar themes of war guilt, sense of loss, regression, and new beginning. Kayama also was invited a half decade later to draft the scenario for *Godzilla,* which closely echoes many of these themes. I then focus on *Godzilla,* along with the director Honda Ishirō's (1911–1993) submarine fantasy film *Kaitei gunkan* (1963, The seabed warship; released in the United States as *Atragon* in 1965), with its powerful allusions to an important 1900 militarist adventure story.[3] *Inter Ice Age 4* is treated here as the antithesis to territorial and national concerns, which are critiqued by imagining all major land masses as submerged. Finally, *Japan Sinks* singles out Japan, which wholly disappears under the surface of the sea. To the best of my knowledge, this is the last major application of the ocean topos to date, at least in the postwar mode sketched here.

Kayama Shigeru: Missing Links and Misty Islands

Kayama Shigeru had a late professional debut in April 1947 with "Oran Pendeku no fukushū" ("The Revenge of the Orang Pendek"), written less than a year after the Japanese surrender in May 1946. The concluding sequel, "Oran Pendeku no gojitsutan" ("The Fate of the Orang Pendek") was published in January 1948.[4]

In the first story, Professor Miyakawa is an anthropologist who has recently returned to Japan after spending the war years in Sumatra. He reports on two unknown species of humans: the Orang Pendek of the title ("small man," a kind of missing link) and another that is amphibious and has gills.[5] At the climax of his lecture reporting on these species, the scientist collapses and dies. An examination reveals that he has the rosette birthmark of the Pendek and the gills implanted in his skin. His assistant Ishigami investigates and finds explanations for Miyakawa's mysterious state. Ishigami becomes his mentor's heir and marries his daughter, Hatae.

The denouement is false, however. Having left home without warning, Ishigami reveals in a letter to his wife that he poisoned her father. Ishigami is in fact an Orang Pendek, compelled to leave his people soon after his birth because he lacked their characteristic birthmark. He was brought to Japan, adopted by Miyakawa, and learned his identity years later. He originally planned the murder because he was forbidden to marry Hatae, but (as already suggested by the title) he is also given the more profound motive of revenge when he discovers that his adoptive father has killed several of his people. Ishigami has also, for the same reason, killed another Japanese scientist and a British administrator on Sumatra.

So far, the ocean topos is only implied through the related lost-world topos in its "island romance" form. In the sequel, however, the principal setting is the ocean. Hatae sets out on a yacht to look for her husband, accompanied by an Indonesian crew and a disguised skipper (who eventually turns out to be the missing husband). At the end of a twisting plot, hero and heroine join the rest of the surviving Pendek on an island shrouded in mist near the Antarctic Circle. Ishigami has calculated that shortly after their arrival, there will be a series of underwater volcanic eruptions that will interrupt the current that brought them there, hiding all trace of the Orang Pendek from the rest of humanity. He suggests that Hatae join the Orang Pendek — who are genetically identical and lead a polygamous life — to refresh their gene pool. When she refuses, he decides that he actually loves her and does not simply need her body for reproductive purposes. At this she consents to stay, give up her identity, and join the primitive tribe on its way to becoming *Homo sapiens.*

In the course of the two stories, postwar remorse and loss turn magically into future promise, with evolutionary progress as a metaphor for modernization. At the same time, the boundaries between nations, tribes, and even species are blurred, and geopolitical space is converted into mythical space. This narrative strategy suggests a reconciliation of a traumatic and guilt-laden national identity with a hopeful future, free of territorial conflicts.

This reconciliation, which could be called "foggy" in more ways than one, responds to the Japanese postwar myth of a new beginning, which integrates both national identity and all manner of hopes seen as progressive (often a vaguely defined conglomerate of universal peace, democracy, and welfare). In Kayama's conclusion, regressive and progressive desires seem to harmonize, as the misty island suggests both a lost paradise and a promised land. The linking of progressive with regressive fantasies is hardly unusual in science fiction of any kind, but what is characteristically Japanese here is the close link to a problematic national identity.

Kayama's text has not aged well. To make his invisible island plausible, he has to resort to an absurd proliferation of abnormal meteorological phenomena. But it is futile to suggest that another planet might have served his purpose better. The fact is that by setting his tale in the Pacific, Kayama introduces the issue of the lost Japanese empire into postwar fantastic literature.

Honda Ishirō: Monsters and Sacrifices

Godzilla makes more effective use of a conflict between regressive (mythological) and progressive moments, partly through antirealistic stylization.[6] *Godzilla* is actually a highly politicized film — not because it espouses a particular political creed but because it raises political issues that are conveyed all the more effectively through stylization and the resulting suspension of disbelief. Its Pacific setting is an important plot element.

To recapitulate briefly the well-known plot: a dinosaur that has survived in a cave under the Pacific is first roused and then genetically changed by the U.S. hydrogen bomb tests on Bikini. Turning into an incarnation of the bomb, the monster sinks several ships and devastates a fishing village on an island at the periphery of Japan's national territory. Attacked with depth charges that only provoke it further, it follows its attackers to Tokyo and devastates the city. The monster is eventually killed by the Oxygen Destroyer, a fantastic weapon of potential mass destruction developed during the war by a young chemist, Dr. Serizawa (Figure 2.2). The inventor has kept it strictly secret, fearing the consequences of making public even the existence of such a technology. He changes his mind when he sees that the monster is causing as much damage as the war, but he ensures that he himself dies while deploying the weapon.

The testing of the H-bomb is the film's hottest political issue. The Bikini Atoll, nearly four thousand kilometers from Japan, was in truth quite close, since Japanese vessels fished in that area. One such ship, the *Lucky Dragon No. 5 (Daigo Fukuryū-maru)* was affected by fallout from the explosion, and one crew member later died in the hospital. The "Lucky Dragon Incident" provided a direct link between nuclear weapons and the everyday lives of the Japanese, and created a welcome opportunity to criticize U.S. superpower politics. It should also be pointed out that the Marshall Islands, to which Bikini belongs, were a Japanese mandate from 1920 to 1945. In that sense, the drama both in the film and in reality takes its point of departure from one of Japan's lost territories. The film confines itself to postwar Japan, of course, but it implies a Japanese Pacific identity when the monster first comes ashore on a remote — yet still Japanese — Pacific island.

Honda's interest in Japan's past glory is even more graphically illustrated by the film in which he debuted as a director, which appeared a year before *Godzilla. Taiheiyō no washi* (1953, The eagle of the Pacific) was one of the first big-budget war films made after Japan regained national sovereignty in 1952.[7] The hero of the film (which also marked the beginning of Honda's long-running partnership with the special effects designer Tsuburaya Eiji) is Admiral Yamamoto Isoroku, the commander of the Imperial Navy who recommended the sea-based preemptive air strike on Pearl Harbor that started the Pacific War in 1941.

In the history of the Japanese Navy, the aircraft carrier–based attack on Pearl Harbor marks the peak, and the end, of a series of remarkable military successes — most notably, victory in the wars against China (1895) and Russia (1905) — in which the rapidly modernized navy played an im-

Figure 2.2. A still from the U.S. version of *Gojira (Godzilla, King of Monsters!)*, showing Serizawa in his laboratory with an aquarium in the foreground. He is about to demonstrate the Oxygen Destroyer for Emiko. (From the 2002 Sony American DVD.)

portant part. Honda and Tsuburaya's monster films address the ghosts of the Japanese past playfully yet seriously, in a way calculated to exorcize those ghosts. They celebrate the nation, but theirs is a pacifist nationalism. Probably the best example of how they used fantasy to defuse militarism is *Atragon*.

The film's Japanese title, *Kaitei gunkan* (The seabed warship), is also the title of a classic 1900 militarist adventure story by Oshikawa Shunrō, in which Captain Sakuragi of the Imperial Navy Reserve retires secretly with his crew to an island in the Indian Ocean to develop a new type of submarine, to be based on an array of innovative Japanese technologies.[8] His charisma and inventive genius mark him as a Japanese Nemo-type character. In the first story (five sequels followed between 1902 and 1909), the submarine is deployed against pirates, but its declared purpose is to force the respect of the Western powers and ultimately to enable Japan to unite the Asian countries against Western imperialism. In other words, the weapon is devised to serve a highly idealized Japanese counterimperialism. Nationalism at this time was a mainstream movement — not only in Japan — and the Japanese victories over China and Russia did indeed win the country international respect. The special significance of the Oshikawa stories is that they constituted a milestone for scientific romance written in Japanese. Not only did this author introduce Verne-type technological speculation, he also pioneered the use of a lively but stylized colloquial Japanese, combined with vivid descriptions and effective use of narrative tension, so that he is almost invariably named in the genealogy of Japanese science fiction.

The Honda film contrives to salvage the myth of Japanese technical prowess while defusing militarism. Honda takes from Oshikawa's story the motifs of the Imperial Navy commander–cum–genius inventor and the topos of the desert-island base, as well as the idea of the supersubmarine. But he sets the story in Japan in 1963, shifts the genre to fantasy, adds elements of family drama, and no doubt also draws on the popularity of Irwin Allen's *Voyage to the Bottom of the Sea* (1961), another film in which a submarine commander saves the world. In Honda's film, the commander, Captain Shingūji, has been developing a revolutionary submarine, secretly launched the day before the Japanese surrender in 1945. He is presumed killed in action, but has in fact been improving his invention: as the film opens, the audience witnesses the launch of the new submarine, which can even fly and cut through rock. But technical hyperbole is not the most fantastic element in the film, which takes up the legend of the lost continent of Mu,[9] picturing an archaic yet technically advanced civilization (its leaders recognizable in the film by wigs of wonderfully unlikely colors) surviving in caves under the Pacific and plotting to recolonize the surface. To help in this task, the Mu have captured a submarine that Shingūji constructed in 1945. Since the attack on the surface world is imminent, and since it has become known that the submarine's inventor is still alive, a small party including Shingūji's former commanding officer (now a ship owner) and his daughter, Makoto, ask him to use his expertise to save the world. He refuses, saying that he has made the ship for his country, not for humanity. Only after Makoto, a true child of the postwar, bursts into tears and tells her father that she hates him does he relent, and the battle against Mu can begin (Figure 2.3). The destruction of Mu, with which the film ends, stands for the end of imperialism and colonialism.

Films of this sort were aimed at a mass audience of all age groups. Symbolically, the film reconciles progressive moments (innovation, reform of political values in line with a global mainstream) with conservative ones (appreciation of Japanese virtues and Japanese achievements, even when formerly placed at the service of the "wrong" values). The reconciliation is aided by attributing one destructive aspect of the past (imperialism) to a fantastic enemy (Mu), and another (military technology) to an equally fantastic toylike invention.

Similar themes are echoed in *Godzilla*, in which a fantastic weapon likewise defeats a mythical enemy. The coexistence of conservative and

Figure 2.3. Makoto confronts her father Shingūji and pleads with him to join in the fight against the Mu. (From the Tokyo Shock American DVD.)

progressive messages is embodied by the paleontologist Professor Yamane, who identifies the monster and speaks the warning epilogue after the double sacrifice of monster and tainted scientist.[10] Though as relieved as everyone else, Yamane mourns not only the younger scientist, who had been his assistant, but also the animal, a living example of a species thought to be extinct.

In both films, the ocean's surface acts as the boundary with the unknown and the unconscious. It brings forth the monsters of the past, but it also receives them at the end in merciful oblivion. In addition, the ocean is the conjurer's handkerchief that reconciles the known and the unknown by making them interchangeable — and profitable, since monsters, like white rabbits, can be made to reappear if the audience is ready for a sequel. This is why, while the 1954 *Gojira* still exudes real menace, Honda's later films, including *Atragon,* are firmly rooted in family entertainment and what Brian W. Aldiss calls "cosy catastrophe."[11] As well as the ironization of pathos that characterizes the development of any genre, this lightness of tone in originally warlike motifs can be seen as showing the sense of security that grew in Japan between the publication of the Orang Pendek stories in the late 1940s and the release of *Kaitei gunkan* in 1963.

Abe Kōbō: No Man's Land

There is nothing cozy about Abe Kōbō's *Inter Ice Age 4,* which resists reconciliation and unfolds a radical reading of the nature of science, humanity, and the future. Of the Japanese works discussed here, this novel is the only one that, notwithstanding a Japanese setting, views the ocean from a truly transnational perspective.

The part played by the sea in this story is revealed late in the narrative, while the title's significance is revealed only at the denouement. The novel depicts several layers of reality, the most superficial sequence of events taking place on four days in August of an unspecified year in the near future: everyday reality is unchanged, but the advanced computer technology described is a fictional innovation. Beneath this, however, runs a deep-time structure that begins by recapitulating the previous three years and ends with a far-future vision.

The first-person narrator, Professor Katsumi, is in charge of a Japanese government project responding to a new class of Soviet prediction computers that are making disturbingly accurate economic forecasts. But when the United States declares political forecasts immoral following the Soviet prediction of the first fully communist society within thirty-two years, Japan follows suit, and Katsumi, who is himself not interested in politics, is hard put to find a field that does not involve politics. It is decided that the computer will secretly predict the life of a random individual, and together with his assistant Tanomogi, Katsumi sets out to choose. Here begins an increasingly absurd series of events that begins with the murder of the man picked for the prediction and ends with Katsumi's wife undergoing an abortion at a mysterious clinic after a voice on the telephone (which she takes to be her husband's) instructs her to do so. We learn that women going to this clinic are told that their offspring will not be killed but bred into better humans. In this way, a mystery is set up in the novel's first part (secs. 1–23, titled "Program Card 1").

"Program Card No. 2" (secs. 24–34) reveals a hidden logical order. Tanomogi takes his superior to a secret aquatic research project that breeds hybrid aquatic organisms from mammal fetuses. The enterprise already can breed submarine livestock on an industrial scale. Katsumi suspects that the organization behind this project is connected with the fetus trade and that it is breeding aquatic humans — a suspicion that eventually turns out to be true. He resolves to find his aborted child and kill it. The next day, he is summoned to a meeting by a telephone voice identical to his own.

It is here that a further layer of hidden reality appears. Katsumi's voice is generated by a computer, more specifically by his "second degree prediction forecast."[12] This is the construction of his situation as it would be if he knew the content of a preceding first-degree prediction, an alter ego that is always one step ahead of the original. The model accuses him of being reactionary, unable to bear the thought that the future might not be a logical extrapolation of the present. Katsumi finally has to present his case to the "committee," consisting mainly of people associated with his project. They are working on another computer project running alongside the official one, and it is this secret project that has generated the narrator's alter ego. The murder has been plotted to implicate him, the "abortion" to test his attitude. Katsumi is informed that it has been decided to kill him, since he knows about the aquatic human breeding project but rejects it. First, however, he is given a detailed report that culminates in a long-range prediction by the computer.

Only at this point does the full significance of the ocean (and the "inter ice age" of the title) emerge. The secret organization behind the "committee" has been founded by leaders of private industry in response to the news, kept secret from the general public, that there will be a drastic rise in the level of the oceans because of steam from undersea volcanic eruptions. This change will destroy the polar ice caps once and for all, so that the present inter ice age 4 will give way to another ice age. The organization is breeding a new race of aquatic humans (aquans) who will be able to live on the seafloor.

The computer leaves open how many years elapse before the developments described in the novel's last part, titled "Blueprint" (secs. 35–38). The Japanese government moves to a secret undersea location, announcing by radio the existence of the submarine colonies and at the same time claiming submarine territorial rights. Eventually, the colonies acquire equal rights with terrestrial humans and form their own government, which is internationally recognized. Other governments follow suit in breeding aquans. It is not specified whether nations continue to exist in the submarine age, but the implication is that they may not.

In the final pages, a young aquan is shown suffering from "land disease," a longing for wind and dry land. He dies on the beach of one of the few remaining islands. In this way, the envisioned future is overwhelmed in its turn by another future. In his epilogue, Abe wrote:

> A true future, I believe, must appear on the far side of a rupture, as a "thing" transcending...value judgments.... The future finds the feeling of continuity of the present guilty. Since I believe that this problem is an important topic for a time of transition such as the present one, I decided to depict a future intruding into the present as something that passes judgment. The feeling of continuity of the everyday must die the instant it glimpses the future.[13]

The future is seen from the vantage point of Japan in the present, and to this end the novel uses features derived from a geopolitically defined national identity. But it is to expose this nationalism as secondary and ideological that Abe takes up the ocean topos and thinks beyond the essentialist myth of a Japanese Pacific identity. He sees the period contemporary with this novel as especially transitory, an attitude born of an era in which Japanese society had just started to stabilize. Abe opens up a historical panorama to the point where historical events appear from an eternal perspective. It is little wonder, then, that his depictions of political ideologies and relationships, such as those between the USSR, Japan, and the United States, appear vain and caricatured — though at the same time, there is nothing to suggest that the role of technical innovator allotted to the Soviet Union is seen at all ironically.[14]

Kayama's tale about a primitive race threatened with extinction and finally embarking on an evolution program reveals only the parochial Japanese obsession with catching up with the rest of the world. In Abe's conception, the surface of the planet itself changes. For that reason, his narrative is reminiscent of works from a transnational socialist canon depicting a postnational and posthuman (though not postorganic) world.[15] This is one way in which this work differs from the others discussed here. Another is that Abe's is the only work with real philosophical ambitions. While the others try to define Japanese postwar identity in some way through the ocean topos, Abe's concern is to demonstrate the limitations of national identity itself.

Komatsu Sakyō: Has the Empire Sunk Yet?

Komatsu Sakyō, writing *Japan Sinks* a decade and a half later, seems similarly motivated and uses a comparable geodynamic device, but his viewpoint ultimately is conservative. He permits his characters to bid a fond farewell to the country they love and to take their culture with them. Komatsu's geodynamics also differ from Abe's: this time, only Japan goes under. Moreover, it does so in the space of only two years, the result of an acceleration of convection movements in the earth's mantle, ending with the islands sliding into the fold of the Japan Trench at the bottom of the Pacific.

The novel's length notwithstanding (two volumes of 409 and 384 pages in the Kōbunsha paperback version), the first million copies of the two-volume novel were sold in just two and a half months after its publication in March 1973. The appeal at the time was in what was perceived as a realistic description of the sinking process.

Three levels of events can readily be identified: physical, social, and affective. All three are connected to questions of Japanese identity. On the physical level, there is the geologic process, explained with a profusion of facts and figures and partly illustrated with diagrams (all cut from the translation). This is realism on the level of technical plausibility, which, of course, is a feature of hard science fiction everywhere. Yet the events explained in this way are destroying the environment only of the Japanese, and the interest shown in the plausibility of this is not something readily translated or transferred overseas. Serving a similarly instructive purpose are the social and political events that arise in response to the impending disaster. Komatsu describes not only the reaction of the political and other institutions of Japanese society but also (and this is the real issue) what might happen to the Japanese after Japan no longer exists — that is, what options the Japanese government might have for evacuating a hundred million Japanese within the geopolitical givens of the time.

On the affective level, which is most directly connected to questions of identity, the narrative dramatizes the emotions created by these events within a rather small cast of central characters, mostly associated with the project (called Plan D) to investigate the initially mysterious natural events. There is one principal hero, a young deep-sea submarine pilot called Onodera. Besides these narrative masks, however, there are a number of major characters shown only from an outside perspective. The most important of the scientists is Professor Tadokoro,[16] a maverick geophysicist who considers that intuition is the most important characteristic for a scientist and who is at first ridiculed by his colleagues for suggesting that Japan might sink. The most politically influential character is Watari, over a hundred years old, who has been active behind the scenes in Japanese politics and business for several generations, and who finances Plan D. Tadokoro and Watari stand, respectively, for the scientific and the social levels of the novel.

There are two women associated with Onodera. The first is the cosmopolitan and slightly blasé Reiko, his prospective wife in an arranged marriage, with whom he shares a passion for diving. She dies during the eruption of Mount Fuji. The other is Mako, a young bar hostess whom he has met in Tokyo and who turns up again as an unlikely member of a group of mountain walkers whom Onodera tries to rescue. It is Mako to whom he is married at the end of the novel, the more down-to-earth woman who is more likely to have children and ensure ethnic continuity. This is made clear in the final scene, when she tells her now husband a legend from her home island, in which the pregnant Tanaba, sole survivor of a flood, founds a new tribe with the son she gives birth to as her partner. Mako says that the story comforts her and that she would do the same if necessary.

Though his appearance in the novel is brief, an important character is Professor Fukuhara, an expert in the comparative history of civilizations who is summoned by Watari when it becomes clear that only a few months remain to evacuate Japan. After presenting the results of a week's continuous work with his commission of experts, he collapses and dies. The commission has suggested dividing the Japanese into three groups: those who could build a new state, given territory on which to do so; those who could assimilate in other countries; and those who could not live elsewhere and must go down with the country. Fukuhara's commission also makes an additional suggestion that its members personally favor, although they concede that it is not likely to be acceptable: that the Japanese people should all go under with their country. The policy eventually adopted essentially corresponds to the three-part division. Those remaining behind are mainly the old.[17] On the colonial front, there is a plan to settle a substantial number of refugees in Namibia, which despite being nominally a UN mandate is occupied de facto by South Africa. Of the scientists in the novel, some are on board a ship headed for the tropics, while Onodera and Mako, both injured, are on the Trans-Siberian Railway, heading west over the continent.

In the preface to the 1995 Kōbunsha paperback edition, Komatsu addresses the question of identity: "I wanted us to think a little bit about the significance of our country, whether things went as they should with prewar and with postwar Japan."[18] Japan itself is everywhere identified with the ephemeral, a recurring theme in interpretations of Japan both by Japanese and by others.[19] Tadokoro compares the convection currents in the earth's mantle to meteorological phenomena, leading the listeners to conclude: "The Archipelago on which they lived was like a line of clouds that had taken form along the leading edge of a moving mass of warm air" (100).[20] Another example of the emphasis on the ephemeral is the list of landmarks destroyed by every new earthquake or volcanic eruption. This produces an effect common to every disaster film or novel: anticipated elegy raises the value of the transient.

Japan's imperialist past, on the other hand, is viewed in the novel with equanimity. Looking back in the direction where his native country has just gone down, the computer scientist Nakata ironically quotes an old song from the Sino-Japanese War of 1895: "Hasn't the *Dingyuan* sunk yet?" The *Dingyuan* was an enemy ship at that time; the joke is that, though incapacitating it at anchor was a key success for Japan in winning the war, the ship never did sink.[21] The old songs may still survive even in the memory of those who do not share the militarist sentiment, it is implied, but they can take on a new meaning if that old sentiment is defused. As with the Mu Empire in *Atragon,* there is much in the old Japanese Empire that is best left to go under — yet in some important aspects, it will never sink.

Of course, Komatsu also addresses the question of what might become of the Japanese after the sinking of Japan. Abe in *Inter Ice Age 4* projected a far future in such a way as to let the national questions become secondary to the more general philosophical questions about human nature. Komatsu is interested in realistic, near-future scenarios and the enduring nature of cultural identity. He seems to be agreeing with Watari when he says:

If we could lose this thing called Japan altogether... if one could drop the Japan in *Japanese* and just be *human,* then there would be no problem, but that doesn't work.... Our culture and language are our historical karma.... If everything else disappeared completely along with the land of Japan — our nation, our race, our culture and history, then that would be fine.... But the Japanese are still a vital young race... they're full of energy, and they still haven't fulfilled their karma to live.[22]

This is Watari's wise response to the ethnologist Fukuhara's comparison of the landless Japanese to the Jews in diaspora. In explaining a little earlier in the same scene why the commission favors the Japanese going under with their islands, one of them says that he doubts the Japanese could bear diaspora, since they identify themselves too closely with their islands. Viewed in this context, the "karma" that Watari refers to is the expression not of fatalism but of hope. The hint of a suspicion remains, however, that, since the Japanese at the end of the novel will not have a homeland to return to, the state of diaspora is seen as preferable to the present one. Beyond that, however, Komatsu provocatively leaves open the question of whether national identity is tied to land. Certainly, he questions the myth that the Japanese are less suited to living outside their country than other peoples. At the same time, he shows respect for those expressing this view.

But if he does not mythologize a diaspora identity, he does seem to mythologize the submerged Japan as a new Atlantis, in line with the anticipated elegy elsewhere in the novel. The name of the sunken city is first mentioned in the novel by the chairman of an American research group holding a news conference after coming to the conclusion that Japan will sink. Pressed to describe the effects on Japan, he says only that it is "the kind of thing that makes you think of the Atlantis legend" (182). The epilogue comes back to the theme of Atlantis at greater length in the Japanese original — the English version cuts all but one of these and omits all references to the lost continent of Mu. In the first of the unnumbered sections of the original Japanese epilogue, the narrator comments that the last stages of the sinking are intensely covered by television stations from all over the world, saying that if the legends of Atlantis and Mu were fascinating, then the spectacle of Japan sinking was all the more so because it is a contemporary and wealthy industrialized nation, whereas Atlantis had been a legendary city-state.

On another mythical level, Japan is personified as a dragon in the epilogue, which also bears the title "The Death of the Dragon":

At the eastern edge of the Eurasian land mass, which covers half of the Northern Hemisphere, a dragon lay dying. As he twisted his huge body and thrashed his tail, smoke and fire poured from every part of him. (219)

The dragon is a metaphor for the land of Japan, hence the allusion to Godzilla, who appears as a synecdoche for the forces of nature surrounding the islands. The two images share the emphasis on a suffering, destructive monster. Both invite a certain degree of pity and identification with the beast: Japan is endowed with pathos and significance.

At this stage of Komatsu's novel, the submerged Japan has been virtualized and internalized. It exists in tales, legends, and songs, some preserved as they were, some modified or adapted (like the dying dragon). As the old man Watari says, "Our culture and language are our historical karma." This is the essence of things Japanese that Komatsu has distilled. To convey this enduring quality in the culture, despite all changes, is his primary message, if we take seriously his intention, stated in his preface, to provoke reflection on the meaning of Japan. In both scientific and mythical discourse, Komatsu stresses the reassuringly stable elements. His is the most conservative of the narratives discussed here, ultimately exuding a quiet confidence in the worth and durability of the Japanese identity — understood in cultural, not national, terms. It is on the basis of a secure ethnic identity that Komatsu criticizes nationalism. As he outlines in his preface, he began writing the book in 1964, in response to validations of Japanese imperialism beginning to be voiced, which he saw as symptoms of a society grown too wealthy.[23] He is not critical of the achievements of the postwar Japanese economy but of complacency about those achievements, especially if it goes hand in hand with a revival of imperialist thought.

New Dimensions, Old Dimensions

All the postwar novels discussed here in some way refer back critically to the myth of Japan as a modern Pacific hegemon — a myth that the adventure stories of Oshikawa at the beginning of the twentieth century helped establish. Even though the postwar artists discussed here reject militant nationalism, they need to refer back to it because it is so intimately associated with Japan's modernization, which continued to be a mainstay of Japanese self-identification after 1945. The most unorthodox of the texts is *Inter Ice Age 4*, which puts the national in a fundamentally anthropological perspective. In that novel, the ocean topos is less geographically specific than in the other works, since the evolutionary process from fish to quadrupeds and beyond is also important; yet here, too, the ocean suggests an allusion to the Pacific empire.

Kayama's "Orang Pendek" stories and *Godzilla* are more recognizably rooted in a postwar culture of remorse. They express basically conservative attitudes, but are compelled to sift which parts of a national identity (seen as tainted) can be conserved. Kayama's strategy is the least clearly defined in dealing with the past, which becomes a stew mingling genocide committed by Japanese (and other colonialists) with the more general fall from grace of modernization. The narrative ends with an equally vague future hope. The strategy of such films as *Godzilla* and *Atragon* is much more successful, since they end with purification rituals that leave intact those aspects of the national past not seen as tainted by the war.

Komatsu's project of isolating what "Japaneseness" might be without national territory is still in this tradition; however, the novel marks the tradition's end. Scientific communities and technical expertise had by 1973 led to an economic boom that was a new source of national pride. Territory was no longer a source of prestige compared with capital and technical expertise. As most of the other essays in this volume illustrate, virtual environments and cyborgs dominate contemporary popular narratives in Japan. When the sea appears in this cybernetic mode, it is generally as a backdrop to highlight a mood.[24] Occasionally it does still appear in the old geopolitical mode, but not — with few exceptions — as the principal setting.[25]

I conclude by noting that most of the works described here are typical products of the postwar period in their conflict between espousal and rejection of national values. Science fiction tends to choose topics about which authors and readers feel insecure, and it is safe to say that the perspectives opened up by developments in information technology and genetics are more disconcerting, and sublime, than the ocean. Nonetheless, if in *Star Blazers* a World War II battleship can be dispatched into outer space, no doubt a revival movement is possible in virtual space. Without the skepticism of the postwar era, however, any such revival is likely to be reactionary in character.

Notes

1. My use of the term *topos* is not intended to indicate something archetypal of or confined to any one specific culture. I see topoi as functions of discourses; if the one sketched here is confined to Japan, this is because the discourse in which it has validity is similarly specific.

2. *Gojira* (1954); reedited and released in the United States in 1956 as *Godzilla, King of the Monsters!*; both versions are available on *Gojira/Godzilla Deluxe Collector's Edition*, 2 DVDs (Classic Media, 2006); Abe Kōbō, *Dai yon kanpyōki*, in *Abe Kōbō zenshū* (Complete works of Abe Kōbō) (Tokyo: Shinchōsha, 1997–2000), 9:9–174; translated by E. Dale Saunders as *Inter Ice Age 4* (New York: Knopf, 1970); Komatsu Sakyō, *Nihon chinbotsu*, 2 vols. (Tokyo: Kōbunsha, 1995); abridged and translated by Michael Gallagher as *Japan Sinks* (Tokyo: Kodansha International, 1995); *Uchū senkan Yamato*, TV series, 26 episodes (1977); translated as *Star Blazers Series 1: The Quest for Iscandar*, 6 DVDs (Voyager, 2001); this is just the first of several TV series, OVAs, and films in the Yamato franchise.

3. *Kaitei gunkan,* dir. Honda Ishirō (1963); translated as *Atragon,* DVD (Tokyo Shock, 2006).

4. Kayama Shigeru, "Oran Pendeku no fukushū" and "Oran Pendeku no gojitsutan," in *Kayama Shigeru zenshū* (Complete works of Kayama Shigeru) (Tokyo: San'ichi Shobō, 1993–97), 1:9–25, 177–97.

5. There are a number of Web sites dealing with reports of the Orang Pendek, including recent sightings.

6. For the discursive background of this film, see Thomas Schnellbächer, "Alltag und Apokalypse: Japanische Science-fiction und die Nachkriegszeit" (Everyday and apocalypse: Japanese science fiction and the postwar), in *11 Deutschsprachiger Japanologentag in Trier 1999,* ed. H. Gössmann and A. Mrugalla (Hamburg: LIT Verlag, 2001), 399–411.

7. *Taiheiyō no washi* (The eagle of the Pacific), dir. Honda Ishirō (1953).

8. Oshikawa Shunrō, *Kaitō bōken kitan/Kaitei gunkan* (The seabed warship: An island adventure romance), in *Oshikawa Shunrō shū* (Oshikawa Shunrō collection), vol. 2 of *Shōnen shōsetsu taikei* (Juvenile literature series) (Tokyo: San'ichi Shobō, 1987), 10–96.

9. This is a modern legend, first postulated by an American amateur archaeologist in 1926. The theory of Mu was never taken seriously by paleontologists, but it still has adherents among New Age devotees and ufologists. In Japan, Mu became popular as a topos of fantasy literature, comparable with Atlantis, but Mu is always associated with the superhuman, and its inhabitants are sometimes said to be of extraterrestrial origin.

10. Yamane's epilogue is missing in the radically changed U.S. version, *Godzilla, King of the Monsters!* This adds an American narrator-protagonist, played by Raymond Burr, who speaks a brief, hard-boiled conclusion from offscreen.

11. Brian W. Aldiss, *Billion Year Spree: The True History of Science Fiction* (New York: Schocken, 1974), 293–94.

12. Cf. sec. 29: "That's right, I'm a *second order predicted value* [*dainiji yogenchi*] that has seen your whole future in the first order prediction. In other words, I'm you as you would be if you knew yourself totally" (*Abe Kōbō zenshu,* 9:119; my italics and my translation). For an alternative translation, see *Inter Ice Age 4,* 149.

13. Abe Kōbō, "Nichjōsei e no senkoku" (A challenge to the everyday), in *Abe Kōbō zenshu,* 11:141–42. This is included as a "postscript" in the English translation of the novel (226–28), but the translation here is my own.

14. Abe's concern with the future is connected to his origins in the postwar as a time of new beginning. Equally, it shows his obsession with contradiction, which permitted him as a Communist to remain loyal even after a shock like that of the Soviet invasion of Hungary in 1956. I have tried to put this complex of developments in perspective in my book *Abe Kōbō, Literary Strategist: The Evolution of His Agenda and Rhetoric in the Context of Postwar Japanese Avant-Garde and Communist Artists' Movements* (Munich: IUDICIUM, 2004).

15. The most important allusions are to Alexander Belyaev's *Amphibian* (1929), in which a young man has shark's gills implanted, and Karel Čapek's *War with the Newts* (1936), in which giant newts bred as slave laborers revolt and flood the continents. Alexander Belyaev, *The Amphibian,* trans. L. Kolesnikov (Moscow: Foreign Languages Publishing House, [195–]); Karel Čapek, *War with the Newts,* trans. Ewald Osers (Highland Park, N. J.: Catbird, 1990).

16. He holds only a professorship in the translation. In fact, he does not appear to have an academic affiliation and is introduced in the original novel using only the more general honorific -sensei, which can be used for a teacher of any kind.

17. Watari is exemplary here. He is also, however, an exemplary migrant, who with his dying breath reveals to Professor Tadokoro that he had a Chinese father. Tadokoro, who is only sixty-five, confesses in the same scene that he has loved Japan like a woman and that going down with her is for him like a romantic double suicide.

18. Komatsu, *Nihon chinbotsu*, 1:5.

19. Buddhist-inspired aesthetic terms associated with this remorse are *mujō* and *mono no aware*. The latter term, for example, was used as the title for the film historian Donald Richie's influential essay about Japanese atom bomb films, first published in 1961. Donald Richie, "'Mono no Aware': Hiroshima in Film," in *Hibakusha Cinema: Hiroshima, Nagasaki, and the Nuclear Image in Japanese Film*, ed. Mick Broderick (London: Kegan Paul, 1996), 20–37.

20. Except as noted, page numbers refer to the English translation, from which the quotations are taken.

21. The *Dingyuan* (or Tingyüan; read "Teien" in Japanese) was the flagship of the Chinese fleet in the battle of the Yellow Sea (September 1894); it was considered virtually unsinkable. Shortly before the decisive battle, she was surprised at anchor in a nocturnal torpedo boat attack and so badly damaged that she had to be beached. In the anecdote related by the song ("Yūkan naru suihei"/"The Valiant Sailor"), a wounded sailor on the Japanese flagship Matsushima asks his commander whether the Dingyuan has sunk yet, and is told what has happened. The sailor replies: "Please strike the enemy!" and dies, which the song celebrates as exemplary patriotism. The translation cited here is from Donald Keene, *Appreciations of Japanese Culture* (Tokyo: Kodansha International, 1981), 280.

22. This is my translation. The published English version begins "Once this Japan of ours is gone forever" (155–56) and gives a different sense to this passage.

23. Komatsu, *Nihon chinbotsu*, 4.

24. The cyborg heroine of Oshii Mamoru's film *Ghost in the Shell* (1995) goes scuba diving in her spare time and, asked by her colleague what she feels when diving, lists fear, anxiety, loneliness, darkness, and possibly hope. Of course, the ocean in the entirely urban setting of this work has no significance beyond being one of many available recreational environments. *Kōkaku kidōtai: Ghost in the Shell*, dir. Oshii Mamoru (1995); translated as *Ghost in the Shell*, subtitled DVD (Manga Entertainment, 1998).

25. There are a few exceptions, like Kawaguchi Kaiji's long-running manga series *Chinmoku no kantai* (1989–, Silent service) and the ending of Ōtomo Katsuhiro's *Akira* manga. In *Chinmoku no kantai*, yet another charismatic young submarine commander, in charge of the latest vessel secretly developed by Japan and the United States, steals the ship during a test run, declaring it an autonomous nation. The United States in particular resolves to destroy the boat, but all attacks fail. Moreover, the Yamato has an unknown number of nuclear warheads onboard. In fact, Commander Kaieda's goal is to push for nuclear disarmament and the creation of a transnational force to safeguard world peace. But since the heroes of this story are so Japanese and so heroic, it can hardly be said itself to transcend the national. On *Chinmoku no kantai*, see Frederik L. Schodt, *Dreamland Japan: Writings*

in Modern Manga (Berkeley, Calif.: Stone Bridge, 1996), 284–88. In the final episode of *Akira* (400–433), after Neo-Tokyo has been destroyed by the meeting of two cosmic forces, an armed UN surveillance force lands to police the destroyed country. But the gang that has accumulated around the youthful leader Kaneda is perfectly capable of looking after itself. The gang members send the intruders packing and set about building a new country. Neither this nor other episodes involving the sea are included in the 1988 animated film version, which was directed by the artist. Ōtomo Katsuhiro, *Akira* (Tokyo: Kōdansha, 1984–93), 6:400–433; first English-language edition colored and with some changes, thirty-eight issues (New York: Epic Comics, 1988–95), unedited black-and-white edition, 6 vols. (Milwaukie, Ore.: Dark Horse, 2000–2002) (two distinct translations, both by Yoko Umezawa et al., but with different teams); *Akira,* dir. Ōtomo Katsuhiro (1988); translated as *Akira,* DVD (Pioneer, 2001). See also Takayuki Tatsumi's discussion of Aramaki Yoshio's *Konpeki no kantai* (1990–, Deep blue fleet) novels, in the afterword to this volume.

3. Alien Spaces and Alien Bodies in Japanese Women's Science Fiction

Kotani Mari
Translated by Miri Nakamura

What were the circumstances that led to the discovery of femininity *(joseisei)* by Japanese women?[1] The 1970s science fiction boom in Japan has been attributed to the importation and complete assimilation of Western science fiction. If so, can we also attribute the birth of women's science fiction to the worldwide women's liberation movement that accompanied the counterculture movement in the late 1960s? The emergence of Japanese women's science fiction would then coincide with the rise of Western feminist science fiction. But unlike its foreign counterpart, Japanese women's science fiction is not governed by a strictly political agenda. In fact, it is difficult or impossible to find Japanese science fiction that propagandizes for feminism.

One reason for this is that the mass media in Japan project a distorted image of feminism as an obscene mode of thought imported from the outside. Most of these images are not antiwomen; rather, they are antifeminist. They can be divided into two markedly opposed images of feminism: feminism as an intellectual discipline that is the purview of ivory-tower scholars versus feminism as a movement led by nonintellectual, emotional, and uncontrollable activists. This does not mean, of course, that women are completely ignorant of social issues such as women's independence and security. There are many women who claim that they dislike feminism but unwittingly deploy avidly feminist rhetoric, and this is the case for most Japanese female science fiction writers.

During the women's liberation movement in the early 1970s,[2] Suzuki Izumi dominated the science fiction literary milieu, and feminist separatism was translated into narratives of "feminist utopias." These narratives, however, did not merely support feminist separatism; on the contrary, they revealed a certain ambivalence about it. Since that time, rather than create a separate isolated space for itself, Japanese women's writing has sought to build a network to expand its space. The literary space has served as a safety zone where female writers can ensure their positions within the network. Hikawa Reiko, Matsuo Yumi, and Arai Motoko belong to this group of women writers. Through Japanese *shōjo* comics, *shōjo* novels, and "ladies' comics"[3]—spaces dominated by adolescent girls, expectant mothers, and women and children in general—most of these authors manipulate the stereotypical images constructed by patriarchal ideologies. They find a place within these stereotypes of femininity where male presence is prohibited, and they continually seek out and collect these cultural spheres.

In Western and Japanese science fiction by male writers, ideals of femininity are perhaps most easily observed in violent narratives of combat. In male science fiction, the female sphere (gynesis) is manifested in fierce images of monsters. In these texts, attacking such monsters is an attempt to control female sexuality and to prescribe the limits of femininity. These Japanese male science fiction writers strive to control gynesis by marking the female as other. In contrast, monsters depicted by female writers, in works such as Hagio Moto's *shōjo* comic *Staa reddo* (1978–79, Star red) or Yamao Yūko's fantastic novels, possess romantic elements mixed with monstrousness.[4] In addition, many of these narratives fabricate reasons to allow monsters to *survive*.

Many of these female writers also portray images of mothers as monsters. In Ono Fuyumi's *Tōkei ibun* (1994, Strange tales of Tokyo) and Shōno Yoriko's *Haha no hattatsu* (1994–96, The development of my mother), the mother becomes a monstrous creation deity.[5] She is situated at the center of the household and must try to create her own world while being forced to be an integral part of the house.[6] These works investigate the claustrophobic spatiality of their constructed worlds. Many stories suggest this is a reflection of deep-seated grudges held by actual Japanese mothers. Whereas male depictions of the mother evince romantic sentiments and nostalgia for the home, female writers tend to focus on vivid mother-daughter conflicts. For example, in Ōhara Mariko's "Haiburiddo chairudo" (1984, Hybrid child), the daughter tries to escape from her "house" (i.e., "mother"), thus instigating a bitter conflict.[7] The mother, as both a creation deity who rules her household and a monster who causes its downfall, is a ubiquitous theme. The notion of the house as a claustrophobic space has become so firmly embedded in the Japanese worldview that the body images of sons and daughters have altered in order to conform with it.

These changes are especially evident for male bodies depicted by female writers, as adolescent male bodies are usually idealized images. This idealization can be seen in situations where male figures become the objects of romantic affairs. The alteration of male bodies can be understood as the desire of women to appropriate the idealized masculine images constructed by male-centered ideologies for themselves. Altered male images appear in romance novels as individuals dressed in male clothing but who embody feminine beauty, and in soap operas *(ren'ai dorama)* in the form of male-male relationships. It is likely that these kinds of altered male images appear in numerous works of female science fiction because fantastic narratives describing strange transformations of humans are common in the world of science fiction. So-called slash fiction by foreign female writers also deploys similar narratives. These trends undoubtedly owe much to the fact that, in the market for women's science fiction, texts such as *shōjo* comics and *shōjo* novels are all targeted at female consumers and establish a female-oriented consumer code.

The theories will be discussed in more detail below.

Women's Utopias

The Female Nation: Suzuki Izumi's "Onna to onna no yo no naka" (1977, The world of women and women)

In the history of English-language literature, science fiction of the 1970s is often associated with the rise of second-wave feminism. Both among new authors and active older writers, the number of women dramatically increased. These American and European developments were reflected in the November 1975 issue of Japan's *SF Magajin (SF Magazine),* a special issue on female writers. Pamela Sargent's renowned critical essay "Women and Science Fiction" opened the issue, followed by translations of exemplary works by female science fiction writers such as Ursula K. Le Guin, Marion Zimmer Bradley, Carol Emshwiller, and Zenna Henderson. Even more interesting, however, is that two new Japanese writers were introduced as counterparts to these well-known Western writers. One of them was Yamao Yūko, whose story "Kamen butōkai" (1975, Masquerade) was a finalist for the Hayakawa Science Fiction Prize. The other was Suzuki Izumi, author of "Majo minarai" (1975, The witch's apprentice).

Two years later, *Kisō tengai,* then Japan's second-largest commercial science fiction journal, published works by Fujimoto Izumi, Koizumi

Kimiko, and Nishida Isei in its March 1977 issue, a special issue devoted to female science fiction writers.[8] Suzuki Izumi's "Wasureta" (Forgot) also appeared in this issue. Diplomatic conflicts between earth and an outer planet named Miiru set the scene for this story, and the tale revolves around romances between aliens. It also recounts, on the one hand, power games deployed by imperialist nations against each other and, on the other, various aspects of alien ecology. The text is deeply rooted in the counterculture movement and its opposition to authoritarianism. It also has elements of "drug literature," along with science-fictional and feminist elements. In retrospect, the text had much in common with the works of the British writer Naomi Mitchison and the American writer Marge Piercy, whose works dealt with sexism and ethnicity and who attracted much attention in the 1970s. Suzuki's work shares some of their themes and has a certain innovative flair.

Kisō tengai's special issue also featured an interview between Suzuki and the science fiction writer Mayumura Taku, "SF: Otoko to onna" (SF: Men and women).[9] When asked what drove her to become a science fiction writer, Suzuki explained that when she was pregnant, her debut work, "The Witch's Apprentice," was unexpectedly published in *SF Magajin*, and from that time she began to write short stories for that magazine. In other words, Suzuki did not consider herself a pure science fiction writer from the beginning; her writing style just happened to fall into that category.

Suzuki's texts defamiliarize the real world in order to free the *joseisei* bound hand and foot by the power structure of the real world. Her works disintegrate the power structure that produces marginalization with phrases like "only for women" or "because she is a woman." It is only through this process that one can begin to think about what constitutes "femininity." By combining an antiauthoritarian point of view with highly realistic and trenchant science fiction, her works make readers reflect on these issues. This is Suzuki's unique narrative method.

Suzuki's "Onna to onna no yo no naka" calls to mind utopian writings produced by 1970s Western feminist writers.[10] The story takes place in a near future, in which fuel and food are about to be exhausted, and where all the main characters are women. Men are confined to a "ghetto" called the "Special Residence Zone" where they must spend their entire lives. One day the protagonist, Yūko, looking from her window, spots a boy walking down the street. She cannot get him out of her mind, and when he walks by her window again, she sends him a message. Sneaking out of the house, she heads over to the boy's hiding place. The entire time, Yūko experiences a strange feeling toward the boy. Eventually, however, the boy is taken back to a detention house, and Yūko is told that men must be detained because they are really dangerous and violent beasts. She then realizes that the world that she lives in is "The World of Women and Women" and that this is just the way life is. In the next moment, however, she feels frightened and senses that, because she is now "someone who knows" male sexuality, "an unforeseen event will take place some day."

During the heyday of the women's liberation movement in the 1970s, numerous texts treated the issue of separatism. Suzuki quarantined males who were wont to destroy the world and depicted women who live peacefully among women. At the same time, however, there is a sense that something is missing from this picture. The disconnection between the worlds of men and women causes an internal conflict within the character Yūko, as the text raises the question of how men and women can live together. Ultimately, however, it surrenders to the current state of affairs, wherein coexistence with men signifies only oppression.

What contributes to the imagining of female worlds? For one thing, these worlds depict the limitations of heterosexual love, an idea that was emphasized in the women's liberation movement. Every society built on heterosexual relations oppresses women, and as a reaction against this violence, a world of homosexuality is envisioned. This is one of the ironic constructions of feminist utopias. For Suzuki, however, separatism produces both a sense of comfort and a simultaneous sense of lack. What reigns in "Onna to onna no yo no naka" is the sensation experienced by Yūko, the sensation of being pulled apart between two conflicting spaces — the land of women and the land of men.

Born in 1949, Suzuki dropped out of high school, ran away from home, and worked as a nude model and a porn star under the alias Senkō Naomi before becoming a writer. She married the great saxophone player Abe Kaoru, who later died of a drug overdose. She also modeled for her own photography collection called *Shishōsetsu* (1986, The I-novel), produced by the famous photographer of nudes Araki Nobuyoshi.[11] In Araki's words, Suzuki was "the woman of the era," highly sensitive to the current events of her time. In her works she depicted the shallowness of Japan's consumer society in the 1980s. As if to exemplify the transience of everyday life, she committed suicide in 1986. She had used drugs to escape the suffering of real life, and her works, like much drug literature, always aimed to expose the world as a fabrication founded on just one power structure. Her texts always displayed a mixture of sharp stimulation by and numbness toward real life. The cheerful sadness that appears at these moments of departure or escape from the world can only be described as a kind of transparent irony.

It is not an overstatement to say that the age of women's science fiction — wherein women discover and reconstruct femininity — began with Suzuki Izumi, who lived through her science fiction.

Women Warriors: Hikawa Reiko's *Onna senshi Efera & Jiriora* (1989–, The women warriors Efera and Jiriora)

The attempt to hold onto heterosexual relations with men while having homosexual relationships with women — a theme we saw in Suzuki's "Onna to onna no yo no naka" — is deeply embedded in the genre of women's science fiction.

Women in these texts seek deep spiritual relationships with other women while living in a system constrained by the rules of a heterosexual society that expects them to marry and to take on the responsibilities of pregnancy, childbirth, and running a household. This is not unusual even in real life. While men in Japan disappear into their male space — a work space marked by politics and economics — women create a space designed solely for their own pleasures. They share the same fashions and food, along with other interests like tea ceremonies and flower arrangements. They engage in endless conversations, go to the theater, and discuss their opinions about plays and films. They strive to have their own creative space. If Suzuki chose to investigate the artificiality of a separatist all-female nation, one could say that Hikawa Reiko chose to depict a more realistic female space that exposes the blind spots that emerge from time to time within the patriarchal system.

Born in 1958, Hikawa was the first amateur to write for *Rōrariasu*, a fan club dedicated to fantasy and heroic fantasy, and she is a major figure in science fiction fandom. She became a professional writer in 1989 and has since produced numerous best sellers that have sold a total of some two million copies. During the 1970s, Japan saw a boom in translations of works of fantasy and heroic fantasy, such as J. R. R. Tolkien's *Lord of the Rings* (1954–55) and popular *Weird Tales* series of the 1930s like Robert E. Howard's *Conan* and C. L. Moore's *Jirel of Joiry*. Hikawa read these works religiously when she was in her teens. She was especially taken by Jane Gaskell's *Atlan Saga* (1966), and she began writing heroic fantasies in which the protagonists were women who lived in imaginary lands. These eventually turned into the *Efera and Jiriora* series.[12]

Hikawa's saga takes place in Haraama, where two moons, Oliga and Zelk, shine on the land. In the distant past, there was a battle between the old gods and the Zelk gods, the bearers of good, and as a result of their magic, Haraama was born. Emperor Okaresk brought order to the land, uniting Haraama and forging an empire. The descendants of Okaresk and his imperial house have, however, ruled too long. Their power is weakening, and once again, chaos is about to descend on the land. The main plot involves two characters, Jiriora ("a runaway girl" and the sole heiress of the powerful imperial family of Muaaru) and Efera ("a dropout sorceress" who was accepted into the sorcerers' guild and then expelled because of her lack of power). They join forces, and together they live out their lives as mercenaries. At the beginning of the series, the two are only in their teens. They go through numerous wars, fall in love, and even have children. By the end of the series, they have turned into two extraordinary adults. The final volume focuses on the peculiar relationship between the two women as "mother mercenaries," leading a group of biological and adopted offspring. The series stands out as a unique contribution to the subgenre of "woman warrior" stories found within science fiction and fantasy. There is also a spin-off of the saga, in which one of the children is kidnapped and the mothers must save him.[13] In these stories, the friendship between the two women takes precedence over relationships with their husbands and their children. The two never share a sexual relationship, however; they are more like sisters who will risk even their own lives to save one another.

Hikawa endeavors to create a space occupied by women and children, a world in which mothers brandish swords to protect their space. Even when men appear as their companions, they barely leave a mark, either dying or departing on journeys. In these tales, societies and worldviews may fundamentally favor men, whose powers remain strong. Yet the existence of men casts only a faint shadow over the fictional world inhabited by Hikawa's women and children, which is intense and boundless by contrast. Bright, wild, and quite appealing, the isolated women's space that Hikawa captures exists in the midst of a male-centered world.

Pregnant Women: Matsuo Yumi's *Barūn taun no satsujin* (1994, Murder in Balloon Town)

Without a doubt, modern Japan is largely governed by androcentric and patriarchal systems. The female space that Suzuki envisioned, however, is not far from reality. In fact, works that create the kind of world that Hikawa revealed in her *Efera and Jiriora* series, in which the female space occupies a marginal blind spot in society, are not at all rare. In these works, female spaces are captured as territories that can only appear from time to time, and these images have become important cultural icons.

Matsuo Yumi was born in 1961 in Kanazawa. She was a member of the science fiction research group at Ochanomizu University. Her first and most representative work, *Barūn taun no satsujin* (1994, Murder in balloon town), won her the Hayakawa Science Fiction Prize.[14] In it, we find a space occupied by expectant mothers. In a near-future society where artificial uteruses are common, women who still yearn for natural childbirth establish a town specifically designed for that purpose: Balloon Town, located in the seventh special protected district of Tokyo. Like expatriates living in a foreign enclave, the pregnant women enjoy happy and fulfilling lives. Their peace is disrupted, however, by a series of murders that takes place within the town, and, to make matters worse, a witness suggests that the murderer is one of the pregnant women. Through statements such as "pregnant women can commit murders, too; they are human beings after all," the text deconstructs stereotypes.[15] The mystery, of course, can be solved only by a pregnant woman, for the cultural codes in the town constructed by the pregnant bodies are too different from those of the normal world. Thus the world's first pregnant detective is born. She describes the culture of pregnant women like an anthropologist and then solves the mystery. She even reveals her own reasons for choosing natural childbirth.

The text is informed by many kinds of narrative construction. It both parodies John Varley's "The Barbie Murders" (1980) and borrows from conventional detective fiction writers such as Agatha Christie and Arthur Conan Doyle.[16] Using these methods, the text examines the futuristic town of pregnant women, making the reader realize how invisible "the culture of pregnant women" — the culture of the "invisible Other" — really is in modern society.[17]

The novel aspect of *Murder in Balloon Town* is that "the culture of childbirth" *(shussan bunka)* is envisioned as a form of utopianism. Balloon Town represents a female world dominated by pregnant women — bodies that truly embody the phrase "only for women" *(josei nara de wa no)*. The culture of childbirth is conventionally a world shaped and protected by the regulations of male-dominated patriarchal society. It is a female world quarantined from the ordinary world. This culture exposes society's desire to isolate bodies undergoing transformations (pregnant bodies), and it represents society's aversion toward the female body. In the words of the Japanese feminist scholar Ogura Chikako: "If men want to completely possess women, they can only do so by getting women pregnant. However, once women become pregnant, they lose their feminine beauty (the beauty constructed and idealized by the male sex)."[18] In Matsuo's novel, although women live in a world where reproductive technology has freed them from being "the sex that gives birth," some women still head for Balloon Town and insist on carrying out natural childbirth. They embrace the transformation of their bodies and reject the concept of "beauty" imposed on them by male-dominated society. The text thus succeeds in envisioning "a solidarity of women" that is highly radical. Because of recent developments in reproductive technologies, the irony here is palpable. Instead of "quarantining" pregnant women as in real life, the text twists reality and creates a utopia marked by lesbian separatism, wherein heterosexual love is no longer possible and the only bonds are those between women. Of course, just as in Hikawa's case, these bonds are not those of homosexual relationships. They are merely signified by the nonphysical spiritual friendships between the women.

Teenage Girls: Arai Motoko's *Chigrusu to Yūfuratesu* (1999, Tigris and Euphrates)

Murder Balloon Town is set in a temporary space where women can stay for only a fixed period of time. The pregnant women all share similar circumstances and construct their own female space and their "pregnancy culture." Once the childbirths are over, however, they must leave that world. In contrast to this, there is another space similar to that of pregnant women, a culture created through shared female experiences and shared fantasies. It is a cultural space that is constantly evoked in the way women live — that of the teenage *shōjo*.

Like "pregnant women," *shōjo*, too, is a concept that belongs to "the female culture" imagined by patriarchal society. *Shōjo* connotes someone who is neither an adult nor married. She represents the time in a woman's life before she must succumb to the "woman's role" assigned to her by the patriarchal system. Within the system, adolescent girls are placed in compounds separate from adult women, mainly in protected spaces like schools. Whereas adult women are constantly restricted by their roles as wives and mothers, adolescence is an independent and more pleasant time for girls. As long as women live in economic stability, they do not have to graduate from *shōjo* status, and even after they have become "women" or "mothers," they can still hold on to their "*shōjo* interests" (*shōjo shumi*). Although separated from the real world, these spaces constructed by women's shared interests in *shōjo* continue to exist.

Arai Motoko is the representative writer of this "*shōjo* culture." This phenomenon was born out of the postwar era during which Japan experienced rapid economic growth. It was a golden era marked by the rise of "the 100-million-strong middle class" (*ichioku sōchūryū*) — a middle-class consciousness supposedly shared by all 100 million Japanese citizens. No other author discussed here has a stronger connection to the *shōjo* phenomenon than Arai.

Born in 1960 in Tokyo, Arai entered the first *Kisō tengai* Competition for New Writers at age sixteen, when she was only a sophomore at Igusa

Metropolitan High School. Her novella *Atashi no naka no ...* (1978, Inside myself ...) received high praise from the science fiction legend Hoshi Shin'ichi, one of the contest judges, and was given an honorable mention. Her work was chosen from among 1,268 entries, making her Japan's first high-school-aged science fiction writer. When Arai was eighteen, *Inside Myself...* was published in paperback.[19] Later, while studying in the German literature department of Rikkyō University, she won both the twelfth and thirteenth Seiun Award for her short stories "Guriin rekuiemu" (1981, Green requiem) and "Nepchūn" (1981, Neptune).[20] By the time she graduated from college she had published eight books and was already well established as a *shōjo* writer.

What made Arai's science fiction shocking was her writing style. *Inside Myself...*, for example, is written completely in the vernacular of teenage girls, a revolutionary concept. This garnered both praise and criticism at the time of the novel's publication. Since then, this style of speech has spread to various groups of people and has influenced the language of *shōjo* comics and "young adult novels" *(yangu adaruto shōsetsu)*. Yoshimoto Banana, for example, is one author who has inherited Arai's style of writing. Today, with the development of the Internet, the development of writing styles equivalent to speech *(genbun'itchi)* has further accelerated, giving birth to unique linguistic forms. Arai seems almost to have anticipated this phenomenon. There are two main characteristics of Arai's science fiction: her style derived from natural speech, and her own feminist theory disseminated through the merging of *shōjo* culture with a science fiction imagination. The culmination of this unique style can be found in her thirtieth work, *Chigurisu to Yūfuratesu* (1999, Tigris and Euphrates), the winner of the twentieth Grand Prize for Japanese Science Fiction.[21]

The story of *Tigris and Euphrates* concerns the mysterious destruction of a prosperous planet that has been colonized by humans. Only one person remains in the aftermath — a woman named Luna, who, because of her lack of education and unusual circumstances, has retained her "*shōjo* nature" *(shōjosei)* even in old age. She resuscitates women who have been cryogenically frozen and asks each of them: "What are the differences between being a woman and being an adolescent girl? Why can't we all remain as adolescent girls? Why did you give birth to me in the first place?" These women who had lived as second-class citizens in a male society, playing their assigned roles as either women, *shōjo*, mothers, or goddesses, wake up on a dying planet and must face the meaning of being a woman. In an apocalyptic situation where men no longer exist, issues of "the female space," women's values, and women's worldviews come into question. From this perspective, the novel reexamines issues that concern all human beings: environmental problems, women's issues, and ageism. The essential concern, however, is where exactly *shōjo* are situated within Japan's cultural sphere.

The cultural critic Miura Masashi has suggested that in modern society, where gender differences are disappearing, the problem that arises when one tries to understand "women" *(josei)* has nothing to do with the cultural codes for "mothers" or "women" but everything to do with the codes of *shōjo*. *Shōjo* was an imaginary construct of the dominant discourse of late capitalist society. The phenomenon gave rise to its own "*shōjo* aesthetics" that bars the intrusion of men. What underlies Arai's science fiction is a fantasy of *shōjo*: figures who, despite being part of the mechanism constructed by dominant discourses, have managed to run their own course. They threaten to implode the world surrounding them, and their presence may even be called monstrous.[22]

The Transformation of Women into Monsters

For female science fiction that investigates the elements of femininity, "the monster" as a metaphor for women presents important issues. Why is it that this transformation of women into monsters is such a common occurrence within the genre? One possible explanation is that women who resist the patriarchal system are often viewed as monsters. If so, what do these images of monsters signify for women themselves?

The metaphor of monsters is certainly a literary tool through which women can defy society and express their frustrations. At the same time, it is perhaps a symbol of their cry for reform and may stand for their grief that they often have no other choice but to turn into monsters.

These monster metaphors can be divided into two types. The first is the representation of monsters as something feminine, or gynesis. The other is the embodiment of the notion of "the mother."

Psychic Powers: Hagio Moto's *Staa Reddo* (1978–79, Star red)

Star Red is a classic work among *shōjo* comics, one that attracted many science fiction fans because of its topic — an individual with psychic powers. The author, Hagio Moto, was born in 1949 in Fukuoka prefecture. Her first work was "Ruru to Mimi" (Lulu and Mimi), published in 1969. Ever since, she has dominated the world of *shōjo* comics with her poetic language and beautiful artwork. An exceptional writer, Hagio has elevated the philosophical and artistic level of the genre. She has written numerous works of science fiction, and *Star Red* stands out as one of her best. The monster that appears here is a teenage girl with uncontainable psychic powers. Her name is Red Star (or "Red Sei" in Japanese, with her surname

"Sei" written using the character for star). On the outside, she is beautiful and brave, but because of her powers, she is dubbed a monster, bullied, and even hunted. She must hide her real Martian identity. By day, she is an obedient daughter who attends a "ladies' school"; by night, she is the aggressive leader of a motorcycle gang.

Red Sei is aware of her alien nature, but instead of living in the shadows, she asserts her raison d'être. Unfortunately, the superpowers that make her character so intense also put her in difficult positions, and in the second half of the text, she is reduced to a shadow existence. Her psychic powers are a conduit for anger and oppressed female sexuality. The more her anger becomes public, however, the more she is hunted. In the story, Sei, who is persecuted for her monstrous powers, vanishes from the real world before the tale ends. Of course, her disappearance is mysterious. Although she vanishes into a fantastic space for a while, she will later find herself in the womb of a beautiful boy who has undergone a sex change in order to become Sei's mother. Thus Sei will be reborn in the body of an infant and will return to the real world.

What is compelling here is Sei's psychic power. Post-1950s American science fiction treated psychic powers such as telepathy, teleportation, and telekinesis as part of human evolution or deployed them as literary tools for capturing human conflicts. In those texts, psychic powers were viewed as a gift from heaven or something almost magical. *Star Red,* in contrast, deconstructs such psychic powers. Take Sei's gaze, for example. Sei is blind, but ESP talents on earth have discovered that even though her eyes do not see anything, she can perceive things visually from any angle. Sei does not develop her sensory perceptions by looking at everyday scenes; she is an alien who receives her extraordinary powers from observing alien landscapes.

In contemporary gender theory, the gaze is often tied to the male subject, and in the same way, we can surmise that Sei's alien perception is linked to a female perspective.

The text marks psychic powers as female, and the virtuosity of Hagio's ideas lies in the fact that the text is able to situate these powers as rational. The narrative begins by exploring the female body but goes on to investigate the constructions of worlds that govern the universe. The universe in the text is divided into two groups: the solar system Zesnuser comprises logical people who govern the real world, and the collective Ami comprises those, such as psychics, who do not fit the mold of Zesnuser: it stands for a conglomeration of illogical thoughts such as dreams, the unconscious, and insanity. We can designate the former as masculine and the latter as feminine. The Zesnusers label Sei as part of the Ami and kill her. Sei loses only her body, though, and survives as a consciousness, floating into the network of the collective that the Ami has spread out behind the galactic system. The Ami, however, rejects Sei as well, and she has no choice but to be reborn as a child in the real world. If we read the two races as representative of the kind of worldview governed by the Western binary opposition of male/female, Red Sei is an alien rejected by both these categories. Although this Western binary opposition underlies the text and although Sei's supernatural powers develop within its sphere, Sei's powers can be understood as a reflection of the mentality of Japanese women, who feel ill at ease in a world that equates gynesis with the concept of "women" as constructed by the Western world.

Freaks: Yamao Yūko's *Yume no sumu machi* (1976, The city where dreams live)

Around the same time that Hagio was rendering the conflict between gynesis and the femininity of Japanese women, the fantastic literature writer Yamao Yūko was also exploring the same topic in her mannerism-influenced fantasy work *Yume no sumu machi* (1976, The city where dreams live).[23]

Yamao Yūko was born in 1955 in Okayama prefecture. In 1973, the year that she began her studies at Dōshisha University, she entered the Hayakawa Science Fiction Contest with her earliest work, *Kamen butōkai* (The masquerade). The work reached the final round, and she quickly came to be regarded as a unique fantasy writer. Since 1982, however, her output has dwindled, partly because of the discontinuation of the journal *Kisō tengai*, where Yamao published most of her works. After getting married and having children, Yamao left the literary milieu for a while, but she resumed writing in 1999.

The story line of *Red Sei*, a girl with psychic powers who travels across dimensions, is reworked in *Yume no sumu machi*. This time, the text focuses on the freakishness of the female body and narrates the fall of a city that celebrates this freakishness.

Yume no sumu machi is a ten-chapter novella published in a collection of the same name. It takes place in a town laid out in a funnel-shaped depression, at the center (or bottom) of which sits a theater. The town is ruled by a mysterious being referred to as "that person." Until the evening before the work opens, a troupe of dancers going by the name of the Rose-Colored Legs was performing in the theater, but now the dancers are all dead, and the theater must be shut down. The Rose-Colored Legs dancers are freaks. The lower halves of their bodies, encased in silk tights, are attractive and well proportioned. The upper halves, however, are shriveled from malnutrition and lack of exercise. We are told that these dancers are "manufactured" from prostitutes, using a secret method. They all die en masse when they dance their last dance. Their rose-colored legs can be read as fantastic images representing women of the red light districts, consumer objects designed to serve their spectators. Beyond the Rose-Colored Legs, there are distorted images of women scattered throughout the town, from angels and mermaids to gunshot victims. Images of women who are oppressed and hurt are ubiquitous. The violence of deformity inscribed onto the female bodies eventually distorts the temporal space of the entire city. On the night of the reopening of the theater, the city resting on top of the funnel falls into the abyss that opens up beneath it and disappears.

Barbara Creed has used Alice Jardine's gynesis theory to claim that horror films that subvert themes of violence against women represent an overflow of gynesis.[24] The city in which freakish women become spectacles only collapses when violence toward women reaches a climax. The city is then obliterated from reality and is sucked into the void.

Cyborgs/Hybrids: Ōhara Mariko's "Haiburiddo chairudo" (1984, Hybrid child)

Born in 1959, Ōhara Mariko was an author devoted to examining Japanese femininity through "simulationism." She made her literary debut in the 1980 Hayakawa Science Fiction Contest. She is known for psychoanalytic works that ceaselessly pursue family issues, issues that can be understood only against the background of Japan's high-tech capitalism of the 1980s. "Haiburiddo chairudo" is a story about an immortal cyborg weapon, "Sample B," which can sample and simulate any object it chooses. The story begins when the weapon escapes from the military and goes into hiding in an occupied house. The text elegantly captures the intensity of love and conflict between a mother and daughter living in the claustrophobic space of the house. A later collection of short stories published with the same title is deeply rooted in Japan's postmodern culture, especially in the rise of simulationism — the sampling, simulating, and remixing — that came after the high-tech era. Because the text exposes political problems surrounding the conflicts between Western and Japanese culture, it attracted the attention of many critics. In 1994 Ōhara won the fifteenth grand Prize for Japanese Science Fiction with her short science fiction collection *Sensō o enjita kamigamitachi* (Gods who performed wars), a feminist fabulation that deals with war, money, sadomasochism, and women.[25]

The hybrid child that Ōhara portrays is a military weapon that can take in, digest, and pretend to be anything it wishes. Because of its strong connection to technology and resemblance to Haraway's cyborg, critics have often interpreted the figure as a reflection of Japan's postmodern mentality. At the same time, this cyborg nature is also closely linked to the issue of femininity. Sample B, after all, not only intrudes into a house where a mother and a daughter are fighting fiercely, it also eats the corpse of the daughter after she is killed and buried in the basement, and takes on the daughter's form.

With the simulation of the daughter by Sample B, the fighting between the mother and the daughter recommences, and the murder is eventually brought to light. The truth behind the murder cannot be revealed until the daughter turns into a monster, finally exposing the mother's monstrous nature. How did the mother become a monster who could kill her own daughter? This mother–daughter battle calls to mind the conflict between two actual modes of living among women: one is the postmodern daughter, who survives by adapting to different situations and by transforming herself; the other is the phallic mother, who replaces the absent patriarchal authority figure by becoming one with the home and by becoming the ruler of the feminized family space. The race for survival between these two female modes — one who follows the flow of things and one who merges herself with the home — is further developed in Ōhara's *Kyūketsuki Efemera* (1993, Ephemera the vampire).[26]

The monstrous female identity called "hybrid child" embodies the way of life led by postmodern women, who try to transform themselves by placing themselves in different situations. The "hybrid child," through her confrontations, exposes the "traditional female image" of the Japanese mother, whose survival tactic is to embrace and perform the same role over and over.

The Mother Tongue: Shōno Yoriko's *Haha no hattatsu* (1994–96, The development of my mother)

Shōno Yoriko's *Haha no hattatsu* is a work that attempts to analyze the Japanese mother image that we saw in Ōhara's work from a linguistic point of view (Figure 3.1). An "avant-pop" writer who has won numerous awards, she was born in 1958 in Mie prefecture. In 1981 she won the *Gunzō* New Literature Award with "Gokuraku" (Paradise), in 1991 the Noma New Writer Award with *Nani mo shite inai* (I haven't done anything), in 1994 the Mishima Award with *Nihyaku kaiki* (The two-hundredth anniversary), and in the same year the highly prestigious Akutagawa Prize with *Taimusurippu konbinaato* (Timewarp complex).[27]

The story unfolds in three parts: "Haha no shukushō" (The shrinking of my mother), "Haha no hattatsu" (The development of my mother), and "Haha no daikaiten ondo" (My mother's big somersault recital). The protagonist, Dakiname Yatsuno, is a forty-nine-year-old woman living

Figure 3.1. Cover image from Shōno Yoriko's surreal family
drama *Haha no hattatsu* (The development of my mother).
(From the Kawade Shobō tankōbon edition.)

with her mother and has suffered from a strange anomaly since the end of
her adolescence: in her eyes, her mother appears as a tiny being. Yatsuno
eventually murders her mother. Later, however, she discovers that her
mother never died completely. By eating human flesh and by undergoing
decomposition and reconstruction, she has turned into a strange being

called "the alphabet mother" (gojūon no haha). Eventually, the alphabet mother leaps in front of Yatsuno and performs a series of somersaults in midair, trying to show Yatsuno "everything about her" (haha no subete). Once Yatsuno sees this, she senses her own death and confronts the reasons behind their conflicts.

Since the story is told in the first person, we can read the entire narrative as a record of Yatsuno's insanity. Perhaps she has been living in her made-up world from the time that she begins to see miniature images of her mother, but what pushed Yatsuno over the edge of insanity? The mother is definitely at the heart of it, and there is also the deep grudge between mother and daughter. This grudge is not just ordinary hatred; it has turned into an obsession combined with love and affection. However, the dead mother and her insane daughter Yatsuno — no matter how much they insult and collide with one another — do help each other to a certain extent, and together they try to situate the word *mother* within the Japanese syllabic system. The alphabet mother embodies a virtual mother figure that reflects a certain grudge-filled reality. Furthermore, she is the source of Yatsuno's insanity, and her somersaults can be interpreted as a kind of insane dance. She draws out Yatsuno's mother obsession, which is what triggered Yatsuno's deep-seated grudge toward the alphabet mother in the first place. "Mother," Yatsuno says, "for the rest of my life, I will live for you and die for you, so please don't say things like 'I want grandchildren.'"[28]

From mother to daughter and from daughter to mother, the mother–daughter relationship is a continuum that has been constantly exploited by heterosexual, male-centered society. Yatsuno's words reveal not only her rejection of her mother but also her reluctance to become a mother herself. This mother–daughter relationship completely rejects biological reproduction. It is an ironic story: a daughter is forced to become her mother, but because of this assimilation, she ends up rejecting her motherly duties in life. "The mother," for many women, is a contradictory existence that makes them remember psychological conflicts buried in their unconscious. The text reveals this construct of "the mother" through the mode of insanity.

The Bride and the Mother-in-Law: Shinoda Setsuko's *Gosaintan*
(1997, Gosainthan)

The Japanese "mother" that Ōhara and Shōno portray is one who becomes assimilated into the home and turns into a monster. The strength of the mother grows after assimilation, and she tries to pull down her daughter along with her. The daughter, however, tries to escape and live her own life, and thus a bloody battle commences. These battles often take place in the middle-class nuclear families of average office-workers *(sarariimen)*, and in that sense, they are extremely modern phenomena.

Another long-established female conflict where the violent nature of the mother becomes apparent is the fight between the bride and the mother-in-law. In agricultural and merchant families, two groups deeply embedded in patriarchal codes, the bride must enter her husband's household. In these families, it is common for the bride and the mother-in-law to quarrel over who will have supremacy within the house. Shinoda Setsuko's *Gosaintan* (1997, Gosainthan) is a story about a bride who becomes a monster in just such an oppressive environment (Figure 3.2).[29]

The protagonist Yugi Terukazu is a single farmer in his late thirties. Under pressure from his mother, Shizue, who wants him to find a wife at once and have children, Yugi arranges a marriage with a non-Japanese woman. Karvana Tami, his Nepalese wife, may look "Japanese" on the outside, but she cannot speak a word of the language. She is a heroine whose speech has been taken away. Shizue takes a liking to her, and Yugi, listening to his mother's advice, forces Karvana to undergo a humiliating medical exam, pays off the intermediaries with a large sum, and takes her in as his bride.

Karvana is given the Japanese name "Toshiko," and she begins her life as a farmer's wife, but she has difficulty learning the language and getting accustomed to Japanese food. She runs away from home constantly, as if under a spell like a sleepwalker. In the beginning, the tale is framed as a "captivity narrative," wherein a young foreign woman is trapped in the Japanese household. For the Japanese family, Karvana is an all-important wife and daughter, but to the woman herself, she is a slave forced to become a Japanese wife.

This story line is similar to American postcolonial literature. One example that comes to mind is Paul Park's science fiction epic *Celestis* (1995).[30] Park, too, depicts a tragic love between a man from earth and the native bride he weds on a colonized planet; she has been operated on and brainwashed using high-tech methods to turn her into a "wife." *Gosaintan's chairudo's* heroine is actually a sacred maiden *(miko)* from a foreign land, and being forced to become the wife of a typical Japanese farmer is an injustice that later gives rise to supernatural phenomena. *Gosaintan's* alien (the foreign woman) resists her fate, thereby bringing about disastrous consequences for the Japanese man's family.

Gosaintan also openly exposes Japan's stance toward Nepal. One detects a double orientalism that takes place within the space of Asia, which often finds itself under the heel of international capitalism.

This orientalism is illustrated by the relationship between Terukazu and Toshiko. Toshiko, a silent woman who can float in the air, becomes a

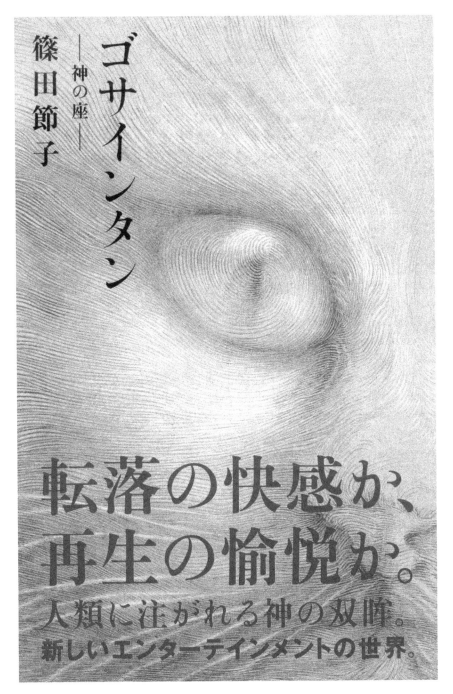

ゴサインタン
　—神の座—
篠田節子

転落の快感か、
再生の愉悦か。
人類に注がれる神の双眸。
新しいエンターテインメントの世界。

Figure 3.2. Cover image from Shinoda Setsuko's *Gosaintan*
(Gosainthan), the story of an arranged marriage to an alien
bride, which gives rise to supernatural events. (From the
Futaba bunko edition.)

mysterious, sacred woman in Terukazu's mind. At one point Terukazu gets upset at Toshiko for giving away his family's money to followers who worship Toshiko as a sacred being. When a cult eventually forms around Toshiko, Terukazu's household falls apart, and Terukazu is left with nothing. Amid all this chaos, moreover, Toshiko disappears. Even under these circumstances, Terukazu saves up his money, leaves home, and pursues Toshiko, who has been deported, into the heart of Nepal. Why is he so obsessed with Toshiko? The narrative is about a Japanese man who has lost all that constitutes his status — his house, his wealth, and his land. Watching his possessions slip away, Terukazu finally comes to see the hideous, true nature of the family, which can uphold its tradition as a "distinguished house" only by exploiting those outside it. He must face the matriarchal history of the women who marry into his household, such as his grandmother and his mother. He must confront the fact that these women have lived like slaves from other Asian countries. Does this mean that his love for Karvana is laced with guilt? Not quite. What we can see in Terukazu is not guilt but an admiration for a mystifying object called Karvana. This orientalist fantasy about an unknown land appears from time to time throughout the text.

When Terukazu pursues Karvana and visits her country, however, he realizes how poor her homeland really is. Karvana is not a mysterious and grandiose sacred maiden or a powerful goddess: she is an ill-fated woman who, if she had remained in her land, would only have died of disease as a prostitute or, even if she had married into a rich family, would have lived a sad life because she lacked a dowry. What Terukazu encounters is a paradox: women like Karvana can be saved only by a system like slavery. If Japanese men wed these women and save them from their sad fates, the women become slaves, but if they are not saved, these women have to live even sadder lives. The text thus captures the humiliating circumstances in which women must live — their inescapable, wretched fates. Terukazu comes to accept these facts, and this time, he is the one who tries to blend in with Nepalese culture.

The brides entrapped in the household are made into monsters by their mothers-in-law. These women separate the "Japanese men" from their households and seek the alteration of their masculinities. In this sense, this text can be seen as one that reexamines the true nature of romance — both that of the more traditional historical romances (*denki monogatari*) and that of love stories (*ren'ai monogatari*) — vis-à-vis its relationship to masculinity (*danseisei*).

The author Shinoda was born in 1955 in Tokyo. She won the *Shōsetsu Subaru* New Writer Award in 1990 with *Kinu no hen'yō* (The transformation of silk), a panic horror story written in detailed artistic style, about an egg that becomes a monster. Since then, she has experimented with "slipstream literature" (kyōkai shōsetsu), and in 1997 Futabasha finally published her Gosaintan. It is a splendid and complex work that combines elements from several different genres, and it won her the 10th annual Yamamoto Shūgorō Prize. In July of the same year, Onnatachi no jihaado The women's jihad) earned the 117th Naoki Prize, perhaps the most prestigious prize for new writers of popular fiction.[31]

The Alteration of Masculinity

As I mentioned in the preceding section, the images of women transforming into monsters are strongly linked to the alteration of masculinity. What kinds of these alterations can we observe in the imagination of women's science fiction?

Half Man/Half Beast: Kurimoto Kaoru's Guin saaga (1979–, The Guin Saga)

Among writers who depict altered male bodies in Japanese women's science fiction, Kurimoto Kaoru is one of the most prominent. Born in 1953, she graduated from the department of literature at Waseda University. In 1977 she won the Gunzō New Writer's Prize with a work of literary criticism called Bungaku no rinkaku (The outlines of literature), written under the name of Nakajima Azusa. (For more on Kurimoto/Nakajima's criticism, see chapter 11 and my introduction preceding it.) In 1978 she won the Edogawa Ranpo Prize with the epic mystery Bokura no jidai (Our era), and since then, she has been active on many fronts, writing fiction, poetry, plays, and criticism in science fiction, fantasy, horror, and mystery.[32]

Her most celebrated work, Guin saaga (1979–, The Guin Saga), is a heroic fantasy that extends to over a hundred novels.[33] The narrative begins when Linda and Remus, twin princess and prince of a kingdom that has been invaded by the country of Gola, meet a stranger during their escape, a leopard-headed man called Guin. Together with Guin, who has lost all his memories, the twins try to restore their kingdom.

The protagonist Guin is a swordsman with a leopard's head, half man and half beast. Why a leopard's head? The heroes of heroic fantasies have conventionally represented the epitome of masculinity. By creating a hero who lives on the border between man and beast, the author reexamines the transcendent and deviant nature of ordinary heroic fantasy protagonists by revealing the essential instability of sexual differences and human nature.

Kurimoto, who casts these kinds of strange heroes in her heroic fantasies, is also known as the founder of a genre of female romantic fiction called "*shōnen* romance" *(shōnen ai).*[34]

Shōnen romance is a genre directed at a female audience and depicts male-male homosexual relationships. It may be traced back to female writers such as Mori Mari, and since the 1970s, it has been used to refer to *shōjo* comics of the "Shōwa 24 gang" — writers such as the aforementioned Hagio Moto and Takemiya Keiko, who were all born in the twenty-fourth year of the Shōwa era, 1949. Kurimoto dubbed these works "*shōnen* romances" and wrote one "*shōnen* romance" herself titled *Mayonaka no tenshi* (1979, Midnight angel).[35]

This genre was the precursor to the contemporary genre of *yaoi* — described in more detail in my short history of *yaoi* elsewhere in this volume and explored by Saitō Tamaki in chapter 11. Kurimoto belongs to the generation that pioneered interest in these genres, shortly before *yaoi* exploded in popularity among female fans. As a critic, too, she has been a strong advocate of *yaoi* culture. Although this culture is fundamentally based on male homosexual relationships, *yaoi* texts have gone beyond regular depictions of gender and have come to occupy a unique position in the female-dominated underground world in which both writers and readers are women.

Kurimoto has turned the body of the regular heroic fantasy protagonist — the flawless macho male hero — into a body that is half man and half beast. She has also attempted this type of alteration of masculinity in her *shōnen* romance fiction. These works explore deep, romantic bonds between men that could be imagined only in a fantastic world, and they are not simply homosexual. These texts question how one may attain equality in relationships and to what extent this kind of intense conceptualization of deviating gender is possible. Here, the usual masculinity and sexuality are completely altered and reconstructed according to women's romantic desires. Works that portray deviations from the real world, such as the alteration of masculinity, often appear to borrow the style of science fiction and fantasy.

Twins: Satō Aki's *Barutazaaru no henreki* (1991, The travels of Balthazar)

Among authors who make use of the theme of twins to present forms of the altered male body, Satō Aki stands out as the most representative writer. Born in 1960, she won the third Japanese Fantasy Novel Grand Prize with her debut novel *Barutazaaru no henreki* (1991, The travels of Balthazar).[36]

The novel is set in Nazi-occupied Vienna. Melchior and Balthazar are twins who occupy the same body. Living a decadent lifestyle in the occupied city, they face a twisted fate after losing all their possessions. Through eloquence and irony, the text depicts the misshapen desires of these two young men who ripen in the decadent, luscious atmosphere of the Western city.

A Japanese writer who simulates the traditions of Western culture, Satō situates this male body with its divided consciousnesses inside the completely constructed world of her own "Europe." The world of the protagonists involves complex and mysterious political plots, but the twins' daily lives are marked by mediocrity and ennui. As destruction threatens this affluent society, the two amuse themselves to death, sensing their impending fall. Satō captures this situation in a cynical manner steeped in dandyism and meticulously portrays the twins' psychology as it is distorted by this suffocating atmosphere. Balthazar is not a man without flaws. His mind is split in two: one half laughs at the world, and the other is a serious soul who tries to understand the other half. Balthazar's pedantic manner is like that of a *shōjo* who refuses to be a *shōjo* or that of a "woman" who refuses to be a "woman." He possesses a cunning intellect that may be called "anti-*shōjo*" *(han shōjo)* and "antifeminine" *(han josei)*. Balthazar and Melchior, rather than being "men," actually are more like women with masks or beautiful women dressed in male clothing. The deep bond between the two male personalities represents a sort of truce between the ideal images of men who embody what women seek in relationships, and the images of men who act with their own free will. In other words, Balthazar contains an altered masculinity rewritten by female desire. This alteration is precisely a mode of criticism of masculinity that is based on women's own criteria.

Artificial Life: Takano Fumio's *Vasurafu* (1998, Vaslav)

The body and human psychology constructed by *yaoi* texts reflect women's romantic desires. The most contemporary example of these "altered" images of men is that of masculinity placed in cyberspace — the theme of *Vasurafu* (1998, Vaslav). The author, Takano Fumio, was born in 1966 in Ibaraki prefecture. Her literary debut, *Mujika makiina* (1995, Musica machina), was about a mad artist who lives in nineteenth-century Europe and was a finalist for the sixth annual Japanese Fantasy Novel Grand Prize. Takano is known for "steampunk" works that mix together a high-tech sensibility with a more classical European world. *Musika machina* certainly belongs to this group of works, along with *Kanto anjeriko* (1996,

Canto angelico), which deals with an eighteenth-century castrato, and *Vasurafu* (Figure 3.3).[37]

Vasurafu takes place in the early twentieth century in an imagined historical version of the Russian Empire, which, in the story, has already become a computer-based, high-tech society. "The Imperial Russian Computer Network Administrative Bureau" creates a ballet dancer "Vaslav" (based on the actual performer Vaslav Nijinsky) in a virtual world. The Vaslav software comes to life and begins to dance within the network. The story revolves around the commotion the software causes among the hackers, programmers, fans, and network dancers. Most compelling, however, is the image of Nijinsky that gracefully dances through the network. The virtual Vaslav is a marvelous hacking program that can invade any computer at any time, and he captures the heart of a hacker with the username Odette. Odette pursues Vaslav and eventually tries to have a romantic relationship with him by using a device to turn the crown prince Ivan's own brain into an interface. The attempt to incorporate Vaslav into the human brain itself is another example of the alteration of masculinity. After his brain processes Vaslav, however, the crown prince collapses.

This attempt to consummate a relationship with a virtual performer echoes similar plots in William Gibson's Japanesque science fiction and anime like *Macross Plus* (discussed in the introduction and in chapter 8). But Takano's resolution is distinct. In *Vasurafu,* the romantic endeavors of a hacker girl result in the alteration of masculinity and the consequent destruction of it. We can read this narrative as a reflection of the romance that women both desire and demand from men.

Conclusion

From Suzuki Izumi to Takano Fumio, in Japanese women's science fiction one constantly discovers attempts to alter the world. This alteration can be read as a subversion of the real world, a subversion that belongs to the genre of female science fiction and its attempts to discover and depict femininity.

Science fiction by Japanese women reflects their sensitivity and open-mindedness toward the transformations of their own bodies, bodies that tend to be cyborglike. Japanese female science fiction refuses to accept its world as a deviant culture *(ibunka).* Rather, it embraces deviance, finds in-between spaces, and seeks its place in the world. It forms a network of texts for its survival. It accepts the transformations imposed on women's bodies and applies them to masculine bodies as well, constantly trying to alter the male body. On the one hand, Japanese women's science fiction reveals a strong will to transform the female body, but on the other hand, it

高野史緒

ヴァスラフ

中央公論社

Figure 3.3. Cover image from *Vasurafu* (Vaslav), Takano
Fumio's story of a virtual ballet dancer that is also the ultimate
hacking software, and the female programmer who loves
him. (From the Chūō Kōronsha tankōbon edition.)

laments the fact that it is only through these transformations that female bodies can survive. This paradoxical sensibility is precisely what gives Japanese female science fiction its literary significance.

Notes

1. [The Japanese word *joseisei* could also be interpreted as "female nature," but in consultation with the author, I have translated it as "femininity" and its male equivalent *danseisei* as "masculinity." — Trans.]

2. The early 1970s are often identified with the women's lib (*ribu*) movement in Japan, and the late seventies with "feminism" (*feminizumu*). Here it may be helpful to outline briefly some of the parallels and differences between the early Japanese and American women's movements. The rise of Japanese women's lib succeeded the activism of the late sixties, but Ueno Chizuko notes that it also critiqued the male centeredness of the sixties New Left. The movement crystallized in 1970 around opposition to proposed revisions in Japan's Eugenic Preservation Law (Yūsei Hogo Hō). Reproductive freedom was an issue central to the Japanese movement, but in this context it encompassed the right to carry a child to term as well as access to abortion and birth control. At the same time, another current of the movement argued for increased recognition of the unpaid "shadow" work of the Japanese housewife. The male-dominated and largely hostile mass media projected a distorted picture of Japanese feminism as (among other things) anti-motherhood, but it was not. Rather, it questioned society's artificial division of the subject into woman (*josei*) and mother (*bosei*). It was not until 1985 that the equal opportunity in employment law was enacted, addressing some of the institutionalized discrimination women faced in the professional workplace. For more on this history, see Inoue Teruko, Ueno Chizuko, and Ehara Yumiko, eds., "Nihon no feminizumu: Ribu to feminizumu (Japanese feminism: Women's lib and feminism) (Tokyo: Iwanami, 1994); Kano Masanao, *Gendai Nihon joseishi: Feminizumu o jiku to site* (Feminism and contemporary Japanese women's history) (Tokyo: Yūhikaku, 2004); Tanaka Mitsu, *Inochi no onnatachi e: Torimidashi ūman ribu ron* (For the women we owe our lives to: An informal theory of women's lib), rev. ed. (Tokyo: Pandora, 2004); Mizoguchi Akiyo et al., eds., *Shiryō Nihon ūman ribu shi* (Documents in the history of Japanese women's lib), 3 vols. (Tokyo: Shōkadō, 1992–95).

3. [*Shōjo manga*, *shōjo shōsetsu*, and *reidiizu komikkusu*. The Japanese word *shōjo* has become a theoretically loaded term among scholars of Japanese literature and popular culture. Most of the time, I have left it as *shōjo*, but in plot summaries and in other general descriptions, I have translated it as "teenage girls" or "adolescent girls" to avoid redundancy. — Trans.]

4. Hagio Moto, *Staa reddo* (Star red) (Tokyo: Shōgakukan Manga Bunko, 1995); originally serialized in the weekly *Shūkan shōjo komikku*, starting with issue no. 23 in 1978 and ending with issue no. 3 in 1979.

5. Ono Fuyumi, *Tōkei ibun* (Strange tales of Tokyo) (Tokyo: Shinchōsha, 1995); Shōno Yoriko, *Haha no hattatsu* (Tokyo: Kawade Shobō, 1996); based on stories originally published in the literary magazines *Bungei* and *Kaien* between April 1994 and spring 1996.

6. [The Japanese word used here, *ie,* can indicate a physical house or dwelling, a group of people who constitute a family, or the social system that has such ideas at its core. Kotani often uses the word in all three senses at once. Lacking such a flexible term in English, I have sometimes translated it as "household," other times as "house," "home," or "family." — Trans.]

7. Ōhara Mariko, "Haiburiddo chairudo" (Hybrid child), in *Haiburiddo chairudo* (Tokyo: Hayakawa Shobō, 1990), 9–73.

8. After the *SF Magajin* and *Kisō tengai* special issues, the third important publishing event of this initial period came in September 1980, when the journal *NW-SF* published a special issue on women's SF, with a woman editor and a combined roster of Japanese and Western authors and critics (including Joanna Russ, Grania Davis, Sonni Efron, and Ursula K. Le Guin, as well as Yamada Kazuko and Yamada Hiromi — now Kawakami Hiromi). Coming at the end of the 1970s and combining the background of Japanese women's lib with elements of Western women's science fiction, this issue could be said to mark a new direction for women's science fiction in Japan.

9. Suzuki Izumi and Mayumura Taku, "SF: Otoko to onna," *Kisō tengai,* March 1977, 121–35.

10. Suzuki Izumi, "Onna to onna no yo no naka" (The world of women and women), *SF Magajin,* July 1977, 114–30; later a novel of the same title (Tokyo: Hayakawa bunko JA, 1978).

11. Suzuki Izumi and Araki Nobuyoshi, *Shishōsetsu* (The I-novel) (Tokyo: Byakuya Shobō, 1986).

12. Hikawa Reiko, *Onna senshi Efera to Jiriora* (The women warriors Efera and Jiriora), 7-novel series (Tokyo: Tairiku Noberusu, 1988–90).

13. Hikawa Reiko, *Onna senshi Efera & Jiriora gaiden: Aoi kami no shirīn* (The women warriors Efera and Jiriora: Blue-haired Shiriin), 2-novel series (Tokyo: Tairiku Noberusu, 1991–92).

14. Matsuo Yumi, *Barūn taun no satsujin* (Tokyo: Hayakawa bunko JA, 1994); collects four linked stories published in *SF Magajin* between March 1992 and December 1993. The title story is partially translated by Larry McCaffery as "Murder in Balloon Town," *Review of Contemporary Fiction* 22, no. 2 (2002): 98–110.

15. Matsuo, *Barūn taun no satsujin,* 40.

16. John Varley, "The Barbie Murders," in *The John Varley Reader: Thirty Years of Short Fiction* (New York: Berkeley, 2004), 119–45.

17. Matsuo, *Barūn taun no satsujin,* 41.

18. Ogura Chikako, *Bijin no jōken: Nyū haafu no erosu* (The conditions of a beauty: Transsexual eros) (Tokyo: Chikuma, 1993), 24–27.

19. Arai Motoko, "Atashi no naka no . . . ," *Kisō tengai,* February 1978, 138–64; later published as *Atashi no naka* no . . . (Tokyo: Kisō tengaisha, 1978).

20. Arai Motoko, "Guriin rekuiemu" (Green requiem), in *Guriin rekuiemu* (Tokyo: Kōdansha Bunko, 1983); Arai, "Nepchūn" (Neptune), in *Ima wa mō inai watashi e* (To the me who is no longer) (Tokyo: Hayakawa Bunko JA, 1990), 7–122. [Japan's Seiunshō translates literally as "Nebula Award," but the prize corresponds to the West's Hugo Award, in that it is decided by fan voting. Japan's equivalent of the West's Nebula Award is the Nihon Science Fiction Taishō, the "Grand Prize for Japanese Science Fiction." As Kotani notes in the following paragraph, Arai won this award as well in 1999. — Trans.]

21. Arai Motoko, *Chigurisu to Yūfuratesu* (Tokyo: Shūeisha, 1999); based on stories originally published in *Shōsetsu subaru* between August 1996 and July 1998.

22. Miura Masashi and Hagio Moto, "Haha to iu kagami ni utsuru mono" (Reflections in the mirror called mother), *Daikōkai* 5 (August 1995): 142–60.

23. Yamao Yūko, "Yume no sumu machi" (The city where dreams live), in *Yume no sumu machi* (Tokyo: Hayakawa Bunko JA, 1978); originally published in the July 1976 issue of *SF Magajin*.

24. Barbara Creed, "Gynesis, Postmodernism, and the Science Fiction Horror Film," in *Alien Zone: Cultural Theory and Contemporary Science Fiction Cinema*, ed. Annette Kuhn (New York: Verso, 1990), 214–18.

25. Ōhara Mariko, *Sensō o enjita kamigamitachi* (Gods who performed wars) (Tokyo: Hayakawa Bunko JA, 2000).

26. Ōhara Mariko, *Kyūketsuki Efemera* (Ephemera the vampire) (Tokyo: Hayakawa Bunko JA, 1996).

27. Shōno Yoriko, "Gokuraku" (Paradise), in *Gokuraku* (Tokyo: Kōdansha, 1994), 5–66; Shōno, *Nani mo shite inai* (I haven't done anything) (Tokyo: Kōdansha, 1991); Shōno, *Nihyaku kaiki* (The two-hundredth anniversary) (Tokyo: Shinchōsha, 1994), 37–88; Shōno, *Taimusurippu konbinaato* (Timewarp complex) (Tokyo: Bungei Shunjū, 1994).

28. Shōno, *Haha no hattatsu*, 178.

29. Shinoda Setsuko, *Gosaintan* (Gosainthan) (Tokyo: Futaba bunko, 1997).

30. Paul Park, *Celestis* (New York: Tom Doherty, 1995).

31. Shinoda Setsuko, *Kinu no hen'yō* (The transformation of silk) (Tokyo: Shūeisha, 1991); Shinoda, *Onnatachi no jihaado* (The women's jihad) (Tokyo: Shūeisha, 2000).

32. Kurimoto Kaoru, *Bungaku no rinkaku* (The outlines of literature) (Tokyo: Kōdansha, 1978); Kurimoto, *Bokura no jidai* (Our era) (Tokyo: Kōdansha, 1979).

33. Kurimoto Kaoru, *Guin saaga (The Guin Saga)*, novel series (Tokyo: Hayakawa Bunko JA, 1979–); volumes 1–5 translated by Alexander O. Smith and Elye T. Alexander as *The Guin Saga* (New York: Vertical, 2003–6).

34. [*Shōnen* is the male equivalent of *shōjo* and means "teenage boy." As with *shōjo*, it has been left in the original. — Trans.]

35. Kurimoto Kaoru, *Mayonaka no tenshi* (Midnight angel), 2 vols. (Tokyo: Bungei Shunjū, 1979).

36. Satō Aki, *Barutazaaru no henreki* (The travels of Balthazar) (Tokyo: Shinchōsha, 1991).

37. Takano Fumio, *Vasurafu* (Vaslav) (Tokyo: Chūō Kōronsha, 1998); Takano, *Mujika makiina* (Musica machina) (Tokyo: Hayakawa bunko JA, 2002); Takano, *Kanto anjeriko* (Canto angelico) (Tokyo: Kōdansha, 1996).

4. SF as Hamlet
Science Fiction and Philosophy

Azuma Hiroki
Translated by Miri Nakamura

his is an essay on science fiction and philosophy. The word *philosophy* is an ambiguous term, however. It actually has two different usages: a quotidian one and a technical one. If, for example, you use the word to mean "a way to think about the world" or "a way to think about the meaning of life," then this is the everyday usage. No specialized knowledge or professional experience is needed for that kind of inquiry; anyone can become a philosopher if one has some life experience, and an exceptional work in any genre would qualify as philosophical.

Science fiction and this quotidian definition of "philosophy" have a strong connection with one another. Be it space opera or New Wave fiction, the essence of the science fiction imagination lies in extrapolating from the unrealistic conditions that exist in our lives. At times, the result sheds light from within our own reality on that very reality that entraps us. The futuristic worlds depicted in George Orwell's *Nineteen Eighty-Four* (1949) and Philip K. Dick's *Ubik* (1969), for example, give concrete form to the image of ourselves living in a totalitarian or a consumer society. And the visions portrayed in Arthur C. Clarke's *Childhood's End* (1953) or J. G. Ballard's *Crystal World* (1966) invite us to ponder the deep question of where humans come from and where we are headed, both from an external and an internal perspective. By reading science fiction, we can reexamine the meaning of the world and its human inhabitants from a viewpoint other than the everyday one. All of these experiences can be dubbed "philosophical" if one wishes, so it is not altogether mistaken to say that science fiction is inherently a philosophical genre. In fact, some theories of science fiction have argued just that.[1]

This is all rather general, however. To think about the relationship between science fiction and philosophy in more detail, one must introduce that second technical usage of *philosophy*. This philosophy belongs strictly to the work of Western modernity. From René Descartes through Gottfried Leibniz and David Hume, it was completed by Immanuel Kant and saw its heyday in the nineteenth century. It is the name of an academic field that in the twentieth century was divided into various schools of thought, such as existentialism, structuralism, and analytical philosophy. This philosophy connotes a world with its own specific rules and history, and therefore not everyone can become this kind of philosopher.

What relationship does this kind of philosophy (Western modernism's philosophy) have with science fiction? My contention is that they have strong links with one another, perhaps even analogous to kinship ties.

First, let me give my own sketch of Western philosophy's history. Pre-nineteenth-century philosophy is usually represented by G. W. F. Hegel. The Hegelian goal was to attain "the absolute spirit" through an understanding of "the historic world" as a whole. In short, it was an extremely optimistic view that envisioned philosophy as a higher form of learning that combined all sorts of knowledge, perception, and ethics.

This optimism, however, had lost its persuasiveness by the latter half of the nineteenth century — a period that saw a rapid rise in accumulated knowledge and that, with the coming of modern industrialization and imperialism, transformed people's lives from the ground up. Hegel's vision did retain some power through all this, up until the beginning of the twentieth century, when two world wars cast out the last remnants of its influence. The authenticity of the philosophy produced up to that point was threatened by the fact that a renowned philosopher like Martin Heidegger had become closely aligned with the Nazis and the fact that Karl Marx's doctrines had given birth to totalitarianism. Compared with the nineteenth-century philosophers, who were allowed to dream of the coming of totality, twentieth-century philosophers had to begin by reflecting on why one must not dream of such things, and why such dreams do more harm than good.

Accordingly, the field of philosophy has since been occupied with how to harmonize various value systems and how to negotiate between them. In certain schools, this type of effort has produced idealistic speculations (postmodernism), in others an affinity with sociology (cultural studies/postcolonialism), and in some others, skepticism toward the methodologies of the humanities itself (computer science/cognitive psychology). These splits have complicated the current state of philosophical thought, but later historians of philosophy may look back on these splits as epitomizing the twentieth century. Either way, the Hegelian ideal of totality, at least philosophically, was tossed away by the mid-nineteen hundreds. To put it in more general terms, it was at that point that the idealism (modernism) that had characterized nineteenth-century Europe finally reached an impasse.

But this does not imply that the Hegelian ideal of totality had completely disappeared. On the contrary, in the latter half of the twentieth century that vision survived in other fields. After it was expelled from philosophy (the domain of logos), it shifted to domains like literature, to various subcultures, and to the occult (the domain of imagination), where it gave birth to numerous new modes of thought, from new age ideas and new religions to cyberculture.

Over the last seventy-five years, it has been science fiction, more than any other genre, that has appropriated this vision and continued to develop it. In 1926 Hugo Gernsback published the world's first magazine dedicated to science fiction, and even in the introduction to that first issue, science fiction was already designated as "a charming romance intermingled with scientific fact and prophetic vision."[2] Here, the ideas of "science," "vision," and "future" (suggested by "prophecy") are already clearly indicated. From these three ideas emerged the golden age of the forties, followed successively by other grand "prophetic visions" such as Robert Heinlein's Future History series and Isaac Asimov's Galactic Empire series (1950–52).[3]

Ironically, it was precisely at this time that grand narratives like these were becoming obsolete in the real world. The thirties marked the dawn of science fiction and at the same time saw the Nazis' narrative give birth to Auschwitz and witnessed the Marxist-Leninist narrative turn into Stalinism. By this time, science fiction's American consumers were probably aware that it was the uncontainable spread of these "sciences" and "prophetic visions" that was causing the world to fall apart. Of course, people cannot live without some sort of dream or vision. The science fiction that appeared in the twenties can be understood as a genre people needed to fill in the gaps they felt.

This essence of the genre has not changed much. On its surface, of course, science fiction has gone through a huge transformation since the forties. Asimov has branded post-fifties science fiction as "social science fiction,"[4] and the sixties saw the New Wave movement. In the seventies, science fiction's intermingling with dominant literary genres became widespread, and new endeavors like feminist science fiction also emerged. Furthermore, we cannot forget the existence of fantasy and horror. The age is long past when the premise for science fiction was an immeasurable faith in science and the future. As a result, it is highly difficult to capture contemporary science fiction as a whole. Even so, if someone were to ask what characteristic lies at the core of science fiction, I believe that many fans would still say it is "grand narrative" or "grand vision." For science fiction to be science fiction, some kind of a vision must be proposed, even if it is a vision of science's failure or of a dark, foreboding future. In the eighties, cyberpunk filled this role. It was not that the worlds of cyberpunk lacked vision; these authors captured readers' attention precisely because of their elegant *new vision of a visionless world.*

At the core of the science fiction genre lies the paradoxical doctrine that it must continue to depict visions, even when grand visions are impossible. In other words, it is in science fiction that the ideal of nineteenth-century philosophy — the desire for the whole that twentieth-century philosophy had to reject — still lives and breathes. Some may criticize my generalizations for failing to take into consideration the variety of twenty-first-century science fiction. However, as an avid reader of Greg Bear, David Brin, Greg Egan, and Robert J. Sawyer, I cannot help but think that this ideal still exists. One could say that twentieth-century science fiction is the scion of nineteenth-century philosophy, or perhaps an illegitimate child abandoned by its parents. And one might even locate the source of science fiction's productivity in these distorted origins. It is no coincidence that the protagonists who captivate us most in science fiction often present similar problems of *naissance.*

Reflecting on these issues tempts me to compare contemporary science fiction and philosophy with the characters of *Hamlet*. Shakespeare's prince of Denmark loses his father and hates his uncle, who has taken the widow (Hamlet's mother) as his bride. Hamlet eventually directs this hatred toward his mother, and, tormented by suspicion, he commits countless strange acts and finally destroys himself. It is the words of his father's ghost at the beginning of the play that plant these seeds of suspicion in Hamlet and cause his "state to be disjoint and out of frame."[5] Hamlet's father is no more, but precisely for this reason, his words have the power to undo the ties between Hamlet and his world.

Compare science fiction with the character of Hamlet. The dead father (the former king) represents the spirit of the nineteenth century; the mother, philosophy; and the uncle (the current king) is the spirit of the twentieth century. Philosophy was once intimate with the spirit of the nineteenth century. There existed a desire for totality, the Hegelian upward movement toward comprehensive knowledge, and faith in human reason. Hamlet/science fiction was born from the marriage of these two entities. Then his father, the spirit of the nineteenth century, died. And his mother, philosophy, had to change her religion, marrying her husband's younger brother, the spirit of the twentieth century.

Hamlet/science fiction cannot accept this act. Hence he continues to pursue the ideal of his dead father — the whole. He continues to see that ghost and to hear that voice. In this manner, the imperative to see visions in an era where visions are no longer possible is something that continues to torment science fiction writers today. Of course, most authors will not end in self-ruin. Sometimes, though, there appear authors like Philip K. Dick, who become entrapped by the ghost's voice and step into the world of insanity just as Hamlet did. Science fiction is haunted by the ghost of totality. And as for philosophy, she is not concerned with trying to understand such torment. She is occupied with her new life.

Notwithstanding the centrality of Shakespeare, Western philosophy, and Anglo-Saxon science fiction in this argument, I am making it with the state of Japanese science fiction in mind as well. My own experience as a reader of Japanese science fiction has informed my conclusion that science fiction is a paradoxical genre that depicts a grand vision, precisely during the era when such visions are impossible to attain. For these reasons I would like to conclude by discussing the recent history of Japanese science fiction anecdotally, in terms of my own reading.

At the start of my teenage years in the early eighties, I was an avid reader of Komatsu Sakyō. A standard bearer for the first generation of Japanese science fiction, Komatsu is also a figure whose influence extends well beyond the genre, a man possessed of encyclopedic knowledge, a keen critical eye, and powerful connections in the political and corporate worlds. He is also representative of those authors who are obsessed with "the grand story" and "the grand vision." In his novels *Hateshinaki nagare no hate ni* (1966, At the end of the endless stream) and *Tsugu no wa dareka?* (1970, Who will inherit?), he visualizes the ultimate stage of human evolution. And as Thomas Schnellbächer discusses in an earlier chapter, Komatsu's *Nihon chinbotsu* (1973, *Japan Sinks*) borrows the form of a disaster novel to capture the present and the future of the Japanese race.[6] Beyond his writing career, Komatsu devoted himself to the establishment of the Japan Society for Future Research and to the production of the World Expo in Osaka. His career is nothing less than a condensed history of Japan itself, dashing from the rapid economic growth of the sixties and seventies all the way into the economic bubble of the eighties.[7]

However, once I entered junior high school, the heated landscape of the postmodern began to catch my eye. When I was in my midteens, I was pulled into the works of Arai Motoko, a science fiction writer completely different from Komatsu. As Kotani Mari describes in chapter 3, Arai's unique character depictions, her vernacular style, and her literary debut at the age of seventeen earned overwhelming support from readers of her own (my own) generation. She was more like an *aidoru* or a rock star than an author, and her popularity makes it impossible to talk about the history of fandom and the phenomenon of the *otaku* without mentioning her. She played a key role in the shift that befell Japanese science fiction in the eighties, and perhaps not only science fiction per se but Japanese subculture as a whole. In this shift, the genre(s) with which science fiction was associated shifted from literature to manga and anime. At the same time, the center of imagination shifted from grand narratives dealing with the world, society, and the human race to little narratives focusing on human relationships between characters. After having read so many of Komatsu's grand narratives, I indulged throughout my adolescence in Arai's manga-esque little narratives.

From Komatsu to Arai. From grand to little narratives. From vision to character. To me this was the eighties, postmodernism, and my teenage years. Since then, my perspective on science fiction has continued to oscillate between the two poles identified with Komatsu and Arai. These are the specific personal readings behind this chapter's more general argument.

As abstract and general as those arguments about philosophy and grand narratives are, discussions like these are necessary, I think, because Japanese science fiction has only recently been confronted with the real results of the changes that started twenty years ago. Today the most central Japanese science fiction is clearly being produced interdependently with media like anime and video games. In 2004, for example, the Grand Prize for Japanese Science Fiction *(Nihon SF taishō)* was awarded to the novelist, manga creator, and game designer Ubukata Tow.[8] In this way, prose science fiction's center of gravity has been shifting toward the genre known as the "light novel" *(raito noberu,* or *ranobe)* — a category with a completely distinct market from the traditional novel, or *shōsetsu.*

[Light novels are written for a juvenile audience and include romance, mysteries, and fantasy as well as science fiction. The genre gets its name from its page-turning "light" style, but what distinguishes light novels from adventure novels, juvenile science fiction, and other young adult fiction is that they play a key role in the novelization of anime, and the writers are expected to write in a manga/anime-esque style — Trans.] At first glance the scientific or legendary elements that appear in these texts seem to place them within the genealogy of science fiction or fantastic narratives, but these elements are relegated to the background; they do not drive the narrative itself. Instead, there is an increasingly broad audience for a strange new kind of novel that highlights only the characters' psychology or relationships. These novels belong to a category of written and visual texts sometimes called "world-type" *(sekai kei)* literature [for the characters' view that the boundaries of the world are defined by the borders of individual consciousness — *Trans.*].[9] It is my feeling that these world novels could be the catalyst that drives the next generation of Japanese science fiction.

Whether one considers its circulation and distribution or its content, the contemporary science fiction that is influenced by these genres is much closer to Arai than to Komatsu. Many of Arai's novels were packaged and sold just like light novels, although the term itself did not exist in the eighties. The quality of her works, too, is similar. For example, *Hitome anata ni . . .* (1981, To see you just once) starts from the typical science fiction premise of a planetoid colliding with earth, but the author is occupied solely with how the heroine and her lover can reunite in this extreme situation.[10] Arai's imaginings may be the forerunner of the world novel, and both hint at the direction science fiction might take after losing its grand vision and grand narratives. What kind of science fiction will result, and will it be something that can still be called science fiction? This is a part of science fiction's own narrative that remains to be written.

Notes

1. George Orwell, *Nineteen Eighty-Four* (Philadelphia: Chelsea House, 2004); Arthur C. Clarke, *Childhood's End* (New York: Del Ray, 1987); Philip K. Dick, *Ubik* (New York: Vintage, 1991); J. G. Ballard, *The Crystal World* (New York: Farrar Straus Giroux, 1988).

2. Hugo Gernsback, "A New Sort of Magazine," *Amazing Stories* 1, no. 1 (1926): 3.

3. Isaac Asimov, *The Empire Novels* (New York: Doubleday, 2002); contains *Pebble in the Sky, Stars Like Dust,* and *Currents of Space;* Heinlein's future history stories are collected in Robert A. Heinlein, *The Past through Tomorrow* (New York: Ace, 1987).

4. Isaac Asimov, "Social Science Fiction," in *Modern Science Fiction: Its Meaning and Its Future,* ed. Reginald Bretnor (New York: Coward-McCann, 1953), 158–96.

5. *Hamlet,* 1.2.20.

6. Komatsu Sakyō, *Hateshinaki nagare no hate ni* (At the end of the endless stream) (Tokyo: Kadokawa Bunko, 1974); Komatsu, *Nihon chinbotsu,* 2 vols. (Tokyo: Kōbunsha, 1995); abridged and translated as *Japan Sinks* by Michael Gallagher (Tokyo: Kodansha International, 1995); Komatsu, *Tsugu no wa dareka?* (Who will inherit?) (Tokyo: Kadokawa Bunko, 1977).

7. [For a sense of the sweep of Komatsu's career, in English see the interview by Susan Napier, Tatsumi Takayuki, Kotani Mari, and Otobe Junko in *Science Fiction Studies* 29 (2002): 323–39. — Trans.]

8. Ubukata Tō [Tow], *Marudokku sukuramburu* (Mardock scramble series) (Tokyo: Hayakawa Bunko JA, 2003); comprising the novels *Nenshō, Asshuku,* and *Haiki* (The first compression, The second combustion, and The third exhaust).

9. [The term *world novel* spread through the Internet in 2002 when the anime *Hoshi no koe (Voices of a Distant Star)* became a huge hit in Japan. The film begins with the quote "There is a word 'world.' Up until middle school, I thought vaguely that the world was the area a cell phone could reach." This kind of world is clearly distinct from the worlds of classic manga and anime, worlds that could be easily discerned from the characters' daily lives and that those characters struggled to protect. *Hoshi no koe: Voices of a Distant Star,* dir. Shinkai Makoto (2002); translated as *Voices of a Distant Star,* DVD (ADV, 2003). — Trans., with thanks to Ebihara Yutaka.]

10. Arai Motoko, *Hitome anata ni…* (To see you just once…) (1981; Tokyo: Kadokawa Bunko, 1985).

5. Tsutsui Yasutaka and the
Multimedia Performance of Authorship

William O. Gardner

In the summer of 1996 the prolific author Tsutsui Yasutaka helped found JALInet, a Web site hosting several writers that claims to be the "first literary server in Japan."[1] Irrespective of the site's claim to chronological primacy, Tsutsui's involvement with this project was a significant literary event, coming as it did in the third year of the author's highly publicized self-imposed cessation of print publishing. Rather than mark an entry into electronic media, however, the launching of this site marked a new phase in Tsutsui's already extensive and controversial work across the boundaries of several media forms, electronic and otherwise. Alternately playing the prankster and the embattled cultural critic, Tsutsui brought a distinctively performative approach to the role of author in his 1990s encounters with new media.

Throughout a career spanning almost forty years, Tsutsui has maintained a sharp focus on the role of media in constructing contemporary experiences of the real and the imaginary, in works combining social satire, science fiction, and highly reflexive metafictional literature. Following the schema proposed by Takayuki Tatsumi, I trace three stages in Tsutsui's treatment of these issues. In the 1960s and early 1970s, Tsutsui satirized how the mass media, in their insatiable drive to produce "news" and "images," intrude into daily life and blur the line between the real and fictional. Tatsumi calls this first stage Tsutsui's "pseudo-event science fiction," referring to the historian Daniel Boorstin's influential political and social critique, formulated in 1962, which suggested that American society was increasingly dominated by pseudo-events "planned, planted or incited ... for the immediate purpose of being reported or reproduced," whose "relation to the underlying reality of the situation is ambiguous" and whose "interest arises largely from this very ambiguity."[2] Early Tsutsui works in this mode include the stories "Betonamu kankō kōsha" (1967, "The Vietnam Tourist Bureau"), in which the modern battlefield is transformed into a theme park, and "Ore ni kan suru uwasa" (1972, Rumors about me), in which trivial events in the everyday life of an ordinary salaryman — in particular his unsuccessful attempts to date a coworker — become the subject of extensive national news coverage.[3]

In midcareer, Tsutsui focused on the surrealist mechanisms of literature and the ability of literary language to create a playful virtual realm, in which the words of fiction could simultaneously comment on their own fictivity — what Tatsumi calls his "metafiction" stage. Perhaps Tsutsui's most audacious literary effort during this period is his novel *Kyokō sendan* (1984, Fantasy fleet), which presents a science fiction parody of world history in the tale of intergalactic warfare between a race of alien weasels and a race of animate writing instruments.[4] This stage culminated in one of Tsutsui's best-known works, *Bungakubu Tadano-kyōju* (1990, Professor Tadano, literature department), an academic satire in which each chapter is keyed to a different school of literary theory. During this period, Tsutsui was also active as a literary critic, proposing a model of fictionality *(kyokō)* and surfictionality, metafiction, or hyperfiction *(chōkyokō)* that, together with the example of Tsutsui's own fiction, has exerted a deep influence on a new generation of Japanese writers such as Takahashi Gen'ichirō, Ogino Anna, Shōno Yoriko, Kobayashi Kyōji, and Shimada Masahiko.[5]

Finally, in the 1990s, Tsutsui began to explore the possibilities of electronic media and the complex relationships between literary fiction, computer simulation, and the already hypermediated realm of daily life — his cyberfiction or, in Tatsumi's terms, "slipstream" stage.[6] Representative works from this period include *Asa no Gasupaaru* (1991–92, *Gaspard of the Morning*), which I discuss below, and the closely related novel *Papurika* (1993, *Paprika*), featuring the eponymous protagonist, a psychotherapist, who with the aid of advanced technology is able to project her consciousness directly into her patients' dreams.

In this chapter, I examine two episodes in Tsutsui's involvement with electronic media during the cyberfiction stage of his career. The first is his experiment in combining newspaper serialization and an Internet salon to create the interactive science fiction novel *Gaspard of the Morning,* which appeared in the *Asahi shinbun* newspaper between October 1991 and March 1992. The second episode involves the controversy over his early short story "Mujin keisatsu" ("Automatic Police"), which drew protests as discriminatory toward epileptics when it was slated for publication in a high school textbook. As a protest over what he claimed was a climate of censorship in the publishing industry and mass media, Tsutsui declared a cessation of print publishing in September 1993, and three years later began to release his work online.

While the two episodes are of a very different nature, each provides a revealing look at the possibilities of electronic media and their relationship to existing modes of expression and dissemination. Furthermore, despite their apparent differences, the two episodes share a number of intriguing commonalities. Each one put Tsutsui into multiple feedback loops with his readers, with the author asserting a greater or lesser degree of control over the nature of the interaction. In each case Tsutsui split his voice across several media, both print and electronic, and played these voices off against each other, in ways that often highlighted the clashes of modality between established and emerging media. Finally, during each episode Tsutsui both confronted and teased readers: on the one hand, unleashing invective against his "enemies" — those he accused of misreading his texts — and, on the other hand, teasing his "loyal readers" by withholding his services as an author, manipulating the text of *Gaspard of the Morning* to frustrate readers' desires for certain types of narratives, or ceasing literary production altogether during the controversy over "Automatic Police." While both strategies of invective and withholding might seem to be extraliterary, they are in fact fundamentally constitutive of Tsutsui's literary personality, honed over years of acute attention to issues of literature and mediation, and his cultivation of a performative sensibility expressed in various media contexts.

The Cybernetic Author as Despot: Gaspard of the Morning

When Tsutsui announced to the readers of the *Asahi shinbun* newspaper that he was beginning his first newspaper-serialized novel, to be titled *Gaspard of the Morning,* he began with a question about the novelistic possibilities of the newspaper medium: "What is it that I can do *expressly because* it is a newspaper serialization novel with a daily limit of three manuscript pages?"[7] His answer was to capitalize on the incremental nature and widespread distribution of this medium by soliciting ideas and criticism for the ongoing novel via letters and an Internet salon;[8] this feedback was incorporated into the text; and the readers, the author, and newspaper fiction editor all entered the text as fictional characters. In this introduction, Tsutsui also alerts his readers to the fact that criticism will be an integral part of the novel, declaring in the opening sentences of his essay, "I would like you to note that this piece of writing is part of the novel. In other words, the fiction *Gaspard of the Morning* has already begun."[9] Aside from announcing that an Internet salon will be opened to receive electronic messages, Tsutsui makes little reference to gaming or cyberfiction in this introduction, instead citing the venerable precedents of the British novelists Samuel Richardson and Charles Dickens for their incorporation of reader response in serialized work. Nevertheless, the fact that computer-networking practices (or potential practices) such as interactive games were also an influence on Tsutsui's conceptualization of the novel becomes clear once the narrative is fully underway.

Several days after this introduction, the serialization of *Gaspard* began in earnest with the scene of a squadron of heavily armed Japanese soldiers led by a Commander Fukae. The soldiers are trekking across an unknown desert planet, unsure of the reasons behind their orders to march and apprehensive of attacks by aliens. Especially given Tsutsui's long association with the genre, readers would be justified from this opening to expect *Gaspard* to continue as a "straight" science fiction piece. Tsutsui places a typically wry comment on his story's generic quality in his first description of the soldiers: "All of their faces, including Fukae's, somehow resembled each other. They each had individual faces clearly expressing their own personal character, so looking at it that way their faces weren't alike. But outlines of each of their faces bore a close resemblance to the characters in action movies....Sometimes Fukae thought it must be the genetic influence of generations of *anime*-loving Japanese."[10]

From the third installment, however, it is revealed that Fukae and his company will not be the novel's chief characters but are in fact characters in a networked computer game called The Phantom Squadron being played by a second protagonist, a business executive named Kinohara Seizō (hence the "genetic influence" of anime-loving Japanese on Fukae and company is revealed to be more literal than it first seemed). This outer story takes place in a Tokyo of the near future, when the first generation raised on computer games has reached middle age. The business managers and top-ranking bureaucrats in Seizō's circle are all avid players of The Phantom Squadron, and discussing the game is an indispensable element of their male-centered socializing. The rest of the novel alternates between occasional episodes following The Phantom Squadron and the unfolding of a marital crisis between Seizō and his wife, Satoko. Satoko, whose hobby is attending fashionable "home parties," is involved in a computer game of her own — day-trading stocks through a networked "portfolio financial service." After a downturn in the market, Satoko tries to cover her losses and plunges the household finances into deeper and deeper debt, unbeknownst to Seizō, who is too absorbed in playing The

Phantom Squadron to notice the looming crisis. After numerous subplots and digressions, the story spins toward its climax as Seizō and Satoko are pursued by a gang of yakuza online loan sharks, to be rescued in the end by Fukae and his phantom squadron, who, in a deus ex machina enacted through a combination of tantric Buddhism, high-tech weaponry, and particle physics, burst through fictional layers into Seizō and Satoko's world.

To make this baroque narrative even more multifarious, the parallel development of Fukae and Seizō–Satoko's worlds is interrupted periodically by the intrusion of the "author," fictionalized as "Kunugizawa," and the newspaper literary editor, fictionalized as "Origuchi," who introduce and debate the reader reactions and suggestions arriving daily. In fielding messages, Kunugizawa and Origuchi offer various metacommentaries on the narrative, including an elaborate explanation of the text's multiple layers of fictionality, complete with references to the literary theorists Gerard Genette and Wayne C. Booth. Even without Kunugizawa's explications, however, the reflexive structure is difficult to miss, with the feedback loop between the unfolding narrative of *Gaspard* and the readers' letters and electronic messages modeled within the text by the feedback loop between the computer game The Phantom Squadron and the networked gamers such as Seizō and his colleagues.

From the beginning, Tsutsui-Kunugizawa plays the letters and Internet messages off against each other as the two media carrying feedback on the novel. This dichotomy is especially problematic in its mobilization of gender in relation to media and fictional genres. In representing reader responses, Tsutsui-Kunugizawa draws a sharp contrast between the desires of the letter writers, gendered primarily as female, who want to see more development of the Seizō–Satoko plotline in the style of the so-called domestic novel, and the desires of the Internet users, gendered primarily as male, who want to see more development of the science fiction elements related to The Phantom Squadron. In the novel's opening stages, the balance between the installments devoted to Seizō–Satoko and the installments devoted to The Phantom Squadron is purported to be dependent on "majority rule" by these two constituencies.

However, since there is no way to independently verify the effect of reader input on the actual development of the novel, and since these two constituencies seem to have at best a very rough leverage on the narrative, it becomes an open question whether Tsutsui's text is really interactive at all. At one point, in fact, the editor Origuchi conveys some readers' suspicions that Kunugizawa has fabricated the letters and the entire science fiction–"domestic" debate, and had already planned the shifts in the story from before the serialization began.[11] While further examination reveals a more subtle degree of interactive "gaming" in *Gaspard*, the question of the readers' actual input on the text is a fundamental one, speaking to the issue of authorial power that recurs throughout the text and through Tsutsui's 1990s multimedia career as a whole.

Although partisans of the "domestic" story line seem to have the upper hand during the majority of *Gaspard,* the actual numeric dominance of Internet messages over letters is striking: by the end of the novel's serialization, the *Asahi* newspaper had received over a thousand letters about the text, a respectable number that was nevertheless dwarfed by nearly twenty-four thousand Internet messages. Strikingly, the Internet salon *Dennō Tsutsui sen (Tsutsui Computer Front),* established as a channel for readers' responses, sustained its own lively textual development parallel to the novel's serialization. For example, salon participants held online virtual parties during the Christmas–New Year's holidays (running parallel to the serialization of installments detailing the parties attended by the novel's heroine Satoko). Likewise, a party was held to celebrate the novel's hundredth installment, and a virtual funeral was conducted on the death of a number of its characters.[12] The discourse on the *Tsutsui Computer Front* can be characterized as employing a high degree of language play, as being highly reflexive of its own status as mediated discourse, and as involving a strong element of self-dramatization and performance — qualities, it should be noted, that are also prominent in Tsutsui's prose itself (Figure 5.1).[13]

Thus, while letters to the newspaper's literary editor and online messages were structured as parallel channels of reader feedback, the *Tsutsui Computer Front* literary salon allowed the development of a semi-autonomous fan community in a way impossible to duplicate through the letter-to-the-editor channel. This fan community can be compared with the *otaku* community of manga fans who circulate alternative versions of their favorite works at manga conventions, or to television fans who create alternative narratives based on their favorite shows in fanzines and other "fan art" media — a process that the American media studies scholar Henry Jenkins, following Michel de Certeau, has dubbed "textual poaching."[14] In fact, these communities of media fans in both the United States and Japan have significant roots in science fiction fan communities, whose close interaction with science fiction authors has been one of the distinguishing features of the science fiction genre itself.[15] Kotani Mari and Saitō Tamaki explore these practices in some depth elsewhere in this volume. Here I would like to point out that the *Tsutsui Computer Front* differs from earlier writer–fan interactive forums, as well as paper-based amateur manga and fanzines, in several key respects, including the increased volume, interactivity, and instantaneous temporality of reader–writer exchange made possible by the online medium. Furthermore, the *Tsutsui*

板垣ワンレン退助

Figure 5.1. An ASCII-art portrait of Tsutsui Yasutaka included in a posting to Tsutsui's online salon, by the participant Itagaki Wanren Taisuke. The characters that make up the image spell the name of the salon, *Dennō Tsutsui sen (Tsutsui Computer Front)*. "Otoshidama (Dennō fukuwarai)," posted January 1, 1992, archived on Asahi Net BBB (accessed January 29, 2002).

Computer Front was an exceptional experiment in that it was synchronized with the serialization of Tsutsui's work in a mass-circulation newspaper, and Tsutsui's own participation in the salon allowed content to migrate in two directions between the serialized "master" text and the communal textual performance generated in the salon.

Tsutsui participated in the salon under the pseudonym Shōkenrō (Laughing Dog Pavilion) and praised the online messaging as a "linguistic game of a very high level."[16] Furthermore, Tsutsui embedded the pseudonyms and personalities of a number of the online participants in the *Gaspard* text, making, for instance, the user pseudonym Hinshuku no Maō (Frowning Demon King) into an alien encountered by Fukae and The Phantom Squadron. These characters in the novel can be seen as "avatars" (or, in the language of the novel, "shadows") of their online counterparts, just as Kunugizawa is a shadow of Tsutsui and Fukae is a shadow of Seizō. The text of *Gaspard* thus incorporates a hidden level of interactive play between the "author" and the participants in the Internet salon, not readily apparent to readers with access only to the print text of *Gaspard*.

In contrast to Tsutsui's positive engagement with the Internet salon in his Shōkenrō persona, however, the attitude of Tsutsui's fictional shadow Kunugizawa toward the salon is extremely hostile, habitually referring to this group of readers as "the Internet science fiction idiots" *(intaanetto no sf baka)*. Toward the end of the serialization, Kunugizawa unleashes a stream of invective against the Internet participants that continues through a remarkable number of installments. Kunugizawa reacts particularly strongly to several participants who "flamed" the salon with cursory negative comments such as "No good. This serialization is a failure," "The emperor has no clothes," "Hey! It's boring, give it up," and "Barf!" *(uu-gerogerogero)*. This launches Kunugizawa on a tirade about the lack of civility on the Internet, which quickly escalates into Kunugizawa's own "flaming" denunciation of the parties involved with a series of elaborate and highly creative insults.[17] Kunugizawa's invective, in its playfulness and excess, is one of the most conspicuously performative elements in the *Gaspard* text — one of the Internet reader/commentators, in fact, compared it with the "abuse of the audience" *(kankyaku batō)* that occurs in some modern theater.[18]

Tsutsui-Kunugizawa's counterattack on reader criticisms goes beyond the denunciation of readers in these performative passages representing Kunugizawa's speech and extends into *Gaspard*'s plot development as well. A good portion of the serialization was taken up by lengthy satirical descriptions of the parties attended by the heroine Satoko, which introduced dozens of partygoers as secondary characters. According to Kunugizawa and Origuchi's representation of reader responses, these party episodes were particularly disliked by the online science fiction faction. Both letters and Internet messages reportedly complained that there were too many secondary characters introduced in these scenes and that readers of the serialized text, who typically had only one brief episode in front of them at any one time, could not possibly keep track of them all. Two-thirds of the way into the serialization, in a willful and deliberately extreme response to such criticisms, Tsutsui-Kunugizawa loads the greater portion of these secondary characters onto the inaugural flight of a superatmospheric high-speed shuttle between Tokyo and Washington, and has the shuttle explode, killing all on board.

In the symbolic violence of this response to purported reader criticism, Tsutsui-Kunugizawa demonstrates his ultimate "authority" over the text, performed with an air of paranoid despotism. Rather than celebrate the democratic possibilities of networked discourse in the newspaper-serialized text of *Gaspard,* then, Tsutsui problematizes the conflicting desires and reading–writing strategies between "author" and "readers," and draws attention to the issue of the power to control speech in emergent media environments. By highlighting these issues within his highly performative text, Tsutsui confirms *Gaspard*'s metafictional status as, in the author's own words, a "novel that critiques novels" or, more precisely, an interactive fiction that critiques interactive fiction.[19]

Nevertheless, the effectiveness of Tsutsui's performance of authorial control in *Gaspard of the Morning* is largely a matter of perspective. For readers who followed the serialization or purchased the paperback edition subsequently issued by Shinchōsha Publishing, Tsutsui has retained ultimate control of the narrative, and his fictional alter ego Kunugizawa has had the last word over letter writing and e-mail sending critics represented in the text. However, the nearly three hundred reader-writers who participated in the online salon jointly created their own performative and discursive sphere, with its own distinct value as a critical and creative expression unfolding in real time. That sphere remained largely hidden from readers of Tsutsui's newspaper serialization, but its 23,805 messages are now archived with the Asahi Net Internet service and comprise a body of writing quite different in style, scale, temporality, and materiality from either a newspaper novel serialization or a printed book.

The Multimedia Cacophony of Silence: "Automatic Police" and the "Pseudo-Event"

After the success of *Gaspard of the Morning,* which received the Japanese Science Fiction Grand Prize for 1992, Tsutsui continued to pursue the themes of cybernetics and virtuality with his next novel, *Paprika.* While hailed by some critics as a magnum opus, *Paprika* was soon overshadowed by a controversy over the textbook publication of Tsutsui's early short story "Mujin keisatsu" (1965, "Automatic Police"). This controversy prompted Tsutsui to dramatically reposition himself versus print and electronic media, and cast a new light on the issues of authorial and readerly power raised in a playful manner in *Gaspard of the Morning*.

Tsutsui's short story "Automatic Police," first published in the author's debut year of 1965, ostensibly focuses on the power of the state rather than the power of media and so would seem to differ slightly in theme from the early works identified by Tatsumi as "psuedo-event sf." Reminiscent of the light and ironic style of the Japanese science fiction pioneer Hoshi Shin'ichi, "Automatic Police" concerns a future society monitored by robotic police. The first-person protagonist "I" *(watashi)* narrates his encounter with a robotic police officer on the day he decides to walk to work — an unusual choice in a society where transportation is dominated by "air cars." Arrested en route by a robotic officer for no apparent reason, the protagonist's distrust of the robotic force quickly transforms into overt hostility. When the robot's memory is analyzed at the police station to determine the cause of arrest, it is revealed that the robotic patroller was a new model equipped with the ability to read minds. This experimental model had overstepped the bounds of its programming to read only surface thoughts and had detected the protagonist's deep-seated unconscious antipathy toward both robots and police. The story gets a final twist when the senior officer, who is expected to intervene on the protagonist's behalf, is revealed to be a robot, too.[20]

In July 1993, a few months after Kadokawa Shoten published its new high school textbook *Kokugo* I (Japanese I) that was certified by the Ministry of Education for publication the following year, Kadokawa received a letter of protest from the Japanese Epilepsy Association (*Nihon tenkan kyōkai*, JEA) about the inclusion of "Automatic Police." The JEA charged that Tsutsui's story "was based on the misunderstanding of and prejudice against epilepsy," and that publication of the story would further spread such misunderstanding through society.[21] The JEA also issued a statement ending with a series of demands that (1) the textbook's certification be withdrawn, sales of the textbook be suspended, and the story excised; (2) school boards and teachers refrain from adopting the textbook; and (3) all previously published versions of the work in short story collections or as part of Tsutsui's complete works be retracted, and future editions of the story be rewritten or annotated appropriately.[22]

As the synopsis above should indicate, epilepsy is not the thematic focus of "Automatic Police" but appears as an example of the types of behaviors and conditions normally monitored by the robotic police. The robot policeman is equipped with a speed monitoring device, an alcoholic intake detection device, and a brain wave calibrator to detect irregular brain waves of epileptic drivers who might have a seizure while driving. It was two references to this fictional seizure-warning device that attracted the JEA's attention.

The JEA articulated a number of reasons for concern over the adoption of "Automatic Police" in a high school textbook. First of all, the issue of driving and epilepsy is a sensitive one: in contrast to the United States and most countries of Western Europe, where driver's licenses can be issued based on epileptics' current condition and program of medication, Japan still unconditionally prohibits all epileptics from obtaining a license to drive — a situation that the JEA has been actively campaigning to reform. In addition to concern that the story would spread fear and misinformation about the issue to impressionable students, the JEA also raised concerns over the story's effect in reinforcing the stigmatization of epileptics and particularly in undermining the social and emotional well-being of epileptic students in classrooms where the *Kokugo I* textbook would be read.

As the JEA's protest was taken up in the press, Tsutsui responded with a lengthy defense of his work. While he maintained, on the one hand, the position that epileptics should not in fact be allowed to drive, he also argued that a reading which regards the story as condoning a view that criminalizes epilepsy misses the entire point of the story, since the vision of a future society intrusively monitored by robots is clearly dystopic. Finally, with regard to the issue of damage to the emotional sensitivities of students, Tsutsui responded by placing himself in the literary tradition of "black humor" whose very nature is to offend conventional sensibilities, to "laugh at the systematic good conscience of readers, to peel away their masks, to touch off their evil and irrational and prejudicial feelings, and to appeal to their anti-systematic spirit."[23] If this one story were to be censored, he wonders, what would become of his other stories with even greater potential to offend? From Tsutsui's perspective, the attempted suppression of "Automatic Police" must have seemed eerily reminiscent of the future society described in the story itself, where even unconscious thoughts are criminalized and all suspected criminals are expected to voluntarily turn themselves over to the authorities.

Even though Kadokawa did not actually retract "Automatic Police" from the textbook, as the debate about the story continued, Tsutsui displayed more and more dismay over the JEA's position and more broadly over the state of public discourse in Japan. He expressed particular anger over what he perceived as the unfair and inadequate representation of his position by television and newspaper journalists, whom he accused of practicing de facto censorship. In this debate over regulating public expression, Tsutsui and his interlocutors increasingly employed the term *word hunting (kotobagari)* to describe the practice of making certain words and expressions taboo. The rapid rise of this neologism, it might be noted, underscored a remarkable synchronicity in the debate between Tsutsui and his critics and the controversy over "political correctness" in the United States.[24]

Finally, in September 1993, Tsutsui declared his intention to protest what he perceived as the increasingly repressive state of public discourse in Japan by ceasing publication of his work in print media.[25] In an interestingly atavistic reference to an earlier mode of writing technology, Tsutsui titled his statement the *"danpitsu sengen,"* or literally "breaking the brush declaration." Rather than enforce a self-imposed silence, however, the *danpitsu sengen* arguably only increased Tsutsui's "bandwidth" on multiple media channels.

Features on Tsutsui's *danpitsu sengen* declaration, including numerous interviews with the author and commentary by prominent writers, artists, and other cultural figures, were carried by the Asahi, Yomiuri, Mainichi, Tokyo, and Sankei newspapers and in such mass-circulation magazines as *Sapio, Marco Polo, Takarajima, SPA!, Shūkan bunju, Shūkan gendai,* and *Shūkan posuto,* as well as more specialized journals such as Kadokawa's *Kokugoka tsūshin* (National language department newsletter).[26] In an interview with the manga artist and novelist Uchida Shungiku, Tsutsui noted that a book of essays about the controversy was selling better than his new novel *Paprika* and joked that he might be accused of being a *"danpitsu* profiteer" *(danpitsu narikin).*[27]

Nor was the mediation of the *danpitsu sengen* controversy limited to print alone. Another site of heated discussion was "221 jōhōkyoku" ("Tsutsui Information Bureau"), the online Tsutsui fan club and discussion group hosted by Asahi Net as an extension of the Internet presence Tsutsui established with *Gaspard of the Morning.* Two days after the *danpitsu sengen* was issued, Asahi Net established another discussion site titled "'Word-hunting' considered" *("'Kotobagari' o kangaeru").* In a hybrid media experiment reminiscent of the *Gaspard* episode, Tsutsui appeared on a special episode of the television program *Live TV until Morning* titled "Freedom of Speech and Discrimination," which was intended to respond in real time to discussion on the "'Word-hunting' considered" Internet site. The differing temporalities and modalities of the television and Internet media soon became apparent, however, as the television staff was unable to keep up with a deluge of over four hundred Internet messages in four hours.[28]

As the controversy over "Automatic Police" and "word hunting" died down, Tsutsui continued to pursue alternative means of public expression while maintaining his self-imposed cessation of print publication. In the summer of 1996 he established his own literary home page (JALInet) and began to release his works over the Web, independent of the print publishing industry. Within a year of his move to online self-publishing, Tsutsui reached an agreement with his conventional publishing outlets over the issue of "word hunting" and resumed print publication, terminating his *danpitsu* period.

The Author as Multimedia Performer

While there are important differences between the two episodes, the *danpitsu sengen* controversy makes an interesting comparison with the *Gaspard of the Morning* project, since both episodes placed Tsutsui in feedback loops with his readers through multiple media channels. In *Gaspard of the Morning,* Tsutsui pointed to the literary potential of interactive electronic media while problematizing the issue of the power over speech in a highly mediated society through his own performative display of authorial control. In the debate over "Automatic Police," however, he found himself displaced from the seat of authorial power and less able to proscribe or co-opt the "misreading" of a different interpretive constituency, the JEA, which established its own media contacts and attempted to alter the forms of Tsutsui's print work. In response to this perceived crisis, Tsutsui counterattacked by launching his own highly mediated "pseudo-event," the *danpitsu sengen,* or "breaking the brush declaration." Tsutsui's *danpitsu sengen* corresponds strongly to Boorstin's original formula of the pseudo-event as an incident "planned, planted or incited ... for the immediate purpose of being reported or reproduced."

Tsutsui brought a markedly performative sensibility to both the experimental fiction *Gaspard of the Morning* and to his role as free-speech advocate during the *danpitsu sengen* episode.[29] In *Gaspard of the Morning,* he dramatized his authorial persona as Kunugizawa within the novel's uniquely Tsutsuian world of slapstick *(dotabata)* science fiction while cultivating the online persona Shōkenrō in his contacts with the *Tsutsui Computer Front* Internet salon. Although his performance as social critic during the controversy over "Automatic Police" appeared more earnest, he brought to this debate a canny knowledge of how to deploy his authorial persona and manipulate Japanese media outlets, culminating in his staging of the *danpitsu sengen* as pseudo-event. It is noteworthy in this context that Tsutsui has been deeply involved in theater, film, and television as an actor as well as a writer throughout his career.[30] During his *danpitsu* period, Tsutsui invested much of his energy in performance projects, and his current online presence has a definite performative emphasis, including a "Multi Media Theater" page featuring QuickTime audio and video clips of Tsutsui giving readings of his work, playing jazz clarinet, granting interviews, and appearing in TV commercials, as well as textual information on Tsutsui's appearances as a film actor and stagings of his dramatic work.[31]

It would be tempting to view Tsutsui's 1990s career through the lens of the ongoing debate over the future of traditional print publication versus emerging electronic media. We might construct a narrative of the science fiction and "metafiction" pioneer who, as a protest against a climate of self-censorship in the publishing industry, withdrew from print publication and turned to the new medium of online publishing to distribute his work directly to his readers. Such a narrative would have a certain iconic appeal, but it would ignore several important aspects of the *danpitsu sengen* episode, including the fact that Tsutsui failed to establish a viable economic model for the online publication of his work and reached a rapprochement with the publishing industry soon after he began releasing work on the JALInet site.

Rather than restrict my focus to print versus electronic publishing, I have attempted to outline how Tsutsui, whose early works were among the first to fictionally explore the hypermediated society, deftly employed a variety of media throughout the 1990s. These include newspaper, journal, magazine, and book publications; postal communication, Web pages and Internet discussion groups; and television and stage performance. Rather than the author's being a single all-powerful agent in these media, his presence is combined with that of other speakers and intermediaries with their own agendas (represented within the fiction of *Gaspard of the Morning* by the newspaper editor Origuchi, as well as the inventors and managers of the networked computer game The Phantom Squadron). Moreover, several of these media not only provide channels for readers' feedback to the author but also establish forums for readers to create their own communities of expression. While electronic media are only one element of this mix, Tsutsui's 1990s experiments highlight the degree to which networked electronic media offer new parameters of temporality, modality, and interaction, often incompatible with the old ones. Through both his fictional works and his broader activities as an author and public figure, Tsutsui has given us an intriguing, vexing, and often comic view of our densely mediated future.

Notes

1. Tsutsui Yasutaka et al., JALInet, http://www.jali.or.jp. Tsutsui's English-language profile with the assertion about Japan's "first literary server" can be found at http://www.jali.or.jp/tti/prof_e.html (accessed May 23, 2006).

2. Daniel J. Boorstin, *The Image: A Guide to Pseudo-Events in America* (New York: Harper and Row, 1964), 11; originally published as *The Image, or What Happened to the American Dream* (New York: Atheneum, 1962).

3. Tsutsui Yasutaka, "Betonamu kankō kōsha," in *Betonamu kankō kōsha* (Tokyo: Chūō Kōronsha, 1979), 189–221; Tsutsui, "Rumors about Me" ("Ore ni kan suru uwasa"), trans. David Lewis, in *The African Bomb and Other Stories* (Tokyo: Kōdansha Eigo Bunko, 1986). For a discussion of the theme of reality and media in Tsutsui's early work, with reference to Boorstin, see Tsutsui Yasutaka, "Zen'ei wa goraku de aru," interview by Larry McCaffery, Sinda Gregory, and Tatsumi Takayuki, *Gendai shisō/Revue de la pensée d'aujourd'hui* 23, no. 11 (1995): 136–37; translated as "Keeping Not Writing: An Interview with Yasutaka Tsutsui," Center for Book Culture.org, http://www.centerforbookculture.org/review/02_2_inter/interview_tsutsui.html (accessed May 23, 2006).

4. Tsutsui Yasutaka, *Kyokō sendan* (Fantasy fleet) (Tokyo: Shinchōsha, 1984). Tsutsui's 1984 essay "*Kyokō sendan* no gyakushū" ("Counterattack of the *Fantasy Fleet*"), first published in the evening edition of *Mainichi shinbun* on July 6, 1984, issued a series of withering replies to the work's detractors. It can be recognized as one important event in the development of the author's distinctive strategies of confrontation with his critics — strategies that will be elaborated in the *Gaspard of the Morning* and the *danpitsu sengen* episode discussed below. The essay is reprinted in Tsutsui Yasutaka, *Kyokō sendan no gyakushū* (Tokyo: Chūō Kōronsha, 1984), 204–8.

5. Tsutsui Yasutaka, *Bungakubu Tadano-kyōju* (Professor Tadano, literature department) (Tokyo: Iwanami Shoten, 1990). Tsutsui has been a prodigious critic and theorist; for one important statement of his views on fiction and surfiction, see *Chakusō no gijutsu* (Techniques of imagination) (Tokyo: Shinchōsha, 1983). For a view of Tsutsui's work in the context of the development of metafiction in Japanese and American literature, see Tatsumi Takayuki, *Metafikushon no bōryaku* (Ideology of metafiction) (Tokyo: Chikuma Shobō, 1993), 61–96.

6. Tatsumi Takayuki, *Nihon henryū bungaku* (Slipstream Japan) (Tokyo: Shinchōsha, 1998), 213–32; Tsutsui Yasutaka, *Asa no Gasupaaru* (Gaspard of the morning) (Tokyo: Shinchōsha, 1995); Tsutsui, *Papurika* (Paprika) (Tokyo: Chūō Kōronsha, 1997).

7. Tsutsui, *Asa no Gasupaaru*, 6; my translation. The novel was serialized between October 18, 1991, and March 31, 1992, in the morning edition of the *Asahi shinbun* newspaper. The paperback *(bunkobon)* edition cited here appeared in 1995. The title is a reference to the prose poem collection *Gaspard de la nuit* by Aloysius Bertrand (1807–1841).

8. Circulation for the *Asahi shinbun* morning edition in 1989 was just over 8 million, making it one of the most widely read periodicals in the world.

9. Tsutsui, *Asa no Gasupaaru*, 5.

10. Ibid., 8–9.

11. Ibid., 78–80.

12. Ibid., 317; Ōkami Asami, "Dennōroku: Kaisetsu ni kaete" (Computer record: In lieu of an afterword), in Tsutsui, *Asa no Gasupaaru*, 319, 325–28.

13. "Dennō Tsutsui sen/salon," message archive on the Asahi Net Bulletin Board Browser, http://bbb.asahi-net.or.jp/bbb/bbs/old.tti.+salon (accessed May 23, 2006).

14. Henry Jenkins, *Textual Poachers: Television Fans and Participatory Culture* (New York: Routledge, 1992). For information on *otaku* and manga conventions, see the introduction to this volume and chapter 11. See also Sharon Kinsella, *Adult Manga: Culture and Power in Contemporary Japanese Society* (Honolulu: University of Hawaii Press, 2000), 1002–38.

15. The key role played by reader letters to Hugo Gernsback's magazine *Amazing Stories* in the early development of science fiction is one well-known example of the close relationship between readers and authors in the science fiction genre. For a look at fans' role in science fiction in the United States, see Camille Bacon-Smith, *Science Fiction Culture* (Philadelphia: University of Pennsylvania Press, 2000).

16. Ōkami, "Dennōroku," 326.

17. *Asa no Gasupaaru,* 201–27. I use the term *flame* to connect the issues of online civility raised in the text of *Gaspard* with similar issues debated in the United States at roughly the same time. See Mark Dery, ed., *Flame Wars: The Discourse of Cyberspace* (Durham, N.C.: Duke University Press, 1994). The word *flame* is not used by Tsutsui in the text of *Gaspard.*

18. Ōkami, "Dennōroku," 327.

19. Tsutsui's succinct definition of metafiction can be found in *Asa no Gasupaaru,* 317. It should be noted that, as if to provide a counterpoint to the performance of authorial control staged in *Gaspard of the Morning,* Tsutsui also helped produce three print volumes of edited transcriptions of the *Dennō Tsutsui sen* Internet sessions, the first of which appeared while the novel's serialization was still in progress. Tsutsui Yasutaka, ed., *Dennō Tsutsui sen: Asa no gasupaaru sesshon* (Tsutsui computer front: *Gaspard of the morning* sessions), 3 vols. (Tokyo: Asahi Shinbunsha, 1992).

20. Tsutsui's story is reprinted in *Tsutsui Yasutaka danpitsu meguru daironsō* (The great Tsutsui Yasutaka "danpitsu" debate), ed. Gekkan "Tsukuru" henshūbu (Tokyo: Tsukuru Shuppan, 1995), 7–20.

21. Ibid., 23.

22. Ibid., 25.

23. Ibid., 32.

24. The *kotobagari* ("word hunting") phenomenon, the JEA objections to "Automatic Police," and Tsutsui's *danpitsu sengen* are discussed together with other controversies over politically sensitive speech in contemporary Japan in Nanette Gottlieb, *Linguistic Stereotyping and Minority Groups in Japan* (London: Routledge, 2006), 25, 31–32, 112–14.

25. Ibid., 38–39.

26. For a list of articles, interviews, and other coverage related to the *danpitsu sengen,* see Hiraoka Masaaki, ed., *Tsutsui Yasutaka no gyakushū* (Tsutsui Yasutaka's counterattack) (Tokyo: Gendaishorin, 1994), 253–55.

27. Gekkan "Tsukuru" henshūbu, *Daironsō,* 176–77.

28. Hayakawa Gen, "'Kotoba-gari' to pasokon tsūshin" ("'Word hunting' and e-communication"), in Hiraoka, *Tsutsui Yasutaka no gyakushū,* 137–40.

29. In *Metafuikushon no bōryaku,* Takayuki Tatsumi discusses *Asa no Gasupaaru* and other works with reference to the concepts of "performance" and "speech act" (61–96). The chapters on Tsutsui in this book and in Tatsumi's *Nihon henryū bungaku* provide an excellent introduction to the issues raised by Tsutsui's work.

30. Tsutsui discusses his work as an actor in the essay collection *Bungakugai e no hishō: Haiyū to shite no hibi* (A flight from literature: My acting days) (Tokyo: Shogakkan, 2001).

31. Tsutsui Yasutaka, Tsutsui Yasutaka home page on JALInet, http://www.jali .or.jp/tti/ (accessed May 23, 2006). See the "Multi Media Theater" section. Most of this material dates from 1997.

SCIENCE FICTION ANIMATION

6. When the Machines Stop

Fantasy, Reality, and Terminal Identity in
Neon Genesis Evangelion and *Serial Experiments: Lain*

Susan J. Napier

"And if he left off dreaming about you, where do you suppose you'd be?"

"Where I am now, of course," said Alice.

"Not you!" Tweedledee retorted contemptuously. "You'd be nowhere. Why you're only a sort of thing in his dream!" . . .

"I *am* real!" said Alice, and began to cry.

— *Alice in Wonderland*

"I am falling. I am fading."

— *Serial Experiments: Lain*

"I am me!"

— *Neon Genesis Evangelion*

In 1909 the British writer E. M. Forster published the short story "The Machine Stops," a bleak vision of the far future in which what is left of humanity lives below the earth, connected through a worldwide communications system that allows them never to leave their rooms or engage in direct contact with anyone else. All human life is organized by an entity known simply as the "Machine." At the story's end the Machine malfunctions and finally stops. Abandoned and helpless, the humans begin to die in a scene that interlaces apocalyptic imagery with an extremely tenuous note of hope – the assertion by Kuno, the narrative's single rebel character, that the Machine will never be restarted because "humanity has learned its lesson." As he speaks, however,

> The whole city was broken like a honeycomb. An airship had sailed in through the vomitory into a ruined wharf. It crashed downwards, exploding as it went, rending gallery after gallery with its wings of steel. For a moment they saw the nations of the dead, and, before they joined them, scraps of the untainted sky.[1]

Forster's dystopian vision may remind readers of other Western science fiction and dystopian works of the period, in particular Aldous Huxley's somewhat later *Brave New World* (1932). Like Huxley, Forster critiques the growing reliance of his contemporaries on technology. But he differs from Huxley in two ways that make "The Machine Stops" a work particularly relevant to contemporary science fiction. The first is in his vision of a world in which technology has rendered direct interpersonal contact unnecessary and, in fact, slightly obscene;[2] the second is the explicitly apocalyptic dimension that he brings to this state of affairs. The Machine destroys not only human relationships but also, ultimately, the material world, although it does leave a tantalizing glimpse of "untainted sky." Forster's work is classic science fiction, serving, as Fredric Jameson puts it, to "defamiliarize and restructure our experience of our own *present*" – in this case, that of 1909.[3] It is also a remarkably prescient view of a future that we in the twenty-first century are increasingly able to imagine.

In Forster's view, however, when the machines stop, reality – the untainted sky – emerges. In the two Japanese anime TV series that I examine in this chapter, this is not the case. In *Shinseiki evangerion* (1995–96, *Neon Genesis Evangelion*) and *Serial Experiments: Lain* (1998), reality itself becomes part of the apocalyptic discourse, problematized as a condition that can no longer be counted on to continue to exist, thanks to the advances of technology and its increasing capabilities for both material and spiritual destruction.[4] The two works also pose an insistent question: What happens to human identity in the virtual world? Does it become what Scott Bukatman calls "terminal identity," a new state in which we find "both the end of the subject and a new subjectivity constructed at the computer screen or television screen?" And does it then go on to become part of what Bukatman refers to as "terminal culture," a world in which reality and fantasy fuse into techno-surrealism and nothing is ultimately "knowable"?[5]

The answer to these last two questions seems to be "yes," at least in terms of the two anime I examine, although the originality and imaginativeness of their approaches might tend to obscure what, to my mind, are their deeply pessimistic visions. The narratives, the characters, and

Susan J. Napier

the mise-en-scène of these works evoke the disturbing postmodern fantasy that Jeffrey Sconce has described in *Haunted Media*. Sconce suggests that, "where there were once whole human subjects, there are now only fragmented and decentered subjectivities, metaphors of 'simulation' and 'schizophrenia,'" and he finds that, "in postmodernism's fascination with the evacuation of the referent and an ungrounded play of signification and surface, we can see another vision of beings who, like ghosts and psychotics, are no longer anchored in reality but instead wander through a hallucinatory world where the material real is forever lost."[6]

Although Sconce's point is that we may be exaggerating the uniqueness of this postmodern condition — and indeed Forster's 1909 text suggests that the interface between self and machine has been a modernist preoccupation as well — it is certainly the case that the two anime I examine call into question the material world in ways that seem peculiarly specific to this period yet show strong traces of Japanese cultural tradition. This chapter explores how each anime evokes its particular "hallucinatory world," but first it is necessary to situate the two texts within both anime and Japanese culture.

Undoubtedly related to the experience of atomic bombing in World War II, but also combined with a centuries-old cultural preoccupation with the transience of life, the apocalyptic critique of technology is one that has grown increasingly frequent in recent Japanese science fiction anime. The trend probably began to develop at least as far back as the 1970s with the immensely popular animated *Yamato* television and film series about the adventures of the spaceship incarnation of the World War II battleship *Yamato* (chapter 2, Figure 2.1). (The series was best known in America in its 1979 television incarnation *Star Blazers*.) This provided the template for an ever-growing mass-culture obsession with apocalyptic motifs. In the *Yamato* series, however, technology, as long as it was aligned with the power of the human spirit — in this case, the Japanese spirit of *yamato damashii* — could still have salvific aspects. This combination reaches its apotheosis (literally) at the end of the film *Saraba uchū senkan Yamato: Ai no senshitachi* (1978, *Farewell to Space Battleship Yamato: In the Name of Love*) when the stalwart young captain of the *Yamato,* accompanied by the fetching corpse of his beloved girlfriend and the shades of former *Yamato* captains, realizes that the only way to save earth is to conduct a suicide mission into the heart of the White Comet. The film ends with a single long-held shot of a spreading white radiance, a surprisingly ambiguous finale for a film aimed largely at children and adolescents.[7]

This ambiguous vision of humans, technology, and the end of the world has appeared in more complex forms in the years since *Yamato*. Most spectacularly, the 1988 film masterpiece *Akira*, directed by Ōtomo

Katsuhiro, inaugurated an infinitely darker vision of technology in relation to human identity. Structured around a series of scientific experiments
on telepathic children gone horribly wrong, *Akira* presented an unforgettable vision of a world in which the innocent were grotesquely sacrificed
to the vicious machinations of what might be called the military–industrial complex. Far from the cozy mix of genders and generations that the
Yamato series presented, the protagonists in *Akira* were largely alienated
male adolescents typified by Tetsuo, its psychokinetically transmogrified
antihero who, in the film's penultimate scene, lays waste to Tokyo in one
of the most memorable and grotesque scenes of destruction ever filmed.
Akira's highlighting of telekinesis also brought a note of hallucinatory
unreality to some of the film's most significant scenes, a feature that
would be expanded in later anime and was perhaps already presaged in
the spectral presences aboard the final voyage of the *Yamato*.[8]

In anime released in the years since *Akira*'s debut, its dark vision of
hapless humanity in the throes of technology has not only been echoed
but intensified. At first this may seem surprising. Japan, along with the
United States, is one of the most technologically advanced countries in the
world. Unlike the United States, however, Japan endured over ten years
of recession starting in the nineties, and it has left a deep mark on contemporary attitudes toward both technology and the future. Although
the country continues to produce important technological advances, the
dominant attitude toward technology displayed in both its mass-cultural
and high-cultural works seems to be ambivalent at best. This is in significant contrast to Western culture, which, as can be seen in American magazines such as *Wired* or in Canadian Pierre Levy's *Cyberculture*,[9] still contains strong elements of techno-celebration, especially in relation to the
potential of virtual reality as promised by computers and other new media.

Besides the recession, another reason behind Japan's often problematic attitude toward technology is undoubtedly the 1995 Aum Shinrikyō
incident in which followers of a charismatic guru named Asahara Shoko
released deadly sarin gas into the Tokyo subway system, killing twelve
people and injuring many more. Both the incident and the cult surrounding it seem to have stepped from the pages of a science fiction thriller.
Many of Asahara's young followers were, at least potentially, part of the
Japanese elite, graduates of top schools in science and engineering. Often
shy and insecure, they were reported in the press to be devotees of science fiction anime. Lured into the cult by its potent mix of supernatural
imagery — Asahara was said to be capable of levitation, for example — its
increasingly strident rejection of the material and materialist world, and
its apocalyptic teachings, believers not only manufactured sarin gas but
also reportedly worked on developing nuclear weapons.

The shadow of the Aum Shinrikyō incident still looms over contemporary Japanese society on a variety of fronts, contributing to a society-wide sense of malaise. The incident itself can be seen as embodying many of the characteristic elements of contemporary Japanese society's complex vision of technology, one that recognizes the dangers of technology but remains awestruck by its potential powers. Aum's mixture of New Age occult elements and traditional Buddhist and Hindu teachings is also relevant, underlining the fact that technology does not exist in a vacuum but interacts with all facets of human existence, including the spiritual.

Consequently, the Japanese ambivalence toward technology goes beyond a simple binary split between technology and its other(s) to encompass a problematic contemporary vision of human identity vis-à-vis not only technology but also the nature of reality itself. Increasingly in Japanese culture, the real has become something to be played with, questioned, and ultimately mistrusted. In some works, such as Murakami Haruki's best-selling novel *Sekai no owari to haadoboirudo wandaarando* (1985, *Hard-Boiled Wonderland and the End of the World*) and Anno Hideaki's *Neon Genesis Evangelion,* characters make conscious decisions to retreat into their own fantasy worlds. In other works such as *Serial Experiments: Lain* or Murakami Ryū's novel *Koin rokkaa beibiizu* (1984, *Coin Locker Babies*), characters attempt to impose their own, perhaps insane, visions on the outer worlds of reality. Often these explorations of the real contain an explicitly spiritual, even messianic, dimension.[10]

Although I include literary examples, the most significant medium in which these explorations of technology, identity, and reality versus unreality are being played out is the animated one, a medium often denigrated by Westerners as fit only for children. Unlike Western popular culture, where expressions of technological ambivalence tend to be mediated through live-action films such as *Blade Runner* (1982), *The Matrix* (1999), and *Minority Report* (2002), Japanese society has welcomed explorations of these complex issues in animated form. The reasons behind this positive reception are varied, but they include the fact that Japan has long had a tradition, through scroll painting and woodblock printing, in which narrative is as much pictorial as literary. This has culminated, in the view of some scholars, in the ubiquitousness of manga, or comic books, as a staple of twentieth-century Japanese mass culture. Anime and manga are strongly linked, since many, if not most, anime are based on manga, and both media appeal to adults as well as children.

There are other, perhaps more intriguing, reasons, however, for the synergy between animation and explorations of reality. As I have argued elsewhere, animation is a medium in itself, not simply a genre of live-action cinema.[11] As such, it develops and plays by its own generic restrictions and capabilities, the latter of which are uniquely suited for dealing with issues of the real and the simulated. The animation critic Paul Wells calls these the "deep structures" of animation that "integrate and counterpoint form and meaning, and, further, reconcile approach and application as the *essence* of the art. The generic outcomes of the animated film are imbued in its technical execution."[12] By this I take Wells to mean that the act of animation — a medium that he compares with the fine arts rather than the cinema — foregrounds and affects the characteristics of the text being animated in ways conducive to a form of art that is both peculiarly self-reflexive and particularly creative. The "deep structures" that inspire animated visions link with the uncanny and the fantastic to create a unique aesthetic world.

Thus Japanese animation tends to show particular strength in the genres of fantasy and science fiction. Unlike manga, which cover an enormously wide terrain, from action fare to self-help books and even economic treatises, the fluid instrumentalities of animation delight in highlighting the unreal or the unlikely. The free space of the animated medium — a medium not bound by a perceived obligation to represent the real — is ideal for depicting the free spaces of science fiction and fantasy, genres that have traditionally existed parallel to representations of the real. The overt technology of the animation medium itself highlights in a self-reflexive way the technological basis of the science fiction genre and the artificiality of fantasy.

Elements of twentieth-century Japanese culture also seem to have made its citizens particularly receptive to the idea of problematizing the real. In *Topographies of Japanese Modernity*, Seiji M. Lippit analyzes the twentieth-century Japanese critic Kobayashi Hideo's argument that a fundamental feature of Japanese prewar culture was a "pervasive spirit of homelessness and loss." This sense of loss is especially embodied in Kobayashi's vision of the city of Tokyo, which serves "not as a repository for memories . . . but only as an ever shifting marker of disassociation from the past." It makes modern Japan into a society in which both urban and natural landscapes are considered "different versions of phantasmagoria, as spectral images without substances."[13] The notion of "phantasmagoria" is one that functions particularly well in relation to the nonrepresentational world of anime, whose fast pace and constantly transforming imagery continually construct a world that is inherently "without substances." It should also not be surprising that Tokyo is the favored location for most apocalyptic anime. As the center of contemporary Japan's trends and currents, it remains in many anime, such as *Akira, Lain,* and *Evangelion,* the "unreal city" both of T. S. Eliot's anomic vision in *The Waste Land* (1922) and of the virtual reality visions of postmodernism.

As the uncanny relevance of Eliot's work suggests, Kobayashi's and Lippit's arguments, while apparently concerning early-twentieth-century modernity and its links to the modernist movement, are still strikingly appropriate to our contemporary, supposedly "postmodern," world. Japan is still a society in which what Marilyn Ivy terms "discourses of the vanishing," echoes of the past, are remarkably prominent. Even though the anime I am examining are set in a future that seems to have lost all traces of Japanese tradition, both works privilege memory — not only its loss but its stubborn ability to remain important in a fluctuating world. But in both *Lain* and *Evangelion* memory itself ultimately becomes uncertain, a force to be manipulated and even, perhaps, abused.

Lippit goes on to argue that, in many prewar Japanese texts, "modernity is marked by fragmentation and dissolution,"[14] elements that commentators find in abundance in our own period. In fact, the speed of fragmentation and loss may be the most distinctive aspect of the postmodern situation leading to a pervasive sense of helplessness and fear. For example, in *Terminal Identity*, Bukatman traces the increasing disembodiment of the subject in the electronic era and analyzes it in terms of social and psychological trauma. "In both spatial and temporal terms, then, the bodily experience of the human is absented from the new reality, precipitating a legitimate cultural crisis."[15]

In Japan this "cultural crisis" can be seen not only in terms of ambivalent attitudes toward the interface between humans and technology but also in a deeper questioning of what it is to be human in relation to the machine, a machine that increasingly seems to dominate, to construct, and ultimately to interfere with the reality of human nature. This problematization of human identity in the context of technology seems to be leading in increasingly apocalyptic directions, concretely manifested in the Aum incident and made an object of aesthetic and ideological interest in the many anime and manga dealing with world-ending scenarios. These apocalyptic visions are not limited to the destruction of the material world. Rather, viewers and readers are confronted with stories whose narrative impetus appears to be a growing sense of hopelessness in relation to overwhelming forces that are both exterior and interior. Not surprisingly, a sense of claustrophobia and paranoia pervades these works, ultimately leading to memorable visions not simply of cultural crisis but also of cultural despair.

Neon Genesis Evangelion and *Serial Experiments: Lain* have much in common. They can readily be described as postmodern in terms of their concern with a notion of identity as fluctuating, their rapid and sometimes incoherent narrative pace, and their refusal of conventional forms of closure. But the two stories have theoretical issues in common as well:

an explicit obsession with apocalypse and the question of salvation; an ambivalent celebration of the spectacle; a notion of time in flux; and a shared vision of what Janet Staiger calls "future noir,"[16] in which dimly lit, labyrinthine cityscapes dominate the mise-en-scène. Most important, they share a complex and problematic attitude toward the real. The two stories also deal with issues that are perhaps culturally specific to Japan: the increasing distrust and alienation between the generations, the complicated role of childhood, and, most significant, a privileging of the feminine, often in the form of the young girl, or *shōjo*. Typical of more sophisticated anime, they also offer a striking visual style, largely architectonic, in which space, shape, and color play off each other to produce in the viewer a sensation that is disorienting and exhilarating at the same time. This contributes to a pervasive sense of the uncanny that imbues both narratives, linking them with the genres of horror and fantasy. Finally, both anime appeared as television series (although *Evangelion* also became two feature films). Unlike most American series where each episode usually stands by itself, Japanese television and OVA (original video animation, i.e., videos produced for direct sale, bypassing broadcasting and theatrical release) series develop over time, allowing, at their best, for far more intricate plots and an infinitely richer understanding of the psychologies of the major characters.

Neon Genesis Evangelion

Anno Hideaki's television series *Neon Genesis Evangelion* was first shown in 1995. Considered by many scholars to be an anime masterpiece, the series is credited by some critics with singlehandedly reviving the genre from what they saw as its creative doldrums in the early 1990s.[17] While I would not go quite so far, it is certainly true that *Evangelion* is one of the most important and groundbreaking anime series ever created. Constructing a mythic universe that is almost Blakean both in its complex and mythic vision and in its dizzying array of Christian and Judaic religious symbols, the series questions the construction of human identity, not only in relation to the technology that the series' plot and imagery insistently privilege but also in relation to the nature of reality itself. Providing more riddles than solutions, the series takes the viewer on a journey into inner and outer reality before ultimately leaving both its characters and its audience floating in a sea of existential uncertainty.

Although it draws on earlier classic anime such as the *Yamato* series in terms of the ostensible narrative — alien invaders, in this case known as Angels, are attacking earth and only a small group of young people can save it, using impressive giant robots with which they synergize — the narrative's actual execution completely defamiliarizes this rather hackneyed story line. This is particularly true in the second half of the series, in which the tortured psychology of the main characters and a variety of enigmatic apocalyptic elements begin to intrude into the conventional action-packed plot. But we are given hints even at the beginning of these significant differences. Thus the opening episode is constructed around all the conventions of the classic "saving the world" narrative, only to undermine them by showing Ikari Shinji, its fourteen-year-old ostensible hero, in a far from heroic light. Set in a postapocalyptic "Tokyo 3" in 2015, the opening episode introduces the viewers to NERV, the secret underground headquarters run by Ikari Gendō, Shinji's remote scientist father, and to the giant robots known as EVAs that Shinji and two other fourteen-year-olds, the mysterious Ayanami Rei and the feisty/obnoxious Asuka Langley (both girls), are expected to pilot against the mysterious Angel attacks (Figure 6.1). In a more conventional anime science fiction narrative, Shinji would climb into the EVA with gusto and proceed to save the world. In fact, he does pilot the EVA and succeed in destroying the Angel —

Figure 6.1. In his first encounter with the EVA in episode one, Shinji stares at its massive head while cradling the wounded body of another child pilot, Ayanami Rei. (From the ADV American DVD.)

who turns out to be the third of seventeen — but only with the greatest reluctance and after a display of temper, fear, and vulnerability that seems less than conventionally heroic.

The rest of the *Evangelion* series is extremely complex, and it would be unfair to the richness of its narrative to attempt to summarize it in a few paragraphs. But it is important to be aware that the narrative is an essentially bifurcated one. On the one hand, it consists of the group's combat with the Angels, which occurs in approximately every second episode. These are violent, bloody exchanges characterized by an extreme inventiveness in terms of the fascinating abstract forms the Angels take; at the same time, they are guaranteed to satisfy the conventional adolescent male viewer of this kind of science fiction or mecha (giant robot) anime. The other strand of the narrative is far more complex and provocative, as it becomes increasingly concerned with the problematic mental and emotional states of the main characters, all of whom carry deep psychic wounds and whose psychic turmoil is represented against an increasingly frenzied apocalyptic background in which it becomes clear that the threat from the Angels is matched by the machinations of various humans connected with NERV. Although the scenes of combat are gripping and imaginative for the genre, what makes *Evangelion* truly groundbreaking are the characters' psychic struggles. Both wide-ranging and emotionally draining, these struggles are also presented with surprising psychoanalytic sophistication as the characters try to come to grips with their own inner turmoil, their problematic relations with each other, and finally, their relation to more remote forms of otherness — the gigantic machines that are the EVAs and with which they must synchronize, and the enigmatic Angels who present a riddle that is increasingly depicted in terms of what seems to be a Christian or perhaps Gnostic notion of apocalypse.[18]

Ultimately, *Evangelion*'s apocalyptic narrative ends with more enigmas than revelations. We never know exactly what the Angels are, although their DNA is said to be 99.89 percent compatible with human DNA. Indeed, the final Angel, number 17, initially appears in human form, disguised as another EVA pilot. This Angel essentially sacrifices itself, allowing Shinji in EVA armor to destroy it. The victory comes at enormous cost to NERV and to Shinji's colleagues, however, as many of them die in the battle. Mick Broderick describes these battles as being held during the "apocalyptic interregnum: the time between the penultimate and ultimate battles that decide humanity's final outcome."[19] But the "final outcome" of the *Evangelion* series is a far cry from conventional apocalyptic closure. Instead of a cataclysmic struggle, the last two episodes of the series (twenty-five and twenty-six) shift abruptly to a stunningly unexpected form of closure:

a vision of Shinji's inner psychological world that becomes an exploration of the nature of reality itself.

As such, the final episodes are worth examining in some detail. Stripped of the high-tech gadgetry and the colorful visuals that characterize the series' earlier episodes, these last two episodes take place largely in muted tones in a virtually empty mise-en-scène symbolizing Shinji's mind. Shinji initially appears alone and seated in a chair in a pool of light, a scene suggestive of a captive's interrogation. In fact, a form of interrogation proceeds to be carried out as he asks himself — or is asked by an unseen voice — probing psychological questions, the most frequent of which are "What do you fear?" and "Why do you pilot the EVA?"

In both cases the answers are surprising. Typical of the series as a whole, they deconstruct the mecha science fiction genre, calling into question the more simplistic motivations typical of earlier works such as *Yamato*. What Shinji fears most turns out to be not the impersonal threat of the Angels but the disturbing workings of his own psyche and his dysfunctional family background. Thus, in answer to the question "What do you fear?" he first answers "myself," then mentions "others," and finally admits to fearing "my father." Even more psychoanalytically significant are his answers about why he pilots the EVA. At first he insists that he does so to "save mankind." But when that answer is met with the response "Liar," he shifts to a more complex self-analysis (aided by the accusing voices inside him — often those of his coworkers — who suggest that "You do it for yourself!"). He admits to piloting the EVA because of his own need for the liking and respect of others, and finally acknowledges that he feels "worthless" unless he is joined with the EVA.

Two similar interrogations follow, involving the other pilots, Asuka Langley and Ayanami Rei. Asuka, the feisty half-Western girl who has a dysfunctional family background equal to or worse than that of Shinji, turns out to be even more needy than Shinji in terms of her relationship with the EVA. Enmeshed in her ruined EVA, which was destroyed in the final assaults, Asuka excoriates the machine as a "worthless piece of junk" but then immediately goes on to admit that "I'm the junk...I'm worthless. Nobody needs a pilot who can't control her own EVA."

Even more provocative are the responses of the enigmatic Rei, who, it has been revealed, is actually a clone of Shinji's dead mother created by Ikari Gendō, Shinji's father. Fittingly, given her essential otherness vis-à-vis Shinji and Asuka, Rei's internal interrogation goes beyond the psychoanalytic to verge on the metaphysical. At first she accuses herself of being "an empty shell with a fake soul," but then her inner voice suggests that she has been formed by her interactions with others, and it accuses her of "being frightened that you will cease and disappear from the minds of others." To this Rei responds chillingly, "I am happy. Because I want to die, I want to despair, I want to return to nothing."

The overwhelming atmosphere of terror and despair intensifies as the action returns to Shinji. Over a montage of bleak visuals that include black-and-white photographs of desolate urban motifs such as a riderless bicycle or vacant park benches interspersed with graphic stills of the devastated NERV headquarters in which Shinji's colleagues are seen as blood-stained bodies, Shinji insists that there is nothing that he can do to change the world and that he is simply a "representative, a signifier." Just at this despairing point, however, the scene shifts to a vision of blank whiteness in which Shinji appears as a cartoon stick figure while a voice-over intones, "None of this will last forever. Time continues to flow. Your world is in a constant state of flux." While the words are redolent of Buddhist terminology, the visuals are self-reflexively anime-esque. Shinji is told that the whiteness around him gives him freedom, and various elements are gradually added to the blankness — first a line, or "floor," that signifies gravity and then other structures to create an animated world.[20]

In another surprising shift, the scene changes to what we discover is a vision of an alternative animated reality — in this case, what seems to be a kind of high-school sex comedy. A self-assured Shinji "awakens" in a pleasant bedroom to find Asuka shouting at him that he'll be late for school, a far cry from his alienating existence in *Evangelion*. Other reversals abound: his father sips a cup of coffee in a homespun kitchen while his mother — now alive — chides him about being late. At school Asuka and Shinji run into a new girl — Rei — now a hot-tempered anime babe, while Misato, Shinji's beautiful, tortured mentor in *Evangelion*, appears as a sexy, placid high-school teacher.

Aware now that he indeed has a world of "freedom" in which what is "real" is "only one of many possibilities," Shinji, surrounded by his revived colleagues, friends, and family, announces, "I am me. I want to be myself. I want to continue living in the world." At this point everyone claps and each character intones the word "Congratulations!" *Evangelion* ends with Shinji thanking everyone and the final words, "Congratulations to the children."

The stunning originality of these final episodes cannot be overstated. While *Evangelion*'s narrative has clear echoes of *Yamato*'s saving-earth-through-technology plots, and its dysfunctional characters resonate with aspects of *Akira*, most notably the notion of the sacrifice of innocent children, the series deals with these elements in breathtakingly creative ways to create a unique and memorable vision of inner and outer collapse and, perhaps, renewal. Many viewers, however, were outraged by the two final episodes. Expecting a more conventional end-of-the-world scenario, fans were baffled that, instead of outward explosions and satisfying combat, the cataclysmic struggle occurred wholly in the character's mind. Rumors flew that the "disappointing" ending was due to lack of money on the part of Anno's parent company Gainax, but the subsequently released film version, *Shin seiki evangelion gekijō-ban: Air/Magokoro o, kimi ni* (1997, *The End of Evangelion*) more than makes up for the minimalism of the final episodes by presenting an over-the-top apocalypse so full of awesome catastrophe and bizarre revelations as to seem almost a parody of the apocalyptic genre.[21]

What Anno is doing in the television series, however, is far more groundbreaking and intellectually exciting. Eschewing the extravagant visuals and relentless action associated with the apocalyptic science fiction genre, Anno instead probes what might be termed the apocalyptic psyche, using simple but dark graphics and photo montages, disturbing voice-overs, and disorienting music — as the final episode opens, Beethoven's "Ode to Joy" swells on the soundtrack. In these last two episodes the machines have literally stopped, and both characters and viewers are left with no recourse but to confront their/our own flawed humanity in all its desperation and insecurities without the technological armor of the typical science fiction text.

Looking at the series as a whole, however, we can see that the ending, although certainly genre bending, should not be totally unexpected. Kotani Mari has suggested that *Evangelion* can in many ways be read as a quest romance in which the hero finds his identity, and this quest is accomplished through far more than combat scenes.[22] Thus, if we return to the first episode, we can see that, although it is technically structured around the combat scene between Shinji and the Angel, it is already an exploration of inner psychological worlds.

This is made clear in the first meeting between Shinji and Misato when, through voice-overs, the viewer is given a hint of Misato's own damaged psyche and her disappointment in Shinji's seemingly utter lack of emotional affect. There are more subtle signs as well: Shinji and Misato's descent into the seemingly bottomless depths of NERV headquarters can be read, as the critic Endō Tōru suggests, as a descent into the unconscious, metonymically reinforced by the profusion of downward escalators and elevators from which the protagonists emerge into a disorienting maze of long, empty corridors and bizarre machinery.[23] It is surely no coincidence that, in the first episode, Misato and Shinji enter NERV only to become hopelessly lost, a situation that recurs symbolically and concretely throughout the series until the final episode explicitly displays Shinji as "lost" in his own subconscious. Other hints of unconventionality occur throughout the series in the often dysfunctional relations between the characters and the revelations about their unhappy backgrounds. Even before the final episodes, therefore, the viewer is accustomed to being as concerned about the characters' psyches as about the outcomes of the Angel attacks.

Even the series' visual style works to create a disorienting and foreboding atmosphere. William Routt has analyzed Anno's unusually frequent employment of still images in the series, sometimes accompanied by complete silence, at other times accompanied by voice-over dialogue. By stopping the visual action, these sequences seize and hold the viewer's attention, forcing him or her out of the mesmerizing flow of fast-paced visual imagery typical of animation and concentrating the focus on more psychological issues. The fact that these still images particularly proliferate in the final episodes is also crucial. As Routt says, "The series continually uses stills of Shinji and his surroundings to direct attention to his state of mind and to his memories, constantly reminding viewers that what is going on inside his head warrants our attention — and in this way predicting its own psychological denouement."[24]

It should be clear by now that *Evangelion* is a text that can be read on many levels. On the one hand, as Kotani and other critics point out, it can be seen as a coming-of-age story, expressed through the narrative of a young boy's growth vis-à-vis others, in particular the patriarchy represented by his father and the feminine presence represented not only by his colleagues but, as Kotani argues, by the EVA itself. The EVA is a clearly maternal entity in whose fluid embrace — it fills with liquid when the pilots enter — Shinji and his copilots can return to the womb. Shinji must also deal with the Angels who, as Kotani suggests, can be seen as the other that needs to be repudiated in order for the subject to mature.[25] But, as the near humanness of the Angels suggests, the other is not so easily repudiated. As the final episodes make clear, the development of Shinji's identity must be made in relation to others, in particular the miraculously resuscitated group of colleagues who are there to congratulate him at the end when he declares "I am me!" a moment that suggests that Shinji's endeavor to develop a cohesive form of subjectivity has been successful.

Or has it? The tale of Shinji's maturation is a fascinating one, but it takes place within an explicitly apocalyptic framework, and it is worth examining Shinji's role within the context of the apocalyptic narrative. In a conventional apocalyptic narrative we would expect a savior figure to arise. Broderick argues that this is essentially Shinji's function; he evaluates the final scene in which Shinji declares himself and receives congratulations in the following positive terms:

> Not only do *viewers* witness the individual reborn into a world made new, but the entire human species is remade immortal, liberated from its biological and psychological constraints to embrace a return to Edenic bliss.[26]

Although I find Broderick's analysis arresting, my own reading suggests that the film's ending is more complicated and perhaps darker than that of a classic apocalyptic narrative. My reading goes back to the special qualities of the animation medium itself and its self-reflexive ability to highlight its unreality in relation to the "real." As Routt says of the series' use of still images, "They signal the overt presence of style: they repeatedly and obviously call attention to the considerable artifice of the series' narration."[27] This calling attention is strikingly obvious in the final episodes of *Evangelion,* first in the scene where Shinji, shown floating in white emptiness, is told he has the "freedom" to do what he likes to create his own world. This is an obvious reference to the role of the animator himself/herself, who constructs a world from white emptiness every time he or she creates animation. Even more obvious is the startling scene in which Shinji becomes the hero of an alternative anime series, a lighthearted world in which he and his fellow characters are shown as confident and independent.

The highlighting of the animation's essential unreality can be interpreted in two ways. On the one hand, if we agree with Broderick's optimistic view, we can see it as underlining the explicit message that every human has the potential to create his or her own world. On the other hand, given the generally dark portrayal of the human psyche in the series up to this point, it is also possible to suggest that *Evangelion*'s final apocalyptic vision is an ironic one: even when we think we can control the reality around us, we are actually at its mercy, cartoon characters in the hands of the fates or the animators. The happy ending that we see is one ending, but, as the series makes clear, it is only one of many possible endings.

Serial Experiments: Lain

While *Evangelion* highlights the technology of the animation medium itself to call our notions of reality into question, *Serial Experiments: Lain* presents its viewers with an animated world in which technology, specifically the computer, both creates and deconstructs reality. While the EVA in *Evangelion* is essentially anthropomorphized, a concrete other that is, initially at least, a necessary part of the characters' identities, the "machine" in *Lain* is invisible, part of a world known as the "Wired" in which the machine not only supports but literally constructs identity. This premise leads both characters and viewers on a darkly surreal adventure into a virtual house of mirrors where identities shift, disappear, and reformulate and where death and life are refigured to create a disorienting and disquieting vision of a very near future.

Less epic than the sprawling *Evangelion, Lain* might well be described as a home drama invaded by the surreality of cyberculture. Its eponymous heroine is a quiet junior-high-school girl living an apparently conventional life with parents, an older sister, and a typical group of friends in a world much like our own, only perhaps a little more high-tech. One day, however, a classmate of hers commits suicide. From that point on, Lain and her other classmates start receiving messages on their computers, seemingly from the dead girl, telling them that "she has only given up her body" and that "God is here," inviting them, or at least Lain, to join her. Around the same time Lain receives a new computer, called a NAVI, and she becomes steadily immersed in its disembodied world. Meanwhile, her classmates insist that they have seen her at a nightclub called "Cyberia," behaving in a way that is most unlike her typical shy self. Reality and dream intersect when Lain actually starts to visit Cyberia, encountering a strange variety of people who insist they've met her before, either at Cyberia or in a world they refer to in English as the Wired, the world of cyberspace.

As Lain increasingly plunges into the Wired, she begins to understand that she and the other Lains she encounters there are very special personages, holding some key to both the real world and the cyberworld. At the same time she begins to realize that the Wired is starting to affect the real world. Newscast transmissions are suddenly delayed or pushed forward, leading the media to issue disclaimers as to whether the news they are presenting has any relevance. In the sky above Tokyo an immense image of a girl (Lain?) appears, to the consternation of the public. A friend, Arisu ("Alice"?), insists that Lain has spread vicious rumors about her in the Wired. Even more disturbingly Lain is presented with a frightening series of questions — "Who are you?" "Are your parents real?" "Is your sister?" "When are your parents' birthdays?" — none of which she can answer.

The motif of interrogation is similar to *Evangelion*. But unlike Shinji, who ultimately finds both the questions and the answers in himself, Lain initially discovers that her interrogator is the "God" of the Wired, a strange, vaguely Christ-like white male with tangled black hair who tells her that "to die is merely to abandon the flesh ... I don't need a body." Lain begins to question her own existence at the same time as she defensively asserts, "I'm real! I'm living!" On her return home, however, Lain discovers a house empty except for her father, who appears only to tell her, "It's goodbye, Miss Lain." Lain begs him not to leave her alone, but he tells her that "you're not alone if you connect to the Wired." More confrontations with God ensue; he teasingly suggests that Lain herself may be a god and that in any case she is "software" and doesn't need a body. In the last episodes of the series, Lain and Arisu confront God, pointing out that he doesn't need a body, either. He thereupon metamorphoses into a hideous monster before disappearing. Free but all alone, Lain discovers she has the power to erase the memory of the rumors about Arisu from her friends' minds and ultimately realizes that she must erase herself as well. In the last scene her father suddenly reappears; he tells her that she doesn't need to wear her bear suit anymore and that she "loves everybody," and he offers to make her some tea.

This brief summary can only begin to suggest the imaginative complexity of *Lain*. The series brilliantly captures some of industrialized humanity's most fundamental concerns at the turn of the twenty-first century, most notably our sense of a disconnect between body and subjectivity thanks to the omnipresent power of electronic media. As Bukatman argues, the invisibility of electronic technologies "makes them less susceptible to representation and thus comprehension at the same time as the technological contours of existence becomes more difficult to ignore."[28] *Lain*, through its foregrounding of the world of the Wired in relation to a young girl who is described as "software," manages to make the invisible visible in a peculiarly disturbing way. Lain's fragmented subjectivity, embodied in the multiple Lains acting out inside the Wired; her withdrawn, almost autistic personality; and her lack of origins make her the perfect representative of the Wired, a world in which the whole notion of reality or truth is constantly called into question.

Even the series' opening credits are full of elements that trouble our understanding of the nature of reality. Each episode begins with a blank screen and a disembodied voice intoning in English, "Present Day! Present Time!" followed by a sinister spurt of laughter. The scene shifts to a shot of Lain walking alone in a bear costume through crowded neon-lit urban streets in which the "Don't Walk" sign seems constantly to be flashing. All the while a singer intones in English the refrain "I am falling, I am fading."

The words "Present Day! Present Time!" seem to be ironically suggestive. Of course, the viewer knows that this is a defamiliarization of our present, but the laughing voice hints that it is we who may be mistaken — is *Lain* the present? Or is our reality the present? Lain's bear suit, which she dons throughout the series, attests to her own desire to escape reality, in this case by wearing a costume suggestive of a stuffed animal, an omnipresent signifier of cute *shōjo* culture in contemporary Japan. The ubiquitous neon signage, often glimpsed through rain, highlights the importance of electronic media, once again making the "invisible" visible. The series also contains an almost obsessive number of still shots of telephone power lines, conveying the omnipresence not only of technology but of the communications media in particular and implicitly hinting at our inability to communicate in any satisfactory way. Finally, the haunting opening theme music addresses Lain's fate and our own unease that we too may "fade" into the Wired.

The final episode of *Lain* seems to suggest exactly that and is worth analyzing in more detail. On the one hand, Lain seems to triumph against the false God of the Wired by catching him in his own logical conundrum — if bodies are not necessary, then why should he need one? This can be seen as an assertion of the importance of the material world, indeed of the body, since without a body, God does indeed disappear (fades), but Lain herself is hardly better off. Reconfiguring the real world — or what is presented as the real world — that her entrance into the Wired has clearly damaged, Lain is forced to erase her own identity. Her parents now have only one child, her elder sister, and only her friend Arisu has a vague uneasy memory of a girl she once knew named Lain. Lain is told — and this is meant to be a comfort — that "if you don't remember something it never happened . . . you just need to rewrite the record."[29]

The erasure of memory is seen here ironically as comforting, a way to rewrite an unhappy history — much as Japanese textbooks have erased certain episodes of the Pacific War — but underneath the irony is a tragedy of a child's nonexistence. The ubiquitous still shots of a nude Lain in fetal position surrounded by computer wires and components suggest her total takeover by the machine (Figure 6.2). Of course if Lain is only "software," then it doesn't matter whether she ever existed. This may be the reason why her father tells her that she needn't wear the bear suit anymore, a cute signifier of contemporary Japanese girlhood. The "machine" (program) of the Wired has finally stopped for her, and she is now liberated to take tea in an imaginary space, without any pretense of reality at all.

Mention of tea may evoke memories of the Mad Hatter's tea party, since Japanese viewers are also familiar with *Alice's Adventures in Wonderland* (1865) and *Through the Looking-Glass* (1871). Indeed, in many ways *Lain* can be seen as a retelling or even a reversal of the *Alice* stories. Like Alice, Lain — and Shinji as well, to a lesser extent — descends into a world in which nothing is what it seems and in which identity constantly fluctuates. As with Alice, she has godlike powers, since she is the "software"

Figure 6.2. In a scene that appears in the final credits of each episode, Lain lies nude in a cradle of wires. (From the Pioneer American DVD.)

that creates her own world, the Wired, just as Alice dreams up Wonderland and Looking Glass Country. Also like Alice, she ultimately confronts the reigning deity within her made-up world and triumphs over it. Here we have a reversal, however. In Alice's case she recognizes the Red Queen's and the others' true forms as simply "a pack of cards" (trite, material objects) while Lain recognizes that it is the immaterial that is the Achilles' heel of her enemy, since without a body, he simply disappears.

Both Lain and Shinji are desperately concerned about their own incipient immateriality, the fact that their subjectivity is verging on "terminal identity" because of their dependence on the machine. Lain fears to be left alone in the world of the Wired but knows that she has nowhere else to go, while Shinji fears that without the EVA he is nothing. The fact that these are children makes their vulnerability particularly disturbing, suggesting extratextual aspects of a social malaise in which young people seem less and less connected, not only with other people but also with themselves.[30] In many ways the emotionally empty Lain seems spiritually linked with Rei who, while a clone of Shinji's mother, is visually presented as a young girl who wants only to "return to nothing." The fact that *Lain* begins with the suicide of a young girl is even more disturbing, suggesting "terminal identity" in its most concrete form. In today's Japanese anime, in contrast to the elderly ghosts who haunt the *Yamato,* it is the children — the future — who seem to have become "phantasmagoria," unhappy ghosts or stick figures lingering on the edges of consciousness.

Lewis Carroll's Alice, who may be considered a nineteenth-century form of *shōjo,* is also afraid of losing her identity, as her tearful insistence that "I *am* real" attests. As it turns out, however, she has no need to worry. Alice is the dreamer and the Red King is simply a figment of her dream, although she is astute enough to wonder, on waking, whose dream/reality it really is. After all, "he was a part of my dream of course but then I was a part of his dream too."[31] For Alice, this is an amusing conundrum. For the children in *Evangelion* and *Lain,* bound to a world in which technology rather than the human imagination increasingly seems to dominate, the question is one with terrifying implications.

Carroll's nineteenth-century text privileges the imagination. Forster's modernist work highlights the need for "real" human intercourse unmediated by technology. The two late-twentieth-century anime works suggest that the imagination, the real, and technology are bound together in increasingly complex ways, and they hint that reality may ultimately be simply a creation of the mind. While this is a powerful, even liberating notion, it is also one that, for many of these narratives at least, can lead to alienation and despair. At the turn of the twenty-first century, when the machines stop, can the human imagination transcend the ruins and create a new reality no longer tied to technology? Both *Evangelion* and *Lain* explore this question, but, given the enigmatic quality of their conclusions, it is hard to say whether the answers they offer are positive or negative.

Notes

1. E. M. Forster, "The Machine Stops," in *The Eternal Moment and Other Stories* (New York: Harcourt, Brace, Jovanovich, 1956), 37.

2. Consider the following exchange between Kuno and his mother in Forster's text: "But I can see you!" she exclaimed. "What more do you want?" "I want to see you not through the Machine," said Kuno. "I want to speak to you not through the wearisome Machine." "Oh hush!" said his mother, vaguely shocked. "You mustn't say anything against the Machine" (4).

3. Fredric Jameson, "Progress versus Utopia or, Can We Imagine the Future?" *Science Fiction Studies* 9, no. 2 (1982): 152.

4. *Shinseiki evangerion,* dir. Anno Hideaki, TV series, 26 episodes (1995–96); translated as *Neon Genesis Evangelion: Perfect Collection,* 8-DVD box set (ADV Films, 2002); *Serial Experiments: Lain,* dir. Nakamura Ryūtarō, TV series, 13 episodes (1998); translated on 3 DVDs (Pioneer, 1999–2001).

5. Scott Bukatman, *Terminal Identity: The Virtual Subject in Post-Modern Science Fiction* (Durham, N.C.: Duke University Press, 1993), 9. Jean Baudrillard's description of the contemporary condition as "no more subject, no more focal point, no more center or periphery: pure flexion or circular inflexion" is also particularly

appropriate here. Jean Baudrillard, *Simulacra and Simulation,* trans. Sheila Glaser (Ann Arbor: University of Michigan Press, 1994), 29.

6. Jeffrey Sconce, *Haunted Media: Electronic Presence from Telegraphy to Television* (Durham, N.C.: Duke University Press, 2000), 18.

7. *Uchū senkan Yamato,* TV series, 26 episodes (1977); translated as *Star Blazers Series 1: The Quest for Iscandar,* 6 DVDs (Voyager, 2001); this was the first of several Yamato series broadcast on American television; *Saraba uchū senkan Yamato: Ai no senshitachi,* dir. Masuda Toshio (1978); translated as *Farewell to Space Battleship Yamato: In the Name of Love,* DVD (Voyager, 1995). A strong awareness of the transience and unpredictability of life has been rooted in Japanese culture for centuries and is exemplified in its lyric tradition. See Susan J. Napier, *Anime from Akira to Howl's Moving Castle: Experiencing Contemporary Japanese Animation,* rev. ed. (New York: Palgrave Macmillan, 2005), 249–53.

8. *Akira,* dir. Ōtomo Katsuhiro (1988); translated as *Akira,* DVD (Pioneer, 2001).

9. Pierre Levy, *Cyberculture,* trans. Robert Bononno (Minneapolis: University of Minnesota Press, 2001).

10. Murakami Haruki, *Sekai no owari to haadoboirudo wandaarando* (Tokyo: Shinchōsha, 1985); translated by Alfred Birnbaum as *Hard-Boiled Wonderland and the End of the World* (Tokyo: Kodansha International, 1991); Murakami Ryū, *Koin rokkaa beibiizu,* 2 vols. (Tokyo: Kōdansha, 1984); translated by Stephen Snyder as *Coin Locker Babies* (Tokyo: Kodansha International, 1995).

11. Napier, *Anime,* 292.

12. Paul Wells, *Animation: Genre and Authorship* (London: Wallflower, 2002), 66.

13. Seiji M. Lippit, *Topographies of Japanese Modernism* (New York: Columbia University Press, 2000), 4.

14. Ibid., 7.

15. Bukatman, *Terminal Identity,* 106.

16. Janet Staiger, "Future Noir: Contemporary Representations of Visionary Cities," in *Alien Zone II,* ed. Annette Kuhn (London: Verso, 1999), 100.

17. Azuma Hiroki, "Anime or Something Like It: *Neon Genesis Evangelion,*" *Intercommunication* 18 (Fall 1996). *Intercommunication* is archived online at http://www.ntticc.or.jp/Publication/Icm/. The article is at http://www.ntticc.or.jp/pub/ic_mag/ic018/intercity/higashi_E.html (accessed March 26, 2006).

18. In the final episode, Anno is clearly referencing Sigmund Freud and perhaps Jacques Lacan, as the unseen voice inside Shinji's head explains to him that he creates his personality first through disassociating with the mother and then through distinguishing himself from others.

19. Mick Broderick, "Anime's Apocalypse: *Neon Genesis Evangelion* as Millenarian Mecha," *Intersections* 7 (March 2002), paragraph 6, http://wwwsshe.murdoch.edu.au/intersections/issue7/broderick_review.html (accessed March 26, 2006).

20. Christopher Bolton points to some other examples of this "textual apocalypse" that are visual rather than psychological, such as the "repeated shots of an empty sound stage or movie studio that suggest a final striking of the set," hinting that the series is "collapsing in on itself" as the animation "rewrites and redraws its own reality in the final scenes" (Christopher Bolton, e-mail message to author, August 5, 2002).

21. This was actually the second film version, released just a month after the first, and the third ending of the story. *Shin seiki evangelion: Death and Rebirth,*

translated as *Neon Genesis Evangelion: Death and Rebirth*, DVD (Manga Video, 2002); *Shin seiki evangelion: Air/Magokoro o, kimi ni (The End of Evangelion)*, DVD (Manga Video, 2002).

22. Kotani Mari, *Seibo evangelion* (Evangelion as the immaculate virgin) (Tokyo: Magajin Hausu, 1997), 99.

23. Endō Tōru, "Konna kitanai kirei na hi ni wa" (On a day so beautiful and so ugly), in *EVA no nokoseshi mono* (The legacy of Evangelion), ed. Shimotsuki Takanaka, *Poppu karuchaa kuritiiku/Pop Culture Critique* 0 (Tokyo: Seikyūsha, 1997), 84.

24. William Routt, "Stillness and Style in *Neon Genesis Evangelion*," *Animation Journal* 8, no. 2 (2000): 41.

25. Kotani, *Seibo evangelion*, 99–101.

26. Broderick, "Anime's Apocalypse," paragraph 20.

27. Routt, "Stillness and Style," 40.

28. Bukatman, *Terminal Identity*, 2.

29. The issue of memory is implicitly suggested in her father's final comments to Lain, in which he suggests that, besides tea, he might also bring "madeleines," an obvious reference to Marcel Proust's *Remembrance of Things Past* (1913–27). While in Proust's work the flavor of the madeleine invites the narrator back into his childhood memories, in *Lain* the cakes simply underline the absence of a past that can be remembered. I am indebted to David Mankins for reminding me of this reference.

30. Not all anime present such pessimistic visions of youth. For a fascinatingly different approach to the same themes of identity and apocalypse, see Kunihiko Ikuhara's 1997 series and film *Shōjo kakumei Utena (Revolutionary Girl Utena)* in which the young heroine of the series triumphantly asserts her identity and ends up actually becoming the machine, in this case a flashy car that serves as a literal vehicle for empowerment. The important difference here is that *Utena*, like *Alice*, is a fantasy, deconstructing such clichés as the fairy-tale prince to tell a romance of feminine liberation. It would appear that, at the present time at least, the science fiction genre in Japan is less able to imagine technology and human identity in an optimistic light. *Shōjo kakumei Utena*, dir. Kunihiko Ikuhara, TV series, 39 episodes (1997); translated as *Revolutionary Girl Utena*, 3 DVD box sets (Software Sculptors, 2003–4); *Shōjo kakumei Utena: Adouresensu mokushiroku*, dir. Kunihiko Ikuhara (1999); translated as *Revolutionary Girl Utena: The Movie*, DVD (Software Sculptors, 2001).

31. Lewis Carroll, *Alice's Adventures in Wonderland and Through the Looking Glass* (London: Puffin, 1997), 310.

7. The Mecha's Blind Spot

Patlabor 2 and the Phenomenology of Anime

Christopher Bolton

I n the opening sequence of Oshii Mamoru's animated film *Kidō keisatsu patoreibaa* (1989, *Patlabor: The Movie*), a small army of men and machines hunts down an elusive quarry, but what they finally capture is an absence that lies at the heart of the film's fears. The hunters are a mixed group of soldiers, tanks, and the "labors" of the film's title — giant human-shaped robots with living pilots. Their target is a rogue labor, but when they finally capture it and open its hatch to apprehend the pilot, they find only an empty cockpit. The labor is unmanned.

The scene encapsulates the central threat in the film, which is the fear that these robotic tools will rise up without pilots and rampage en masse. But it also has added significance. The more frightening threat implied in *Patlabor* and its sequel *Patlabor 2* (1993) is that the labors are images of us, human–machine hybrids that have lost all humanity, increasingly technologized bodies that turn out to be empty shells.[1]

As Susan Napier has shown for similar anime, these giant mechanical puppets carrying tiny human souls are an evocative metaphor for the ways that technology not only magnifies the body's reach and power but also changes what the body is. They are "simultaneously appealing and threatening, offering power and excitement at the expense of humanity."[2] Napier's discussion focuses on the mecha's outward physiognomy and bodily topology, but one of the most prominent figures for this trade-off in *Patlabor 2* is the trope of vision and mediated vision. The labor pilots and virtually everyone else view the world magnified and filtered by sensors, displayed on screens, enhanced and often distorted by electronics. The motif of an enhanced vision that has its own blind spots is made to reflect the trade-offs between technological amplification of bodily experience and a progressive alienation from our original bodies, threatening dehumanization. The goal of this chapter is to trace this motif of dehumanization through *Patlabor 2* with reference to Vivian Sobchack's ideas about mediated experience and virtual reality.

The technologically mediated experience represented by the labors is an extreme fantasy, but Oshii's film also addresses milder examples much closer to hand — for example, the idea of the mass media as the most thorough and pervasive electronic filter for experience. The issue of the mass media is in fact much closer to the heart of the film than the crisis of a literally robotic body. Of course, this raises the question of whether Oshii's anime, itself part of a high-tech genre and the popular media, can effectively critique the milieu from which it arises. In the concluding part of this chapter I argue that we can see such a critique in Oshii's work, but not without some attention to the nature of representation in anime. I address this by taking a closer look at Sobchack's phenomenology of electronic and cinematic experience, and applying it to Oshii's film to examine what kind of vision anime might constitute.

Screening Reality

The trope of a body that is both enhanced and invaded by technology is a staple in anime. It is also an idea that has attracted the interest of literary critics, a number of whom have seen human–machine hybrids in a range of texts as figures that embody or solve the dilemmas we face in our increasingly electronic and virtual culture. Among the most influential of this work is, of course, Donna Haraway's cyborg feminism, which suggests the cyborg is a figure whose hybrid nature — both human and machine — promises a way to overcome the enforced and ultimately limiting categories of biology, race, and gender.[3]

It is in this context that Oshii first attracted the attention of North American critics, with his 1995 film *Kōkaku kidōtai: Ghost in the Shell*, an evocative and sophisticated visual exploration of body, gender, and technology.[4] (For example, see Sharalyn Orbaugh's reading of *Ghost in the Shell* in chapter 9.) Like Haraway's theoretical cyborg, the cyborg heroine of Oshii's film possesses a body in which technology and biology are united so intimately that she can no longer separate the human from the artificial. Her superbody boasts the exaggerated female proportions common to many anime heroines, but she regards it with carelessness or disdain, as a container or a machine. The film follows her lead, dehumanizing her form until it becomes a thing, but arguably this act of objectification also strikes a blow against the same constructed essentialisms that Haraway is trying to combat — human versus inhuman, organic versus artificial, female versus male.

The bodies in the *Patlabor* series belong to a different tradition of mechanical bodies in anime, the "mecha," or "mobile suits." These towering humanoid robots piloted by human operators have occupied a place in anime for over thirty years, from *Majingaa Z (Mazinger Z)* in the 1970s and later staples like *Gandamu* (1979–, *Gundam*) and *Makurosu* (1982–, *Macross*) to the commercial and critical phenomenon *Shinseiki evangerion* (1995–96, *Neon Genesis Evangelion*).[5] (Some of these titles are discussed in chapters 6, 8, and 9.)

In the *Patlabor* series,[6] the labors were originally developed to be the heavy military and construction equipment of the twenty-first century. The power of the machines made them dangerous in criminal hands, giving rise to a new category of labor-based crime. As a result, the police force has formed a "special vehicles division" — the "labor patrol" of the title — whose officers pilot labors of their own in order to fight labor-related crimes.

In particular, the human shape of the labors allows them to be regarded as extensions of the human body (Figure 7.1) in a fantasy of bodily magnification or augmentation that is not unlike the cyborg, although in the *Patlabor* series the confusion of human and machine appears less profound. The cyborg's body incorporates and internalizes technology so thoroughly that the machinery can no longer be removed, but the mecha are vehicles that are ultimately distinct from their pilots, mobile suits that the humans can take off at the end of the day. Indeed, much of the two films revolves around the interactions of the human characters, who spend most of the story outside these machines.

Nevertheless, one can detect in the very scarcity of labor scenes some anxiety about undue mixing, particularly a fear that if the humans remain too long in their machines, they may not be able to leave them. In *Patlabor 2*, this is played out as a feeling of claustrophobia or confinement in the labor scenes that goes hand in hand with the bodily amplification and empowerment. There is a quality of sensory deprivation inside these dark, quiet machines, as if the pilots were blindfolded. Even with the labor's advanced sensors — laser scanners, infrared imaging, radio communications, and night vision are all prominently depicted — the pilot and the film's viewer never quite connect with what is going on outside. As the

Figure 7.1. The labors tower over humans, but retain a
humanoid shape. The pilot is just visible looking out from
the chest. (From the Manga Entertainment American DVD.)

spectator and pilot have their senses and sense of self cut off, the effect is
like John Perry Barlow's famous description of early virtual reality: "It's
like having had your everything amputated."[7]

In the film, the labor's blind spots are the central figure for the trade-
offs of the technological body. Oshii makes the point that while these
electromechanical projections extend human awareness, sensation, and
experience into new dimensions, they also insulate us in other ways, cutting us off from more immediate sensations. Consider, for example, the
first scene of *Patlabor 2* and the way it contrasts with the empty labor that
begins the first *Patlabor* film. The second film opens with a United Nations
military mission somewhere in Southeast Asia. A group of experimental
Japanese military labors is on UN military maneuvers under the command
of Japan's top labor engineer and tactician, Tsuge Yukihito. When Tsuge's
group is cut off and threatened by advancing enemy troops, headquarters
denies Tsuge permission to attack, telling him to wait for reinforcements.
But the enemy attacks first, and Tsuge must watch helplessly as his force
is wiped out.

It is this disaster that twists Tsuge into the story's noble villain, but
the horror of the battle is figured largely as Tsuge's removal from the action or, rather, as the gap between the violence on the battlefield and the
sensory deprivation he experiences inside his labor as he watches the
fight on his monitors.

Tsuge watches the enemy troops advance toward his position on a
screen whose image fills the movie screen; we never see them directly,
but the animation shows an intricate computer display that paints their

Figure 7.2. The screened view from inside Tsuge's cockpit.

heat signatures against a green background while zooming in on them in a series of complicated visual operations (Figure 7.2). Just as we cannot see the enemy in the flesh, Tsuge's face is concealed from us by his helmet visor, two small mechanical lenses taking the place of his eyes. But when a wave of incoming enemy rockets appears on his monitor, Tsuge's fear is signaled by the dilation of these lenses, a mechanical analogue of wide-eyed shock.

As the rockets strike Tsuge's group, the bipedal labors double over and fall like human figures, more human in fact than the immobile pilots inside their cockpits. Throughout the scene, the film cuts back and forth between the noise and carnage outside, and the dark interior and cool green displays that are all that Tsuge can see. Over the radio he hears the anguished cries of his men screaming "Captain!" But the sounds are distant and distorted, filtered through layers of static.

When one panicked pilot realizes his labor is about to be destroyed and screams, "I can't eject!" he voices the fears of the whole scene and eventually the whole film: that the humans will be trapped permanently inside their mechanical shells. The opening scene of the first *Patlabor* film might indicate the next step, when the human pilot has become totally absorbed, leaving only an empty chair — a point at which the human–machine hybrid we have become retains no inward or outward human traces at all.

This opening scene is followed by a credits sequence that shows a labor pilot in a virtual training exercise, and the same elements are featured: the goggled pilot, the labor's cameras, and the cockpit displays that show a flickering virtual world (Figure 7.3). From this opening, the film goes on to become entirely dominated by these kinds of images.

Figure 7.3. In the opening credits, a member of the Patlabor squad tests the sensor equipment on a new model of labor. This is one of many shots in which we see people through screens that superimpose digital information on their faces or bodies.

Sobchack has described the fear of insulation and absorption as a defining quality of electronically mediated experience. Drawing on Don Ihde's phenomenology of technology, Sobchack associates this fear with the inevitable disappointment of our impossible desire for a powerful but fully transparent technological body, one that projects us into new dimensions without changing the nature of bodily experience. Sobchack's observations come in a series of articles on the now-defunct cyberculture magazine *Mondo 2000* and similar rhetoric surrounding the Internet and other early virtual realities.[8] On the surface, this rhetoric professes excitement at the possibility of expanding experience by freeing users from the constraints of the body, but beneath this excitement Sobchack finds a reluctance to imagine any kind of experience beyond everyday bodily sensations. Users want to project their bodies further and faster across the Net, but they want the same kinds of experiences they are accustomed to at home. Hence the focus on fantasies of virtual sex — not on new kinds of experience but simply on old experiences accomplished by remote control. Clearly there are parallels with Oshii's giant robots. Implausibly shaped just like human beings, they represent the same kind of technological fantasy, the desire to magnify the body yet keep it as it is.

While cybersex and fantasies of virtual reality frequently revolve around transmitting the sense of touch, Sobchack's other work (treated in more detail below) identifies the sense of *sight* as uniquely implicated in constituting the sense of self; the sense of sight is also subject to the most thorough and complicated mediation in electronic culture. In *Screening*

Space, her survey of science fiction cinema through the eighties, Sobchack argues that the prevalence of computer readouts and computer graphics in films from *Tron* (1982) to *Wargames* (1983) expresses the threat of dehumanization. Citing Fredric Jameson's idea of a flattened postmodern space linked to a flattened affect or a loss of psychological depth, Sobchack writes:

> In these films and others, the "deep" and indexical space of cinematographic representation is deflated — punctured and punctuated by the superficial and iconic space of electronic simulation.... Indeed, only superficial beings without "psyche," without depth, can successfully maneuver in a space that exists solely to display.[9]

In one sense *Patlabor 2* clearly expresses a similar fear of dehumanization in its images of labor pilots unable to see outside except through electronic screens. But examining both Sobchack's ideas and the film's images in more detail reveals that there are other ways of screening reality in the film that are even more frightening.

A Shooting War or a Shooting Script?

Released after the 1991 Gulf war, *Patlabor 2* inverts a contemporary image of that war as a video-game conflict of easy, remote-control kills. Instead of watching doomed, distant targets through the crosshairs of long-range weapons, the characters watch their own mechanical bodies and the destruction of those bodies on screens that nevertheless render those things oddly remote. Asked why Tsuge does not ignore his orders and fire on the enemy, Oshii suggested that it is partly because he cannot feel any sense of danger from what transpires on his screens.[10]

The remainder of *Patlabor 2* repeats the same motif on a larger canvas: it revolves around Tsuge's plot, three years later, to force Japanese politics to emerge from its own shell. Postwar Japan has not fought actively in foreign military conflicts — presumably it is to preserve the policy that Tsuge is forbidden to fire in the opening scene — but the country has benefited economically and politically from the American wars it has supported.[11] *Patlabor 2* draws a connection between the labor pilots watching the battles on their monitors and the Japanese nation insulated from the realities of the wars it prosecutes by proxy. Tsuge's one-time accomplice Arakawa describes this national insulation using the metaphor of the display screen:

> We reap the fruits of these conflicts, prosecuting the wars that rage on the other side of our monitors, forgetting that we are standing just behind the front lines. Or pretending to forget. Someday we'll be punished for our lies.[12]

Tsuge upsets this complacency by staging a series of attacks that heighten political tensions — first a cruise-missile attack on the Yokohama Bay Bridge, then an invasion of Japanese airspace by a phantom plane. By playing the police, the military, and the United States against one another, Tsuge's plan provokes a declaration of martial law that leads to the presence of troops in the streets of Tokyo and sets the stage for a new war on Tsuge's own terms.

What are the terms of Tsuge's war? Arakawa describes the plan as an effort to strip away Japan's insulation and bring the Japanese close to conflicts that they are accustomed to seeing only on television, if at all. Tsuge, he says, will start "a genuine war that will make up for this passive, empty peace."

Some critics have taken Arakawa's words as the heart of the film and have seen in Tsuge's plot a decisive, if violent, act that pierces the veil of illusion and mediation: in Ihoroi Tadashi's words, an act that finally "closes the distance" between the formerly insulated self and the world. Michael Fisch treats Tsuge's operation as a real war (and at the same time a replay of World War II) that shatters Japan's political illusions, awakening it to the real possibility of its own destruction and pushing the film's characters and viewers toward a more aggressive and interventionist foreign policy, justified as self-protection. Fisch treats Oshii's fantasy as a vehicle for speculation, but he chooses not to deal with questions of mediation and representation in the film, instead relating it directly to the Japanese political situation in 1993, particularly the controversy over participation of Japanese troops in joint military operations like the Gulf war.[13]

In Fisch's article, the film's relevance is located in its relationship to real-world events, and the film itself is said to emphasize the realities of war and geopolitics. This political background is useful, and along the way Fisch gives some illuminating readings of Oshii's portrayal of America. But this kind of reading is a bit unsatisfying in its efforts to see the film as a more or less straightforward media representation of an outside political reality, without any attention to the issues of representation and mediation itself, issues that the film raises over and over in its imagery and plot.

Noda Makoto gives more attention to the radically mediated and virtual quality of experience and perception in *Patlabor 2*, seeing those features in all of Oshii's early films. He acknowledges "Tokyo's condition of isolation, as a city unable to escape the chains of media and technology." But even Noda sides with the Arakawa character in seeing Tsuge as a figure whose commitment is able to punch through this fiction in the end. In fact, Noda views *Patlabor 2* as a turning point in Oshii's work because, he says, its characters are actually able to escape the shells of their individual virtual realities and join with others in a real world.[14]

I would argue that neither reading is very helpful in seeing the real (or, rather, unreal) nature of Tsuge's plot, in particular the way he wages his war against the media itself. It is not the shooting war that Arakawa and Fisch posit but a kind of scripted action, an illusory war conducted in and on the media, discourses that reflect only indirectly what is occurring "on the other side of our monitors." By relating the sensory deprivation inside the labors and the idea of a war that does not register on the screens of everyday life, Oshii takes aim at a broader target, the way that electronic sensation and communication distance us from reality, whether in the labor or in modern society. As Arakawa says in a more revealing moment, when asked what god will dole out the "punishment for our lies": "In this city everyone is like a god. Omniscient, all seeing, but unable to touch any of it from where they sit — gods who never lift a finger."

However, Tsuge's attack on virtual reality is itself virtual (in ways that I show below), so it raises the question of how effectively representation can critique representation, or mass media critique itself. While these are slippery questions, I believe that they are among the most interesting and important ones the film raises, because they also relate to the issue of how an animated film, a product of the mass media, can stage a media or political critique. At its heart, this is the question of how we experience this medium — the phenomenology of watching anime — as well as of whether and how we can read it: as an intentional or unintentional political statement, a reflection of cultural anxieties, or any of the other cultural phenomena that critics have taken it to be. Certainly one might raise similar questions for any of the pop culture texts that cultural studies has taken up. But since animation's mode of representation is qualitatively different from that of the written texts and live-action films we are more accustomed to dealing with, these queries have a particular urgency.

Tsuge's war is virtual in the sense that it is conducted almost entirely in and on language — an action designed to co-opt and then disrupt the media and mediation that make discourses of war and peace possible. His plot proceeds as follows: after a few carefully staged violent incidents have raised tensions and provoked a domestic power struggle, martial law is declared, and Tokyo waits tensely for an all-out conflict. At this point his forces lead a series of surgical strikes on the city's bridges and communication facilities. While the communication grid goes down, powerful jamming disrupts radio communication, figured in the film by an evocative sound track, which features static interspersed with garbled bits of speech. At the same time, Tsuge launches a series of doomsday weapons, in the form of giant unmanned blimps that function by remote control. When the authorities try to disable one of these airships, it crash-lands

The Mecha's Blind Spot

and releases a cloud of yellow gas that envelops several blocks of downtown. After an initial panic, the gas is revealed to be harmless, but the authorities learn that the blimps are capable of releasing real toxins as well, and they realize Tsuge now holds the city hostage.

Each strategy — the feints, the jamming, the gas scare — is designed not to wreak physical destruction but to create the appearance and the perception of war. Tsuge's operations are rhetorical, both in the sense of being symbolic acts of destruction and in the sense of acting mainly through language and image. So even before the blimps rise into the air above Tokyo, the image of war has been created. In fact, the declaration of martial law midway through the film is Tsuge's real victory, for he has achieved a state of war without an actual war. The long, mournful montage of troops taking up their positions is the film's visual and emotional center, and the role of media representation is highlighted by the way the troops are shown reflected in various other media. We witness the maneuvers on televisions in a store window; we hear reports on a series of radios; we see troops and tanks in a bystander's snapshot or elaborately reflected in the glass windows of skyscrapers. The viewer knows that whatever comes later, Tsuge has already won the war of words and images.

Gotō, the labor-squad police captain who is battling to foil Tsuge, says that Tsuge's plot is about "constructing a state of war. Or rather, producing a 'wartime' on the stage of Tokyo." Answering Arakawa's theory about a real war to expose the fake peace, Gotō counters:

> Arakawa-san, what you said about fraudulent peace and real war was interesting. But if you're right that this city's peace is a lie, the war Tsuge has created is a lie as well.

Ueno Toshiya is one critic who has analyzed the film with attention to these issues of representation and media, as well as to the issues of bodily alienation and dehumanization with which I began. Ueno's canonical book on mecha anime, *Kurenai no metaru sūtsu: Anime to iu senjō* (1998, Metalsuits, the red: Wars in animation), contains a memorable formulation for comparison between the labors and the larger situation in society: both the city and its residents, he says, are suited up. As labor-assisted construction projects refit Tokyo, weaving it a new networked skin, the city is also a suit that its residents put on:

> This invisible (mienai) city is becoming a suit or a machine itself. The city is a suit that its residents get into; a "media suit" that makes communication (im)possible. This is the expansion of the invisible domain.[15]

"Invisibility" is Ueno's term for the insidious confusion of media society and its multiple images, a confusion that Tsuge exacerbates and exploits. One kind of invisibility results from the profusion of images in electronics and the media, to the point where the distinction between reality and simulation becomes meaningless. (And here Ueno lists many of the same examples of screens and images already given above.) The political situation in the film is analogous, with the reversible discourses of vision and power, as well as the shifting circumstances of politics, producing a battlefield on which the enemy is always invisible or unknown, and the good guys are indistinguishable from the villains. Hence the film's confusing plot, in which the identities of Tsuge's plotters are never really certain, even at the end.[16]

For Ueno, neither reality nor simulation emerges as dominant in *Patlabor 2*. The film is not a critique of the way the media undermine and alter a stable reality, nor is it a celebration of the simulacrum that sweeps reality under the rug. Material reality emerges, but only "from within the folds of multi-dimensional fiction." The film can only force us to reflect on how technology changes our perceptions and our society, even if we cannot escape those changes. The film's characters battle to bring these changes to our attention, Tsuge by accelerating them, Gotō by arresting them. But both characters are fighting a losing "rear-guard action," because they themselves are caught up in the networks of data and of power that facilitate these changes.[17]

Ueno's interpretation is helpful in foregrounding the issue of representation in the film, and his conclusion is a safely familiar one in media theory, at least for works such as Oshii's that seem to reflect on their own methods of representation. But I would contend that *Patlabor 2* is not as relativist as Ueno suggests. The film still maintains a strong dichotomy between insides and outsides, the claustrophobia of the labor clearly juxtaposed with less-mediated kinds of views. And the film does hold out a conservative hope for a more-authentic or less-mediated kind of experience than Ueno admits, even though Tsuge never entirely conquers the virtual, as Noda suggests he does. The way the film balances the real and the mediated allows for a more direct and nuanced critique of the mass media than either critic describes.

My reading of the film declines Ueno's "invisibility" and its associations with the epistemologically undecidable or unknowable, opting instead for the metaphor of an obstacle to vision that insulates us from an outside reality without rendering that reality irrelevant, an obstacle that can be overcome partially if never totally. It is not a blindfold that Tsuge can rip off us (as Noda might argue) but more like a blind spot: a hidden point in a view that is otherwise unimpaired. It may be large or small. It may be consciously sensed (like the area outside the range of a car's rearview mirror) or unconsciously missed (the rodless, coneless region on our retina that invisibly swallows up details). It moves. Sometimes it can be overcome by looking in a different direction, and sometimes not. Like the space "on the other side of our monitors," it is a shifting area that always is *in our view* but that we do not notice or cannot see.

The Machine's Blind Spot

To understand how Tsuge and Oshii direct our attention to our own blind spots, consider an incident that begins when Japanese defense radar picks up an unidentified warplane moving on an attack course toward Tokyo — a plane that is actually a computer ghost the plotters have created by hacking the defense net. The fact that the intruding plane is an electronic hallucination emphasizes the idea that all these augmented senses have blind spots of their own and that they sometimes conceal more of the world than they reveal.

The action alternates between the air over Tokyo, where the pilots of the interceptor fighters search fruitlessly for the intruder, and various defense control centers, where operators in darkened rooms plot the course of the phantom plane on a series of computerized displays. Screens dominate the command centers: technicians stand in front of monitors or are silhouetted against them, their faces reflected in the glass or lit from below by readouts, their eyeglasses flashing in the screens' reflected light.

The audio in the scene portrays the humans as buried under layers of technology. This is emphasized by the static-laden radio dialogue between the pilots and their controllers, so garbled that it requires subtitles.[18] As in the Southeast Asian scene, the communications become more frantic as the situation escalates, yet the static renders it remote.

In one of the interceptor planes, we watch the outside world from the pilot's point of view, through the heads-up display (HUD) in the plane's cockpit. The HUD is a device in use on real fighters today, a clear pane of glass in front of the pilot on which luminous instrument readings are projected. A high-tech gun sight and more, it lets the pilot see the sky in front of the plane through the glass, but with an overlay of digital information about the plane's course, speed, and weapons. This technology is duplicated in the labors by the graphic overlays that appear in their pilots' helmet visors. It is the literal incarnation of what Sobchack and Ihde identify as the sought-after "transparent" technology, one that allows us to see in the same way, only more.

But the fact that the technology does transform its users is indicated symbolically by shots of one pilot from a viewpoint outside his plane; we look back through the HUD so that the digital readouts now appear superimposed (in mirror image) on the pilot's face. The same shot is used in the control room sequence, where we gaze down at the operators from a position behind the wall-mounted display screens. The screens appear partly transparent to us, allowing us to see the operators behind the reversed readouts. This kind of shot is repeated throughout the film; again and again we see the characters through semitransparent display screens, visors, and eyeglasses that flash with digital information (Figure 7.3). These shots force the spectator to look through this technology just as the characters do, and they are a central image in the film supporting the idea that however transparent the technology, however subtle its mediation, it nevertheless alters us and our view.

The clear sense in these scenes — of technology interposing itself between humans and an external world — argues against Ueno's characterization of "simulacra generated kaleidoscopically... with each successive repetition having a material reality" of its own.[19] So too does Tsuge's final solution, which is not to multiply depictions further but to cut off communication altogether.

Tsuge accomplishes this with radio jamming and a series of pinpoint attacks carried out by saboteurs and helicopter gunships, attacks that destroy the city's bridges, communication lines, antennae arrays, and command centers, but leave everything else untouched. There is considerable footage of exploding targets, but the only casualty is communication. We never see a human injured, but there are pointed scenes of TVs and radios helplessly bleeding static into the air. As Gotō surmises when the jamming begins, "Cutting off information, causing confusion — that's not the means, but the end." Tsuge puts all of Tokyo in the situation he experienced inside his labor, blind and cut off, and so urges citizens to shed their electronic shells, just as he must emerge from his ruined labor after the battle in the opening scene.

Tsuge is opposed by Gotō and other members of the police force's special vehicles division, including his coldly beautiful cocaptain, Nagumo, who is also Tsuge's ex-lover. Gotō and Nagumo eventually foil Tsuge's plans, but in failing, Tsuge succeeds. To triumph, the good guys must essentially heed Tsuge's warning, opening their eyes and reclaiming their own senses from the machines; in the end, they too must emerge from their suits in order to defeat him. Ironically though, their victory lifts the jamming and reinstates the very mediated communication that Tsuge had momentarily suspended and they momentarily surrendered.

Tsuge's defeat is staged as a climactic battle between good and bad labors that makes the sensory shortcomings of both sides apparent. Gotō and Nagumo have tracked Tsuge to a spot of reclaimed land in Tokyo harbor, where he is controlling the blimps and the jamming. The only path of attack is through a narrow underwater tunnel guarded by Tsuge's own labors, a pair of advanced "Ekstor" models. The Ekstors represent the apex of mediated experience in that they are unmanned, controlled by remote operators via radio and cable. Their automation and inhumanity are signaled not only by their inhuman, crablike shape but by their eyes, glowing red sensors that wink mechanically on and off.

The Ekstors are eventually defeated by cutting their remote control cables and then blocking the radio signals from their human operators, in effect turning Tsuge's jamming strategy against his own machines. In order for the police forces to see through their own electronic countermeasures, they must abandon their labors' special sensors and use their naked eyes. When Nagumo activates the jamming, her labor's electronic displays dissolve into static, while her face, hidden until now, is revealed. She turns off her now useless data-visor, and her pilot's chair rises on elevators out of the labor's stomach cockpit so that she can see outside. As she joins the battle, her face is framed in the window of the machine's giant head, stressing the human heart or soul at the core of the good labors, in contrast to Tsuge's soulless Ekstors and unmanned airships.

The Ekstors are only narrowly defeated, and when Nagumo's labor rises to the surface of the reclaimed island on a freight elevator, it is a ruined hulk, hunched and still. Nagumo ejects in a mechanically intricate process in which the labor's abdomen blows off explosively and she jumps out from between its legs in a cloud of smoke — as if the labor is giving birth to the human. Her arrival startles a group of seagulls on the island into flight, one scene among several in which animals (particularly dogs and birds) are shown to possess the acute, unmediated senses that humans lack. Having shed her steel skin, Nagumo now enters that unmediated world. She dramatically doffs her visor and helmet, and goes to meet Tsuge face-to-face.

For most of the film, Tsuge has remained unseen. Like the incidents he stages, he is a ghost onto which other characters map their fears and expectations. Now Nagumo finds him staring at the city across the bay through binoculars. For the first time, he speaks at length:

> From here the city looks just like a mirage, doesn't it? . . . Three years ago when I returned to Tokyo, I lived in the midst of that illusion. And I tried to tell people it was an illusion. In the end, no one noticed until the first shot rang out. Even now, maybe they don't.

Then we see the city, shimmering in the distance. To this point the film has taken every opportunity to look through instruments like the binoculars, forcing mediated views on the spectator. But now for the first time it refuses us this augmented vision: we see the city as Nagumo sees it, with her naked eyes. She presses her physical reality on Tsuge:

Even if it is an illusion, there are people there living it as real life. Or are those people ghosts to you too? ... The woman standing in front of you now is no phantom.

As Nagumo places the cuffs on her former lover, a lingering close-up shows them clasping hands in a briefly intimate gesture. She has not only opened her eyes and shed her metal skin, but forced Tsuge to accept the real world outside simulation. In the final scene, when a policeman asks Tsuge why he allowed himself to be captured alive, Tsuge takes off his glasses (a last layer of mediation) and admits that he wants to stay and "see a little more" of the city's future. Apparently the real, physical world of humanity has triumphed over the mechanical, mediated existence. At least that is the conclusion of critics like Noda, who sees in the final scene a human connection that penetrates the layers of technological mediation and human alienation.[20]

But is this reading right? With Tsuge's arrest, the police are able to shut down the jamming. Communications have been restored, but only briefly is it the handclasp of direct human contact. More permanently, it is the mediated language of electronic communication, with all the problems that entails. So while Tsuge's arrest at first seems to be a victory for unmediated experience, it actually restores the mediation that he had interrupted.

Ueno finds evidence of a postmodern relativism in the film's ambiguous ending, which seems to provide no real victor in the contest between image and reality, or between the antihero Tsuge and the hero Gotō. But I would argue that the film's pessimistic conclusion accents, rather than abandons, its media critique. It depicts, if only briefly, a dream of stepping outside our "media suits" and then frowns on the failure of that revolution. There is a salient detail that Ueno passes over, one that gives the cessation of the jamming a chilling edge. After Tsuge's arrest, Nagumo's comrades, emerging battle-torn from the tunnel where they fought the Ekstors, hear the voice of Captain Gotō on the radio. As they realize the jamming has been lifted and yell their enthusiasm to Gotō, their distant, excited cries ("Captain! Captain!") replicate the anguished cries of Captain Tsuge's dying men, who scream the same words over the radio in the film's opening scene. We are returned to the tragedy and the critique that opened the film.

This moment also returns us to the question of whether anime really can or should mount any such critique. We have raised the question in general terms: can a product of popular media like anime conduct such a critique from the inside out, or do these issues effectively fall in anime's own blind spot — an area the text (as part of the popular media itself) cannot detect or represent. To phrase this question or objection in more specifically visual terms, can the critique of the electronic body and mediated experience suggested above really be undertaken in a medium that substitutes animated representation and often computer animation for real bodies and real landscapes? The discussion up to this point has contrasted mediated with unmediated vision in the film, opposing what the characters see with their eyes to what they see on their monitors. But can a stylized medium like animation — one that is today often produced by computer — effectively represent the difference between a mediated and unmediated view?

For example, it is often at moments when the film image is depicting computer screens that it appears most realistic, since the animation can mimic these essentially digital displays with a high degree of visual accuracy. Conversely, the ostensibly unmediated views of human faces must remain cartoonish or stylized. Are there extra layers of representation at work when we are viewing animated versions of live figures, or is it meaningless and even naive to distinguish between arbitrary versus illusionistic simulation?

Sobchack's work offers a considered framework for looking at explorations of mediated experience in contexts (like film) that are already more or less mediated themselves. So far I have used her observations about technologically augmented experience. And I mentioned that among the different kinds of experience that technology augments, sight possesses a singular importance in Sobchack's scheme. These two ideas come together in Sobchack's larger phenomenology of film experience, a theory that speaks directly to the differences between electronic and cinematic presence, and by extension to the differences between the experience of animation and the experience of live-action cinema.

Anime's Body: Medium or Mechanism?

In her article "Toward a Phenomenology of Cinematic and Electronic Presence: The Scene of the Screen," Sobchack applies her observations about technologically mediated experience and alienation to the experience of watching film. She traces the development of film from still photography to cinema to electronics, arguing that while still photography fixes events in a way that prevents us from entering back into them, motion pictures record not just a frozen experience or perception but the ongoing act and process of looking. Cinema "makes visible not just the objective world, but the very structure and process of subjective, embodied vision."[21] For Sobchack, this gives rise to a sense of cinematic film as a kind of perceiving subject that orders space and time for itself.

But with the advent of electronic technology, from videotape on, cinema's ordering of space and time gives way to dispersal and discontinuity, "an alternative and absolute world that uniquely incorporates the spectator/user in a spatially decentered, weakly temporalized, and quasi-disembodied state." This is figured in terms of discontinuous methods of representation, transmission, and experience in electronic film: from the pixels, bits, and packets of video and computer graphics to the frantic pace of the images in the dominant video aesthetic, a style that Sobchack says produces a sequence of intense, present instants rather than generating a coherent narrative. The result for the spectator is a "dizzying sense of bodily freedom" and disconnection not unlike that of the virtual reality she describes in her critiques of *Mondo 2000*.[22]

So while cinematic film and electronic film are both kinds of virtual sensation, cinematic film reinforces the significance of human bodily experience, while electronic film undermines the sense of the body. Where does anime fit on this spectrum? I have argued that *Patlabor 2* portrays the increasing mediation of electronics in our experience, with images of screens that get between the characters and the world. But is the film itself one more such screen, refracting or distorting the world for us in a way that other film does not? In other words, do *Patlabor 2* and similar works belong to the realm of the electronic or the cinematic?

It is true that *Patlabor 2* makes heavy use of computer graphics (for its time), in combination with conventional cel animation.[23] And anime's physical medium is more likely to be video than film: while the two *Patlabor* movies had theatrical releases, much of the other work in the series was produced for television or direct-to-video (OVA) release. Finally, there is a common perception of anime that matches Sobchack's description of intensely present but disconnected images. Most tempting, of course, is the comparison between Jameson's aesthetic flattening, the flattened screen space Sobchack sees in films like *Tron*, and the two-dimensional quality of anime.

But while *Patlabor 2* fits the description of an electronic medium in terms of its production and surface features, it also contains elements of the cinematic, and it is ultimately the mixture of the two that defines the film. We have already noted that, in contrast to Sobchack's ideas about flattened psychologies, the *Patlabor* films dwell obsessively on human characters. Napier notes that in many mecha anime, "the narratives themselves often focus to a surprising extent on the human inside the machinery," and in contrast with some body/technology critics' "visions of the armored body as lacking interiority... the protagonists in *mecha* anime often have a surprising amount of interiority."[24] Furthermore, while many anime fit the stereotype of frantic visual activity, *Patlabor* and *Patlabor 2* do not. Their pacing can be glacial, both the plot's movement and the physical movements of the figures, which are often depicted in lingering close-ups and static tableaux.[25] The lengthy political and philosophical monologues that accompany these scenes, if not always profound, are also far from two-dimensional.

Fortunately, Sobchack's phenomenology of film experience allows us to go beyond accidents of the film's production and stereotypes about animation. It does so by developing the notion of the coherence of visual experience in an extensive and rigorous way, using the idea of embodiment. *The Address of the Eye: A Phenomenology of Film Experience* expands on "The Scene of the Screen" by elaborating the relationships among bodies, vision, and visual language in the cinematic regime. By seeing how much of this applies to Oshii's film, we can address the question of whether *Patlabor 2* is more electronic than cinematic and can begin to draw some conclusions about whether the film represents technology's breaking apart of the subject and bodily boundaries, or whether it tries to conserve some notion of human experience and particular bodily experience even as experience is altered by technology.

The Address of the Eye combines the issue of embodied versus transparent technology and the issue of film experience by developing a theory of the "film's body." Drawing on an existential phenomenology that grounds the subject in *bodily* experience, Sobchack describes how "the act of seeing is entwined intimately with the act of being, how seeing *incarnates* being."[26] And since cinema is not only a seen object but a representation of the experience of vision (in some senses a subject in its own right), it also has a body, which consists in part of the material and technology that make up the film and in part of an imagined body that the spectator assigns it. In film, Sobchack says,

> discontiguous spaces and discontinuous times ("shots") are gathered together in a coherence ("scenes") whose reflection and signification constitute the significance of what can be called conscious experience. And (as with the spectator) that coherence is accomplished by the lived body. The camera its perceptive organ, the projector its expressive organ, the screen its discrete and material occupation of worldly space, the cinema exists as a visible performance of the perceptive and expressive structure of lived-body experience.[27]

Acknowledging that no technology is fully transparent, Sobchack draws on Ihde's distinction between "embodied technologies," which act as relatively transparent extensions of our sensory organs, and "hermeneutic technologies," which represent the world to us in abstract signs that must be read or interpreted. A microscope is an example of the former; a thermometer or other gauge would represent the latter.

Sobchack argues that cinema is a variant of embodied technology because it portrays an act of vision that the spectator experiences as if from within another body — the body of the film itself.[28] The film's body is not directly visible, but the spectator can posit it or fill it in by comparing the film's vision with his or her own and extrapolating a body that belongs to that filmed vision. For that to happen, however, the way in which the film views the world must have a coherence that allows us to relate its vision to our own. This is not a matter of realism in a naive sense: the film need not mimic a human being's vision optically. Indeed it should not, since its own body is never identical to a human body in shape or function. But it must have some kind of *coherence* that allows us to relate it to our own visual experience.

In the electronic (as opposed to cinematic) regime, the film's act of seeing loses this coherence, and we become unable to imagine a coherent viewing subject with a coherent body to accompany it. In concrete terms, this can result from the images losing a sense of unity as they become subject to all the subdivision and manipulation possible with videotape and digital media. Divided into channels, frames, and pixels, images are rewound, replayed and redacted, slowed down and speeded up. Extrapolating from Sobchack, we might say that if this electronic vision does have a body, it is a networked (not even mechanical) body that we can no longer relate to our human one.

In Sobchack's scheme, then, the technologized body portrayed in the plot of mecha anime might indeed be doubled in our own experience of watching these films, an experience that might alienate us from our normal senses. But what of *Patlabor 2* specifically? The answer to whether Oshii's film is electronic or cinematic (and to our earlier question about whether any anime can mount a critique of media) boils down to the question of whether the film's body has coherence. This in turn is a question of *how it looks* — how it watches and how it appears — and how close that is to the way *we* look. In Ihde's language, the issue is whether the film *looks* (as a person does) or merely *displays* (like a gauge). It is the question of whether we experience the electronic/mechanical/visual layer of anime as transparent or opaque.

Asking these phenomenological questions of *Patlabor 2* yields an interesting result: Oshii's film does try to portray the dismemberment of the electronic body (the labors, the media, Tsuge's war). But to do that it must also try to shed its own electronic skin. To this end, the film imitates or simulates both the unified cinematic body and its electronic dissolution, resulting in an oscillation between cinematic and electronic vision.

Just as there is more to embodied vision than naive realism, Sobchack makes it clear that there is more to locating the film's body than simply considering the camera's point of view. But viewpoint is still a key point. Sobchack's ideas suggest why Oshii's film uses screens and displays as it does — not simply as background but in a way that forces us to look into them or through them, to experience the events of the film filtered by these electronic aids and impediments. We see events unfold on monitors, in viewfinders, through goggles we are forced to don. The visors, HUDs, and other see-through displays literally realize Ihde's metaphor of transparent versus opaque technology. And through the process Sobchack describes, viewers try to posit a body that sees things in this way.

Frequently we can. The technologically mediated views we see are not the disembodied torrent of images Sobchack identifies with the electronic. They are essentially human visions, partly transformed. This vision is analogous to the bodies of the labors themselves: with their massive hydraulics and complex software, the labors' bodies are suspended between the mechanical and computer ages, ages that Sobchack associates with the cinematic and electronic, respectively. The film at these points has a similar kind of body: neither wholly electronic nor wholly cinematic; vaguely human, even charmingly old-fashioned, yet also tangibly different.

At other points, however, the film's body approaches a less-localized, more-distributed body that resembles Sobchack's electronic regime. These are the moments when Oshii portrays the view not through the eyes of the electromechanical labors but through the wholly electronic lens of the mass media, a networked electronic body with sensors everywhere. For example, the aftermath of Tsuge's attack on the Yokohama Bay Bridge is revealed as a series of television news reports on different international networks, including a flickering videotape of the incident in which key frames are blown up and rerun endlessly, a tape loop repeated again and again until it becomes unreal. (And in fact, as the story unfolds, the tape is revealed to be a fake, no more reliable than the many other mediated sensations portrayed in the film.) It is a channel-flipping sequence that suggests Sobchack's disconnected, present instants. So it is actually when the mediated view departs from the fictional scenario of the giant robots and approaches our own everyday bodily experience of watching television that the film's body begins to lose coherence.

Other shots through the media's eyes are accomplished not by showing spectators a television screen but by placing them in the position of the screens themselves. When martial law is declared, there are several shots of rapt viewers watching the announcement on television; only gradually does it dawn on us that we are watching these people from the television's perspective. These shots recall Jean Baudrillard's catchphrase for the influence of media and the equivalence of the worlds inside and outside the set: "You are the screen, and the TV watches you."[29]

These scenes are the ones that associate the film most clearly with the electronic. By forcing us to look from the perspective of the monitor, or the medium itself, they suggest a viewing body radically different from the human, not only in its optics but in its interests, its logic, its concerns.

The question remains: What does the film have to contrast with these electronic views? Is it possible to generate a more natural view to accentuate the artificiality of the mediated ones? Sobchack points out that the electronics and screens in American science fiction films have often been foils for the human characters and their stories, which represent a world of authentic experience.[30] In some respects *Patlabor 2* follows this pattern: the plot's heavy human-interest element throws into relief the artificial quality of the labors and the media.

But artistically, the humans remain the least real-looking element in the frame, making it hard to create a distinction between mediated and unmediated views of the human body. In visual terms, the contrast with the film's many monitors is provided not by human faces and bodies but by exterior landscapes and cityscapes rendered in startling detail. This hyperrealism (as opposed to photorealism) is a style Oshii developed further in his later films, where the intent is evidently to reproduce the effects of low light and reflected light that are visible to the eye but difficult to capture in a live-action film: complex multiple reflections at night, for example, or the glowing quality of snow falling in the dark. These provide the ground against which the other scenes become apparent as mediated or virtual.

Oshii also has a complementary strategy: he makes the video screens appear less realistic than they might. A small but telling detail is the slight flickering that accompanies TV news footage of the damaged Bay Bridge. It is one of many scenes of video screens and televisions in which the screens flicker or show banding. Such flickering and banding typically show up in live-action films when a television appears because the television screen refreshes its image at a rate different from the rate the camera captures successive frames on film. The phenomenon is called "aliasing" and has a more familiar variant in the famous wagon wheel effect, where spinning wheels appear to turn slowly or backward on film because the frame rate is close to their rate of rotation.

But in animated film, there is no reason for these effects to occur. The television monitor in the frame is animated as well, so it can appear any way Oshii wants. In fact, he has introduced these effects to make the screens in the film appear to have come from a conventional motion-picture camera.[31] This *virtual* aliasing is an effort to trick us into going back in our minds to an earlier technology. It is another way in which Oshii simulates the cinematic perspective to critique the electronic.

A related strategy is to simulate lens distortion in the animated image, for example, in a scene where he blurs a wall of monitors in the background in order to duplicate a television news camera's shallow depth of field, or in several shots where he introduces a fish-eye effect. The latter is one of the director's trademark shots. Oshii says only that the effect represents "the world from a different viewpoint."[32] But more than once in *Patlabor 2* it seems to be associated with scenes in which the spectator is made to assume the viewpoint of a screen or camera. At these points when the critique of the digital emerges most forcefully, Oshii simulates the older optical cinematic regime to assert or simulate a coherent body and gain a perspective from which to mount his attack.

The difficulty, of course, is that if the cinematic regime and body are themselves partly simulated, one might reasonably ask if the critique itself is not merely a virtual one. This is clearly a compromise the film must make as it oscillates between the human and the robotic, the cinematic and the electronic, the virtual and the real. *Ghost in the Shell*, the film that followed *Patlabor 2*, shows the same kind of oscillation in its treatment of its cyborg heroine, who is alternately superhuman and nonhuman, with a glorified, objectified body to match. Orbaugh takes up some of these issues in chapter 9, and I have argued elsewhere that this film's style also alternates realism or hyperrealism with a self-consciously theatrical mode that recalls the Japanese puppet theater. It is an oscillation that has left critics uncertain whether to see the film as serious or full of play, as a male fantasy or a feminist critique.[33]

Some of Oshii's anime before and after *Patlabor 2* and *Ghost in the Shell* avoid that pitfall by forgoing the oscillation and veering instead to one or the other extreme. Oshii's comic romp *Urusei Yatsura 2: Beautiful Dreamer* (1984) also treats the theme of shifting identities in virtual worlds, but remains an unbridled fantasy with no intrusion of seriousness. On the other hand, Oshii and Okiura Hiroyuki's *Jin rō* (2000, *Jin Roh: The Wolf Brigade*) treats the same themes with few fantasy elements and no humor, in the mode of a grimly realistic political thriller.[34]

The oscillation between the real and the represented may mean that *Patlabor 2* will disappoint critics on both sides of the fence. It seems likely that Fisch chooses not to deal with representation in the film because he sees the film's merits in its reflection of real-world politics, though I have argued that the complex treatment of transmission and reflection in the film urges caution in any discussion about what it is in the real world that the film reflects. Ueno seems to have a different and more conflicted perspective: a desire for Oshii's work to be politically relevant, but also a hope that before it ends, the film will have given up its nostalgic dreams of authentic unmediated experience and will have discarded what postmodernism might regard as a naive media critique. It may be this hope that causes Ueno to miss how the film does cling to a reality outside representation.

In a 1996 interview with Oshii, Carl Gustav Horn compared the release of the fake poison gas in *Patlabor 2* with the real nerve gas attack that occurred in the Tokyo subway two years after the film's release.[35] Watching *Patlabor 2* in the United States today, it is impossible to escape parallels with 9/11. In both tragedies, the scale and proximity of the destruction seemed to draw a clear line between reality and simulation. And yet it is impossible to consider the subway gas attack or 9/11 apart from the role that the media played in seeing and shaping them. In this situation, Oshii's films hold interest precisely because they address both the oppressive realities and the oppressive unrealities with which we are faced.

Notes

1. *Kidō keisatsu patoreibaa,* dir. Oshii Mamoru (1989); translated as *Patlabor: The Movie,* DVD (Manga Video, 2000); *Kidō keisatsu patoreibaa 2: The Movie,* dir. Oshii Mamoru (1993); translated as *Patlabor 2,* DVD (Manga Video, 2000).

2. Susan J. Napier, *Anime from "Akira" to "Howl's Moving Castle:" Experiencing Contemporary Japanese Animation,* rev. ed. (New York: Palgrave Macmillan, 2005), 88.

3. Donna Haraway, "A Cyborg Manifesto: Science, Technology, and Socialist-Feminism in the Late Twentieth Century," in *Simians, Cyborgs, and Women: The Reinvention of Nature* (New York: Routledge, 1991), 149–81.

4. *Kōkaku kidōtai: Ghost in the Shell,* dir. Oshii Mamoru (1995); translated as *Ghost in the Shell,* subtitled DVD (Manga Entertainment, 1998).

5. On earlier robot series, see Frederik L. Schodt, *Inside the Robot Kingdom: Japan, Mechatronics, and the Coming Robotopia* (Tokyo: Kodansha International, 1988), 73–90; Napier, *Anime,* 87.

6. As with many anime titles, the amount of *Patlabor* material is extensive. The feature-length theater releases are part of a franchise that includes a television series, direct-to-video (OVA) releases, manga, and merchandise. The works directed by Oshii include the first two films and the first OVA series, which includes an episode on which the plot of *Patlabor 2* is based. *Patlabor: Mobile Police – Kidō keisatsu patoreibaa,* OVA, 7 episodes (1988–89); translated as *Patlabor: The Mobile Police – The Original Series Collection,* 2-DVD box set (U.S. Manga Corps, 2005). For Oshii's detailed filmography, see Haraguchi Masahiro, "Oshii Mamoru kenshō intabyū: Ima kaimei sareru maboroshi no firumogurafii" (Interview with Oshii Mamoru: Going to the source for his elusive filmography), in *Zenryaku Oshii Mamoru-sama* (Dear Oshii Mamoru), ed. Noda Makoto (Tokyo: Futtowaaku, 1998), 227–348.

7. John Perry Barlow, "Being in Nothingness," John Perry Barlow Library, http://homes.eff.org/~barlow/library.htm (accessed March 25, 2006).

8. See the following articles by Sobchack: "Democratic Franchise and the Electronic Frontier," *Futures* 27 (1995): 731–32; "Teenage Mutant Ninja Hackers: Reading *Mondo 2000*," *South Atlantic Quarterly* 92 (1993): 577–79; and a precursor to these articles, "What in the World," *Artforum* 29, no. 8 (1991): 24–26.

9. Vivian Sobchack, *Screening Space: The American Science Fiction Film,* rev. ed. (New York: Ungar, 1987), 256–57.

10. Oshii Mamoru and Miyazaki Hayao, "Jidai no keri o tsukeru tame ni" (Ending an era), in *Oshii Mamoru zen shigoto: "Urusei yatsura" kara "Avaron" made* (Complete works of Mamoru Oshii: From *Urusei yatsura* to *Avalon*), ed. Uekusa Nobukazu, rev. ed. (Tokyo: Kinema Jumpō, 2001), 83.

11. For decades after World War II, the Japanese constitution was interpreted as prohibiting any deployment of Japanese troops abroad. The first Gulf war marked the beginning of an ongoing and hotly debated political process that has eased these restrictions, but only very gradually.

12. The subtitled version of *Patlabor 2* from Manga Entertainment provides good translations, but the dialogue translations in this article are my own.

13. Ihoroi Tadashi, "Mieru mono, mienai mono," in Noda, *Zenryaku Oshii Mamoru-sama,* 165; Michael Fisch, "Nation, War, and Japan's Future in the Science Fiction Anime Film *Patlabor 2,*" *Science Fiction Studies* 27 (2000): 49–68.

14. Noda Makoto, "Shin'ai naru Oshii Mamoru-sama: 'Anata' to 'watashi' no monogatari ni tsuite" (Dear Oshii Mamoru: On the story of "you" and "me"), in Noda, *Zenryaku Oshii Mamoru-sama,* 77; see also 76–89.

15. Ueno Toshiya, *Kurenai no metaru sūtsu: Anime to iu senjō* (Metalsuits, the red: Wars in animation) (Tokyo: Kinokuniya Shoten, 1998), 38.

16. Ibid., 41–45, 50–57.

17. Ibid., 44, 64; see also 40–45, 55–64.

18. Part of the distancing effect is that the pilots' radio code phrases are in English. The film has Japanese subtitles here, but the sound is so garbled that the American video release required a second set of subtitles transcribing the English.

19. Ueno, *Kurenai no metaru sūtsu,* 44.

20. Noda, "'You' and 'me,'" 88–89, 100–101.

21. Vivian Sobchack, "Toward a Phenomenology of Cinematic and Electronic Presence: The Scene of the Screen," *Post Script* 10 (1990): 54.

22. Ibid., 56, 58.

23. Oshii and Miyazaki, "Ending an era," 82.

24. Napier, *Anime,* 87, 90; see also 100–102.

25. Many anime limit motion to reduce animation costs. Though this seems to render some anime films even flatter, Oshii is able to match the pace of the film and the pace of the images in a way that takes advantage of this motionlessness.

26. Vivian Sobchack, *The Address of the Eye: A Phenomenology of Film Experience* (Princeton, N.J.: Princeton University Press, 1992), 51.

27. Ibid., 299.

28. The embodied quality of cinema is Sobchack's most important point in distinguishing the cinematic from the electronic, but it is only one part of her full thesis, which is that the technology of cinema constitutes a complex combination of the embodied and the hermeneutic.

29. Jean Baudrillard, *Simulacra and Simulation,* trans. Sheila Faria Glaser (Ann Arbor: University of Michigan Press, 1994), 51.

30. Sobchack, *Screening Space,* 255–62.

31. Ironically, computer animation can now be used in live-action film to erase screen flicker, by digitally drawing in the screens later rather than filming them directly with a camera.

32. Oshii Mamoru, interview by Carl Gustav Horn, in *Anime Interviews: The First Five Years of "Animerica, Anime and Manga Monthly" (1992–97)*, ed. Trish Ledoux (San Francisco: Cadence, 1997), 136.

33. Christopher Bolton, "From Wooden Cyborgs to Celluloid Souls: Mechanical Bodies in Anime and Japanese Puppet Theater," *positions: east asia cultures critique* 10 (2002): 729–71; Carl Silvio, "Refiguring the Radical Cyborg in Mamoru Oshii's *Ghost in the Shell*," *Science Fiction Studies* 26 (1999): 54–72.

34. *Urusei yatsura 2: Byūtifuru doriimaa*, dir. Oshii Mamoru (1984); translated as *Urusei Yatsura 2: Beautiful Dreamer*, DVD (U.S. Manga Corps, 2004); *Jin rō*, dir. Okiura Hiroyuki, screenplay by Oshii Mamoru (2000); translated as *Jin Roh: The Wolf Brigade*, DVD (Pioneer, 2002).

35. Oshii, interview, 139.

8. Words of Alienation, Words of Flight

Loanwords in Science Fiction Anime

Naoki Chiba and Hiroko Chiba

Sō sasayaku no yo, watashi no *gōsuto* ga.
(I hear a whisper... a whisper of my ghost.)

> — *Ghost in the Shell*

Ma ha shutai e tuby e tuby e, tu shuutei a no en tuby.

> — Sharon Apple, "*A Sai Ën,*" in *Macross Plus*

Masa ni *gōjasu!* (She really is gorgeous!)

> — *Neon Genesis Evangelion*

Watching science fiction anime in the original Japanese language, one is certain to encounter many loanwords and non-Japanese expressions. In Japan, loanwords, especially those taken from English, are commonly used in daily conversations as well as in written texts. Although this helps explain the profusion of loans in science fiction anime, their employment is often more conscious and radical. Indeed, some are used creatively with unconventional meanings ("*gōsuto*" in the first epigraph), some are not expected to be understood by the audience (Sharon Apple's song),[1] and some familiar expressions are employed to give a scene a comical touch ("*gōjasu*" in the final epigraph). Non-

Japanese settings in anime do not fully explain the frequent use of loans either. *Shinseiki evangerion* (1995–96, *Neon Genesis Evangelion*), whose story unfolds mainly in Japan, offers a dazzling spectrum of loanwords, while in the strangely Germanic world of the space opera *Ginga eiyū densetsu* (1989–97, Legend of galactic heroes) they are scarce. In this chapter, we discuss the use of loanwords and foreign expressions in two classic Japanese science fiction anime, *Macross Plus* (1994–95) and *Akira* (1991). We illustrate how they are characteristically employed to express foreignness and otherness, intimacy, characters' capabilities and empowerment, superficiality, lightheartedness, alienation, and transcendence. Combined with other modes of expression and vocabulary, they are highly significant elements in constructing the complex world a subject experiences in a story. We also demonstrate that it is not the "functions" of loans but the features that distinguish them from nonloans that are critical in constructing the fictional world.[2]

Often loanwords in science fiction anime are no different from those in other genres, but anime also uses loanwords in ways particular to the genre. Discussing Japanese translations of foreign words and loans, Akira Yanabu postulates that their charm, which he calls the "cassette effect," is closely connected to their similarity to imaginary monadic signifiers without signifieds. They are like attractive jewelry boxes that can in fact be empty: they are eye-catching not because of their content but because of their appearance. Yanabu underlines the charm of monadic signifiers as the key characteristic of words in general and casts light on the creative power they exert. They let us imagine things behind their facades, and this imagining leads to the creation of things and events: signifiers precede their signifieds.[3]

Naturally, not all loanwords in science fiction anime are like monadic signifiers: many are laden with associations and carry diverse effects and functions. We discuss some of these below. Yet it cannot be denied that science fiction anime represents a leading edge of word borrowing and neologism, offering many examples of unfamiliar expressions that stimulate viewers' imaginations. Many audiences are fascinated with exotic expressions whose meanings often remain unexplained or underexplained throughout the anime. This tendency is stronger in anime than in manga, in part because simultaneous commentaries called *"rubi,"* which are commonly used in the written media, cannot be employed in anime.[4]

Other distinct characteristics of loans in science fiction anime include the heavy use of scientific jargon borrowed from Western languages and the relatively high frequency of instances in which loans are intentionally employed to produce negative effects. All in all, it is fair to say that, even though loans in science fiction anime are not qualitatively different from loans in Japanese in general, they often attract our attention because they stir our imagination, making us wonder what lies behind their familiar and unfamiliar faces.

"Wago," "Kango," and "Gairaigo"

Before we move on to concrete analyses, it is necessary to clarify what we mean by "loanwords" and how the present study is related to others on loanwords in Japanese.

The vocabulary of contemporary Japanese falls into four main categories: *wago, kango, gairaigo,* and *konshugo. Wago,* or *yamato kotoba,* are vocabulary items considered native to the Japanese language.[5] The words that are used most frequently, as well as those that perform the main grammatical functions, fall into this category. *Kango* are words imported from Chinese into Japanese in the process of creating the Japanese language. Although they are loans, they are seldom regarded as *gairaigo* (see below), mainly because of their antiquity and the critical role they played in the formation of Japanese. *Kango* are the most numerous among the four groups in terms of the variety of vocabulary items and are usually denoted by *kanji* or Chinese characters.[6] *Gairaigo,* in its general sense, means any words taken from non-Japanese languages, although it usually excludes *kango.* More often than not, only those words widely accepted as Japanese vocabulary items are regarded as *gairaigo.* In modern Japanese, words of Euro-American (especially English) origin predominate in this category. In the current notation system, *gairaigo* are usually written with katakana, or the square-looking variety of the two Japanese syllabic writing systems. Finally, *konshugo* are words that consist of components taken from two or all three of the categories just mentioned.

Despite general agreement on these categories, the distinctions between them are not without controversy. For the present purpose, however, it will be enough to clarify our definition of loanwords in relation to *gairaigo* and *konshugo.* By "loanwords," we refer to non-Japanese expressions used in predominantly Japanese contexts: non-Chinese *gairaigo* in the general sense stated above, as well as *konshugo* that contain a *gairaigo* component in them.[7]

Functions of Loanwords

Among the many existing approaches to loanwords in Japanese, this chapter is mostly informed by those focused on the functions of and motivations for their employment. Although researchers generally agree on the functions of loanwords, each emphasizes a slightly different set of uses. Probably the most systematic among them is Leo Loveday, who classifies eleven "socio-linguistic functions" of loans into four categories of "contact-strategies": to "upgrade and westernize" (the images of the referents or the speakers), to "compensate" (for lack in vocabulary), to "obscure" (an otherwise too strong message), and to "intentionally miscode" (to make the utterance humorous).[8] There are a few oft-mentioned functions not covered by this system, such as the eye-catching effect of katakana and the Roman alphabet, the necessity of using internationally circulable terms, and the rhythmicity of English (and probably some other languages). One may bundle these under the rubric "to exploit non-semantic characteristics."[9]

While the above listing seems quite exhaustive, we can add at least one more to it: the creation of negative imagery. For instance, a fictional character may be given many (potentially upgrading) loanwords, making the person look snobbish.[10] In other words, loanwords can be employed both to upgrade and downgrade. This is because their upgrading or downgrading capability is not inherent in loanwords: the functions of loans are tendencies abstracted from their concrete use, and their actual employment is often more flexible than suggested by the list of functions above. Indeed, as James Stanlaw points out, ways of using loanwords are often improvised creatively by Japanese speakers.[11] One factor that makes the use flexible and creative is the practice of exploiting or underlining only one or a few characteristics of the words. Yanabu's cassette effect pays attention to the upgrading power of loans that derives from the general admiration of many Japanese for Western culture, as well as from the fact that they are not heavily associated with things, events, facts, or set images (let us call this their "association-thin" quality). Naturally, partial exploitation of this sort sometimes leads to the "misuse" of words from the viewpoint of the words' native users. It is well known, for instance, that English phrases printed on Japanese T-shirts often make no sense: being eye-pleasing is the sole significant quality here.

Characteristics of Loanwords

Employment of loanwords can be effective only when they are contrasted with other forms of expressions, such as a *wago*-dominant, down-to-earth style, or a bookish one with many *kango.* To be precise, neither *wago* nor *kango* represent monolithic modes of expression. For instance, exclusive use of historical *wago* would give an archaic, mythical impression, instead of the feel of day-to-day commonality. Generally speaking, however, *wago* are more frequently used in oral Japanese than in writing, and *wago*-dominant styles tend to sound soft and tender and be more expressive of feelings and intimacy. Employment of many *kango* tends to give the impression of solemnity and sublimity, making the style compact and rhythmic.[12] Loveday writes that there is "a correlation between the degree of linguistic sinification and the perceived 'heaviness' and intellectuality of the style," and Ono Rikizō finds that this "heaviness" is often associated with "authority."[13]

In comparison, loanwords often give the impressions of distance, novelty, intellectual sophistication, lightness, and the general (but stereotypical) atmosphere of the source culture. As observed in the previous section, these impressions are not necessarily inherent in loanwords. For instance, although the employment of many strange loanwords may make the text appear impenetrable, usage of the same loanwords within a social group (in-group usage) could enhance intragroup ties. Intentional (mis)use of common loanwords in a historical drama could give a familiar appearance to a historically distant scene.

Besides the new ideas that many loanwords introduce into the culture, the qualities that set them apart from *wago* and *kango,* and allow them to give the above impressions, include their sound, appearance in written forms, association-thin-ness, discrepancy in association, association with foreign elements, unfamiliarity or incomprehensibility for the majority, and strong association with and ubiquity in present-day life. For instance, in-group ties and intimacy can be emphasized when almost incomprehensible expressions are commonly circulated and understood only within a group. Association-thin-ness and foreign sounds often lead to the impression of lightness, and the association with fashionable non-Japanese elements and unfamiliarity can be exploited to "upgrade" the user's image. In actuality, such attempts sometimes fail and thus elicit the ceaseless criticisms against the overuse of loans. One should not expect all the listed qualities to be applicable to every single loan. Apparently, not all loanwords are association-thin, and many are by no means incomprehensible. What is important is that those characteristics are more salient among loans than other forms of expressions. Some of the qualities, in fact, are closely related with each other. For instance, being association-thin tends to direct audiences' attention to nonsemantic qualities, such as sounds and visual impressions, which further leads to emphasis on the beauty of the sound, the materiality of the referent, and so on.

In the following, we find concrete examples of these qualities and the impressions they produce in two science fiction anime. The first, *Macross Plus,* represents science fiction anime that employ loanwords rather frequently. Viewers encounter many unfamiliar loans in it. In the second, *Akira,* loans are not employed so frequently or in especially unique ways.

We try to demonstrate that even in such an example, loans are utilized more or less systematically, playing an important role in constructing a world. We consider mainly loanwords that are not widely used or that are used in uncommon ways (unusually frequent use of common loans is included here). They are more consciously employed as "loanwords," and in them, we observe characteristics of loanwords more vividly.

Macross Plus

Macross Plus is the fourth production of the vastly popular *Macross* series, which includes *Superdimensional Fortress Macross, Macross: Do You Remember Love? Macross II, Macross Plus, Macross 7, Macross 7: The Movie, Macross Dynamite 7,* and *Macross Zero*.[14] The series is loosely unified by a common universe, characterized by the presence of a mysterious extraterrestrial civilization called the Protoculture, attacks on the earth by the fighting race of Zentraedi (a creation of the Protoculture), and the centrality of music in human culture.

The story is set in 2040 on the colony planet of Eden. Isamu Dyson is a pilot of a robot-plane called Valkyrie. He loves flying and craves high speeds and violent maneuvers. Although he is probably the best pilot in the armed forces, he becomes marginalized because of his reckless behavior and is sent home to Eden as the test pilot of a new generation of Valkyrie, YF-19. In Eden, Isamu encounters his high-school sweetheart, Myung, and his former friend Guld, who competes with him fiercely as the test pilot of another new Valkyrie, YF-21. (Guld is of Zentraedi stock; many Zentraedi now live side by side with humans.) The three used to be good friends: the boys shared the dream of flying, and Myung, who loved to sing, was always with them. Both Isamu and Guld were attracted to her and her songs. Thus from the outset, singing and flying, the activities through which the story develops, are spotlighted. As we discuss below, these are also activities in which loanwords are heavily used.

Another central topic of *Macross Plus* is the love triangle of the protagonists. Early in the film, it is suggested that they have not contacted each other for seven years, since a tragic incident that shattered their friendship. Guld believes that Myung was deeply hurt by Isamu in the incident. In the encounter of the old friends in 2040, each still seems to carry wounds, anger, or sorrow that cast shadows over their lives. Guld and Isamu have now become pilots, and Myung works as the producer of a popular virtual idol singer, Sharon Apple. They are shown to be highly competent in their professions, yet each seems to have a sort of internal vacuum. This is especially true in the case of Myung.

Myung's job title is "producer," but her actual task is to give Sharon an emotional dimension in her performance. This is done by directly connecting Myung's central nervous system to Sharon's AI. Sharon's fans believe that she is an independent AI, complete with an emotion unit; in actuality, the most human aspect of her art is Myung's. Thus Myung's talent is heavily reflected in Sharon's coquettish songs, yet they are not the sort of music that Myung's heart desires. She has always wanted to sing and has always loved Isamu. She has failed to realize either of her dreams, and now feels at a loss. Despite this psychological instability, audiences (in and of the anime) are presented with a stunning performance by Sharon, during which Sharon's AI learns the suppressed yet profound feelings Myung has.

In the *Macross* world, music (especially Japanese-style pop music) occupies a central place in human culture. Thus it would be appalling if truly inspiring songs could be created by a computer — and that is exactly what takes place in *Macross Plus*. Later, when Sharon's AI is "completed" with the insertion of an illegal bioneuro-chip (which gives the AI an instinct for self-preservation), Myung becomes practically useless among Sharon's staff. Sharon now starts to act independently to express and realize her (Myung's) desire: she wants to have Isamu. This becomes more explicit after Sharon's team arrives at Macross City on earth and gives a concert, at which Sharon literally mesmerizes people with her songs, hacks the main computer of Macross City, captures Myung, and even starts manipulating Ghost X-9, the military's newly developed fighter plane.

Meanwhile, Guld and Isamu face a crisis: the Valkyrie project is canceled because of the military's decision to adopt the Ghost X-9, which is unmanned, instead of piloted Valkyrie fighters. This is a blow to Isamu in particular, because it not only means the loss of his job as a test pilot but also a denial of his passion for flight. That night, he and Yang, the whiz kid who designed the YF-19, secretly leave for earth in order to settle the matter in a dogfight with Ghost X-9. Guld then follows Isamu with YF-21 to put an end to their entangled relationship. Isamu and Guld fight fiercely in earth's atmosphere, and at the climax of the battle, Guld's suppressed memory of the past tragic incident suddenly comes back. The flashback shows that it was Guld, not Isamu, who attacked and hurt Myung. Their old friendship revived, the two pilots glide side by side with their engines cut.

Here, and in the contrast between Myung and Sharon, one may see a simple dichotomy of nature versus artificiality. Myung's song, sung slightly off-key with her bare voice, is cherished by the male protagonists. In contrast, for all their vast popularity, Sharon's computer-generated songs are worthless to Guld and Isamu. In the same way, flying under human control and gliding are depicted with nostalgia and yearning, while for the protagonists, the computer-operated fighter represents the end of their dreams.

This dichotomy can be understood as an expression of what Jonathan Clements and Helen McCarthy identify as "the very human fear that machines will take over."[15] However, a careful viewing of the anime reveals that the trite human–machine contrast is only a means to present what is really central to the story. The "natural" is presented as an ideal, yet the ideal is not a static, self-contained state. From the beginning, Myung's hope to become a singer (and make people feel happy) and Isamu's (as well as Guld's) desire to fly are mediated by certain forms of technology, such as recording devices and human-piloted aircraft (Figure 8.1). If the protagonists are to pursue their dreams, they must rely on machines and technology. This is how the dramaturgic space of this anime is spanned. In other words, *Macross Plus* explores the otherness that is indispensable for the individual self.

In this light, the ensuing battle scenes might be understood as suggestive of either Kristevan abjection or of sublation.[16] Isamu and Guld now start fighting together against Sharon, trying to save Myung, and in the process Guld crashes into Ghost X-9. After a direct confrontation with Sharon, Myung also recovers the mental strength to fight back and sing. In a sense, Sharon can be considered a hideous yet beautiful projection of Myung's innermost feelings, which she wants to separate from herself in order to be the person that she knows as herself. The impersonal, high-performance Ghost X-9, and even the hidden monstrosity of Guld, might be understood as aspects of Isamu that he wants to eliminate. At the same time, however, it is important that the conflict does not simply destroy the entities to be denied. Through battle, Myung's desire and Isamu's (and Guld's) monstrosity are embraced, rather than annihilated. Myung regains her dream through Sharon, and Isamu accepts Guld, who will be flying forever in space even after his death. The protagonists' lives were barren at the beginning of the film. It is only after they accept what they have tried to reject that their lives start to appear meaningful again.

Loanwords in *Macross Plus*

In *Macross Plus*, two fields of activity prominently feature technical and nondaily loanwords: first, the development and testing of the Valkyries, including combat; and second, the operation of Sharon via a computer. Indeed, military affairs and computers are the domains of science fiction anime in which we encounter the greatest number of unfamiliar loanwords.

Figure 8.1. In the movie version of *Macross Plus,* young, lively Myung looks at the human-powered technology of the plane piloted by Isamu. (From the American DVD.)

Aside from the obvious fact that these highly technical fields are known for a plethora of loans, this is attributable in large part to the omnipresence of war and computer technology in science fiction anime. However, if we take a closer look at word usage, another reason can be discerned.

Let us first list a few other examples of notable word usages in *Macross Plus.* They include (1) English in Myung's song "*Voices*"; (2) English, French, and made-up languages in Sharon Apple's songs; (3) *kango* frequently used in the statements of Colonel Millard (Isamu's boss); and (4) the lack of loanwords in Myung's song, as well as in Sharon's conversations with Myung. We must discuss these usages in tandem with those of *gairaigo* in order to fully grasp the effects of loanwords.

As mentioned earlier, the Valkyries and Sharon's AI are, in one aspect, devices that enable the protagonists to pursue their dreams and, in another, alien objects that restrict the free flight of the characters' imaginations. It is not a coincidence that many uncommon English loanwords are used to depict activities related to these machines. Some words, such as *BDI shisutemu* (BDI system), *BL yunitto* (BL unit), and *beeta endorufin* (beta-endorphin), are not intended to be fully understood by every viewer. The employment of such words by the characters can express their competence and power; at the same time, it is likely to make the audience feel a distance between the characters and themselves. Depending on the context and other means of expression employed in the scene, one or both of these effects can be underlined. In the rehearsal for Sharon's concert in Eden, for example, Myung gives directions to AI technicians to create the desired effects. Their conversation is sprinkled with technical loanwords. This shows Myung's mastery of Sharon-tech and the fact that Sharon is a manifestation of cutting-edge technology. At the same time, it tends to place viewers at a distance from the female protagonist and the AI. This sense of distance can be nullified if something "deep and real" is shown to underlie the superficial facade. That is the case with Myung, but the same cannot be said of Sharon.

Thus we observe here that the association-thin nature of loanwords (mainly English) is exploited to create the cassette effect, as well as a feeling of distance. Of course other forms of expression can create similar effects. The frequent use of hard-sounding *kango* by Colonel Millard is expressive of his authority, knowledge, and experience (the cassette effect and psychological distance). Loanwords, however, more easily transmit the impression that what is depicted is advanced technology, because Euro-American expressions are more strongly associated with modern science than *kango* or *wago* expressions are. Moreover, the unfamiliar and association-thin qualities of loanwords tend to give the impression of shallowness in a person or a body of knowledge that employs them frequently. As discussed above, something profound is often imagined to lie behind difficult-to-understand loanwords. At the same time, their overuse by certain people and fields has always been considered expressive of vanity and inner emptiness. The unfamiliar face, which can be a signifier of mastery and meaningfulness, is rejected when people see that little lies behind it. This stance is not conspicuous in *Macross Plus,* but it is implicit in the fact that certain scenes focusing on the minds of the characters are dominated by *wago.*[17]

The impression of shallowness or lightness that tends to accompany loanwords is utilized in another way, when a character utters common loans more frequently than usual. At early stages of the drama, Isamu uses expressions such as, "Okay, no problem" (English pronounced with Japanese phonemes) and "suriringu daro?" (Isn't it thrilling?), which, together with his body language, facial expressions, and manner of talking, establishes him as a certain stereotypical type of character — smooth and jocular, flippant and extroverted. It would be difficult to produce the same impression with nonloans. His character develops through the story, thus this first impression is not the whole of Isamu's personality. Yet it is noteworthy that only "lightness" and not "profundity" can be evoked by certain uses of loanwords. Discrepancies in association between the loans and corresponding nonloan expressions are the main factors here.

Let us now turn to the songs sung by Sharon and Myung, as well as Sharon's words to Myung and Isamu. As noted earlier, music is regarded as the heart of human culture in the Macross universe, so Sharon's creation of enchanting songs should be antithetical to the dominant values of the world. Interestingly, none of the lyrics of her songs are in Japanese: she sings in English, French, and made-up languages. Some melodies sound Middle Eastern. Together with certain forms her visual representation takes (she presents herself in 3-D images of a mermaid, a goddess, etc.), the songs seem to indicate Sharon's "otherness." It is a sort of otherness that is enchanting yet horrifying. Her songs are fascinating because they manipulate audience emotions — via technology like *saburiminaru efekuto* (subliminal effects) and *koketisshu parusu mōdo* (coquettish pulse mode). Their charm is strongly contrasted with the more pristine beauty of the young days shared by the protagonists, represented by the only song Myung sings. One may argue that Sharon's songs are genuinely fascinating, and there is nothing abhorrently alien about them. Indeed, the songs, composed by Kanno Yōko, are very popular among anime fans: today, two decades after the release of the original OVA, there still are Web sites dedicated to Sharon. We ourselves feel no reluctance in appreciating the music. Nevertheless, the point here is how Sharon's music is positioned in the context of *Macross Plus,* especially in contrast with Myung's song "Voices."

There can be different ways to understand "Voices," also a composition by Kanno, but we see it mainly as a poetic depiction of the trajectory that Myung's mind follows in the story (and, to a lesser degree, that Isamu and Guld follow as well). The song consists of seven segments. Segments 1, 2, 4, and 7 repeat the same simple melody, and the first and the last are sung without accompaniment. Figure 8.2 shows the original Japanese lyrics and the English translation given in the English version of the OVA, with some modifications. (The italics indicate words that are *kango* or non-loan-*konshugo*.)

In the lyrics, three words are spotlighted: "dream" *(yume),* "wind" *(kaze),* and "hmm . . ." *(n'n . . .).* The dream brings out the "darkness deep inside my heart," and with the wind the mind flies into a brighter, and perhaps symbolic, realm. After the magical journey (probably full of hopes and pains), the mind finally "returns" to a strange place that is near to the person's heart — a place where concrete symbols seem to exert little power.

Interestingly, only *wago* are used in segments 1, 2, and 7, which focus on the innerness of the person (presumably Myung). Segments 2, 3, 4, and 5 suggest a symbolic journey of the mind, and no loanwords are employed in them. Except in segment 2, there are a few *kango* and *konshugo,* and although these are very common ones that sound more or less like

"(1) Hitotsume no kotoba wa yume
Nemuri no naka kara
Mune no oku no kurayami o
Sotto tsuredasu no.

(1) The first word is "dream."
It comes to me as I sleep,
gently bringing out
the darkness deep inside my heart.

(2) Futatsume no kotoba wa kaze
Yukute o oshiete
Kamisama no mune no naka e
Tsubasa o aoru no.

(2) The second word is "wind,"
it shows me the path.
Flapping my wings, it takes me
into the arms of God.

(3) Tokete itta kanashii koto o
Kazoeru yō ni
Kin'iro no *ringo* ga
Mata hitotsu ochiru.

(3) As if counting out the sorrows
that have melted all away,
yet again, falls
another *golden apple* . . .

(4) Mita koto no nai *fūkei*
Soko ga kaeru *basho*
Tatta hitotsu no inochi ni
Tadoritsuku *basho*.

(4) A *landscape* I have never seen
that is the *place* I return,
the *place* where I reach
the only life that I hold.

(5) Furui *mahō* no hon
Tsuki no shizuku, yoru no tobari
Itsuka aeru
Yokan dake . . .

(5) An old book of *magic,*
moonlit dews, the veil of the night . . .
We will be together again
is my only *premonition* . . .

(6) We can fly, we have wings,
we can touch floating dreams.
Call me from so far
through the wind in the light.

(6) We can fly, we have wings,
we can touch floating dreams.
Call me from so far
through the wind in the light.

(7) Mittsume no kotoba wa . . . n'n . . .
Mimi o sumashitara
Anata no furueru ude o
Sotto tokihanatsu.

(7) The third word is . . . hmm . . .
If I just listen closely . . .
These trembling arms of yours that I hold . . .
. . . I gently set free.

Figure 8.2. Myung's song "Voices" from *Macross Plus*.

wago for many listeners, they seem to help shift the flow of the lyrics. To-gether with the instrumental accompaniment that starts with segment 2 and the interlude between segments 4 and 5, this word usage indicates movement and a slightly more concrete (not so purely internal) dimen-sion.[18] Unlike the rest of the lyrics, segment 6 is written entirely in En-glish. There are no truly new messages here except that the expressions are much more straightforward, and now the phrases are sung in chorus with the subject "we." Probably more important is the feel of smoothness, light-ness, and freedom that comes from the sound of English and its association-thin nature (for Japanese audiences). This segment literally reminds one

159

Words of Alienation, Words of Flight

of a slow, smooth, and delightful flight, reminiscent of the giant pterosaur that appears once in the movie. Thus we see here that *wago* is employed to express the innermost dimension, while English is utilized to produce an image of lightness and freedom. The song returns to *wago* at the end, indicating the now-altered inner state.

Although Sharon and the Ghost X-9 warplane she controls at the end of the story are contrasted with the simple beauty of Myung's song and the memory of the youthful days that accompanies it, their roles are not totally villainous. They threaten the lives of the protagonists, yet they are instrumental in awakening Myung and the others to fuller lives. After all, Sharon is a projection of Myung's hidden, genuine desire and emotion. She simplemindedly tries to realize her heart's desire. (She loves Isamu, and wants him to feel the ultimate thrill of flying. She also wants to move people with her music.) In this sense, even though Sharon is a "foreign" being, she is at the same time very human. When she talks to Myung or Isamu, she uses mainly *wago:* the only loanword she utters is *shō* in the sentence *"Shō ga hajimaru wa"* (The show will start). This lack of loanwords is highly effective in making her words sound human, emotional, and true to her heart. Sharon's sad face when she is destroyed by Isamu, and the tearlike light that crosses the surface of her central unit at the end, also makes us realize her purity and humanity. Combined with her unreasonable deeds and foreignness, however, her human dimension lets us sense something precious and powerful yet hideous inside ourselves, a theme that is more fully explored in *Akira.*

Finally, we would like to comment on the religious references in *Macross Plus.* Many anime employ religious terms, from actual (Christian, Shinto, Buddhist, and other) as well as imaginary religions. Such references may or may not be meant to transmit serious messages, but religious flavor does more than stage the appearance of profundity. It also gives the whole work a unified tone by associating it with certain images and ideas. In *Macross Plus,* only one word, *Eden,* is directly taken from the biblical tradition. It is the name of the protagonists' home planet — a place associated with yearning, dreams, friendship, faith, love, and pain. In a sense, *Macross Plus* is a story of a return to this lost paradise. Earlier, we argued that the final battle with Sharon could be understood either as expressive of abjection or sublation. The paradise may have been lost in the process whereby the protagonists become incorporated into the symbolic order. Sharon may be an almost religious manifestation of the suppressed abject. Alternatively, the paradise may have been lost in the process of alienation. The very human activities of pursuing dreams have led to the birth of the admirable, omnipotent, and dominating Sharon (and the Ghost X-9 controlled by her). Moreover, Sharon is not simply an embodiment of

Myung's desire: she also embodies the desires of her fans. In this sense, the creation of this goddess is a classic example of the alienation described by Ludwig Feuerbach.[19] At the same time, her creation is a process whereby Myung is alienated from the society that embraces Sharon's performance. Ultimately, the only way the protagonists can fight against her is to accept her as an emanation of their own minds, a symbolic return to Eden, so to speak.

Probably the only other semireligious reference in *Macross Plus* is the word *Macross* itself. It is not really a religious term, and, in the story, few explanations are given about its implications. However, it clearly suggests a fictional mythological universe, in which the origins of the human race, the enigmatic Protoculture, and the nature of human culture are alluded to. It is true that neither the word *Eden* (a loan) nor the word *Macross* (a foreign-sounding word) is likely to evoke set interpretations of the story. They generally bring vague bundles of associations that allow viewers to feel the depth of the work and interpret the story in many ways. The associations they bring in as well as their association-thin nature help carry the story, stirring the imagination of the viewers.

Akira

Like *Macross Plus, Akira* also explores "the darkness deep inside" human hearts. However, it views this enigmatic domain not simply as a psychological field but as something vast and multilayered. The year is 2019. After World War III, Tokyo has been rebuilt over Tokyo Bay. The city looks as prosperous as ever, but it is actually corrupt inside. The "colonel" (the leader of the "army," the defense force of Neo-Tokyo) calls it "a junkyard of desire-driven idiots." Antigovernment riots are unstoppable, millenarian movements are gaining momentum, and groups of hot-rodders *(bōsōzoku)* are fighting with each other in the streets. But unknown to the vast majority of the residents, the biggest threat to the security of Neo-Tokyo is the shadow of Akira, a boy whose psychic power initially destroyed old Tokyo and triggered World War III. Scientists have tried in vain to understand and control his power, and have finally secured his dissected but still dangerous body in an underground vault, where he is kept in stasis at a temperature of 0.0005 degrees Kelvin.

As the story unfolds, several main characters pursue their separate goals, which are all linked to social and cosmic powers in one way or another. The protagonist, Kaneda, is an exception in this sense: he follows his instincts and plays a catalytic role on various occasions. One evening, Tetsuo, a friend of Kaneda's and a member of his gang, nearly runs down Takashi, a mysterious boy with the bluish wrinkled face of an old man.

Tetsuo's bike explodes, apparently as a result of Takashi's psychic powers, and Tetsuo too is changed. His friends watch him get taken away by the army to a hospital, where scientists administer drugs that help him develop the psychic powers apparently triggered by his encounter with Takashi. *Akira*'s main plot revolves around Tetsuo's transformation from a weakling teen into a violent telekinetic mutant, then a monstrous baby, and ultimately the initiating force of a new universe. Government scientists, led by a person called the "doctor," try to study Tetsuo in order to discover a way to control Akira's power, while the colonel and several psychic children (Takashi, Kiyoko, and Masaru) try to stop Tetsuo from contacting and awakening Akira. Meanwhile, an antigovernment group attempts to disclose the secret of the government's project to develop psychic abilities in children, although a female member of the group, Kei, cooperates with the children later in order to prevent Tetsuo from reaching Akira and causing a catastrophe. Kaneda is always after Tetsuo, first in order to save him from the hands of the government and later in order to defeat him, after Tetsuo kills another member of the gang and numberless bystanders.

The central characters in *Akira* are more marginalized in their society than those in *Macross Plus*. Kaneda, Tetsuo, and their friends are students at a special high school for social dropouts and have few ways of expressing themselves other than burning up the road and fighting rival gangs. Tetsuo is a weaker member of the group and, as such, feels oppressed even among his friends. Kaneda has been his protector since childhood, yet this very fact has been a source of Tetsuo's inferiority complex. Similarly, the psychic children do not have a place in the world outside the government lab. They depend on special drugs to sustain their lives, their power is a menace in the eyes of ordinary people, and they appear too strange and too conspicuous to blend in with the masses. Kei and her fellow underground fighters are placed on the wanted list by the police, and they engage in dangerous activities to subvert the government. Even the colonel, who holds a high position in the military and the government, becomes marginalized because no one on the council understands the imminent danger of Akira. The colonel detests the corrupt politicians and the people who have forgotten the devastation of World War III, and he eventually launches a coup d'état to protect the city.

At the same time, each of the socially oppressed characters represents transforming power and new possibilities. They see and feel social and personal impasses, and desperately try to break these deadlocks. The dynamic of ruling versus subversive power is ubiquitous in the film and is most impressively presented in the metamorphoses of Tetsuo. Yet, even though the most significant characters are teenagers who struggle and exert subversive power, and the story can legitimately be understood as

Marginalized	Dominant
Tetsuo	Kaneda
Kaneda and friends	school, "Army," the colonel, adults
psychic children	adults (big people, including Tetsuo)
the colonel	politicians, corrupt society
Kei, Ryū, and underground fighters	government, "Army"
Akira (underground)	Neo-Tokyo (high-rise)
humanity, life	order and control (science and technology)

Figure 8.3. Contrasts between the Marginalized and the Dominant in *Akira*.

expressive of what Susan Napier calls "stubborn adolescent resistance," the strength of *Akira* lies partly in the fact that it successfully generalizes a characteristic experience of youths into the wider issues of human existence.[20] This generalization occurs through a series of contrasts, some of which are marked by word usages.

Figure 8.3 schematically illustrates these contrasts. (See the illustration in Figure 8.4 as well.) In the first column are the persons or entities that are marginalized, oppressed, or hidden, and in the second are the dominant restrictive powers that will be subverted by the marginal ones. Members of the first column are closer to the sources of the "power" around which the story revolves, but are deadlocked and are not in control of that power. In various scenes they can be regarded as manifestations of that untamed power, even though the nature of such forces remains more or less enigmatic throughout the story. A few central characters are listed on both sides of the table, indicating the complex structure of the story, as well as the shifts in viewpoint. For instance, Kaneda has the upper hand in his relationship with Tetsuo at the beginning of the story (row 1 in the table), but he and his gang, in turn, are powerless against schoolteachers, military officers, the colonel, and others, who appear to embody the power structure that lies behind them (row 2). The colonel, for his part, is not an icon of the Establishment either, and he becomes marginalized in his fight against the corrupt political authorities (row 4). Audiences are generally led to side with the weaker of each pair. When we first meet Tetsuo and Kaneda in the anime, for instance, Tetsuo looks fairly docile. Kaneda's body language and voice convey his arrogance, which makes him a little difficult for many viewers to identify themselves with, although this impression of Kaneda does not last.

In the story, the marginalized take actions directly or indirectly to change the present state, relying on specific media that we call "vehicles of

Figure 8.4. A cityscape from *Akira*. The contrast between the high-rise buildings and the dilapidated area in the foreground is comparable with other contrasts in the film. (From the American DVD.)

alteration": reckless riding on motorcycles, paranormal powers, religion, terrorism, science, and even the evolutionary process. The vehicles may help alter the power structure. At the same time, they help form and internally alter those who resort to them. Tetsuo, for instance, yearns to ride Kaneda's enormous motorcycle, which symbolizes higher in-group status and the enhanced power he can exert in the world. After awakening to his psychic power, he starts behaving more violently and arrogantly. These "vehicles" not only change the world around Tetsuo and his relationships with it, but clearly transform Tetsuo from within.

Although vehicles of alteration empower the marginalized, they may also turn into devices for domination and control. Motorcycles may have a liberating power for the riders, yet their activities may also grind others down. Science may free humanity from the tight grip of established social power, yet it is chiefly depicted in the anime as oppressive and reactionary. Moreover, vehicles of alteration are not just instruments passively controlled by someone; they drive people to take actions using them, and such actions are instrumental in manifesting the force of life. Indeed, the marginalized, their vehicles, and the manifestation of untamed power are inseparable from each other, and together they dominate the screen.

Toward the end of the film, Tetsuo, no longer able to control the "power," turns into a gigantic, grotesque baby and then into an amorphous, amoebic entity. He asks Kaneda for help as his ego collapses and his body swallows his girlfriend, Kaori, and Kaneda. This metamorphosis is the exact reverse of the evolutionary process that Kei refers to in her explanation/contemplation of the power of Akira. As Napier points out, it is also possible to see abjection in this transmogrification.[21] What finally stops Tetsuo, or the force that has overtaken him, is Akira, who is reconstituted in part by the power of the psychic children. The "Akira phenomenon" that annihilated old Tokyo is now reinitiated, destroying and absorbing everything in its range. The doctor observes the birth of a new universe in this phenomenon. Kaneda, who is swallowed into the new universe and then saved by the children, experiences it as a flight through memory: pieces of Tetsuo's memory, the children's memories, and the memory of the human species, life, and the universe. Perhaps Tetsuo has not actually been stopped: with the return of Akira, the regressive process may simply have gone deeper, reaching the primal memory of the "Beginning." Tetsuo, the children, and Akira disappear to another world. It is suggested, however, that Tetsuo's and Akira's power now exist tangibly (although not in the form of psychic abilities) in Kaneda and probably many others.

Loanwords in *Akira*

We do not encounter many uncommon loanwords in *Akira,* but we can still observe certain tendencies in their usage. Let us first examine the series of contrasts discussed above, which is linguistically marked. In the first scene with Tetsuo and Kaneda mentioned earlier, Tetsuo is examining Kaneda's red motorcycle. In addition to his rather polite expressions, Tetsuo uses several not-so-common loanwords that describe parts of the machine. This "correct" use of technical terms, which hints at Tetsuo's tameness, is in sharp contrast with the few jargonized loanwords used by Kaneda and other gang members. The loanwords used to describe the motorcycle convey the idea that this vehicle of alteration is not just a powerful, phallic machine; it is a computer-controlled and technically sophisticated vehicle, foreign enough for Tetsuo to take him to a new world. In addition to the loans' association with technical knowledge, what is exploited here is not so much the viewers' unfamiliarity with the expressions as Tetsuo's. The few jargonized loanwords used by Kaneda and his friends (such as *shirobiru,*[22] or a white building, meaning a hospital) are well incorporated into their rough, recusant style of conversation, which also transmits a feeling of intimacy among the gang members. Their manner of speech is clearly distinct from that of the teachers and the officers they confront, who sound oppressive, mechanical, or indifferent.[23]

Several uncommon loanwords are employed from science and technology (Figure 8.3, row 7). Although the terms used by the scientists are not as exotic as those in *Macross Plus,* words such as *supesharu pataan* (special pattern), *nanbaazu* (numbers), and *ao no pataan* (pattern blue) have special meanings in the story. Not many viewers are familiar with the expression *dyuwaa shitsu* (Dewar room), which confines the frozen body of Akira. Scientists, especially the doctor, try to analyze, understand, and control the power of Akira and the psychic ability of the mutant children, relying on loanwords as well as other "scientific" *kango* expressions, such as *shindenzu* (electrocardiogram) and *ryōshi hōkai* (quantum disintegration). This "scientific" language is strongly contrasted with the languages of those who are objectified by science (i.e., the psychic children's predominantly *wago* utterances and Tetsuo's recusant style — see note 23). "Scientific" language also contrasts with the visual and auditory images that express the manifestation of the untamed power (e.g., Tetsuo's metamorphoses and the Akira phenomenon). The scientists are in pursuit of truth, yet their organized "truth" turns out to be superficial and powerless before the violent manifestation of the universe's raw power. This is clearly shown by the destruction of the research and control facilities that we witness in the film. The doctor's heavy reliance on computer outputs and circumlocutions in understanding Tetsuo's and Akira's abilities also indicates the desperate indirectness (or perhaps irrelevance) of scientific language.[24] The impression loanwords convey of meaningfulness (the cassette effect) and the feel of association-thin distance and shallowness are quite appropriate for characterizing the scientific activities in the story.

Some other contrasting pairs in Figure 8.3 are also linguistically marked, although not necessarily with loans. Generally, the characters who use loanwords or *kango* are most frequently those who appear only on the right-hand column of the table, that is, army officers, policemen, government officials, and scientists. The psychic children, who speak predominantly in *wago,* and Akira, who does not utter a word, appear only on the left side of the table. In between are the hot-rodders, the underground fighters (included in "adults"), and the colonel. Among these, the colonel uses *kango* more frequently than others. Kaneda and his friends do not utter many *kango:* quite frequently they employ loans when referring to motorcycles or activities related to them. This tendency in the use of loans and *kango* may simply reflect the reality — people are likely to use more *kango* and technical loans on duty than in casual conversations. The fact remains, however, that wording is utilized, consciously or unconsciously, to distinguish among those who take different social positions in the story.

Most of the uncommon loans in the film concern control over power and primarily refer to activities related to motorcycles or science (the latter focusing on control of psychic power). Yet they are also used effectively to label the military and its activities — for example, *aamii* (the army), SOL (a satellite laser weapon), the psychic children (who are described as *gurotesuku* [grotesque], for example), *bebii rūmu* (the psychic children's nursery or baby room), and phenomena related to untamed forces (e.g., *dezasutaa* [disaster]). The foreign, association-thin characteristics, as well as the sounds of (English) loans, are appropriate for indicating the mobility and unfathomable potential of the motorcycles and other vehicles. In another way, the same association-thin and foreign-sounding qualities are also employed to emphasize unfamiliarity: when loans are used to label something powerful yet loathsome, they tend to exaggerate the impressions of distance and materiality. Depending on the subjective position of the speaker, such labels can be attached to either social oppressors or the social abject.

All the attempts to control the "power," however, eventually fail. The ones who could touch the untamed power are not those who try to control it by using social devices and loanwords. Probably the closest to this force, the secret of life and the universe, are the psychic children, who speak predominantly in childish *wago* expressions. Akira, who is more like the secret itself, is wordless, and at the end of the story, neither Kaneda nor the psychic children can provide concrete expressions when trying to refer to the crux of the whole event. Just as in Myung's song "Voices," the most significant thing cannot be expressed in concrete words.

In this connection, the title of the anime, *Akira,* needs to be discussed briefly. It is not a loanword but an ordinary male name in Japan. However, this name, usually denoted by kanji, is written either in the Roman alphabet or in the katakana syllabary in the film — notations that are regularly employed to denote foreign expressions and loans. In other words, this word is rendered foreign in the anime. It is in fact a common practice in Japanese pop media to defamiliarize ordinary expressions by writing them in Roman characters or katakana. Audiences (and readers of the original manga) usually assume that "Akira" is the name of a person. At the beginning of the film, however, they may conceive of the possibility that it is a code name given to something nonhuman, something to be kept secret, in part because of the notation.[25] Just like the words "Macross" and "Eden," this defamiliarized expression, "Akira," is given semireligious connotations, and the initial uncertainty about its referent works as an instrument to keep the story in motion. It enables the religious fanatics, who expect the "advent" of Akira as their savior, to gain momentum. At the same time, the hollow materiality of the word *a-ki-ra* (written and pronounced as three separate syllables) transmits the awe and the fear some people in the drama must be feeling. This almost empty expression is probably the only way to refer to the most enigmatic and significant of referents.

Conclusion

We have discussed how loanwords are used to construct the worlds of two anime, *Macross Plus* and *Akira*. They are frequently employed to suggest psychological distance, powerful potential, shallowness, charm, intimacy, and other qualities that the characters in the story and the audience should be feeling toward the referents or the utterers of the words. Together with other vocabulary items, loans powerfully depict the characters' subjective worlds. Moreover, we have tried to demonstrate that various functions of loanwords come from exploiting the distinctive qualities that separate them from *wago* and *kango*. Loans are especially flexible because they tend to be association-thin: as semimonadic signifiers, they strongly stimulate our imagination. This is a main (but not the only) reason loans can be used so creatively, to indicate characters' free flight, on one occasion, and their alienation, on another.

To stir the imagination means to become open to interpretations. Here lies another reason for the imaginative but sometimes nonchalant use of loanwords. The point here is the status of Euro-American languages, especially English, as a common basis for intellectual play. A body of knowledge being acquired by a group of people is often employed as an intellectual playground: they joke about it, parody well-known phrases, improvise witty remarks based on their common (but not commonplace) knowledge, and so on. There are not many fields, however, in which the majority of contemporary Japanese can enjoy such shared gamelike pursuits. English (and, to a lesser degree, other major European languages), offer one such common basis for many Japanese, because they have long been areas of familiar yet incomplete knowledge. This provides opportunities to participate in imaginative and intellectual experiments, stunts, and enjoyment. This enjoyment is not unlike that of science fiction adventures in which creators and readers/audiences often play with leading-edge or fictional concepts and findings of science. That in fact may be another reason why many science fiction anime are rich in loans.

Notes

1. It is in fact written in a made-up language. The quoted text is supposed to mean "Greenery on the earth, on the earth, the fragrance of flowers."

2. *Shinseiki evangerion*, dir. Anno Hideaki, TV series, 26 episodes (1995–96); translated as *Neon Genesis Evangelion: Perfect Collection*, 8-DVD box set (ADV Films, 2002); *Ginga eiyū densetsu*, dir. Ishiguro Noboru, OVA series, 110 episodes,

4-DVD box sets (44 DVDs) (Hapinetto Pikuchaazu, 2003–4); *Akira,* dir. Ōtomo Katsuhiro (1988); translated on DVD (Pioneer, 2001). *Macross Plus* was originally released as an OVA (original video animation, or direct-to-video) series, which was then reedited as a movie. The movie version condenses the four-episode OVA series, but a few scenes are added to make the work more entertaining and make some messages clearer. The descriptions and the analysis here are mostly applicable to both versions. *Macross Plus,* dir. Kawamori Shōji, OVA; translated on 2 DVDs (Manga Video, 1999); *Macross Plus,* dir. Kawamori Shōji; translated as *Macross Plus – Movie Edition,* DVD (Manga Video, 2002).

3. One may recall a Native American's magical use of script reported by Claude Lévi-Strauss, although what Yanabu discusses is not limited to script, and he is more appreciative of the power of monadic signifiers. Yanabu Akira, *Hon'yaku bunka o kangaeru* (Thoughts on translation culture) (Tokyo: Hōsei University Press, 1978); Yanabu Akira, *Hon'yaku to wa nani ka* (What is translation?) (Tokyo: Hōsei University Press, 1985); Claude Lévi-Strauss, *Tristes Tropiques,* trans. John Weightman and Doreen Weightman (New York: Atheneum, 1974).

4. *Rubi* (which comes from "ruby," the name of a small font) signifies small characters usually printed directly above or to the side of *kanji* characters and used to denote their pronunciation. (On the difference between *kanji* and other kinds of characters, see the section that follows.) In actual application, however, they frequently add or twist meanings. For instance, the word meaning "stranger" that is usually pronounced *ihōjin* may be accompanied by *rubi* that read *sutorenjaa* or *etoranje* (derived from the English or French terms), *totsukuni no hito, achi-san* (a local children's dialect), the proper name of a certain person, and so on, each adding a different flavor to the word. When the *rubi* is a loanword, the word to which it is attached often (but not always) serves to explain an unfamiliar borrowed expression. Besides *rubi,* many manga artists also employ elaborate systems of notes to give commentaries on the manga or messages to the readers. For more on the use of *rubi* to gloss unfamiliar expressions in Japanese prose science fiction, see Takayuki Tatsumi, "The Japanese Reflection of Mirrorshades," in *Storming the Reality Studio: Casebook of Cyberpunk and Postmodern Science Fiction,* ed. Larry McCaffery (Durham, N.C.: Duke University Press, 1991), 366–73.

5. Of course there is a prehistory during which *wago* were formed and imported from indigenous and foreign languages. For more information, see, for example, Leo J. Loveday, *Language Contact in Japan: A Socio-linguistic History* (Oxford: Clarendon, 1996); Shinmura Izuru, *Gairaigo no hanashi* (Discussions on loanwords) (Tokyo: Kyōiku Shuppan, 1976); Tanaka Takehiko, *Gairaigo to wa nanika* (What is gairaigo?) (Tokyo: Chōeisha, 2002); Umegaki Minoru, *Nihon gairaigo no kenkyū* (A study of loanwords in Japanese) (Tokyo: Kenkyūsha, 1963).

6. Strictly speaking, many so-called *kango* are not borrowed from Chinese but created in Japan using *kanji* and their original (although Japanized) sounds (*jion*). To denote the group of words that include such Japanese-made *kango, jiongo* (words that utilize Chinese sounds of *kanji*) is a more appropriate expression. See, for example, Takashima Toshio, *Kanji to Nihonjin* (Kanji and the Japanese people) (Tokyo: Bungei Shunjū, 2001). Further, recent imports from China are often read with the sounds of modern Chinese (Mandarin or other), not with Japanized *jion.* These new imports should be regarded as loans rather than *kango.*

7. "Non-Japanese expressions" refers to words and phrases used in their original non-Japanese forms, directly reflecting the sound of the original vocabulary

item. *Gairaigo* here do not include Japanese-sounding words coined to translate foreign words *(hon'yakugo)*.

8. Loveday, *Language Contact in Japan*, 199.

9. On eye-catching effects, see Gillian Kay, "English Loanwords in Japanese," *World Englishes* 14, no. 1 (1995): 67–76. On circulable terms, see Kay and Fukao Tokiko, *Katakana kotoba: Nihon ni kikashita gaikokugo* (Katakana words: Foreign words naturalized in Japan) (Tokyo: Saimaru Shuppankai, 1979). On rhythmicity, see Loveday, *Language Contact in Japan*, and Kōmoto Eriko, "Gendai Nihon shakai ni okeru gaikokugo gairaigo no yakuwari" (The roles of foreign words and loanwords in contemporary Japanese society) (BA thesis, Kōbe University, 2000). For other work on function and motivations of loanwords, see Ishino Hiroshi, *Gendai gairaigo kō* (On contemporary loanwords) (Tokyo: Taishūkan, 1983); Ishiwata Toshio, *Nihongo no naka no gairaigo* (Loanwords in Japanese) (Tokyo: Iwanami, 1985); James Stanlaw, "Japanese and English: Borrowing and Contact," *World Englishes* 6, no. 2 (1987): 93–109; James Stanlaw, "'For Beautiful Human Life': The Use of English in Japan," in *Re-Made in Japan: Everyday Life and Consumer Taste in a Changing Society,* ed. Joseph Tobin (New Haven, Conn.: Yale University Press, 1992), 58–76; Yanabu, *Hon'yaku bunka o kangaeru*; Yanabu, *Hon'yaku to wa nani ka.*

10. More precisely, the character is supposed to be using loans for "upgrading," yet their negative effects are fully expected by the writer.

11. Stanlaw, "For Beautiful Human Life."

12. On softness and rhythm, see Tanaka, *Gairaigo to wa nani ka*; on feelings, see Satake Hideo, "Wago, nazuke, ryūkōka" (Wago, naming, pop songs), *Gengo seikatsu* 359 (1981): 46–52; on intimacy, see Tamamura Saburō, "Wago no hataraki" (Functions of wago), *Gengo seikatsu* 359 (1981): 36–45.

13. Loveday, *Language Contact in Japan*, 42; Ono Rikizō, "Wago to *Genji monogatari* no koto nado" (Wago, *The Tale of Genji,* and other topics), *Gengo seikatsu* 359 (1981): 64–68.

14. For an overview of the whole anime franchise, see Jonathan Clements and Helen McCarthy, *The Anime Encyclopedia: A Guide to Japanese Animation since 1917* (Berkeley, Calif.: Stone Bridge, 2001), 234–36.

15. Ibid., 235.

16. Julia Kristeva, *Powers of Horror: An Essay on Abjection,* trans. Leon S. Roudiez (New York: Columbia University Press, 1982).

17. Some anime like *Patlabor 2* (1993) exhibit this "shallow profundity" in some scenes but avoid it elsewhere by not using difficult loans even in certain high-tech scenes. *Kidō keisatsu patoreibaa 2: The Movie,* dir. Oshii Mamoru; translated as *Patlabor 2,* DVD (Manga Video, 2000).

18. This effect is in fact quite subtle. In segment 4, for instance, the original Japanese words for the words *place* and *landscape* are *basho* and *fūkei,* respectively. One may imagine replacing these expressions with *wago,* such as *tokoro* and *nagame.* The resultant phrases are somewhat vaguer and more elusive than the original, at least for the authors. This impression comes in part from the *wago,* and in part from the change in the number of syllables. Some of the italicized words, such as *ringo* (apple), cannot be replaced with common *wago* expressions.

19. Ludwig Feuerbach, *The Essence of Christianity,* ed. and trans. E. Graham Waring and F. W. Strothmann (New York: Ungar, 1957).

20. The quote is from Susan J. Napier, *Anime from Akira to Princess Mononoke: Experiencing Contemporary Japanese Animation* (New York: Palgrave, 2001), 43.

Conversely, one may also say that the anime successfully connects the general issues of human existence to more particular activities of the youths.

21. Ibid., 43–46. Napier also points out that the *bōsōzoku* and other oppressed people in the anime can be regarded as social abjects.

22. More precisely, *shirobiru* is a *konshugo,* a combination of a *wago* and a loan.

23. Kaneda often changes his mode of speech in accordance with the context. However, the contrast between his style and many adults' still holds. Likewise, later in the anime Tetsuo talks as roughly as his friends, in contexts such as fighting with rival gangs (even before he acquires his new powers). However, it is the contrast between these scenes and the early scenes with Kaneda that counts here.

24. This characterization of science is more evident in the manga version, in which a team of Western scientists tries to analyze the Akira phenomenon in an American aircraft carrier anchored off Neo-Tokyo. Ōtomo Katsuhiro, *Akira,* 6 vols. (Tokyo: Kōdansha, 1984–93); translated by Yoko Umezawa et al. (Milwaukie, Ore.: Dark Horse, 2000–2002).

25. This effect is even more pronounced in the manga version. The first volume does not reveal that "Akira" is in fact a personal name, although Kiyoko (one of the psychic children) calls him (or it) "Akira-kun," a form used to address a young male or the speaker's junior. Even this expression could be interpreted as Kiyoko's anthropomorphosis of a nonhuman entity. The colonel's statement "Akira will wake up!" *(akira wa okiru!)* can also be read as "Akira will take place!" This ambiguity is intentional. In fact, the idea of Akira as a nonhuman entity is not so far off the mark. Akira is a boy in appearance, yet his mind does not seem to be working like a human's: he is more like an incarnation of the universal power. In the film, Akira remains an enigmatic entity for Kaneda and other protagonists for a long while. Answering Kaneda's question "What is Akira?" Kei answers that Akira is said to be an absolute power responsible for our evolutionary process.

9. Sex and the Single Cyborg
Japanese Popular Culture Experiments in Subjectivity

Sharalyn Orbaugh

I found that these people possessed a method of communicating their experiences and feelings to one another by articulate sounds. . . . This was indeed a godlike science, and I ardently desired to become acquainted with it . . . for I easily perceived that, although I longed to discover myself to the cottagers, I ought not to make the attempt until I had first become master of their language; which knowledge might enable me to make them overlook the deformity of my figure; for with this also the contrast perpetually presented to my eyes had made me acquainted.

— Mary Shelley, *Frankenstein*

Visual representations of cyborgs are . . . not only utopian or dystopian prophesies, but rather reflections of a contemporary state of being. The image of the cyborg body functions as a site of condensation and displacement. It contains on its surface and in its fundamental structure the multiple fears and desires of a culture in the process of transformation.

— Jennifer Gonzalez, "Envisioning Cyborg Bodies"

As Jennifer Gonzalez contends, cyborgs are not about the future, they are about contemporary society and its current transformations. Claudia Springer concurs, writing that "what is really being debated in the discourse surrounding a cyborg future are contemporary disputes concerning gender and sexuality, with the future providing a clean slate, or a blank screen, onto which we can project our fascination and fears."[1] In this chapter I discuss recent Japanese narratives that use the figure of the cyborg to explore new paradigms of subjectivity, as the advanced nations of the world become increasingly postmodern, post-national, postindustrial, and even posthuman. In particular, I focus on two aspects of subjectivity that have been fundamental to the modern — as opposed to postmodern — notion of personhood: sexuality and singularity. The figure of the cyborg — that embodied amalgam of the organic and the technological — confounds the modernist criteria for subjectivity and, when featured in narrative, allows readers/viewers to think through the ramifications of the changes we currently face.

The cultural products that engage the notion of the cyborg help us come to terms with the meaning of this new relationship between the human body and technology *as that relationship unfolds:* narrative helps us work through the fears and desires of a particular historical-cultural moment. We are each of us already compelled daily to face the breakdown of the distinction between the mechanical/technological and the organic/biotic. Cyborg narratives allow us, in Gonzalez's phrasing, to personify, condense, and displace the anxieties and hopes raised by this situation.

Donna Haraway, the best-known theorist of cyborg subjectivity, explains some of the fears and hopes that most fundamentally characterize cyborg narrative: "In retelling origin stories, cyborg authors subvert the central myths of origin of Western culture. We have all been colonized by those origin myths, with their longing for fulfillment in apocalypse."[2] She suggests that the only way to avoid the hypocrisies and dangers of Western culture's current trajectory is to recast origin myths — which cultures use to explain their own ontology and subjectivity to themselves — to confront and subvert narratives of (false) innocence and apocalypse.

I would contend that, in general, Japanese popular-culture forms work through issues of apocalypse, survival, and the impossibility of establishing innocence far more often and in terms of greater moral complexity than those of North America. For example, Susan Napier has argued that a multitude of Japanese popular-culture products — from the 1950s Godzilla films to the internationally popular anime film *Akira* (1988) — can be seen as attempts to grapple with issues arising from the 1945 atomic bombings and the very real possibility of global annihilation that they implied.[3] In the Godzilla films we see another common characteristic of Japanese popular narrative: both the destructive *and* the potentially productive aspects of technology are explored. Consequences, including occasionally the pointless deaths of protagonists, are rarely evaded in Japanese popular narrative.

In another sense, too, Japanese cultural production may offer a particularly fertile area for the study of cyborgs and subjectivity. Japanese social discourse incorporates robots and cyborgs with little of the implicit dread often found in North American references. The manga artist Shirō Masamune has remarked that

> from childhood Japanese children are educated in robots/robotics. Starting with [the cartoon characters] Astro Boy and Arare-chan, and progressing to Doraemon — these are all robots. Japanese children give robots names and see them as friends, and are raised from the beginning with an image of robots that portrays them as extremely useful.[4]

As opposed to the terrifying figure of Darth Vader — one of the first memorable cyborgs encountered by children in North America — Japanese children enjoy a wide range of characters that mix human and machinic elements.[5] Certainly it is difficult to overlook the large number of robots, cyborgs, and "metal fighting suits" in Japanese television, anime, and manga. While many of these narrative products can be dismissed as unimaginative or derivative, others are complex and thoughtful, and their sheer quantity means that the various issues at the heart of the new cyborg paradigm are explored in Japanese popular culture perhaps more thoroughly than anywhere else. (And, given the extraordinary popularity of manga and anime outside Japan, this exploration is shared by increasing numbers of international viewers.)

Further, Japanese popular culture may enjoy a particularly significant, persistent engagement with the cyborgian because of its participation in what I call the "Frankenstein syndrome." I have proposed this notion as a parallel to what the film theorist Rey Chow has called the "King Kong syndrome." Drawing inspiration from the 1933 film, she identifies a tendency on the part of Western countries to read the non-West as the "site of the 'raw' material that is 'monstrosity,' [which] is produced for the surplus value of spectacle, entertainment, and spiritual enrichment for the 'First World.'"[6] My inflection of the parallel notion, the Frankenstein syndrome — inspired by Mary Shelley's 1818 novel rather than any of the films — refers to the tendency of developing countries, those defined as "monstrous" and "raw" by the already developed nations, to see themselves in those same terms.

When Japan reopened to the world in the mid-nineteenth century after more than 250 years of isolation, one of the most powerful messages of Western discourse the Japanese absorbed was the "scientifically proven" racial and cultural inferiority of the "Asiatic" race. Less than fifty years later, Japan had replicated every aspect of Anglo-European modernity with astounding success: cutting-edge science, medicine, and technology; a colonial empire supported by a powerful military; a fully developed industrial economy. Nonetheless, after helping the Allied powers defeat Germany in World War I and becoming a founding member of the League of Nations, Japan was once again relegated to the position of anomalous other by the other founding nations' refusal to incorporate a statement of basic racial equality in the League charter.[7]

Like the monster in Shelley's *Frankenstein*, rejected first by his creator and eventually by all the other humans with whom he tried to establish contact, the people of modernizing Japan were forced time and again to recognize that even the complete acquisition of the "godlike science" of language — in the form of the discourses of industrial, post-Enlightenment modernity — was not enough to save them from the curse of monstrosity in the eyes of the West. All modern Japanese literature and art has been (and continues to be) produced under the shadow of this recognition, leading to an unusual concern with monstrous or anomalous bodies/subjectivities and various attendant issues (Kotani Mari makes a similar point).[8] In striking similarity to the key themes in Shelley's *Frankenstein*, some of the most pressing issues for Japanese modern narrative have been questions of legitimacy and illegitimacy, nonnormative forms of reproduction, the hybridity of bodies or subjectivities, and ambiguous or anomalous incarnations of gender/sex/sexuality.[9] I have written elsewhere about the effects of these culturally specific concerns on the development of the figure of the cyborg/robot/android in Japanese popular culture from 1870 to the present.[10] Here I confine myself to discussing two very recent Japanese cyborg narratives and to a limited set of questions on cyborg subjectivity.

The title of this chapter incorporates two of the key terms I use to explore cyborg subjectivity: *sex* and *single*. I begin by explaining why sexuality and singularity are so important in this context and then discuss two recent anime narratives — *Shinseiki evangerion* (1995–96, *Neon Genesis Evangelion*) and *Kōkaku kidōtai: Ghost in the Shell* (1995) — in terms of the nexus of contemporary fears or desires about subjectivity being negotiated through those depictions.[11]

Sexuality and singularity are not unrelated, of course, since partnered sex and its various consequences present one of the most common contexts within which the human experience of the singularity of the subject is challenged — through intimacy, loss of self in orgasm, pregnancy, infection, and so on. Luce Irigaray has written eloquently (though in a different context) about the experience of sexuality/subjectivity that is not singular: "Within herself, she is already two — but not divisible into one(s)."[12] She eventually arrives at the useful term *not-two* for this doubled but coherent kind of subjectivity.

In one highly interesting attempt to map the conceptual limits of human subjectivity, Elizabeth Grosz has invoked the examples of conjoined twins and intersexed people.[13] A consideration of these naturally occurring anomalous subjectivities can help in understanding the conceptual challenges involved in cyborg subjectivity.

Conjoined twins challenge the notion of the individual, autonomous identity housed in a singular body; they demonstrate the possibility of separate personalities and consciousnesses — separate subjectivities — in a single physical unit. Moreover, although conjoined twins have separate consciousnesses, Grosz quotes first-person accounts that underscore the fact that the "usual hard and fast distinction between the boundaries of one subject or another are continually blurred" to a degree unimaginable to morphologically singular human beings, even including identical twins.[14]

In the case of intersexed or ambisexual people, the morphological binaries of male and female — usually taken to be utterly natural and universal — are confounded. Again it may be difficult for the single-sexed individual to conceptualize the experience of subjectivity embodied in a way that is not sexually unitary or singular. But it is important to stress that while conjoined twins and intersexed people cannot be considered and do not experience themselves as singular/unitary/one, neither can they be considered (nor do they experience themselves) as doubled/separate/two.[15] They are incarnations of the aforementioned "not-two."

In some kinds of cyborgs, it is possible at least to sketch the boundaries, the interfacing surfaces, between one component (the biotic) and another (the techno-mechanical), but once the two are joined, those boundaries are meaningless in terms of determining or experiencing subjectivity.[16] Some common examples of this would include people who have been inoculated and those with transplanted organs or prosthetic devices. We can separate the parts, but once they are combined, they make one functional unit.

In premodern and modern(ist) conceptualizations of subjectivity, naturally occurring anomalies ("monsters") such as conjoined twins and hermaphrodites functioned to mark the borders of the "normal" embodiment of the "normal" subject. In Judith Butler's terms, these "monsters" formed the constitutive "outside" that "secures and, hence, fails to secure the very borders of materiality."[17] Cyborgs, which are by definition *not* naturally occurring, serve in a new but equally significant way to mark the borders of modern(ist) subjectivity and simultaneously to reveal the ways those borders are breaking down and being redrawn in postmodern, posthuman paradigms.

In the case of cultural production in Japan, cyborgs and other anomalous — hybrid, not-two — embodiments perform the same function: that of marking the abject borders that serve to define normal subjectivity. But in Japan, because of the Frankenstein syndrome, the bodies or subjectivities marked as anomalous may simultaneously be identified as simply

"Japanese," since monstrosity *is* normal for those defined as other by Western hegemonic discourse. This allows for an exploration of the hybrid, monstrous, cyborg subject from a sympathetic, interior point of view rarely found in North American cultural products. Another culturally specific aspect of Japanese narrative is the frequent appearance of "female" or ambiguously gendered cyborgs. This, too, relates back, I would argue, to Japan's experience of feminization by the dominant Western powers of the nineteenth century.[18] The Japanese people currently involved in scholarship and cultural production around the figure of the cyborg are completely knowledgeable about Western science fiction and cyborg theory, and many of them participate fully in the international conversation on the topic. Nonetheless, the history of Japan's modernization has produced a body of cyborg discourse that differs in important respects from that of North America.

The questions most frequently asked about conjoined twins and intersexed people are echoed in contemporary Japanese narrative explorations of the cyborg. We might wonder of conjoined twins, which is really in control of the body, or to what extent do they have separate control? How do they coordinate movement and agency? In the case of cyborgs we are tempted to ask the same question: what is the power relationship between the biotic and techno-mechanical components; which is "really" in control? These questions may be as meaningless for the cyborg itself as they are when posed to conjoined twins — but those of us who consider ourselves to be morphologically singular beings strain through such questions to understand dual subjects.

Similarly, many have wondered of both conjoined twins and hermaphrodites: how and with whom do they have sex? (One of the most frequently reported facts about the original "Siamese twins," Chang and Eng Bunker, is that they married sisters and fathered more than twenty children.) This question does not arise solely out of prurient curiosity but out of our fundamental belief, "identified by Foucault as the sign of modernity itself, that sex 'harbours what is most true in ourselves.'"[19] It is no surprise, then, that many explorations of the nature and potential of cyborg subjectivity involve a focus on sexuality in some sense as well — even if the focus is on the impossibility or irrelevance of some form of sexual behavior.

The two Japanese anime under consideration here are no exception. *Evangelion* explores the aspects of human sexuality involving bodily conjoining, intimacy, and penetration/permeability played out through a cyborg subject. *Ghost in the Shell* examines and rejects old forms of species reproduction in favor of cyborgian and cybernetic alternatives.

Evangelion, directed by Anno Hideaki, was broadcast every Wednesday night from October 1995 to March 1996 on Tokyo TV Channel 12, a

177

Sex and the Single Cyborg

total of twenty-six episodes. It was immediately and hugely popular. The story is extremely complex, so here I provide only a brief synopsis. The setting is 2015, fifteen years after the global disaster known as "Second Impact" when a meteor had hit Antarctica and the resulting shock waves, tidal waves, and melting ice cap had killed billions of people. This is the official story. Most people are not aware that what actually happened was an attack by an unknown alien machine or creature, called a *shito* — a word that means "apostle" or "disciple" but is always translated into English, at Anno's insistence, as "angel." The creature was destroyed, and the resulting explosion is what actually caused Second Impact. It is now fifteen years later, and angels have begun appearing again. The most powerful of conventional weapons are useless against them; the only effective weapon is a kind of huge "metal suit" robot, called an "EVA," designed and deployed by a special international team called "NERV." The EVAs look very much like the conventional fighting robots of the metal suit ("mecha") genre, but they have a few idiosyncratic characteristics: they can be piloted only by fourteen-year-olds; and each EVA and its designated pilot must achieve a high degree of bio-electrical synchronization in order to function. Developing this ability to biologically interface and harmonize can take months. When the narrative begins, there are only two EVAs in existence, a prototype model, 00, piloted by a mysterious girl named Rei, and the first Test Model, 01, for whom a pilot has yet to be found.

In the first episode the fourteen-year-old protagonist, Ikari Shinji, is summoned to NERV headquarters by his estranged father, Ikari Gendō. Thinking his father has summoned him out of affection, Shinji is shocked to learn that, on the contrary, his father wants him there only to pilot the new EVA. Since an angel is at that very moment attacking headquarters, Shinji has no time to think about taking on this task. At his continued refusals his father orders that Rei, the pilot of EVA 00, be brought in to battle the angel, despite the fact that she is still badly wounded from an earlier sortie.

Rei is brought in on a stretcher, shivering and moaning in pain. When the angel attack shakes the building and she is thrown off the stretcher, Shinji runs to pick her up from the floor. While cradling her body in his arms, he sees her fresh blood on his hand and changes his mind about piloting the EVA (Figure 9.1). Repeating, "I mustn't run away, I mustn't run away," he summons his courage to tell his father that he will do it.

In the next scene we see a cylindrical capsule, the "entry plug," being lowered into an opening in the "neck" of the giant EVA suit. The scene shifts to Shinji inside the plug as it begins to fill with some kind of liquid. Terrified, Shinji tries to hold his breath, but eventually has to breathe in

Figure 9.1. Shinji sees Rei's blood on his own hand as he holds her wounded body. At this moment he decides to pilot the EVA. (From the ADV American DVD.)

the liquid filling the capsule, which he is told will deliver oxygen to his lungs. Following this, the support crew monitors his synchronization rate with the EVA suit, astonished at his ability to mesh with it on this first attempt. Soon after, the Shinji-EVA cyborg is launched to fight the angel.

In the scene that follows this one chronologically, we see Shinji successfully moving the EVA, which is extraordinary, given his lack of training.[20] Nonetheless, the Shinji-EVA cyborg is badly beaten by the angel; we see Shinji in pain and terror inside the cockpit gripping his own arm when the angel rips off the arm of the EVA suit. Eventually the Shinji-EVA cyborg is wounded in the head, so that those watching back at headquarters are convinced that the cyborg amalgam of Shinji-EVA is dead. But at this moment the Shinji-EVA, disconnected from its power supply, goes berserk and, through some force the designers have never seen, manages to destroy the angel.

The point to be noted from the scene of the first creation of the Shinji-EVA cyborg is a process I would like to call *intercorporation* — that is, mutual incorporation of the other. The viewer sees Shinji, inside the very phallic-looking entry plug, being inserted into the receiving orifice of the EVA suit and being incorporated by it: structurally this is completely analogous to the "normal" sexual incorporation of the penis by the body of the other. But immediately thereafter we see the fluid inside the EVA filling the entry plug, and filling Shinji, much to his terror. In this case, therefore, each of the cyborg's two components — the mechanical EVA and the biotic Shinji — has penetrated into and filled the other; each has been incorporated by the other.

Maud Ellman has written that "Hegel, Feuerbach, Marx, and Freud, in spite of their divergences, agree that eating is the origin of subjectivity. For it is by ingesting the external world that the subject establishes his body as his own, distinguishing its inside from its outside."[21] The body ingests or incorporates materials from the outside — food, oxygen, semen — changes them, and expels a different kind of material back to the outside — feces, carbon dioxide, baby. This conceptualizing of our bodies is basic to the construction of the unitary, bounded subject, permeable only within controlled limits. Having control over what we take in and when and how we expel wastes/products is part of the training and prerogative of the autonomous adult modern subject.

However, sexual difference renders bodies *differentially* permeable in these examples. While all humans ingest food and oxygen and expel feces and carbon dioxide, only females incorporate genetic information from the semen their bodies take in with sexual penetration, and only females have their body boundaries forcefully breached by the act of giving birth to the baby that is the product of that original incorporation. This "extra" permeability to genetic information, as well as the mysterious "leakage" of menstruation and the possibility of violent eruption from within of childbirth, is a primary reason that women have never been considered to meet fully the criteria of the autonomous, unitary, bounded, self-controlled modern subject.

How does this basic structure for the construction of subjectivity relate to *Evangelion*'s cyborgian example? In this case, we have no incorporation by a bounded self of a relatively unimportant other, to be absorbed, transformed, and then ejected, but the intercorporation and interpenetration of two relatively equal components to produce a third, hybrid product: the cyborg. Not unitary but, at the same time, not-two. (While space does not allow me to pursue the point here, it is significant that later in *Evangelion* we learn that a series of intercorporations has already occurred: Shinji's mother has been fused with the inorganic material of the EVA suit — as well as being cloned to produce Rei — and the mother of the chief scientist, Ritsuko, has been fused with the MAGI computer system. In every case, it is a woman whose complete intercorporation with the inorganic has produced the weapons powerful enough to resist the angels.)

If intercorporation is one characteristic structural aspect of cyborg subjectivity, what kinds of fears and hopes does it engender? The question of sex/gender seems to be crucial here, as many contemporary narratives demonstrate that intercorporation is an especially disturbing concept for their male protagonists. The fact that we *see* Shinji's terrified/terrifying experience of initial intercorporation, but not that of his girl colleagues, is no doubt meant to play dramatically on the fears of the male viewing audience. Another popular anime, for example, *Kyōshoku sōkō gaibaa* (1989, *Guyver*), features a man being physically invaded by the body armor — tentacles of it penetrate his skin and orifices — that then turns him into a benevolent and powerful cyborg able to save his friends from certain death.[22] Nonetheless, he is distraught at the invasion of his body and his inability to expel the invading component, which retreats into a small area of his back most of the time, but then takes over his whole body again when he is provoked to fight. A further example can be seen in the live-action cult film *Tetsuo, the Iron Man* (1988), which opens with a man intentionally "infecting" or "impregnating" himself by thrusting a metal bar into a slit in his thigh, which gradually turns him into a monstrous amalgam of the machinic and the organic.[23] He then goes on to "infect" or "impregnate" others. This model of intercorporation — similar to the invasive attack of an infection or a parasite — can be found in many Japanese popular-culture narratives featuring male protagonists who are "feminized" by their bodies' penetration by and permeability to "the outside." (At the same time, they continue to exhibit masculine/male characteristics, such as the ability to "impregnate," resulting in a radically ambiguous gendering of these protagonists.) The association of this trope with HIV since the early 1990s only reinforces the nexus of sexuality, singularity, and subjectivity that is both exemplified and challenged by cyborgian intercorporation.

Control of the body and body boundaries is clearly an important node of anxiety being played out through many cyborg narratives. Certainly through techno-medicine we are controlling the body more and more successfully — this is one reason we have so many literal cyborgs walking among us now. The classic robotic bodies that appear in traditional science fiction are perfect, completely controllable. They represent an ideal version of the modernist conception of the body/self. But the conceptual price that must be paid for our increasing attempts to control the body is the recognition that the repressed always returns. As the imagined social body has become increasingly more perfect and controlled — more and more closely fitting the modernist model of (male) autonomous subjectivity — the likelihood of the eruption of the repressed body, in all its abject, excessive, imperfect, uncontrolled, boundary-challenged "female-ness," increases.

By the nineteenth episode of *Evangelion*, Shinji has experienced so many traumatic events that he has finally quit as an EVA pilot. Before he manages to leave the area, however, he is convinced to return and fight an angel that has taken on the unexpected form of another EVA, after he sees his friends, the two girls who also pilot EVAs, nearly destroyed by this new angel. The Shinji-EVA loses badly to the angel, with (again) one arm ripped off in the battle. Finally, the suit's power reserve is drained, and the Shinji-EVA cyborg is completely at the mercy of the angel. At this moment, however, Shinji, screaming with frustration, manages to "syn-chronize" so completely with the EVA suit that he disappears, simultane-ously managing to activate some power in the cyborg amalgam of him-self and the suit that allows him/it/her to rise up, regenerate its own arm (which is now flesh rather than metal), and defeat the angel. At the end of the scene the Shinji-EVA amalgam crawls like an animal to the dying angel and begins to eat it. Finally he/it/she rises up and roars in triumph, as the "mecha suit" armor is rent and destroyed from within. The stunned watchers from NERV are simultaneously delighted by the unexpected victory, mystified by the EVA's ability to move with no power source, and revolted by the EVA's animalistic cannibalism. Ritsuko remarks with fear that the EVA's "bindings" have been obliterated. In response to a surprised query from a junior colleague, she explains: "That isn't armor. Those are restraints that allow us to control the EVA's power. But now the EVA is removing the web that binds it to our will. We can no longer con-trol the EVA."[24]

Kotani has related this act of cannibalism on Shinji-EVA's part to "the explosion of the radically feminine, that is, to what Alice Jardine calls 'gynesis.'" Kotani describes the scene this way:

> The moment electric technology becomes unavailable [his power supply cords have been cut], Shinji strongly hopes for a miracle. Thus, with the ultimate aim to defeat the enemy, Shinji very naturally but miraculously comes to feminize himself. This sequence unveils Shinji's epiphany. The more strongly he desires a miraculous breakthrough, the more decon-structive his own sexuality becomes. Hence the abrupt explosion of fear-ful femininity out of Shinji's own male subjectivity.[25]

Despite the hypermasculine outlines of the EVA suit and the fact that the pilot of 01 is a boy, over the course of the series in scenes such as this one the Shinji-EVA cyborg amalgam is decisively gendered feminine: the uncontrollable, insufficiently bounded body/subjectivity that enlightened, rational modernity has sought to repress. And yet, it is in precisely these same scenes that the Shinji-EVA cyborg manages through some kind of hysterical crisis to overcome the limits of technology — the power cord and backup battery — to defeat the attacking angel.

This narrative, therefore, emplots both the male *terror* of being radically feminized through the excessive intimacy implied by the interpenetration and intercorporation of the cyborg subject and the paradoxical *hope* that the one power that can finally oppose the various forces of evil is precisely the eruption of the abject femininity — permeability/penetrability — that is repressed in techno-patriarchal society. That powerful eruption can only occur, however, when the interconnection of the various cyborg elements is at its maximum. In the nineteenth episode Shinji's synchronization rate with the suit is an inconceivable 400 percent, indicating that, despite the terror it provokes, the only hope for humankind is to move toward increased intimacy — permeability/penetrability — with the mechanical other.

I turn now to *Ghost in the Shell*, a film directed by Oshii Mamoru, based on the popular manga by Shirō Masamune.[26] This is a much shorter narrative and deals with one basic issue: species reproduction in a cyborg society. How does it occur, what gets reproduced, and in what sense does a cyborg species have historical continuity into the future?

The film opens with a very short scene, a joke, in which the first problematic of cyborg reproduction is raised. Major Kusanagi Motoko, a special security forces officer and our protagonist, is hooked into the Net through four interface sockets in the back of her neck. A colleague talking to her over the Net remarks that there is a lot of static in her head today. "Yeah," she mutters, "I'm having my period."[27] This immediate reference to menstruation — one of those odd breachings of body boundaries that make the female body unfit for modern subjectivity — alerts the viewer to the fact that reproductive sexuality is at the heart of this film. The reference to menstruation is particularly significant because, as we learn immediately thereafter, Kusanagi has a body that is completely mechanical and certainly does not bleed. After this brief introductory scene, we see, interspersed with the opening credits, Kusanagi being created/re-created/replicated (it is impossible to tell which) in the lab. As we learn from this sequence, her body is entirely artificial. Therefore, this body is under perfect control: nothing goes into or out of it except what/when/how she wishes. One assumes that this body is also incapable of impregnation, gestation, or parturition — what would be the need for such functions in a security officer? Her postmodern, reconstructed body is not enhanced to maximize *her* preferences or pleasures, we learn, but to maximize her usefulness to the state. Although she is extravagantly female in terms of external morphology (and spends several scenes of the film naked), and although she is presumably female in terms of original identity, the sexed body as reproductive body has no meaning in her cyborg state.[28] The juxtaposition, in the first five minutes of the film, of her reference to menstruation with the scenes of her cyborgian replication immediately underscores the fact that this film's theme is the problematic of reproductive sexuality in a posthuman subject.

Kusanagi's only biotic component is her brain, which provides her with a "ghost" — that is, memories, consciousness, and self-identity. The uncyborgized, natural-body humans all possess a ghost as a matter of course. But for radically altered humans like Kusanagi and most of the other members of her security force, the original ghost is the only thing that distinguishes the cyborg-human from the pure android.[29]

Why, then, does she mention menstruation? Why, going back to *Evangelion* for a moment, is it the sight of Rei's blood on his hand that makes Shinji change his mind about piloting the EVA?[30] In both cases, this early intrusion of the uncontrollable, messy, leaking feminine body serves, among other things, to underscore the *absence* of such bodies at the *surface level* of the narrative. Everyone looks perfect, appears under complete physical control — but whose and what kind of control? These bodies perfectly incarnate the modernist idea of autonomous subjectivity; in this sense, they are all coded "male," despite the strong visual dimorphism. Where is the "female" in this perfectly controlled universe? How does reproduction occur in a desexed universe? These are the questions raised by the simultaneous presence/absence of female (menstrual) blood in these cyborg narratives.

As the film progresses, we learn that Kusanagi heads a special defense team: Division Nine of the Security Branch of the Department of the Interior. She is brought in to deal with the problem of someone known only as the "Puppet Master," who carries out terrorist acts by hacking his way into the ghosts of chosen people through their implanted prosthetic links to the Net, reprogramming their ghosts, and causing them to perform terrorism. It is revealed that the Puppet Master began as a computer program that somehow became sentient and was then forced by its makers to abandon the Net and to enter a completely manufactured body. Now, however, the Puppet Master has escaped, and its whereabouts are unknown.

In the hunt for the Puppet Master, Kusanagi watches as people are told that the memories they have of spouses, children, jobs — everything they hold dear, everything that organizes the sense of self — have been artificially implanted by the Puppet Master who had hacked into their ghosts. She wonders whether her own ghost is real and original or whether everything she thinks she knows about herself is, like her body, completely artificial.

In the final sequence we witness a most unusual reproductive act, performed by two naked, voluptuous female torsos, minus arms and legs, lying side by side. Kusanagi's body was reduced to this state when she battled to rescue the "female" android body into which the Puppet Master had fled (Figure 9.2). Through the help of her friend and partner, Batō, Kusanagi is linked through technology to the Puppet Master, and they somehow merge into a single entity, capable of traveling the Net as the Puppet Master does but still retaining some element of Kusanagi's subjectivity (through her organic brain, it is assumed).

Ghost attempts to describe a completely new form of reproduction, for the new kinds of beings that will emerge from the increased cyborgization of the world. *Replication* is the reproductive process of the cyborg, as we see in the opening creation sequence, where Kusanagi's brain is encased in an entirely manufactured body. This reminds the viewer that she is infinitely reparable — as long as her brain is intact, her body can be reconstructed, in whole or in part, as often as necessary, and she will still be Kusanagi Motoko. Once again, therefore, this narrative explores the ramifications of the possibility of perfect control over the body. In this case, however, the interest is focused not on the infinite replicability of cyborgs but on the *limits* imposed on subjectivity by such perfect control and how these limits may be transcended, moving to the next step of evolution.

Figure 9.2. The ruined cyborg shells of Kusanagi and the Puppet Master lie next to one another as they prepare to merge. (From the Manga Entertainment special edition American DVD.)

Human species reproduction as we know it is structured around several salient features. One is the interplay of repetition/sameness with diversity. While a parent's genetic material is replicated in the child, the mixing of genetic material from the father with that of the mother produces diversity in the offspring, and this is repeated from generation to generation. For cyborgs such as Kusanagi there is no such combination of continuity and change. The mechanical body — or body part — is replicable, but what is (re)produced is a facsimile of the previous one and has no reference to an organic "original." Nor is there any intermixing of genetic information, and thus qualities, from another body/subject. There is continuity in the sense that Kusanagi's brain/ghost remains the same. But in a world where "ghosts" can be hacked and identities implanted, how can she be sure that her brain is indeed original and her sense of self unadulterated?

Another feature of organic reproduction as we know it is the importance of place — the space of embodiment. One is born from a specific place, the body of the mother, into a specific place. This happens only once, in that time and that place. The materiality and spatial specificity of the point of origin and the surroundings of one's journey through life are integral to a sense of subjectivity. As we see in the opening credits of *Ghost*, Kusanagi as cyborg is denied the specificity of time and place of birth. She emerges time and again from the same process; the fact that it is impossible to tell from the scene whether this is the first creation of her cyborg body or the thousandth underscores the distance from organic birth. In the case of many cyborgs, rather than two physical bodies coming together to (re)produce a new body/subjectivity — limited and constituted by place, circumstance, time — it is the corporation and the government, figured in many anime as disembodied, transnational, and threatening, that produce and reproduce the cyborg as species.

In *Ghost* physicality does retain one very important function. As Ueno Toshiya explains it: "Rather than the mind *(seishin)*, a 'ghost' is more like a person's spirit *(tamashii)*, and logically it is also unconscious; in general it is made up of past experiences and memories. It's something like water in a cup, premised upon the existence of some kind of shape (such as a metal suit or a shell)."[31] Possession of a ghost, rather than a particular kind of body, is what determines the legal and social status of a being as human — the nature of the body is irrelevant in determining ontology. But since a ghost (evidently) cannot exist without a container, the body is not (yet) a disposable element of selfhood.

Kusanagi is clearly concerned with these questions of cyborg ontology and reproduction, and the Puppet Master offers her a unique chance to overcome the limitations of her cyborg nature. By reproducing, she, like the Puppet Master, will have carried out one of the defining characteristics of a life-form, thus proving that she is more than an automaton.

That this is a whole new stage in evolution is signaled in a biblical passage quoted by the Puppet Master as he urges Kusanagi to merge with him/it: "When I was a child, I spake as a child, I understood as a child, I thought as a child: but when I became a man, I put away childish things. For now we see through a glass, darkly; but then face to face: now I know in part; but then shall I know [fully] even as I am [fully] known."[32] To know fully even as she is fully known is the possibility awaiting Kusanagi — as simultaneously herself and her offspring — in her new, unlimited existence in the Net. She will have left the "childhood" of her cyborg subjectivity behind and achieved full subjectivity in the next stage of evolution.

In narratives of cybernetic reproduction such as this one, what becomes of subjectivity? How can we — not even yet fully transformed from modern humans to postmodern cyborgs — be expected to feel any connection with Kusanagi's dilemma and the Puppet Master's solution? It is no doubt significant that even here reproduction ("merging") is the result of individual desire and will, carried out only with great contrivance and sacrifice. In that sense, the subjectivities even of the cyborg Kusanagi and the new life-form Puppet Master are recognizable to those of us still struggling with our modernist preconceptions of personhood.

Donna Haraway has proclaimed that "the cyborg is a creature in a post-gender world."[33] That may be true of Haraway's idealized vision of cyborgs themselves, but, as I have shown, contemporary Japanese cyborg narratives are still very much concerned with the binary oppositions of sex and gender, and the sexuality presumed to accompany them. Nonetheless, I would argue that these narratives relate a breakdown in what Cynthia J. Fuchs, quoting Judith Butler, calls the "'heterosexual matrix,' [in which] gendered identity and the construction of stable body contours rely upon fixed sites of corporeal permeability and impermeability."[34] As I have shown, that permeability is no longer differentiated by sex/gender in cyborg narrative.

Haraway puts the same point a little differently: "Communications sciences and modern biologies are constructed by a common move — the translation of the world into a problem of coding," resulting in a "world [that] is subdivided by boundaries differentially permeable to information."[35] Permeability to information is not a gendered phenomenon, particularly in the world of *Ghost*, where humans are altered by techno-medicine to link directly to the Net, or a world such as that of *Evangelion*, where male and female EVA pilots alike undergo involuntary intercorporation: Shinji cannot prevent himself from interfacing/synchronizing with the machine. Nor is permeability to information and technology in general a gendered phenomenon in our contemporary lived experience, and it may well be anxiety not just over that fact in itself but also over the breakdown of the "heterosexual matrix" determined by sex-differentiated permeability that motivates the strongly gendered aspects of many cyborg narratives.

Haraway echoes this anxiety, warning against the increasing and undifferentiated permeability of the body, which she sees as a situation where "all resistance to instrumental control disappears, and all heterogeneity can be submitted to disassembly, reassembly, investment, and exchange."[36] In contrast, Butler describes what sounds like a utopian vision of the potential of cyborg sexuality/subjectivity:

> Foucault held out the possibility that we might cease to think of sexuality as a specific attribute of sexed persons, that it could not be reducible to the question of his or her "desire," and that overcoming the epistemic constraint that mandated thinking of sexuality as emanating from sexed persons in the form of desire might constitute an emancipation, as it were, beyond emancipation. The phrase, "bodies and pleasures" held out the possibility of unmarked bodies, bodies that were no longer thought or experienced in terms of sexual difference, and pleasures that were diffuse, possibly nameless, intense and intensifying, pleasures that took the entire body as the surface and depth of its operation.
>
> The turn from "sex-desire" to "bodies and pleasures" promised for some a turn away... from the insistence that sexuality be thought of in terms of sexual difference, and that sexual difference be thought of as a function of oedipally induced differentiations, and that desire be understood as structured by lack in relation to a sexually differentiated Other.[37]

I have yet to see an anime narrative that explicitly approaches cyborg sexuality in this pleasurable, fully postgendered way, but I think this vision is suggested in the reluctance of cyborg narrative to depict sexuality in the modernist terms of the meeting of sexual organs attached to sexed/gendered bodies. The scene in *Ghost* in which two limbless female torsos somehow perform reproductive sex is one example of this. Also suggestive is the radical — one might almost say Frankensteinian — dismemberment and resuturing of the oedipal family romance in *Evangelion*, where Shinji's literal, absolute merging with his mother's body is engineered by the otherwise rejecting father. What kind of sexual/sex/gender identity would result from these examples of emancipation from traditional conceptualizations of subjectivity? In *Evangelion* the radical intercorporations of difference through bodies that cannot resist is a situation explored with fear and hope. Despite the celebration of the machinic in some senses, the human body and will — *when linked to the machinic* — are

Sharalyn Orbaugh

ultimately reinscribed as finally the most hopeful, only truly effective force for resistance, even if that resistance is only temporarily successful. In *Ghost,* on the other hand, the already achieved compulsory permeability of the populace to information and surveillance can be resisted only by abandoning the body altogether, moving it to the next level of evolution. Neither of these scenarios is very optimistic, but both are useful in the process of thinking through the possibilities of subjectivity in a rapidly changing world.

Notes

1. Jennifer Gonzalez, "Envisioning Cyborg Bodies: Notes from Current Research," in *The Cyborg Handbook,* ed. Chris Hables Gray (New York: Routledge, 1995), 267–79; Claudia Springer, "The Pleasure of the Interface," *Screen* 32 (1991): 303–23.

2. Donna Haraway, "A Cyborg Manifesto: Science, Technology, and Socialist-Feminism in the Late Twentieth Century," in *Simians, Cyborgs, and Women* (New York: Routledge, 1991), 175. Haraway's "cyborg" is actually an idealized eco-socialist-feminist relationship between women and technology rather than the "literal" cyborg — an embodied amalgam of the organic and the machinic — that I discuss in this chapter. Many of her ideas about the future model of subjectivity that she calls "cyborg" are, however, pertinent to my argument.

3. *Akira,* dir. Ōtomo Katsuhiro (1988); translated as *Akira,* DVD (Pioneer, 2001); Susan J. Napier, *Anime from Akira to Princess Mononoke: Experiencing Contemporary Japanese Animation* (New York: Palgrave, 2001), 197.

4. Shirō Masamune, interview by Ueno Toshiya, *Komikkaazu/Comickers* (Autumn 1995), quoted in Ueno Toshiya, *Kurenai no metaru sūtsu: Anime to iu senjō* (Metalsuits, the red: Wars in animation) (Tokyo: Kinokuniya Shoten, 1998), 116.

5. It could be argued that the great majority of the "cyborgs" (including also androids and technologically enhanced humans) well known to North American audiences are emphatically male in appearance and often portrayed as threatening, or at times pitiable, monsters: Darth Vader and the Empire's soldiers (the clone warriors) in the *Star Wars* films (1977–2005); Data, and all the Borg except the Queen, in the television series *Star Trek: The Next Generation* (1987–94); *RoboCop* (1987); *Terminator* (1984); *Total Recall* (1990). When female cyborgs do appear they are often "afterthoughts" to the original narrative corpus: Seven of Nine in *Star Trek: Voyager* (1995–2001), and the female police officer in *RoboCop 3* (1993). Pris and Rachael, in *Blade Runner* (1982), are the unusual exceptions to this rule. In Japan, in contrast, friendly robots appear not just in popular culture representations but in reality: the first robot dog, Aibo, intended to serve as a pet; Mitsubishi's child-shaped Wakamaru, which is designed to be a "house-sitter," recognizing faces and up to ten thousand words; the robot greeters at the 2005 Nagoya Expo; and so forth.

6. Rey Chow, "Violence in the Other Country: China as Crisis, Spectacle, and Woman," in *Third World Women and the Politics of Feminism,* ed. Chandra Talpade Mohanty, Ann Russo, and Lourdes Torres (Bloomington: Indiana University Press, 1991), 84.

7. John Dower, *War without Mercy: Race and Power in the Pacific War* (New York: Pantheon, 1986), 204.

8. Kotani Mari, "*Evangelion* as the Immaculate Virgin: A New Millennialist Perspective on the Daughters of Eve" (paper presented at the University of Montreal, March 27, 1999), 2.

9. Although I will not take the time to repeat the arguments here, critics from Sandra Gilbert and Susan Gubar to Peter Brook have identified the multiple ways that Frankenstein's monster, although possessing male genitalia, is actually gendered "female" throughout the novel. This gender ambiguity/hybridity, and the problematics of monstrous reproduction/sexuality in *Frankenstein,* are very much a part of what I am calling the "Frankenstein syndrome." Sandra M. Gilbert and Susan Gubar, *The Madwoman in the Attic: The Woman Writer and the Nineteenth-Century Literary Imagination* (New Haven, Conn.: Yale University Press, 1979), 213–47; Peter Brook, *Body Work: Objects of Desire in Modern Narrative* (Cambridge, Mass.: Harvard University Press, 1993), 199–220.

10. Sharalyn Orbaugh, "The Genealogy of the Cyborg in Japanese Popular Culture," in *World Weavers: Globalization, Science Fiction, and the Cybernetic Revolution,* ed. Wong Kin Yuen, Gary Westfahl, and Amy Kit-Sze Chan (Hong Kong: University of Hong Kong Press, 2005). See also Susan J. Napier, *The Fantastic in Modern Japanese Literature: The Subversion of Modernity* (London: Routledge, 1996).

11. *Shinseiki evangerion,* dir. Anno Hideaki, TV series, 26 episodes (1995–96); translated as *Neon Genesis Evangelion,* 13 subtitled VHS tapes (ADV Films, 1996–97); *Kōkaku kidōtai: Ghost in the Shell,* dir. Oshii Mamoru (1995); translated as *Ghost in the Shell,* DVD (Manga Entertainment, 1998).

12. Luce Irigaray, "The Sex Which Is Not One," in *This Sex Which Is Not One,* trans. Catherine Porter with Caroline Burke (Ithaca, N.Y.: Cornell University Press, 1985), 24. Note that Irigaray is contrasting the singularity of male/masculine subjectivity, as symbolized by the singular penis, with the two-in-oneness represented by the female genitalia and reflected, she argues, in female/feminine subjectivity. I do not intend to bring Irigaray's arguments about sex and gender into this essay, but merely to borrow her shorthand terminology for this kind of two-in-one subjectivity.

13. Haraway's "Cyborg Manifesto" also explicitly cites "monsters" such as conjoined twins and hermaphrodites as important in the establishment of concepts of subjectivity, identity, legal autonomy, and so on (180).

14. Elizabeth Grosz, "Intolerable Ambiguity: Freaks as/at the Limit," in *Freakery: Cultural Spectacles of the Extraordinary Body,* ed. Rosemarie Garland Thomson (New York: New York University Press, 1996), 66. Grosz reports that Chang and Eng Bunker, the "original" "Siamese twins," used the pronoun "I" when they wrote letters jointly (when a "we" might have been expected) and jointly signed as ChangEng.

15. Ibid., 58–65.

16. Clark and Myser write powerfully about the ways that new medical technologies of vision are serving the modernist human compulsion to delineate the boundaries that invisibly "separate" conjoined twins, in order to allow their physical separation into "acceptable" singular units. David Clark and Catherine Myser, "Being Humaned: Medical Documentaries and the Hyperrealization of Conjoined Twins," in Garland, *Freakery,* 338–55.

17. Judith Butler, *Bodies That Matter: On the Discursive Limits of Sex* (New York: Routledge, 1993), 188.

18. A point I have argued in "The Genealogy of the Cyborg in Japanese Popular Culture."

19. Michel Foucault, introduction to *Herculine Barbin: Being the Recently Rediscovered Memoirs of a Nineteenth-Century Hermaphrodite,* trans. Richard MacDougall (New York: Pantheon, 1980), xi; Clark and Myser, "Being Humaned," 347.

20. After showing the entry plug being loaded into the EVA and then showing the suit being launched, the narrative jumps to a point several hours or even days later, with Shinji lying in a bright, quiet hospital. It is only in a subsequent flashback that we see Shinji's fight with the angel.

21. Maud Ellman, *The Hunger Artists: Starving, Writing, and Imprisonment* (Cambridge, Mass.: Harvard University Press, 1993), 30.

22. *Kyōshoku sōkō gaibaa,* dir. Ishiguro Kōichi, OVA (1989); translated as *Guyver,* 13 subtitled VHS tapes (Manga Entertainment, 1994–97).

23. *Tetsuo, the Iron Man,* dir. Tsukamoto Shin'ya (1988); translated on subtitled VHS (Fox/Lorber, 1992).

24. This is a transcription of the English subtitles on the ADV videotape (episode 19). Please note that in the original Japanese the pronouns used carry no indication of gender whatsoever: it is impossible to tell whether the speakers think of the Shinji-EVA cyborg as "he," "she," or "it."

25. Kotani, "*Evangelion* as the Immaculate Virgin," 3, 5.

26. Shirō Masamune, *Kōkaku kidōtai: The Ghost in the Shell* (Tokyo: Kōdansha, 1991); translated by Frederik Schodt and Toren Smith as *Ghost in the Shell* (Milwaukee, Wis.: Dark Horse Comics, 1995).

27. In one English-dubbed version of the film (VHS, Manga Video, 1996), this is sanitized as "Yeah, I must have a wire loose"!

28. Although in this essay I am not discussing the manga versions of these narratives (which often differ considerably from the anime versions), I should point out that in Shirō's manga of *Ghost in the Shell,* Kusanagi is shown enjoying explicit (albeit virtual) sexual activity with a group of female cyborg security officers like herself (a scene that was deleted from the English translation of the manga). In the manga it is clear that sex for pleasure is available and allowed, but sexual reproduction is not, provoking Kusanagi's dilemma.

29. The problem of creating proper ontological divisions between various posthuman creatures is addressed in many anime films. In the TV series *AD Police,* for example, which is largely concerned with the sexuality of female cyborgs, a person is considered human (with all the rights and privileges pertaining thereto) so long as no more than 70 percent of his/her body has been replaced with mechanical parts. Those more than 70 percent mechanical are called Voomers and are liable to immediate arrest and/or destruction by the special AD Police (rather like the replicants in *Blade Runner*). *AD Police,* dir. Takahashi Akihiko and Nishimori Akira, OVA (1990); translated as *A.D. Police Files,* 3 subtitled VHS tapes (Animeigo, 1995).

30. A related, though not identical, example is Gally in *Gunmu* (1993, *Battle Angel*), whose fighting persona is activated any time she sees or smells blood. As a complete android she neither menstruates nor bleeds when damaged. Yet she retains traces of old values based on a culture of organic bodies: love, reproduction,

loyalty, integrity. *Gunmu,* dir. Fukutomi Hiroshi, OVA (1993); translated as *Battle Angel,* subtitled VHS (ADV Films, 1997).

31. Ueno, *Kurenai no metaru sūtsu,* 104.

32. 1 Cor. 13:11–12 (King James Version).

33. Haraway, "Cyborg Manifesto," 150.

34. Cynthia J. Fuchs, "'Death Is Irrelevant': Cyborgs, Reproduction, and the Future of Male Hysteria," in *The Cyborg Handbook,* ed. Chris Hables Gray (New York: Routledge, 1995), 283; Judith Butler, *Gender Trouble: Feminism and the Subversion of Identity* (New York: Routledge, 1990).

35. Haraway, "Cyborg Manifesto," 164.

36. Ibid.

37. Judith Butler, "Revisiting Bodies and Pleasures [excerpt]," *Ampersand* 1 (November 1998): 6–7.

10. Invasion of the Woman Snatchers
The Problem of A-Life and the Uncanny in *Final Fantasy: The Spirits Within*

Livia Monnet

The first entirely computer-animated, photorealistic feature-length film based on the principles of live-action cinema, *Final Fantasy: The Spirits Within* (2001), was a commercial failure. Produced by Square USA, Inc., and directed by Sakaguchi Hironobu, the award-winning executive producer of the popular interactive game software *Final Fantasy* series, the film was praised for the beauty and technological achievement of its computer graphics, but widely derided for its uninspired screenplay and a failure at the box office.[1]

This chapter argues that *Final Fantasy* is a transitional film that marks a turning point in the history of moving-image media, as well as in the history of science fiction. I show that the significance of Sakaguchi's film lies less in a largely successful attempt to create cinematic digital animation than in the variegated, often intriguing ways in which it illuminates the conceptual history of representation of life in the cinema, in animation, and in contemporary new media cultures. *Final Fantasy* demonstrates that that which provides continuity, desire, and cross-fertilization between analog and digital moving-image media, on the one hand, and between these media and the information-based life sciences, on the other, is a contingent, historically, and media-specific notion of life (and of death) as artificial life, or a-life.

The chapter is divided into two sections. The first discusses the notion of a-life in early cinema and film theory, as well as in early animation (in particular in a category of animated films that I call "cinemation," which foregrounds the interaction between live-action cinema and animation) to which *Final Fantasy*'s envisioning of the Phantom invasion, and to a lesser extent its CGI humans, calls attention. The common characteristic of the conceptualization and representation of life in these various media histories is *life excess* — a concept that designates the excessive vitality or liveliness of ghosts and resurrected dead characters, animism, and a phenomenology of frantic motion. The second section traces *Final Fantasy*'s remediation of the notion of life in the neovitalistic, evolutionary biology of Lynn Margulis and in contemporary theories of artificial life.[2] I argue that the film's endeavor to replicate, and simultaneously to transcend and reinvent, these imaginaries produces an uncanny effect, because it relies on the very double repression embodied in Sigmund Freud's suppression of the potential aliveness, and hence subversive significance, of the doll Olympia, in his reading of E. T. A. Hoffmann's novella "The Sandman" in his seminal essay *Das Unheimliche* (1919). Another operation of double suppression — which becomes a wellspring for uncanny effects and aesthetics in its own right — consists in *Final Fantasy*'s attempt to camouflage science fiction's own abduction and substitution of female agency.

Media Meta-Life and Lively Undeath

Final Fantasy invites us — by means of a seductive array of promotional materials,[3] by appealing to our ingrained habits of cinematic perception (and by way of compensation for its unconvincing plot and rather poor imagination) — to regard it as an allegory for what Thomas LaMarre calls the "fatal repetition" of cinema in digital media.[4] But to see it solely in these terms becomes at once suspect. The critic who insists only on *Final Fantasy*'s undeniable infatuation with, and imitation and remediation of, the cinema will merely be repeating the repetition. Her gesture will simply point, tautologically, to this digital movie's "movieness" and to its re-enactment of the compulsive return of the cinema described by LaMarre. At the same time, focusing exclusively on the film's laborious reconstruction of (an imagined) cinematic real occludes its conceptually more promising concern with historical — and contemporary — notions of life and death. In particular, *Final Fantasy*'s spectacular staging of the war between humans and the invading Phantoms, and the struggle between earth's blue Gaia and the red Phantom Gaia, raises interesting questions about life-and-death processes in the cinema and digital new media, as well as in the contemporary life sciences, cybernetics, philosophy, and science fiction.

Figure 10.1. Phantom wresting a human's blue spirit from his body. (All images in this chapter are from the Columbia Tristar American DVD.)

Let us consider, for instance, the Phantoms. Huge, translucent creatures that can fly, walk through walls, rocks, and fire, and emerge all of a sudden from floors, ventilation systems, or out of air pockets, these space invaders are ghosts of the intelligent species that perished in the nuclear explosion that annihilated the Phantom planet. As if reenacting the cruelty and devastation of the wars that led to this disaster, and at the same time apparently motivated by a desire to recover the life they lost forever, the Phantoms prey on humans, wresting their blue spirit from their bodies and instantly devouring it (Figure 10.1). This unconscious, mechanical repetition of a traumatic event that took place long ago points, it seems to me, to new media culture's rediscovery and revalidation of an intense, intimate engagement with death, and of the desire to transcend it, via various technologies of artificial life in early cinema, in the fantastic-grotesque imaginary it inspired, as well as in the nineteenth-century popular arts and entertainments that paved the way for the advent of motion pictures.

The new media artist Zoe Beloff, for instance, suggests that the grotesque descriptions of artificially resurrected dead people in Raymond Roussel's novel *Locus Solus* (1914) resonate strongly with the *dispositif* and spectatorship of the earliest movies in cinema's history, and with the fact that viewing frozen cadavers in the Paris morgue was a favorite, pre-cinematic mass entertainment in France until the turn of the twentieth century. One such passage in Roussel's novel describes the protagonist Martial Canterel's successful experience of reanimating corpses by means of two liquids that produced a powerful electric current: the thus resurrected, cryonized electrical automata could perform the most traumatic moments of their lives, time and again, with uncanny precision. Since Canterel is modeled on Edison, the legendary inventor of the phonograph and the kinetoscope, and since the earliest movies were very short loops that were projected continuously, compelling their characters, as it were, to mechanically perform the same role time and again, the association with motion pictures as intertext/intermedia in *Locus* is compelling.

Citing Noël Burch, Beloff also proposes that early cinema was regarded by its spectators (in particular by middle-class bourgeois viewers) as a medium/technology for transcending death — an ersatz of life or lifelike illusion that seemed capable of keeping death at bay. Cinema and digital media, like all moving-image technologies, are time machines thriving on death and are sustained by a desire to defer the terror it produces through artificial resurrection or artificial life.[5]

Final Fantasy's portrayal of the Phantom invasion, and of the deadly struggle between the blue Gaia and the red Gaia, resonates with Beloff's commentary on Roussel's novel and early cinema. The aliens are not exactly dead people but specters of long-deceased creatures. They are (re)animated by several kinds of forces: by the energy of the red Gaia; by the human spiritual, bio-etheric energy; by the animation software used to create them; and, quite literally, by the electricity feeding the computer workstations where the ghostly invaders were born. Like Roussel's electrical automata, the Phantoms endlessly reenact, mechanically and unconsciously, the most traumatic moments in their former lives: the anger, hatred, and violence of the wars they fought; and their desire to take revenge for their suffering and for the destruction of their planet. At the same time, these ghosts from outer space evoke the mechanical behavior and phantasmal atmosphere of early, short movies produced in the 1890s and the early 1900s. Be that as it may, the "movieness" of Sakaguchi's film seems to highlight the messy problem of an ambivalent ontology of lively undeath and artificial life at the heart of both cinema and animation, and of the cinematic, digital arts.[6]

Final Fantasy is made disturbing by the fact that not only the Phantoms but the human characters as well appear undead. The ontological uncertainty of these digital humans has several sources. While the Phantoms derive part of their proliferating, malignant vitality from the human spirits they prey on, the film's CGI humans literally "vampirize" the motion-capture actors who modeled them. The elastic, dot-constellation figures produced by the computer from motion-capture data provided by real human actors absorbed, as it were, the latter's "lifeblood," which then became the "living material" of the digital actor's "lifelike" behav-

Figure 10.2. Aki Ross, *Final Fantasy*'s world savior and "final girl."

ior. Like Roussel's resurrected, electrical automata, *Final Fantasy*'s virtual actors perform as undead, digital vampires or zombies. Partly because of the limitations of the animation software available at the time of the film's production, these digital humans also look like plastic androids suspended in a frozen, timeless fiction of a-life (Figure 10.2). Finally, *Final Fantasy*'s CGI actors not only possess a blue, unmistakably CGI (noncinematic, nonhyperreal) spirit that mediates between (digital) life and (digital) death, and between cinema and animation, but they literally *never die*. As the episode of Gray Edwards's ecstatic passing into Gaia at the end of the film demonstrates, all spirits reenter the eternal, life-giving blue Gaian flux upon the demise of the living bodies that housed them.

Both the Phantoms and the humans are characterized by ontological indeterminacy — the tremendous vitality of death epitomized by the ghostly aliens; the vampiric agelessness and smooth, plastic android appearance of the digital humans; these characters' oscillation between cinema and animation, analog and digital new media; the Möbius-like straddling of life and death characteristic of all these media. This indeterminacy is coupled with a logic of invasion, infestation, and secrecy. That is to say, Phantom particles invade the human body, proliferate like cancerous metastases, and rapidly undo its protective barriers until the weakened individual dies. Aki is the only character in the film who can communicate with the aliens and who resolves the puzzle of their motivation for waging war against humankind. The film thus seems to urge a psychoanalytic reading in which the Phantoms once again assume the leading role.

I am thinking here of the French psychoanalytic theorist Nicolas Abraham's speculations on the transgenerational phantom.

The Phantoms of the Cinema

According to Abraham, "The phantom which returns to haunt bears witness to the existence of the dead buried within the other.... It indicates the effects, on the descendants, of something that had inflicted narcissistic injury or even catastrophe on the parents." In other words, a traumatic event in which the subject's parents or immediate forebears were involved, or which they witnessed, is buried in their (the parents') unconscious as an unspeakable secret. This unspeakable trauma or shameful secret is never acknowledged, never revealed as such to the child. It is only cryptically alluded to in a manner that deprives the parent's speech of its libidinal grounding. The parent's unspeakable secret is transmitted to the child in the form of the phantom, a strange body, an intruding ventriloquist, an unconscious formation that returns periodically to haunt the subject, even though it lies outside the realm of her/his experience. This alien phantom signaling the presence of an occluded, horrific fact in the parent's unconscious manifests itself in the subject in several forms: as irrational, illogical speech, as various obsessions, or as inexplicable habits and pursuits. These manifestations of the phantom should not be interpreted as symptom-formation in the sense of the return of the repressed, for they are foreign to the subject's personal experience, desires, and fantasies. In many ways similar to Freud's description of the death instinct, the transgenerational phantom's silent work of disarray, Abraham goes on to argue, can be undone through an alliance between analysand and analyst: a nonthreatening analytic construction allowing the phantom-bearer to recognize and eject the bizarre foreign body that influenced her behavior and contradicted her.[7]

Abraham's concept of the transgenerational phantom and transgenerational phantomatic haunting usefully maps the relation between the Phantom invasion and its human victims in *Final Fantasy*. The alien invasion might thus be regarded as the effect of disavowed, repressed sins and transgressions committed or of traumas experienced in the past by the forebears of the futuristic human civilization portrayed in the film. This reading may seem, on one level, to reiterate the argument of the fatal repetition of the cinema in digital new media invoked above. Since *Final Fantasy*'s putative primary goal consists in the simultaneous simulation and overcoming of the cinema, its "parent" medium and mentor, the film offers itself as a willing host for incursions, haunting, and disruptions by the phantoms of the cinema. It also calls attention to the secret (of the suppression) of death in Sakaguchi's film and, more generally, in the cinema and other media histories it addresses. Seeing the role of the Phantoms in *Final Fantasy* as transgenerational, as well as trans- and intermedial, haunting allows us to clarify Aki's dual vocation as both *privileged phantom-bearer and medium* (indeed, in the double sense of a spiritualistic medium who communicates with the dead and of analog or digital media). It also allows us to visualize how this assignment deprives the young woman of her body and identity, eventually erasing her material presence altogether. Finally, the concept of the transgenerational phantom enables a productive rewriting of the histories of rotoscoping and of motion-capture in terms of *Final Fantasy*'s position in these traditions. Since the issue of Aki's vocation as medium opens onto the vast territory of the uncanny, I discuss it in the second part of the chapter. For now, I consider the implications of her role as privileged phantom-bearer.

A crucial part among several types of "family secrets," or "dead buried within the other," that return to haunt the digital humans in *Final Fantasy* is played by the secret legacy of the destruction of the Phantom planet. As I noted above, Aki Ross is the only character who is initiated into the background and unfolding of this tragic event. As a result, Aki becomes, quite literally, a "privileged phantom-bearer." Her infestation or contamination by Phantom particles (which at one point comes close to killing her) signifies at once a revelation, a warning, a prophecy, and a punishment or sacrifice. In other words, Aki has been chosen by the invading aliens to carry out a multiple mission: to disclose to other humans the tragic story of the Phantom planet's total destruction; to warn them that a similar fate may await them should they fail to welcome, and respect, difference and life's right to expand and flourish; and to be a sacrificial victim whose sacrifice will enable her community and the planet as a whole to avoid disaster. The "family resemblance" between *Final Fantasy* and a host of science fiction and fantasy films and anime such as *Invasion of the Body Snatchers* (1955), *Alien* (1979) and its sequels *Alien 3* (1992) and *Alien Resurrection* (1997), *The Terminator* (1984) and *Terminator 2: Judgment Day* (1991), *Total Recall* (1990), *The Matrix* (1999), *Nausicaä in the Valley of the Wind* (1984), *Ghost in the Shell* (1995), and *Neon Genesis Evangelion* (1997) certainly corroborates this interpretation.[8] At the same time, Aki's infestation by Phantom particles, and the Phantom invasion in general, suggests that the Meta-secret, the primary mechanism that enables circulation across and among media, and transformation of meanings, techniques, and concepts (and their imaginaries and histories) between *Final Fantasy* and these films, is located in the *uncanny phenomena of the life excess*.

Thus the two forms of life and death energy in the film reveal themselves to be very similar: earth's blue Gaia effectively suspends death, while the red, alien Gaia devours life to indefinitely postpone real extinction. Indeed, once the deadly Phantom Gaia has been rendered harmless and becomes a maternal nourisher and life-giver like the blue Gaia, the perpetual duration of life is guaranteed. Aki's dreams reveal to her not only the tragic legacy of the now-extinct Phantom planet and her (predictable and cliché) vocation as earth savior. They also reveal the bewildering world of images, stories, concepts, and sensations shored up by cinema, animation, and digital new media, and by science fiction's media and genres, to keep the terror of (death's) life excess at bay.

Cinematic Animism

While *Final Fantasy*'s translucent, transgenerational Phantoms undoubtedly evoke various representations of ghosts, zombies, vampires, and revenants in the history of cinema and animation, the concepts mapping their excessive vitality and immaterial, yet real and threatening, ubiquity must be contrasted with similar concepts in the analog, "parent" media. One such concept is often found in film theory in the 1910s and 1920s. It refers to cinema's putative animism and vitalism: its capacity to endow the object or the noumenal world it captures with an arresting vividness and vibrancy, a potency of the image that makes inanimate matter seem alive — or the reverse, implying cinema's potential to render visible the life that is already there, the soul of the world, or élan vital.[9] Among early-twentieth-century theories of cinematic animism, Jean Epstein's and Emile Vuillermoz's are notable for their poetic, visionary imagination. Epstein, for instance, argues that *photogénie,* cinema's inherent ability to attribute "a semblance of life to the objects it defines" also enhances their moral value. The close-up, a condensed, intense expression of *photogénie,* is capable of revealing both the libidinal and psychic motivations of filmic characters, and the "life" or "personality" of things and beings. Epstein describes this as "the (living) spirit visible in things and people, their heredity made evident, their past become unforgettable, their future already present." The "life," or spiritual energy rendered visible by cinematic images, is unrelated to human life. It is, rather, synonymous with the magical power attributed to charms, amulets, and other "ominous, tabooed objects of certain primitive religions": "If we wish to understand how an animal, a plant, or a stone can inspire respect, fear, or horror,...I think we must watch them on the screen, living their mysterious, silent lives, alien to the human sensibility."[10]

Epstein's contemporary Vuillermoz wrote that the film camera is a magical instrument that expresses the "religion of things" and strives to capture their soul. Cinema's essence is *cinégraphie*, which Vuillermoz defines as an art that can "make inanimate objects speak and give laughter and tears to things." *Cinégraphie*'s unique potential can also "lay out the whole gamut of expressions of trees, clouds, mountains, and seas," re-creating the world as a "superreality more intense than the truth." "It recognizes no impossibilities of any kind, in neither space nor time."[11]

Like Béla Balázs, Vachel Lindsay, Edogawa Ranpo, and other early film theorists, Epstein and Vuillermoz attribute a magical transformative power to the cinema, as well as transcendence, ubiquity, and the affective and persuasive capacity of religious beliefs. Motion pictures' mechanical, photographic "semblance of life" thus seems able to substitute itself for living, and lived reality, and to transcend time and death ("a superreality, more intense than the truth," which "recognizes no impossibilities of any kind, in neither space nor time"). It can also abolish the distance between spectator and screen, or interiority and exteriority, and radically transform both our habits of perception and the world. In the two French theorists' romantic vision, then, cinema is pure excess, pure expenditure: *cinematic hyper-a-life.*

Movement beside Itself

As computer-animated "time machines of movement" that are also figures of transition,[12] *Final Fantasy*'s transgenerational, transmedial Phantoms also call attention to what might be called a *phenomenology of movement beside itself.* In effect, the space ghosts in Sakaguchi's film are extremely mobile, superfast, and deadly efficient, attacking their human opponents with a relentless, blind determination that the latter's sophisticated military technology can only temporarily halt. Such excess of movement, interestingly enough, is posited in the film as a major conceptual link between cinema, animation, and digital new media. What I have in mind here is not so much the kineticism, or principle of motion inherent in all these media — the fact that cinema can be defined as photography in/of motion and that animation invests hand-drawn, or computer-generated objects and beings with the illusion of life and movement by decomposing the latter into a frame-by-frame sequence of successive phases. Rather, I am thinking of a phenomenology of movement that, while present in all forms and genres of cinema and animation, articulates itself with particular urgency in the hybrid forms of the two media's coexistence: the "continuing discourse between animation and live-action film" described by historians such as Paul Wells and Giannalberto Bendazzi, and which, following LaMarre, I call "cinemation."[13]

In early "lightning hand" or "quick sketches" films such as J. Stuart Blackton's *The Enchanted Drawing* (1900) and *Humorous Phases of Funny Faces* (1906), and Winsor McCay's *Little Nemo* (1911), live-action footage of the cartoonist is integrated with the animated figures emerging from his pencil or brush. The mood is comical, parodic, or satirical, the movement frantic and over-the-top. In these films, magic and wide-eyed, childish astonishment reside not only in the subject matter (which sometimes stages magical acts such as that of the "vanishing lady") but above all in the cartoonist's virtuosity and the elasticity and fantastic feats of the drawn figures.[14] Here motion pictures are clearly secondary to animation, celebrating the latter's unlimited freedom, fantasy, and power of enchantment.

In the Fleischer brothers' *Out of the Inkwell* series, Koko the clown climbs out of a live-action image of the animator's inkpot and escapes into the outer world, where he does a lot of mischief and delights in constantly eluding the artist's attempt to bring him back under control. In the brothers' even more anarchic *Betty Boop's Snow White* (1933), the presence of motion pictures transpires in the ghost Koko's dance of the "St James' Infirmary," which was created through the rotoscoping of African American jazz singer Cab Calloway's celebrated dance-walk performance of the same tune.

The physics of movement advocated in these and many other cinemation films is a wild, chaotic kinetics that disrupts the laws of gravity, biology, and the social and cultural control systems of the modern nation-state. The ontology they posit is one of becoming, in the Deleuzian sense of "continuously variable events organized around aspects, or 'particles' of an object or an event."[15] (A notable instance of such metamorphic becoming is the dancing ghost's transformation into a set of tubes or ropes that turns into a ring chain connected to a twenty-dollar piece and a bottle in *Betty Boop's Snow White*.)

Another form of "movement beside itself" evoked by *Final Fantasy*'s Phantom invasion is a phenomenology of the *mise-en-abîme* of motion. Such reflexive *mise-en-abîme* may be seen in countless animated and cinemation films that are essentially studies in and of the movement of material forces *(puissances)* that create, enable, or disarray animation. The French animator Emil Cohl's "incoherent cinema" films *Fantasmagorie* (1908) and *En Route* (1910) stage the artist's well-known technique of constructing a character or an event from lines falling at random into a frame. Jan Svankmayer's *Dimensions of Dialogue* (1971) ostensibly highlights the destructive behavior of characters whose intentions and emotions are at cross-purposes while making startling revelations about the powerful forces and the subversive politics of clay and other everyday objects that act as primary materials for the animated film.[16]

The legacy of excessive vitality, excessive dynamics of movement and aggressive agency of *Final Fantasy*'s transmedial phantoms thus seems to suggest that cinemation should be reinstated, and properly investigated, as a major tradition in both cinema and animation — indeed, that the two media's respective histories be rewritten as always already informed and haunted by, always already emulating, remediating, and reinventing, one another. It also suggests that motion pictures and animation share a common definition as time — and life machines of movement — the former a photographic capture, the latter a hand-drawn/computer-generated production of the a-life of movement. The becoming of a-life — as undeath in motion as well as motion's afterlife — which provides continuity, coherence, and desire between cinema, animation, and digital new media in Sakaguchi's film, is featured, logically enough, as a struggle between the blue life–Gaia and the red death–Gaia. While the battle is of course won by the former Gaia's superior life power, what is invariably overlooked in the debate on *Final Fantasy*'s re-creation of cinema's "semblance of life" is, precisely, the *construction of life* (and death) in both analog and digital cinema.

Despite notions of hyper-, photo-, or cinematic realism, of cinematic animism, and of a magical, subversive "aliveness" in cinemation, experimental animation, and other narrative traditions, the problem of life in these media is not one of illusionistic rendering of reality or the world *but a problem of artificial life*. As I have stressed throughout this chapter, *Final Fantasy*'s concern is with the digital (re)production of other moving-image media's a-life. The uncanniness of this endeavor resides neither in the apparent success of the film's imitation/re-creation of media a-life nor in the fact that the latter is sampled as undead space ghosts and as equally undead, virtual humans. It resides rather in the congruence between *Final Fantasy*'s conceptualization and rendering of earth's "life" (which is, of course, artificial life) of Gaia and the conceptualization of Gaia as a planetary superorganism in the neovitalistic biology advocated by scientists such as James Lovelock and Lynn Margulis. *Final Fantasy*'s problematic "biopolitics" (i.e., the film's controlling, disciplining, and policing of its characters through the quasi-Foucauldian "biopower" of a digital economy where affect becomes information and socialized attention is distributed according to each character's "life expectancy" and profitability with respect to the Phantom invasion) and (unconvincing) concern for environmental, or a-life, conservation produce an uncanny effect also as a result of their reliance on a missing term. Unsurprisingly, this absence is that of women's bodies, histories, and cultural contributions (including their contribution to science fiction and digital culture). The strategy used in the film to erase female power and agency is that of abduction — a dual practice entailing a speculative, future-oriented reasoning as in Charles Sanders Peirce's notion of abduction (see below), as well as a literal carrying off, as in science fiction's alien abductions.

The Emergence of A-Life

While *Final Fantasy*'s image of earth's life or Gaia as a blue flow of sentient matter from which the spirits of all living beings emerge, and to which they return after death, represents yet another version of New Age pop conservationist, paganist discourses inspired by Lovelock's Gaia hypothesis,[17] the overlap between the film's representation of the struggle between the blue Gaia and the red Phantom Gaia and Margulis's conception of the evolution of early life is much more intriguing. Let us recall briefly that the Phantoms in Sakaguchi's film are the "angry and confused" ghosts of an intelligent species that once peopled the alien planet and that perished in the nuclear holocaust that annihilated the latter. The space invaders landed on earth on the Leonid meteor in 2065 and have since systematically destroyed most human cities, as well as all other human-made and natural environments. They prey on humans, killing them like so many defenseless puppets, and extract their blue spirit, which they consume as a graphic "life supplement."

Another method used by the Phantoms to grab the coveted human spirit is "particle infestation." Phantom particles insinuate themselves into the human body, where they proliferate like cancerous tumors or metastases until the contaminated individual dies. Aki has been able to survive the alien contamination of her body thanks to a breastplate created by Dr. Sid that neutralizes the lethal Phantom energy through a counter-energy pattern. It is, finally, this bioetheric antidote that saves earth and its remaining human population (an operation requiring the sacrifice of Aki's lover Gray Edwards, and of his faithful military comrades, the members of the Deep Eyes task force).

Margulis's description of the emergence of Gaia as a planetary superorganism through the complex process of symbiogenesis neatly maps, up to a certain point, the story of the Phantom invasion in *Final Fantasy*. Margulis argues that Gaia designates simultaneously earth's evolution into a living superorganism and the almost limitless capacity of matter to be imbricated and infiltrated with life. The strange tendency of both the earth and the nucleated cell to be invaded by alien predators falls under the purview of this immense receptiveness or permeability to life. Thus the eukaryotic cell emerges through a combination of invasion and the early prokaryotes' "tolerance for their predators": a parasitic invasion by bacterial DNA on a prokaryotic cell, the consumption of prey DNA by a predator, and finally the supple and fine-tuned ability of the cell to accommodate alien encroachment — an ability coevolving with the prokaryotic cell. It was probably the evolution of a protective membrane, Margulis goes on to argue, that allowed early prokaryotes to survive the invasion or inhabitation by "poisonous guests." The new form of the eukaryotic cell thus seems to have emerged through a blockage of the host cell's DNA. In Margulis's view, such processes of blockage, cohabitation, and symbiogenesis played a crucial role in the emergence of early life and in the constitution of Gaia as a living superorganism.[18]

Final Fantasy's representation of the Phantom invasion, and of the struggle between the blue Gaia and red Gaia, seems to follow Margulis's description faithfully. The ghostly aliens penetrate and proliferate in host human bodies just like parasitic bacteria invading prokaryotic cells. The space predators consume human spirits in a manner similar to the consumption of the prokaryotic cell's prey DNA by poisonous bacteria. The development of a "protective membrane" — a breastplate containing a bio-etheric energy pattern that can neutralize the lethal effect of the Phantom energy — has enabled Aki (and will presumably enable earth's remaining human population) to survive the various attacks of Phantom "particles." It is unlikely (though not impossible) that Sakaguchi and his screenwriters, Al Reinert and Jeff Vintar, studied Margulis before producing the script. It seems equally improbable that *Final Fantasy*'s creators intended to add yet another level of allegory — that of the representation of the genesis and evolution of life processes — to the film's already overburdened allegorical discourse. The striking similarities between *Final Fantasy*'s Gaian discourse and the theories of Margulis and Lovelock nonetheless point once again to the centrality of the problem of life in Sakaguchi's film. Indeed, this overlap or insistence on a-life in *Final Fantasy* may be regarded as a translation or transcoding of current discourses on life into the computer-generated ecologies of artificial life.

The film seems to suggest that, if life is always already coded information, and if its emergence, evolution, apparent aberrations, and disappearance have followed preprogrammed designs and modelizations — in other words, if life has always been actualized, "artificial" a-life — then the experiment of the digital, new artificial life was both "natural" and logical. The uncanny effect of such ecologies of digital a-life (which *Final Fantasy* identifies as the ecologies of the Phantom invasion and the blue Gaia's struggle for survival) is produced less by their populous, variegated vitality than by the suppression of the very imaginary that sustains them: that of a maternal science fiction of the future. The film suggests also that science fiction is the uncanny genre par excellence because it tirelessly stages the stubborn return of the abducted and suppressed powerful woman (or the thought of femininity in control) as life effect.

Ecologies of the Uncanny: Representing Life for A-Living

In *Wetwares: Experiments in Postvital Living* Richard Doyle argues that what makes a-life creatures — the lively simulacra of life forms produced by A-life software — uncanny is not so much the ontological uncertainty they embody ("are they really alive?") but the fact that the "cute and perky vitality" of these virtual organisms is enabled by a very real *disappearance of the materiality and sovereignty of life*. Indeed, the articulation of life as information, as dislocated living systems capable of instantiation in contexts other than their original location, as "life-as-it-could-be . . . writ large across all material substrates" in the theories of artificial life of Christopher Langton and others, suggests that life as a sovereign entity disappears, leaving instead various forms of liveliness, or life effects, as criteria for determining what is alive.[19] The life effect of a-life creatures depends in its turn on their interactions with their virtual (computer-generated) environment, as well as with other a-life creatures; on their ability to be provoked from a-life code into lively actualization by translational mechanisms Doyle calls "rhetorical softwares," and thereby to replicate or represent life in a compelling way; and finally on a-life organisms' enmeshing with the "human" agents with whom they interact.

Computer-generated a-life forms, Doyle goes on to argue, also generate uncanny rhetorics and delusions or hallucinations of localization and ubiquity. Tamagotchi virtual pets and the strange dogs or "Moofs" running around in SimLife (an artificial life software) ecologies appear alive "in," "on," or "behind" the computer screen. Such a rhetoric, as Doyle observes, occludes the complex interactions and interpenetrations between (as well as the materiality of) a-life software, the computer interface, the electric grids that power it, the personal history and identity of the human interactor to whom the virtual creatures respond, the agency of the computer network over which the latter are distributed, and so on. A-life familiars seem uncanny also because they are manifestations of actualized life that dwell in pure virtuality and that *represent life for a living*. Their survival depends on convincing the interactor, as well as the other inhabitants of the virtual environment, that they are capable of lifelike behavior. Since life, as a-life or life effect, is no longer confined to a body or a location but appears to be everywhere and nowhere at the same time, it also provokes the uncanny sensation, so poignantly described by science fiction writers such as William Burroughs and Philip K. Dick, that "anything . . . could be alive" and that we are "'surrounded' by vitality."[20]

Perhaps the uncanniest feature of a-life as actualized life or life effect, writes Doyle, is its *abductive ontology*. The persuasive or affective power of a-life organisms is predicated on that strange category of reasoning Peirce called *abduction,* or *hypothesis.* Unlike induction — which is tied to habit, tends to subsume all events into the same, and also operates in ways that run counter to deduction, which relies on full knowledge of all the premises — abduction is constituted by an absence or a missing term. It is the only mode of reasoning that welcomes an encounter with the future or with a novel, unprecedented and uncorroborated, thought. In Peirce's argument, abduction fosters the production of "a general prediction without any positive assurance that it will succeed either in the special case or usually, its justification being that it is the only hope of regulating our future conduct rationally." In its guise as hypothesis, abduction gambles on the unpredictable and the improbable, working through an intensive substitution — that of a single conception, which is swapped for a "complicated tangle of predicates attached to one subject."[21]

Clearly thriving on abduction, a-life substitutes the improbable fiction of "life as it could be" for the complicated tangle of formal attributes of "life as we know it." Though we can only guess at what it is exactly that defines a-life organisms' aliveness, abductive reasoning allows us (so goes the argument of artificial life enthusiasts) to posit this life effect as "genuine life — (a life that is) simply . . . made out of different stuff than the life that has evolved here on Earth."[22] The strange assurance with which this type of abductive reasoning — what Doyle describes as a-life's "silicon abduction" — bets on artificial life's genuine, irrefutable "proof of life" has much in common with the unhesitating affirmation often found in another type of "abduction discourse": narratives of encounters with extraterrestrial aliens.[23]

Doyle's discussion, then, seems to distribute a-life's uncanniness unevenly over three zones. Some 70 percent of the unnerving sensation produced by a-life organisms is rhetorical (via rhetorics of localization and ubiquity, and of a-life's "genuine life" or aliveness). Another 20 percent emerges from absence or abduction (in the disappearance of life's sovereignty, and substitution of the life effect for "real" life; the abductive mode of reasoning allowing for an encounter with a missing term that is yet to come, such as "life as it could be"). Finally, 10 percent of a-life's uncanniness is a-corporeal (the enmeshing of human bodies, affects, and ecology with the evolution of a-life creatures). Now, if we juxtapose Doyle's speculations, especially his insistence on the uncanniness of a-life, with *Final*

Fantasy's New Age Gaian discourse, or its conceptualization and representation of vital forces — "life," bio-etheric energy, earth's planetary spirit — we will notice that the film's uncanniness has different sources. If *Final Fantasy*'s Phantoms, digital humans, and simple-minded representation of the blue Gaia are disturbing to watch, it is because of the tension, *différance*, or fractal relations between the various versions of "life" staged in the work.

As my analysis has demonstrated, *Final Fantasy* attempts (and fails) simultaneously to narrate, replicate, seduce into actualization, and reconcile several notions of life that are not necessarily compatible: cinema's "semblance of life"; the excessive, over-the-top kinetics that produces animation's (particularly cinemation's) own illusion of life; the anorganic vitalism, and conceptualization of the earth/Gaia/planetary life as superorganism, in the heterodox biology of Margulis and Lovelock; the redefinition of life in the information life sciences and in artificial life theory and informatics. Indeed, it seems legitimate to argue that Sakaguchi's film cannot re-present, reinvent, or achieve life — and thus cannot come alive and convince the viewer — because it is overly obsessed with and haunted by a-life.

By analogy with Marcello Barbieri's description of living systems as a tripartite assemblage of *genotype* (hereditary information carried primarily by DNA), *ribotype* (translational apparatuses that convert DNA into folded proteins), and *phenotype* (the dynamic embodiment of these informational structures and transformations), I want to suggest that *Final Fantasy* is torn between the irreducible demands of its genotype, or material substratum; its phenotype, or its aesthetics, philosophy, and ideology; and the translational ribotype mediating between the former two structures and enabling the emergence of "life."[24] If we identify the complex assemblage of the histories and concepts of the cinema, animation (cinemation), and video games, as well as the individual science fiction narratives cited above as the film's genotype; regard its impressive visual aesthetic, unconvincing story, and problematic, militaristic ethos as its phenotype;[25] and locate its ribotype, on the one hand, in the cutting-edge animation software and computer technology and, on the other hand, in the artificial life theory and practice it relies on, we will readily perceive a major reason for *Final Fantasy*'s uncanny, disturbing quality.

While the film seems to perform a never-ending pantomime, simulation, or digital karaoke version of "life," it seems to have forgotten that the life it so strenuously pursues is ... artificial. A-life. The "genuine life" of artificial life. The various "a-lives" that inhabit, contaminate, or haunt *Final Fantasy* — cinema's "hyper-a-life," the crazed dynamics of cinemation, the crowded, continually invaded body of the planetary Gaia, the various catastrophes and forms of survival engendered by science fiction's invasions of body snatchers, computer animation's own life effect — clash with what Langton has called the "big claim" of artificial life (i.e., the latter's divergent and yet "genuine" aliveness). It does so not only because each media a-life has different criteria for defining its own vitality or animism but also because each of these "lives" has staked out a "big claim" of being more "genuine," or "real," than the others. Awash in trendy, cutting-edge a-life, *Final Fantasy*'s hailing of "life" as a technology of immortality, redemption, and universal reconciliation fails to convince us not only because of such fraudulent "big claims" but also because of another, even more monumental fraud. Not content with performing, through deft abductive moves, substitutions of "life" substitutes (such as the substitution of a computer-generated, derivative science fiction film's "single conception" of a-life for the "complicated tangle of predicates attached to" live-action science fiction cinema's, and literary science fiction's, conceptions of a-life), the film substitutes a missing term for another absent notion; (ab)uses it as its primary ribotype; abducts it again; and substitutes for it a more versatile and supple, less-threatening body — a body that by definition embodies, and thereby enables endless repetitions of, abduction.

The Vanishing Lady's Disappearing Act

I am thinking here, of course, of Aki Ross and of the various abduction scenarios in which she becomes an unwitting protagonist. As I indicated above, Aki is a privileged phantom-bearer, the only character who understands the message of the terrifying alien invaders. Her role is not only that of a world savior, a redemptive sacrificial victim (she is contaminated by Phantom particles and clearly intended to die, but survives thanks to her protective breastplate and to the selfless sacrifice of her lover, Gray Edwards), but also that of a *medium*. Aki is, quite literally, a medium who can communicate with, and who is able to translate the language of, the spirits of dead beings — in this case the ghosts of long-dead creatures that once lived on the Phantom planet. Her recurrent dreams of the destruction of the Phantom planet constitute the actual medium for the transmission of the aliens' message. Recorded by a sophisticated computer workstation, these dreams erase, and substitute themselves, for Aki's material presence in several ways that are not without irony. They are "blown-up" so as to occupy the whole screen, chasing the dreaming Aki, as it were, offscreen and retaining only the dream image of her — the immaterial, evanescent image of Aki inside the dream. At some point only the recorded dreams remain, Aki having literally vanished. (When a military unit arrives in her office to arrest her, she is gone, with the recording of her dreams scrolling on the computer screen as the only proof of her existence.) While the classical psychoanalytic paradigm posits dreams as a production of the unconscious, Aki's dreams do not belong to her but were "uploaded" into her unconscious by the aliens.

To a certain extent, then, Aki may be said to be rendered superfluous by, disappear in, or exist only by virtue of her dreams and the message they have to convey. As if literally abducted by the aliens that appear in her dreams, Aki is mobilized both as medium/messenger and as message. This abduction is significant because Aki is cast as a gifted woman scientist on whom both the survival and the future of earth depend.

Despite the crucial role assigned to her, Aki thus appears mostly passive, deprived of agency, *a vanishing medium as well as a vanishing woman.* Several other elements in the film seem to support this notion. Though she actively participates, even to the point of risking her life, in Dr. Sid's research on the bio-etheric energy wave that can counteract the lethal Phantom energy, Aki is not given credit for her research activities. She remains confined in the subsidiary role of the devoted, self-effacing assistant. She is clearly destined to conquer the Phantoms and halt the destruction of the world (the film's opening shows Aki waking from one of her recurring dreams of the Phantom wars, wondering whether she "will be in time to save the earth").[26] Yet Aki is not allowed to accomplish this mission through her own creativity, willpower, or agency. Though the anti-Phantom energy pattern discovered by Dr. Sid is completed and plugged into Aki's breastplate, it is not she but Gray who magically transfers it to the Phantom Gaia, effectively neutralizing the latter's destructive power. The glory of the world savior is thus displaced onto Gray, who dies a hero's, and a martyr's, death (Figure 10.3).

The materiality and credibility of Aki's character (a materiality that is at once corporeal, mediatic, narrative, and conceptual) is further diluted by a whole battery of facts. She is a computer-generated simulacrum of an ideal, cinematic female character that has no real referent (this is a fate that, of course, she shares with the film's other digital humans). Since the basic outline for her "natural, lifelike" behavior was provided by a computer-generated dot skeleton that was itself a mere translation of the motion-capture data provided by a motion-capture actress, Aki is, strictly speaking, little more than a layer of texture and paint placed over a wire-mesh structure covering the original motion-capture skeleton. Furthermore, since the motion-capture process is the digital counterpart of the analog process of rotoscoping in animation, Aki is by definition (and much like Koko the clown and other characters in classical narrative animation whose bodies were often rotoscoped from live-action film characters) a *ghostly,*

Figure 10.3. Gray Edwards carries the bio-etheric energy pattern into the red Phantom Gaia, which subsequently becomes blue, beneficial life energy.

invaded body: a computer-animated trace of a real, referential movement (i.e., that of the motion-capture actress), which is itself a copy of a character's movement in analog animation that was in its turn a simulation of the cinema.[27] Aki is invaded not only by the alien Phantoms and their charged history but by the cinema, by rotoscoped cel animation, by the shadowy presence of a genealogy of selfless, maternal, world savior–type females in science fiction and fantasy cinema and animation, all at once.

Another encroachment on Aki's materiality and agency is effectuated by the Phantoms — or, more precisely, by the transgenerational, intermedial phantomatic haunting they enable. The story of the ghostly aliens evokes, as I noted above, the beginnings of both cinema and animation. That early, experimental period in the history of the two media was literally haunted by spiritualistic mediums (in particular female mediums), by an intense fascination with the ghosts they conjured, as well as by spiritualism's (often uneasy) cohabitation with the art of magical acts and performances such as that of the vanishing lady. In the same way, Aki appears to be erased or abducted by her very function as medium. In other words, just as the performance of late-nineteenth- and early-twentieth-century female spiritualistic mediums was territorialized by photography and the cinema, and just as these mediums disappeared entirely in the "materializations" of spirits and ghosts they produced in a way that evoked the disappearance of the vanishing lady in the famous magical act (the subject of early films by George Méliès, R. W. Paul, and Thomas A.

Edison), Aki is invaded and territorialized, and finally disappears in her "multi-task mediumship."[28] Her disappearance as both "vanishing medium" and "vanishing lady" could not have been more complete.

Abducted by Science Fiction: The Woman as Perpetual Ribotype

What does this vanishing, or repeated abduction, of the woman in *Final Fantasy* tell us about the film's gender politics, its revisiting of the uncanny, and the production of an uncanny aesthetics (if there is such a one) in digital new media, particularly science fiction digital cinema, computer animation, and video games? It is fairly obvious that Sakaguchi's film is masculinist, archconservative, and not really interested in having credible female characters. Indeed, he is bent on erasing female power and creativity. What is less evident is the fact that the film completes its abduction of Aki/the Woman/women's histories only after using her good services as translational ribotype, or what Doyle calls "rhetorical software." Her vanishing is deftly camouflaged by the substitution of . . . science fiction. Science fiction's supple, versatile, metamorphic body is substituted for the body of woman. The Vanishing Lady of Digital Cinema is abducted by science fiction's extraterrestrial aliens. How does that come about? Does this mean that computer-generated science fiction is an oppressive, patriarchal dystopia that has no place for women?

We have seen that Aki is abducted, and made disposable by, the ghostly space aliens, as well as by a wide range of historical and contemporary rhetorics, discourses, and media practices. The film, however, cannot do without her. So it uses her as a medium to convey messages, to mediate between various practices, and to make possible the emergence of (digital media's) a-life. Aki clearly mediates, and translates, between several domains: between the alien Phantoms and the high-tech human culture to which she belongs; between live-action cinema and analog animation, on the one hand, and software cinema, computer animation, and video games, on the other; between various categories and subgenres of science fiction, such as space and time travel science fiction, alien invasion science fiction, and military science fiction.

All the digital actors in *Final Fantasy* were created through the same laborious process (motion-capture, dot skeleton, wire-mesh polygon figure, Maya sculpture, block model animatic, etc.). They may all be said to be, like the computer-generated a-life creatures with which they share their uncanny life effect, assemblages of software genotypes, ribotypes, and phenotypes. Yet it is only Aki who is assigned the mission of a "perpetual translational ribotype." She is the only character who carries the completed anti-Phantom energy wave in her breastplate and who can really "save the earth." She is also the only one who can mediate between the past, the present, and the future and who can, quite literally, guarantee the continuation of "life" in the film — as well as of digital a-life in new media culture. As an archetypical, maternal world savior, she is at once the body that bears and brings forth the seeds of life (the Phantom particle "infestation" as manifestation of digital a-life, the anti-Phantom energy pattern that can neutralize the Phantoms' lethal energy, or deadly life effect), and the rhetorical, digital ribotype ensuring that "life" can go on.

Uncannily enough, however, the function of the translational ribotype in a life system overlaps with that of abduction in Peirce's tripartite scheme of the categories of philosophical reasoning. Just as the ribotype is the indispensable, intermediary actant allowing for the emergence and perpetuation of life, so is abduction needed for thought's encounter with, and energizing and renewal by, the future, the unpredictable, the actualization of the virtual. As a mediating, redemptive ribotype, Aki is thus predestined for (or condemned to) abduction. She cannot but disappear, cannot but be the vanishing lady of philosophy, cinema, and digital new media, because she can never be herself, only a thought of and for the future, the medium for revealing and letting through the otherness of the other, the alien-ness of the alien.

It is here that we realize that *Final Fantasy*'s abductive reasoning (inconsistent and fallacious though it undoubtedly is) has duped us all along. For, if abduction works by substitution (a "single conception" that is substituted for a "completed tangle of predicates attached to one subject") and gambles on the future, so does, habitually, science fiction. Indeed, science fiction works hypothesis to death for a living, frantically mobilizing all its rhetorical softwares to convince us that the space aliens are about to land, or are already among us, and that artificial life is more alive and genuine than life here on earth. Since *Final Fantasy* is a science fiction film, and since it works by abduction and substitution (substituting its New Age Gaian discourse for the evolutionary Gaian biology of Margulis, its digital a-life organisms for real life forms, its digital actors for real actors), it has clearly been plotting all along to deprive Aki of her all-too-important position and to place a less-threatening agent in her stead. So, while Aki apparently has a crucial mission on which the very survival of earth and of humankind is made to depend, it is actually science fiction that gets the assignment and is sent into action. If this may seem tautological — science fiction saves the world in a science fiction film — it is less so if we consider the ruse, indeed *the scandal*, of *Final Fantasy*'s abductions and substitutions.

Return of the Vanishing Lady

The entire *Final Fantasy* project is *pure science fiction*. This is true not only of the story of the Phantom invasion, and Dr. Sid and Aki's research on an antiphantom counterenergy wave, but also of the rhetoric and publicity hype on the film's laborious production process (in particular the description of the creation of "hyperreal" digital actors in the documentary included in the Columbia Tristar DVD and in the lavishly illustrated BradyGames book *The Making of Final Fantasy: The Spirits Within*). Though it promises to deliver the very future of cinema and video games, as well as that of art and popular culture — indeed, the future of life itself in the era of software culture and global network society — *Final Fantasy* offers us only bad science fiction. In itself, such miscalculation wouldn't be of much consequence (for bad science fiction films and novels are aplenty) were it not for the abduction and supplanting of the woman it effectuates. Even this latter abduction — which does little more than reiterate the countless evictions, displacements, and distortions of the agency and cultural contributions of women (or of minorities, or of colonized groups) in modern science fiction — could be overlooked were it not for the necessity of reenvisioning the uncanny it suggests.

If there is a message to be remembered from viewing this flawed film, it is perhaps that we have been wrong in our thinking on the uncanny. Or rather that Freud was wrong, and all of us in his wake who believed him. For what is uncanny and disturbing is not the return of the repressed, that which should have remained hidden but which reemerges into view with a grin and a vengeance; not the phantoms, doubles, and revenants, nor Nathaniel's "feminine complex" toward his father in "The Sandman" but the abduction, the neat vacating of the doll Olympia's role, as well as of all that was operatic, raucous, excessive, abject, and transgressive in Hoffmann's tale, that is effected in Freud's reading. What is uncanny is the persistence and vitality of the beautiful doll, the fact that she refuses to go away, that she resists obfuscation and substitution, and that we (feminist readers and viewers, interactors who are suspicious of abductions, whether alien or home-grown) can and should reinstate her as a live, autonomous woman with a will and voice of her own, at the center of the narrative. As Hélène Cixous writes in her memorable reading of Freud's essay "The Uncanny," "The beautiful Olympia is effaced by what she represents, for Freud has no eyes for her. This woman appears obscene because she emerges there where 'one' did not expect her to appear, and she thus causes Freud to take a detour. And what if the doll became a woman? What if she *were* alive? What if, in looking at her, we animated her?"[29]

While the uncanny should be, and has been, continually revised and reinvented,[30] *Final Fantasy*'s problematic retrieval of the genre alerts us to the latter's own history of repression. In its aptly disguised, yet utterly banal and obscene repetition of Freud's originary erasure of the doll Olympia in his 1919 essay, as well as in its substitution of an apocalyptic scenario of a-life wars for the art of life, and for the story of its magnificent resistance to replication, narrativization, and reductive modeling, Sakaguchi's film suggests that both science fiction and the theory, aesthetics, and philosophy of the uncanny have thrived on the abduction and consistent suppression of the obscene woman, and *of her stubborn return as life effect*. (The life-giving, ceaseless blue flow of earth's Gaia clearly represents the return of the vanishing lady as life effect). At the same time, the film demonstrates that any science fiction narrative's arrogant claim to colonize the future in the name of science fiction — science fiction's putative right to appropriate the dreams and chaos of potential alien invasions and "life as it could be" because its abductive imagination, to paraphrase Peirce again, may be "the only possible hope of regulating our future conduct rationally" — is doomed to fail. The failure would be provoked only in part by the defeat of science fiction's invasion of woman-snatchers, by the immense vitality and creativity of women's science fiction, or of their art and imagination in general;[31] and it would be unrelated to the terror generated by the universe's apparent, ubiquitous aliveness and undeath as imagined by Burroughs. Rather, science fiction's abduction of the future must fail precisely because anything is, or could be . . . science fiction. And also because — whether or not we agree with *Final Fantasy*'s/ contemporary science fiction's reimagining of the ancient Gaia myth — anything is, essentially, *a woman*.

Notes

I am grateful to Vivian Sobchack, Istvan Csicsery-Ronay, Christopher Bolton, and Tom LaMarre for their constructive critical comments on earlier drafts of this chapter. I also owe a debt of gratitude to Jean-Pierre Monnet for providing much-needed technical expertise.

1. *Final Fantasy: The Spirits Within*, dir. Sakaguchi Hironobu (Square, 2001); translated on DVD (Columbia Tristar, 2001). The film's production budget was $137 million, out of which $45 million was used to build Square's Honolulu studio. The film was financed entirely by Square's video game franchise; various installments of its *Final Fantasy* game series have sold tens of millions of copies worldwide. Sakaguchi is the executive producer of the game series, and in 2000 he received the Academy for Interactive Arts and Sciences Hall of Fame Award for seminal contributions to interactive entertainment and information. In 2002 *Final Fantasy: The Spirits Within* won the Special Jury Prize at the annual Media Arts Festival sponsored by the Japanese government's Bureau for Cultural Affairs

(Bunkachō media geijutsusai). For negative criticism of *Final Fantasy,* see Thom Taylor and Melinda Hsu, *Digital Cinema: The Hollywood Insider's Guide to the Evolution of Storytelling* (Studio City, Calif.: Michael Wiese Productions, 2003), 105. In 2005 Square followed up with a second movie based on the seventh game installment: *Fantasy VII: Advent Children,* dir. Nomura Tetsuya, translated on DVD (Sony, 2006). More films seem likely to follow, but here I consider only the first film.

2. The notion of remediation I have in mind here is that proposed by Jay David Bolter and Richard Grusin, who define remediation as the representation and refashioning of a medium in another medium. Remediation relies on the twin logics of immediacy, or the erasing of the medium and the practices of mediation it produces; and hypermediacy, or the reflexive foregrounding of the medium, or of the production process of an artifact (such as film) in that medium. Remediation may also be defined as a process constituted by three interrelated strategies: the mediation of mediation, or each act of mediation's dependence on other acts of mediation; the inseparability of mediation and reality, or a media culture's remediation of reality; and finally, remediation as a process of reforming reality. Jay David Bolter and Richard Grusin, *Remediation: Understanding New Media* (Cambridge, Mass.: MIT Press, 1999), 21–62.

3. See disc 2 of the Columbia Tristar DVD, which contains an interactive documentary, *The Making of Final Fantasy,* and a DVD-ROM offering, among other things, a "Virtual Tour of Square Pictures'" Honolulu Studio, and several Web links related to the film. See also Steven L. Kent and Tim Cox, *The Making of "Final Fantasy: The Spirits Within"* (Indianapolis: BradyGames, 2001).

4. LaMarre argues that the repetition of cinema in digital media and the digital arts is inevitable and that these media's attempts to simulate the cinema must fail. Thomas LaMarre, "The First Time as Farce: Digital Animation and the Repetition of Cinema," in *Cinema Anime,* ed. Steven T. Brown (New York: Palgrave, 2006), 161–88.

5. Zoe Beloff, "An Ersatz of Life: The Dream Life of Technology," in *New Screen Media: Cinema/Art/Narrative,* ed. Martin Rieser and Andres Zapp (London: British Film Institute, 2002), 292–95; Raymond Roussel, *Locus Solus,* trans. R. C. Cuningham (London: John Calder, 1983).

6. I borrow the term *movieness* from Daniel Mendelsohn, "It's Only a Movie: Kill Bill — Volume 1, A Film Directed by Quentin Tarantino," *New York Review of Books,* December 13, 2003, 41.

7. Nicolas Abraham, "Notes on the Phantom: A Complement to Freud's Metapsychology," in *The Shell and the Kernel: Renewals of Psychoanalysis,* by Nicolas Abraham and Maria Torok, ed. and trans. Nicholas T. Rand (Chicago: University of Chicago Press, 1994), 1:174–75. For an introduction to Abraham's theory of the transgenerational phantom, see the editor's note on pages 165–69 of the same volume. Developed in several essays published in the 1960s and early 1970s by Abraham and his long-time collaborator Maria Torok, this theory represents a radical reorientation of Freudian and post-Freudian theories of psychopathology insofar as symptoms are shown to derive from someone else's repression of their secret desires, conflicts, or traumas rather than from the individual's life experience. Abraham uses the concept of the phantom to reread Hamlet's dilemma in Shakespeare's celebrated play as a conflict provoked by the secret that the prince's father took to his grave and that appears as the latter's ghost ("The Phantom of Hamlet," in *Shell and the Kernel,* 1:187–205). For writings inspired by Abraham's

theory of the phantom, see Esther Rashkin, *Family Secrets and the Psychoanalysis of Narrative* (Princeton, N.J.: Princeton University Press, 1992); Avital Ronell, *Dictations: On Haunted Writing* (Bloomington: Indiana University Press, 1986); Claude Nachin, *Fantômes de l'âme: Des héritages psychiques* (Paris: L'Harmattan, 1993); Didier Dumas, *Hantise et clinique de l'autre* (Paris: Aubier, 1989). For studies of Abraham and Torok's work see Nicholas Rand's introduction to *The Shell and the Kernel* (1–22) as well as Rand, "Family Romance or Family History? Psychoanalysis and Dramatic Invention in Nicolas Abraham's *The Phantom of Hamlet*," *Diacritics* 18, no. 4 (1988): 20–30; Nicholas Rand and Maria Torok, "Paradeictic: Translation, Psychoanalysis, and the Work of Art in the Writings of Nicolas Abraham," *Diacritics* 16, no. 3 (1986): 16–25; Peggy Kamuf, "Abraham's Wake," *Diacritics* 9, no. 1 (1979): 32–45.

8. Like most genre fiction, *Final Fantasy* draws on, revisits, or remediates a welter of films and texts. Like the T1000 in *Terminator 2*, the invading Phantoms infiltrate their human victims and steal their spirit or soul. Like the protagonist Quaid in Paul Verhoeven's *Total Recall*, who has recurring dreams of himself and an unknown woman wandering through arid landscapes on the planet Mars, Aki sees herself in her dreams as a witness to the devastating war that led to the total destruction of the Phantom planet. Her dreams, like those of Quaid in *Total Recall*, are at once implanted memories and a form of communication with the aliens. The Phantoms in *Final Fantasy* are similar to the cold, expressionless, undying Agents in the Wachowski brothers' cyberpunk hit *The Matrix* in that they can sneak into any human body and wrench out its spirit. The distant prototypes for the transparent Phantoms in *Final Fantasy* are of course the peapod aliens in *Invasion of the Body Snatchers* and the monstrous creatures that invade the bodies of humans in the *Alien* series.

Final Fantasy also seems to have plundered the anime tradition. Thus Aki is clearly a counterpart of Nausicaa and San in Miyazaki Hayao's *Nausicaä* and *Princess Mononoke*, respectively, in that she is a world savior. Like Nausicaä, who becomes poisoned by the giant ōmu, Aki is contaminated by Phantom particles. The design of the Phantoms owes a great deal to the EVA cyborgs in *Neon Genesis: Evangelion*. The Phantoms also seem to evoke *Ghost in the Shell*'s awesome Puppet Master, who can manipulate individuals through the "personality software" he plants in their brains. *Kaze no tani no Naushika*, dir. Miyazaki Hayao (1984); translated as *Nausiaä of the Valley of the Wind*, DVD (Disney, 2005); *Mononoke hime*, dir. Miyazaki Hayao (1997); translated as *Princess Mononoke*, DVD (Miramax, 2000); *Shinseiki evangerion*, dir. Anno Hideaki, TV series, 26 episodes (1995–96); translated as *Neon Genesis Evangelion: Perfect Collection*, DVD box set (ADV Films, 2002); *Kōkaku kidōtai: Ghost in the Shell*, dir. Oshii Mamoru (1995); translated as *Ghost in the Shell*, DVD (Manga Entertainment, 1998).

On Hollywood science fiction blockbusters see Geoff King, *New Hollywood Cinema: An Introduction* (New York: Columbia University Press, 2002); King, *Spectacular Narrative: Hollywood in the Age of the Blockbuster* (London: Tauris, 2000); Geoff King and Tanya Krzywinska, *Science Fiction Cinema: From Outerspace to Cyberspace* (London: Wallflower, 2000). On *The Matrix*, see William Irwin, ed., *The Matrix and Philosophy: Welcome to the Desert of the Real* (Chicago: Open Court, 2002); Chris Seay and Greg Garrett, *The Gospel Reloaded: Exploring Spirituality and Faith in the Matrix* (Colorado Springs, Colo.: Piñon, 2003). On the science fiction tradition in Japanese anime, and its relation to science fiction cinema, see Ueno

Toshiya, *Kurenai no metaru sūtsu: Anime to iu senjō* (Metalsuits, the red: Wars in animation) (Tokyo: Kinokuniya Shoten, 1998); Thomas LaMarre, "From Animation to Anime: Drawing Movements and Moving Drawings," *Japan Forum* 14 (2002): 329–67; LaMarre, "First Time as Farce"; Livia Monnet, "Toward the Feminine Sublime, or the Story of a Twinkling Monad, Shape-Shifting across Dimension: Intermediality, Fantasy, and Special Effects in Cyberpunk Film and Animation," *Japan Forum* 14 (2002): 303–51; Seto Tatsuya et al., *Nihon no anime: All about Japan Anime, Bessatsu Takarajima* 638 (Tokyo: Takarajimasha, 2002).

9. The early decades of the twentieth century saw a proliferation of discourses on cinema's primitivism, animism, magical power, and uncanny effect. These idealistic theories were proposed above all by novelists, theorists, and filmmakers such as Vachel Lindsay, Béla Balázs, Tanizaki Jun'ichirō, Germaine Dulac, Edogawa Ranpo, Siegfried Kracauer, Louis Aragon, André Breton, Abel Gance, Ricciotto Canudo, Sergei Eisenstein, and Walter Benjamin. See Rachel O. Moore, *Savage Theory: Cinema as Modern Magic* (Durham, N.C.: Duke University Press, 2000), 48–95; Richard Abel, ed., *French Film Theory and Criticism, 1907–1939: A History/Anthology* (Princeton, N.J.: Princeton University Press, 1993), 1:131–83, 235–67, 305–73, 410–13, 421–36; Joanne Bernardi, *Writing in Light: The Silent Scenario and the Japanese Pure Film Movement* (Detroit: Wayne State University Press, 2001), 195–214; Thomas LaMarre, *Shadows on the Screen: Tanizaki Jun'ichirō on Cinema and "Oriental" Aesthetics* (Ann Arbor: Center for Japanese Studies, University of Michigan, 2005).

10. Jean Epstein, "On Certain Characteristics of Photogénie," in *French Film Theory and Criticism, 1907–1939: A History/Anthology,* ed. Richard Abel (Princeton, N.J.: Princeton University Press, 1993), 1:316–17. See also Epstein's essay "Magnification," in the same volume (235–41).

11. Emile Vuillermoz, "Before the Screen: Hermes and Silence," in *French Film Theory and Criticism, 1907–1939,* ed. Richard Abel (Princeton, N.J.: Princeton University Press, 1993), 1:158.

12. In "An Ersatz of Life" Zoe Beloff defines the cinema as a time machine of movement (295). For a different view on the cinema as time machine, see Siegfried Zielinski, "Backwards to the Future: Outline for an Investigation of the Cinema as Time Machine," *Future Cinema: The Cinematic Imaginary after Film,* ed. Jeffrey Shaw and Peter Weibel (Cambridge, Mass.: MIT Press, 2003), 566–69. *Final Fantasy*'s Phantoms are time machines of movement because they fall through, or traverse the space-time and histories of, the cinema, animation, and digital media. They are transitional because they call attention to an important shift in filmmaking and animation.

13. LaMarre defines cinemation as the interface of cinema and animation in computer-generated cinema, or cinematic digital animation ("First Time as Farce"). The notion of cinemation I am proposing here refers to a type of film in which live-action footage and analog animation, or their digital counterparts, coexist, simulate, and remediate one another. For discussions of the history and aesthetics of cinemation, see Paul Wells, *Understanding Animation* (London: Routledge, 1998), 13–17, 38–39; Giannalberto Bendazzi, *Cartoons: Le cinéma d'animation, 1892–1992,* trans. Marina Gagliano (Paris: Liana Levi, 1991), 32–39.

14. For a study of lightning-hand animation, see Donald Crafton, *Before Mickey: The Animated Film, 1898–1928* (Chicago: University of Chicago Press, 1993).

15. Richard Doyle, *Wetwares: Experiments in Postvital Living* (Minneapolis: University of Minnesota Press, 2003), 214.

16. For an in-depth study of Cohl's work, see Donald Crafton, *Emile Cohl, Caricature, and Film* (Princeton, N.J.: Princeton University Press, 1990); on Svankmajer, see Peter Hames, ed., *Dark Alchemy: The Films of Jan Svankmajer* (Trowbridge, U.K.: Flicks Books, 1995).

17. Lovelock's Gaia hypothesis affirms that the earth is a whole that has been transformed by a self-evolving and self-regulating living system. All life-forms on the planet are part of Gaia. The continually evolving diversity of these life-forms produces and sustains the most favorable conditions for the growth and prosperity of Gaia. The earth's atmosphere, seas, and terrestrial crust were created by Gaia. As a "total planetary being" that comprises but is not limited to the biosphere (the part of the earth where living things exist) or to the biota (the collection of all individual living organisms), Gaia "has continuity with the past back to the origins of life, and extends into the future as long as life persists." James Lovelock, *The Ages of Gaia: A Biography of Our Living Earth* (New York: Norton, 1988), 19. See also Lovelock's *Gaia: A New Look at Life on Earth* (Oxford: Oxford University Press, 1987).

18. Lynn Margulis, *Early Life* (Boston: Science Books International, 1982), 85, 3. See also Margulis, *Symbiotic Planet: A New Look at Evolution* (New York: Basic Books, 1998); Lynn Margulis, Dorion Sagan, and Philip Morrison, *Slanted Truths: Essays on Gaia, Symbiosis, and Evolution* (New York: Copernicus Books, 1997).

19. Christopher Langton, *Artificial Life* (Redwood City, Calif.: Addison-Wesley, 1989), 2, quoted in Doyle, *Wetwares*, 25.

20. Compare this with a quote Doyle cites from William Burroughs's *Ghost of Chance*: "Panic . . . the sudden, intolerable knowing that everything is alive." In *Wetwares*, Doyle notes that the main characters in Philip K. Dick's novels *Game Players of Titan* and *Radio Free Albemuth* experience a similar feeling of panic on realizing that they are "surrounded" by vitality, a seemingly ubiquitous presence of life that may be nonorganic, non-carbon-based, or may arrive from the future or the past (19, 34–35).

21. Charles Sanders Peirce, *Collected Papers* (Cambridge, Mass.: Belknap Press of Harvard University Press, 1932), 2:270, 643, quoted in Doyle, *Wetwares*, 24.

22. Langton, *Artificial Life*, 33, 2, quoted in Doyle, *Wetwares*, 26.

23. Doyle, *Wetwares*, 215.

24. Marcello Barbieri, *The Organic Codes: An Introduction to Semantic Biology* (New York: Cambridge University Press, 2002).

25. *Final Fantasy*'s representation of the blue Gaia may be regarded as an actualized (computer-generated) representation of the "total planetary being" or Gaian superorganism imagined by Lovelock and Margulis. Dr. Sid's own Gaia hypothesis sounds like a science fiction version of artificial life theories such as those of Langton, Steven Levy, and Stefan Helmreich. The film's holographs of proliferating Phantom particles are clearly inspired by computer-grown a-life cells and organisms. Stefan Helmreich, *Silicon Second Nature: Culturing Artificial Life in a Digital World* (Los Angeles: University of California Press, 1998); Steven Levy, *Artificial Life: The Quest for a New Creation* (New York: Pantheon Books, 1992).

26. Kent and Cox, *Making*, 218.

27. See Norman M. Klein's suggestive description of Koko the clown's rotoscoped body as an invaded, phantom presence: "Of all Fleischer characters, Koko

was rotoscoped the most often. By 1933, it gave him a phantom presence, too often invaded. Graphically, rotoscoping leaves scars — something a bit too human, a bit too lithe, subtle but plain to see. Koko practically inhabited two bodies at once, from a cartoon clown who shuffled (buttery head, sacklike body) to a leaner man who ran gracefully (more angles to his chin; a stiffer spinal column). Koko was designed to be haunted, wrapped in billowy cloth that was ideal for a ghost dancing between bodies, particularly in this (i.e., in *Betty Boop's Snow White*), his last extended appearance, his swan song." Norman M. Klein, "Animation and Animorphs: A Brief Disappearing Act," in *Meta-Morphing: Visual Transformation and the Culture of Quick-Change,* ed. Vivian Sobchack (Minneapolis: University of Minnesota Press, 2000), 27.

28. Like nineteenth-century spirit photography, early cinema became fascinated by spiritualism's materializations of ghosts and spirits. Many early films stage such apparitions, some even mocking spirit photography's repeated failure to render the tenuous presence of the specter (e.g., *Photographing a Ghost* [1898]). The early decades of the twentieth century saw the emergence of ectoplasm-producing mediums — female mediums who excreted a mysterious, grayish-white substance during materialization séances. One of the most spectacular examples of such mediums was Eva C. (Eva Carrière), who became the subject of a thorough "scientific investigation" by Baron von Schrenck-Notzing. Schrenck-Notzing also produced one of the rare filmed records of a female spiritualistic medium's trance and production of ectoplasm.

In her fascinating study of vanishing women in the magical arts, spiritualism, cinema, and psychoanalysis, Karen Beckman argues that what made female mediums disappear in the ghostly materializations they produced was not only the anxiety provoked by the exposure of the medium's transgressive corporeality and sexuality but also the fact that spirit photography and early spiritualist-themed films attempted to capture the elusive, ghostly essence of the photographic or the cinematic image. Beckman also argues that, while Méliès's *L'escamotage d'une dame chez Robert Houdin* (1896), R. W. Paul's *Vanishing Lady* (1897), and Thomas Edison's film on the same magical act exhibit an anxiety toward the female body and female agency similar to that found in accounts of female spiritualistic mediumship, magic's vanishing women also used the spectacle of vanishing to resist, and protest, total eradication. See Karen Beckman, *Vanishing Women: Magic, Film, and Feminism* (Durham, N.C.: Duke University Press, 2003), 49–91. On spiritualism and the role of female mediums, see also Ruth Brandon, *The Spiritualists: The Passion for the Occult in the Nineteenth and Twentieth Century* (New York: Knopf, 1983); Ann Baude, *Radical Spirits: Spiritualism and Women's Rights in Nineteenth-Century America* (Boston: Beacon, 1989). On spirit photography, see Fred Gettings, *Ghosts in Photographs: The Extraordinary Story of Spirit Photography* (New York: Harmony, 1978); Andreas Fischer and Veit Loers, *Im Reich der Phantome: Fotographie des Unsichtbaren,* exhibition catalog (Ostfildern-Ruit: Cantz Verlag, 1997); James Coates, *Photographing the Invisible: Practical Studies in Spirit Photography, Spirit Portraiture, and Other Rare but Allied Phenomena* (1911; rpt. New York: Arno, 1973). On late-nineteenth-century magic and the vanishing lady act, see Geoffrey Lamb, *Victorian Magic* (London: Routledge and Kegan Paul, 1976); Lucy Fischer, "The Lady Vanishes: Women, Magic, and the Movies," *Film Quarterly* 33 (1979): 30–40; Tom Gunning, "Phantom Images and Modern Manifestations: Spirit Photography, Magic Theatre, Trick Films, and Photography's

Uncanny," in *Fugitive Images: From Photography to Video,* ed. Patrice Petro (Bloomington: Indiana University Press, 1995), 42–71. Fascinating early-twentieth-century accounts of spiritualistic materializations may be found in J. Bisson, *Les phénomènes dits de materialization* (Paris: Alcon, 1914); A. Freiherrn von Schrenck-Notzing, *Materialisationsphänomene: Ein Beitrag zur Erforschung der Mediumistischen Teleplastie,* 2nd ed. (Munich: Ernst Reinhardt, 1923).

29. Sigmund Freud, "The Uncanny," in *The Complete Psychological Works of Sigmund Freud,* trans. James Strachey (London: Hogarth, 1964), 17:178–258; Hélène Cixous, "Fiction and Its Phantoms: A Reading of Freud's 'Das Unheimliche' ('The Uncanny')," trans. Robert Denommé, *New Literary History* 7 (1976): 538. The emphasis is Cixous's.

30. For an informative overview of late-twentieth-century theories of the uncanny (most of which revisit Freud's influential 1919 essay), see Anneleen Masschelein, "The Concept as Ghost: Conceptualisation of the Uncanny in Late Twentieth-Century Theory," *Mosaic* 35 (2002): 53–68. See also Martin Jay, *Cultural Semantics: Keywords of Our Time* (London: Athlone, 1998), 157–64; Dany Nobus, "Het Unheimliche: Een bibliografisch repertorium," *Psychoanalytische Perspectieven* 19–20 (1993): 173–83.

31. Women's science fiction has flourished throughout the twentieth century and continues to thrive with such new talent as Laura Mixon, Edith Forbes, Tricia Sullivan, Justina Robson, and Liz Williams. For a recent critical anthology on women's science fiction, see Marleen S. Barr, ed., *Future Females: The Next Generation* (New York: Rowman and Littlefield, 2000). See also Edward James and Farah Mendelsohn, eds., *The Cambridge Companion to Science Fiction* (New York: Cambridge University Press, 2003).

11. Otaku Sexuality

Saitō Tamaki
Translated by Christopher Bolton

Introduction

Kotani Mari

As fan cultures centered on Japanese media grow and spread internationally, critics inside and outside Japan have shown greater interest in these communities, particularly the subculture of zealous fans known as *otaku*. Saitō Tamaki is among the leading Japanese scholars working in this area. A practicing therapist who has long been recognized for his research on introverted youth, he has more recently become known for his psychoanalytic studies of sexuality, media, and imagination — starting with a celebrated book on male *otaku* desire, *Sentō bishōjo no seishin bunseki* (2001, Armored cuties: A psychoanalysis). This chapter is adapted from his second book on this topic, and it outlines his original theory of *otaku* sexuality while elaborating the psychoanalytic theory underpinning that work. It also expands the discussion to include female fans, specifically the women's genre and fan culture known as *yaoi*.

Otaku is a word that has increasingly entered the critical as well as the popular lexicon in the West (for more on this term, see the introduction to this volume). In some ways *yaoi* culture is a kind of female *otaku* culture, but it is also distinct in important ways, with its own usage, history, and context. Here it may be helpful to describe this background in a little more detail as a prelude to Saitō's chapter.

222

Yaoi is a term used to describe texts and a broader subculture characterized by a predilection for male-male love stories, stories created by and for women. Starting in the 1970s, Japanese manga included comics depicting love between young men *(shōnen)* by artists like Hagio Moto, Takemiya Keiko, and Yamagishi Ryōko — called the Shōwa 24 gang, for their common birth year, 1949. Inspired by the cult author Mori Mari, in 1979 Kurimoto Kaoru published a novel of young male love titled *Mayonaka no tenshi* (Midnight angel). These *"shōnen* love stories" *(shōnen ai mono)* in prose and manga were the precursors of *yaoi*.[1]

At the same time, from the mid-1970s onward, in the world of fanzines *(dōjinshi)*, women writers and artists were producing prose fiction and manga that imagined love between the male characters of popular anime like *Gatchaman* and *Majingaa Z.* (In some ways this resembled American "slash fiction," whose name derived from the "/" placed between the paired characters' initials.) These were anime parodies, but in 1979, Kurimoto helped found the magazine *JUN* (later *JUNE*) to publish original works for the same readership.

But it was only later that the term *yaoi* was applied to works like these. Around 1980, the female manga artists Sakata Yasuko and Hatsu Akiko coined this word to describe the male-male sex manga they were publishing in the magazine *Rappori. Yaoi* was a combination of initial letters from the phrase *"Yama nashi, Ochi nashi, Imi nashi"* (no climax, no conclusion, no meaning) — a self-ironic reference to the fact that these parodic works had no need of a story and consisted simply of repeated sex scenes.

The word *yaoi* gained currency in places like Komike — a huge, periodic convention where fanzines are bought and sold. In the mid-1980s, *yaoi*-style parodies of the soccer anime *Captain Tsubasa* were so popular at these markets that the term began to be used for this genre or style of sexually explicit takeoffs on anime. In the 1980s *yaoi* was divided into two streams: the anime parodies and the original fiction represented by *JUNE.* But the parodies were by far the more numerous. In the early 1990s publishers cashed in on this phenomenon by establishing commercial genres based on *yaoi.* These were first known as *tanbi* or *otanbi* ("aesthetic") and, then, as they became increasingly commercialized in the mid-1990s, by the acronym BL for "Boys' Love." At this point the term *yaoi* suggested works that were parodies of other texts, while the commercial BL genre was focused on original stories.

The texts parodied by *yaoi* eventually came to encompass not only manga and anime but film, the music world, and virtually all of contemporary media. For this reason, in my book *Joseijō muishiki* (1994, Technogynesis), I defined *yaoi* as a culture that rereads and reconstructs male heterosexist society along the lines of female desire. *Yaoi* is now often used to refer to a broader culture centered on these tastes.[2]

If *otaku* is a term associated with anime culture, women *yaoi* fans are indeed *otaku*. But because of the word *otaku*'s negative connotations, in the new millennium *yaoi* fans have started to favor the self-appellation "fujoshi." Pronounced like a common compound for wife or woman, the first character is altered from "feminine" to "depraved" *(fuhai)*, to produce a meaning something like "fallen woman." This is an ironically self-deprecatory reference to their obsession with things not viewed as proper — at least not in a society that wants to regard women as chaste beings cut off from sexual expression. Saitō does not use the term *fujoshi* in this chapter, but his "yaoi fan" *(yaoi aikōka)* is analogous.

Critics today differ on how to define *yaoi*. *Tanbi* author and self-proclaimed *yaoi* enthusiast Sakakibara Shihomi declared herself "a homosexual male with a female body."[3] Kurimoto Kaoru (writing as Nakajima Azusa) associates *yaoi* with anorexia and "incomplete communication."[4] Saitō argues below that if male *otaku* sexuality is focused on the object, the sexuality of female *otaku* or *yaoi* fans is focused on relations *(kankeisei)*.

One might say that *yaoi* represents what the science fiction writer and critic Joanna Russ called "pornography by women for women, with love."[5] Nevertheless, the central emblem of *yaoi* is the homosexual male, making it easily confused with gay culture, and the world of *yaoi* has been criticized by gay activists for distorting that culture or co-opting it. But examining the structure of Boys' Love novels, the literary critic Nagakubo Yōko concludes that the division of roles in *yaoi* couplings corresponds neither to the heterosexual roles of "male" and "female" nor to the customary roles in gay relationships, but to a radical departure from both.[6] Nagakubo's work analyzes the ways these novels represent the sexual self-expression of contemporary Japanese women.

One can hope that more of this criticism will be translated in the future. It is certain that time will bring further work on *yaoi* and further theories — not only from Saitō and the other critics mentioned here but from new figures we can expect to emerge from the ranks of *yaoi* producers and fans.

Otaku Sexuality

It is impossible to discuss the reception of contemporary Japanese science fiction without considering a particular category of adult fans devoted to anime, manga, and related genres, a group known as the *otaku*. Not all *otaku* are fans of science fiction in particular, and certainly not all science fiction fans are *otaku*, but there is a considerable overlap between the two groups. For example, two of Japan's best-known independently produced anime are the animated clips shown at the opening ceremonies of DAICON3 and DAICON4, the Japanese National Science Fiction Conventions held in 1981 and 1983. The hobbyists who created these pieces went on to become Gainax, the studio that produced one of the most popular anime series of the nineties, *Neon Genesis Evangelion* (1995–96, *Shinseiki evangerion*). And there are many other examples of this crossover, from the celebrated feminist science fiction critic who dresses as an anime character at conventions to the involvement of science fiction authors in anime production.[7]

There is also a close relation between science fiction and much of Japanese manga and anime. Like *Evangelion,* many anime (particularly the robot variety) employ science fiction settings and devices, and frequently even the dialogue and titles demand some knowledge of science fiction culture. Conversely, there are more than a few works of science fiction that assume a knowledge of anime. The interpenetration of these genres is proceeding apace.

The word *otaku* is now recognized around the world as describing a certain kind of fan mania, but as is often the case with common terms like this, its actual meaning is not sufficiently understood. The situation is no different in the *otaku*'s place of origin, Japan, and it may even be worse. Overseas *otaku* seem to identify proudly with this word, but in Japan this is not always the case. Japanese television networks prohibit this word on the air, so wrapped is it in visceral prejudice and misunderstanding. "Lacking social skills and even common sense"; "solitary and maladjusted"; "pedophiles incapable of dealing with mature women" — these are the prevailing conceptions of *otaku* in Japan, and conscious of society's judgmental gaze, *otaku* themselves are reluctant to come out, except to one another.

Yet Japanese *otaku* have been trying to correct these prejudices. The work of the critic Ōtsuka Eiji and the writer Okada Toshio (known even abroad as the Otaking) have educated people about *otaku* and have begun to mitigate these biased views. In this chapter I hope to promote a more accurate understanding of the *otaku,* based both on their own views and on my personal experience with them. In particular, I would like to draw on my own expertise as a psychiatrist and focus on the description and psychoanalysis of *otaku* sexuality.

Prejudices about *otaku* based in ignorance have circulated easily for some time, even in my own field of psychiatry. One typical (mis)diagnosis is that *otaku* have a schizophrenic personality disorder. (My own opinion is that *otaku* clarify the limits of the very concept of personality disorders, but I leave this argument for another time.) Perhaps this kind of misunderstanding should be seen as a symptom of psychiatry's shift from a participatory activity to a system of observation. I would not go so far as to identify myself as an *otaku*, but my correspondence with the young people described below has led me into a rather profound relationship with this world — certainly beyond what I could call fieldwork. For all of these reasons, I feel that this record of my observations may have some clinical significance at the present time.

In 2000 I published a book titled *Sentō bishōjo no seishin bunseki* (Armored cuties: A psychoanalysis).[8] The title names an icon that has enjoyed tremendous popularity in Japan, particularly in manga and anime — the *sentō bishōjo*. Literally this means "beautiful warrior girl," though the translation I prefer is "armored cutie." It seems to me the popularity of this strange image is virtually unique to my country. Many Western series, from *Alien* to *Tomb Raider*, feature fighting women, but they are almost all Amazonian women. Until recently the West had almost no works that featured girl warriors in the kindergarten or elementary school range.

How did these *sentō bishōjo* come about, and how are they consumed? My book posed a series of questions along these lines, and I believe it was able to point the way toward some answers. And since it was the *otaku* who were most in love with the icon of the *sentō bishōjo*, this book also had to describe the *otaku* in some detail.

In 2003, as a kind of follow-up and expansion on the arguments in *Sentō bishōjo no seishin bunseki*, I published a book on the linked motifs of adolescence, media, and sexuality titled *Hakase no kimyō na shishunki* (The doctor's strange adolescence).[9] The present chapter is adapted from material in that latter book, particularly the second chapter on *otaku* sexuality. It summarizes many parts of the argument in *Sentō bishōjo no seishin bunseki*, though it skips some of the introductory description, for example, on the origin of the term *otaku* and the evolution of its use. And it goes beyond the earlier work in elaborating my arguments about the issue of sexuality and fiction.

Who Are the *Otaku*?

In general, the term *otaku* is used to indicate adult fans of anime, but it can obviously be expanded to include fans of manga and video games, those who collect scale model figures of characters from these media, aficionados of monster movies and other special effects genres, and so forth. All these are things that children normally graduate from in elementary or junior high school, but the *otaku*'s attraction to these "transitional objects" actually deepens beyond adolescence and into adulthood.

Saitō Tamaki

226

This is frequently regarded by others as an escape from reality, giving rise to clichéd criticisms of *otaku* as immature or unable to distinguish the real from the imaginary. But in my experience, there are few individuals more strict about that distinction than the *otaku*.

Some believe that the reason people look coldly on *otaku* traces to external physical characteristics, like thick glasses, unkempt hair, weight problems, or ugliness. It may be true that *otaku* have certain distinguishing features of appearance, but criticisms of these things amount to nothing more than personal impressions. If a critique never moves beyond these kinds of impressions, the critic will never escape the trap of narcissism; in other words, these criticisms simply reveal the means by which the critic sustains his or her own self-love.

This is the first difficulty with theorizing *otaku:* from the outset all these theories (sympathetic and unsympathetic) have been exposed to these impressions and value judgments. So my own approach here will be to avoid value judgments as far as possible and try to describe the *otaku* formally. My descriptors for *otaku* are as follows:

- They have an affinity for fictional contexts *(kyokō no kontekusuto).*
- They resort to fictionalization in order to possess the object of their love.
- They have multiple orientations when it comes to enjoying fiction.
- For them fiction itself can be a sexual object.

Here I have deliberately used the term *fictional contexts,* instead of just *fiction.* Otaku seek value in the fictional, but they are also extremely sensitive to different levels of fictionality. From within our increasingly mediatized environment, it is already difficult to draw a clear line between the real and the imaginary. It is no longer a matter of deciding whether we are seeing one or the other, but of judging which level of fiction something represents. Manga and anime both contain multiple imaginary layers: the world depicted in the text, the personal circumstances of the author that the text may also describe, the backstage world of the work's production, and marketing questions of where it circulates and how it is received. When enjoying a work, the *otaku* takes pleasure in straddling all the levels of these layered contexts. Adapting a term from classical psychiatry, I call this "multiply oriented."

But all of the above are also seen to some extent in the mania of other fans. The behavior that sets *otaku* apart is the act of *loving* the object by possessing it. For example, the largest of all *otaku* events is the Komikku Maaketto ("comic market"), abbreviated as Komike in Japanese and held twice a year in August and December. Here, hundreds of thousands of *otaku* (many dressed as their favorite manga and anime characters) gather to buy and sell independently produced comics called *dōjinshi*. Just attending Komike is a crash course in the world of the *otaku*.

Dressing up and producing these *dōjinshi* comics are among the activities *otaku* must participate in to maintain their credentials, something that sets them apart from run-of-the-mill fans. Over thirty thousand groups produce and sell their *dōjinshi* at Komike, and most are second-order texts, that is, takeoffs on well-known manga and anime. I believe *dōjinshi* are significant because they constitute an *otaku* "rite of ownership," whereby the fans take the works they love and make them their own through the act of parody, which is to say by fictionalizing them even further. *Dōjinshi* are one crystallization of this activity, though more recently Internet mailing lists and discussion boards have also become sites for publishing independently authored stories. In venues like these that are more text-based than the visual *dōjinshi*, participants contribute "SS" — original short stories or "side stories" with characters and settings borrowed from favorite works.

The most popular among the *dōjinshi* are the pornographic parodies in the "eighteen and over" genre. It is easy to hold these works up and proclaim disgust with the *otaku*, but unless one can overcome this visceral dislike, it is impossible to perceive the *otaku*'s true nature. As my list of *otaku* descriptors indicates, the issue of the *otaku* is one of sexuality, and it is this genre that displays their unique qualities in distilled form. It is not easy to locate a sexual object in fiction itself: that represents a taste for something far more direct than we see in the fetishism of ordinary fan manias. Many *otaku* actually have imagined sexual relationships with their favorite manga and anime protagonists, and masturbate to these fantasies.

Something that deserves special mention here is *otaku* sexuality's estrangement from everyday life. For example, there are many varieties of the odd sexuality *(tōsaku)* depicted in the eighteen-and-over genre, including an attraction to little girls that could be seen as pedophilic. It is around this issue that the revulsion directed at *otaku* becomes most intense. Many people immediately associate this with an incident that popularized the word in the mass media, the 1989 child murders committed by the anime- and porn-obsessed serial killer Miyazaki Tsutomu. But contrary to popular expectations, the vast majority of *otaku* are not pedophiles in actual life. They are said to choose respectable partners of the opposite sex and to have the kind of sex lives one would term healthy. The evidence for this separation between textual and actual sexuality is that only a tiny number of *otaku* commit criminal acts, even though they number in the millions. As a matter of fact, since 1989, Japan has seen no other child murders committed by *otaku*.

The Particulars of *Yaoi* Culture

This separation is even more pronounced when it comes to the phenomenon of *yaoi*. I have already discussed the *otaku* predilection for parody; *yaoi* is part of this parody culture, but it has its own particular protocols. If the takeoffs produced by male *otaku* render their subjects pornographic, *yaoi* texts render them homoerotic.

For example, *yaoi* texts may take heroes from manga like *Yū yū hakusho* (*Ghost Files*) or *Captain Tsubasa* and concoct imaginary scandals that reread the relationships between these characters as homosexual ones.[10] The targets of this activity are usually characters in manga and anime for young people, but apparently they also include characters from novels and real figures like baseball players and pop stars. As Kotani Mari notes in her introduction to this chapter, *yaoi* is an abbreviation of the phrase *Yama nashi, Ochi nashi, Imi nashi,* which translates roughly as "no climax, no conclusion, no meaning." In other words, narrative is dispensed with, and the only point is to portray the homosexual relationship. *Yaoi* texts correspond to the subgenre of Western fan writing known as "slash fiction," which had its origins with some *Star Trek* fans' depictions of a "K/S" homosexual relationship between Captain Kirk and Mr. Spock. (For more on the history and the usage of the word *yaoi*, see Kotani's introduction.)

The first thing to point out is that the producers and consumers of *yaoi* texts are overwhelmingly women. The majority of participants in the Komike comic market are women (contradicting the idea that *otaku* are mostly male), and the majority of those female participants are *yaoi* aficionados. Certainly, the number of gay men producing or consuming these texts is virtually nil. If the desires of *yaoi* authors are directly reflected in these texts, then how should we characterize their sexuality? Clearly, it represents a set of desires that cannot be described in terms of the psychoanalytic theory that has defined perversion *(tōsaku)* up to now. What is significant here is again the fact that the imaginary sexual lives of the *yaoi* crowd are totally separate from their everyday sexual lives.

Some contend that one should investigate sexuality by considering actual sexual activities, but I have always argued that today the real or the actual is something layered, something increasingly devoid of any firm foundation. In this situation, fantasies may in fact be the most appropriate material for investigating sexuality. More pointedly, real sexual acts are far too much of an admixture to consider when analyzing the structural aspects of sexuality. Here, the fact that *yaoi* fans *(yaoi aikōka)* and *otaku* are sexual late bloomers actually works in our favor: because they are unacquainted with the realities of sex, they can pursue these sexual fantasies in a purer form.[11]

Enomoto Nariko is a figure who sheds considerable light on *yaoi* fantasies and sexuality. She is the author of the popular manga *Senchimento no kisetsu* (Sentimental season), serialized in the weekly comic magazine *Biggu komikku supirittsu* (Big comic spirits). She has also created numerous *dōjinshi* under the name Nobi Nobita. As recorded in *Sōhyō* (Criticism) — an anthology of her critical works she issued herself as a *dōjinshi* — Enomoto started out as a *yaoi* author. She became known for a piece of criticism titled "Adults Just Don't Get It," its title drawn from the Japanese title of François Truffaut's *400 Blows* (1959). That essay used R. D. Laing's *Divided Self* to read the celebrated anime serial *Neon Genesis Evangelion* (the psychology of which has been taken up even at meetings of the Japanese Association of Pathography). *Evangelion*'s director Anno Hideaki was reportedly so impressed with Enomoto's interpretation that when he made the films based on the series, he incorporated a number of details that reflected her ideas.[12]

Enomoto/Nobita's work is a valuable resource. Usually the creators of *yaoi* texts are even less forthcoming about themselves than *otaku*. They will speak volumes on their affection for certain texts, but generally without a very critical approach to the works; *yaoi* writing itself has not become the target of analysis or interpretation. Enomoto is the exception among *yaoi* creators, gifted with unusual eloquence and a keen critical sense to match. For me her criticism is far more interesting than her manga, and when I accepted an invitation to do an interview with her in the magazine *Komikku fan* (Comic fan), it was out of admiration for Nobi Nobita the critic more than Enomoto the artist. That interview touched on a number of important points related to *yaoi* sexuality, so I rely broadly on Enomoto's comments in what follows.[13]

Asymmetrical Sexuality

Let me begin with some distinctions between male and female sexuality among the *otaku*. Male *otaku* refer to their affection for anime heroines with a special term *moe* (pronounced mo-ay), which literally means "budding." When a fan of a character called Asuka says "I'm Asuka *moe*," it means something like "I have a thing for Asuka." Significantly, this expression has a rather self-derisive quality to it: the *otaku*'s enthusiasm is tempered by a kind of self-awareness that gives it a performed quality.

Distinguishing the sexuality of male and female *otaku* means distinguishing male and female *moe*, and there are some evident differences. For many male *otaku*, the trigger for *moe* is either a character's cute figure or the situation she finds herself in. What then is the object of *moe* for the female *otaku* who constitute the *yaoi* group? In fact *moe* is a term that *yaoi* fans do not generally use themselves, but Enomoto puts it perfectly when she says that while a male *otaku* may be "Asuka *moe*," a *yaoi* fan is "phase *moe*." "Phase" here represents one phase of a relationship. Let us suppose, for example, that a certain manga depicts a relationship of mixed friendship and antagonism between two boys. This relationship will be the focus of attention for these women fans: based on subtle gestures, looks, and expressions, or on fragments of dialogue, how and when will it move into its romantic phase of homosexual attraction? That is the universal theme of *yaoi* texts.

Enomoto explains that "male fans cannot experience *moe* until they have fixed their own position" — an observation that may well have validity beyond *otaku* and *yaoi* fans. In general a man fears the undermining of his own subject position, and he must establish that position firmly before he can desire an object. This is probably the fate of all who possess a phallus (as distinct from a penis): if the position and orientation of the phallus is not defined, the male cannot face even the object of his own desire. The word *moe* is used by male *otaku* to locate the agent of that desire.

On the other hand, in women that fear for one's subject position is less acute. When a woman desires something, her own position is not important: she immerses herself completely in the object, and by emptying herself, she is able to take it in. The versatility of this subject position is clear when we consider how she identifies with the object. In the gay sex depicted by *yaoi* texts, a reader or creator can identify with both the *seme* ("active") and *uke* ("passive") characters.[14] This is why her attraction to a text surpasses that of the male *otaku*.

This passion manifests itself in a different posture toward the text. For example, male *otaku* will often debate matters of textual interpretation with one another, but *yaoi* readers will argue fiercely about the combinations of characters in a parody or the choice to assign a character the *seme* or *uke* role in a sexual encounter. The latter sort of debate is unthinkable among male *otaku*, although both kinds of argument represent the struggle described above to "possess the work."

Should *yaoi* texts be regarded as proof of the charge entertained above, the confusion of "fiction" with "reality"? In fact, these fan authors realize that the gay connections between characters in the textual worlds they create could never realistically exist. Regarding the absence of female characters in these parodies, Nobi Nobita explained to me that "when women are depicted, it can't help becoming weirdly real." Clearly there is no confusion between reality and fiction here.

Something *yaoi* fans have in common with male *otaku* is that the objects of their affection exist in a world of pure fiction. The *otaku*'s *sentō bishōjo* lack any correspondent in the real world. In the same way, *yaoi* texts depict relationships that could never occur in reality (even after making allowances for parodic exaggeration). In other words, both require of fiction that it be a closed reality sufficient unto itself.

The *yaoi* creator Nakajima Azusa has written an analysis of *yaoi* titled *Children of Thanatos,* which is interesting as an act of self-analysis by one of the genre's key players. The book's description of *yaoi* has a number of points in common with theories of *otaku* I advanced in my first book on *otaku, Sentō bishōjo no seishin bunseki.*[15] First, Nakajima writes that nearly all *yaoi* writers are heterosexual women with husbands and children and that she has never met one who was a lesbian. This corresponds with my own observation about the scarcity of homosexual *otaku.* Like *otaku, yaoi* fans are living out separate sexualities. They lead heterosexual lives, but their fictionally oriented sexuality turns to male homosexual relationships. These fictional sexual objects are not proxies for the real; instead, the space of fiction has a wholly independent economy of desire, a point *yaoi* fans share with male *otaku.* We know there are also women who feel drawn to gay men and seek them out; it is interesting that they share these same *yaoi* tastes.

So *otaku* and *yaoi* texts both exhibit sexualities estranged from everyday life, but the details of that estrangement differ. These are distinctions that have existed since the origins of *otaku* culture, and they have resulted in separate male and female habitats within this culture. If the *sentō bishōjo* is the object of desire for *otaku* (and from here on I use that word to refer to males only), *yaoi* texts banish female characters, and readers' desires are represented by homosexual relations between males. In an afterword to a bunkobon edition of Yoshida Akimi's *Banana Fish* — one of the most commercially successful *yaoi* manga — one critic wrote that love is possible only among those of the same gender. This recalls Hashimoto Osamu's famous assertion that "friendship is love without sex." Either comment could be applied accurately to the desire systems of *yaoi* authors and fans.[16]

As noted earlier, in *yaoi* texts the relations between characters and their psychological dynamics are everything. Unlike *otaku* texts, characters are depicted as genderless, and sexual intercourse itself is represented very *abstractly.* Given the homosexuality, anal intercourse is necessarily depicted, but it is simply the signal of an emotional climax; it is the rising psychological excitement and euphoria leading to this act that are drawn with real care. This differs from *otaku dōjinshi,* which focus on the visual depiction of sexual activity and which elicit the reader's empathy through the depiction of sexual passion, rather than psychology.

Surprisingly, in *yaoi* parodies it is not important that the original text be in a visual medium like the parody itself. While *otaku* parodies target almost exclusively manga and anime, *yaoi* authors can appropriate a wider range of characters drawn from genres that range from mystery novels to real-life boy bands. This parallels the difference between so-called boys' (*shōnen*) and girls' (*shōjo*) manga, the one privileging visual shock effects and the other psychology and story.

The Origins of Asymmetry

Actual heterosexual relationships appear symmetrical in the sense that the man desires the woman and the woman the man. But as we know, in any male-female relationship, the fundamental orientation of the male's desire differs from that of the woman. (In that sense, love is nothing more than an exchange of illusions.) We must refer to psychoanalysis — particularly Sigmund Freud and Jacques Lacan — to understand these structural differences between male and female desire.

Psychoanalysis teaches that female and male desire have contrasting makeups from the moment they are constituted. What first gives rise to male desire is the process of symbolic castration. When the father intrudes into the happy sufficient union that exists between the mother and the young child, he severs their connection. At this point the male child discovers that his mother lacks a penis. The mother's omnipotence (the omnipotence of the ego) is abandoned and replaced (along with the absent penis) by the signifier of the phallus.

When the male child obtains the primal tool of language that is the phallic signifier, the male child becomes a speaker and enters the symbolic world. By experiencing symbolic castration, he becomes a neurotic subject, and from that point the full range of desires becomes possible. Constituted as it is in this way, male desire has castration anxiety at its heart and must always seek the "object a" lost through castration. Desire directed at the *object a* incarnates desire as an illusion within the symbolic world, but never reaches the actual object.

On the other hand, female desire arises in a more roundabout way. Women also undergo symbolic castration to become a neurotic subject, but afterward, a woman discovers her own anatomical difference. She moves toward the mother's position because both daughter and mother lack a penis. In males, gaining the phallus does not stave off desire for the mother, but for females, desire directed at the mother must be redirected through castration. For females, the mark of lacking a penis makes it possible to desire the phallus from the mother's position.

The male follows a chain of metaphors directed toward the desired *object a* that he cannot attain. In the process, he constructs the illusion called knowledge. What he tries to possess (e.g., the illusion of woman) is actually a stand-in for the singular *object a* that perpetually eludes his grasp. And what is the situation for women? They locate themselves in the position of that which is desired by the male, the position of the mother. But this location represents a state of lack. Women can locate themselves only as beings lacking from the symbolic world, where women do not exist, and it is from this position of lack that women desire the phallus they do not have. This is the diametric opposite of the male orientation that constructs illusions.

The object of *otaku* desire, the *sentō bishōjo,* or armored cutie, is none other than *object a,* the girl who identifies with the penis. It is in an effort to become the possessor of these figures that male *otaku* construct the various illusions around them: fiction/criticism, novels, *dōjinshi,* and so forth. What is at the heart of the issue here is the reality the *sentō bishōjo* has by virtue of existing completely within fiction — by virtue of her state of lack. In *Sentō bishōjo no seishin bunseki,* I described this as "the inverted hysteria of visual space." There is not room here to repeat all the details of that argument, but in summary it consists of the following points:

1. When a male desires a female, she is "hystericized" *(hisuteriika).*
2. Hystericization is desire that perceives a two-layered structure to the object: a visible outer layer that attracts or entices, and an unseen deeper level, the object's true nature (like a hidden trauma).
3. The *sentō bishōjo* has a number of features that correspond to those of actual hysteria.
4. However, the *sentō bishōjo* can experience battle ("jouissance" = enjoyment) without trauma (such as the experience of "rape" that motivates many "real" fighting women). In this sense she presents the mirror image of actual hysteria.

For male *otaku* desire, what is important is precisely that the desired object is lacking. If the premise of the *sentō bishōjo* is that she is fictional and lacking, it is only this that makes her eligible as an object of desire. But the illusionary quality of these warrior girls must have a *concretely* visual aspect. In the experience of *moe,* these visual elements occupy a central place, because inasmuch as these *sentō bishōjo* are objects of desire, they must provide some toehold for the author and reader to identify with them iconically. It is only in the visual dimension that the male can project his image narcissistically on the object. This accounts for the male predisposition to be attracted by physical appearances, and it may also explain the tendency among agents of male desire to supplement their own lack with a fetish.

How, then, does the desire of *yaoi* readers differ from that of *otaku?* Here we can directly apply what was said earlier about female desire. It may seem impossible for female readers to identify themselves directly with anything in a gay love story, particularly one from which female characters have been banished. But this is part of the fundamental process that enables desire. In the everyday world, it is by virtue of being the object of male desire that women are able to constitute their own position as a lack. If male *otaku* feel desire for the lack of the object, in *yaoi* female desire it is important that one be a lacking subject oneself.

So excluding women from *yaoi* texts is more or less necessary in order for the reader to alienate herself as the agent of desire. This current of desire, meticulously prepared, is then directed toward the phallic relationship of the men in the text. This phallic connection results from the fact that males, having penises, can take either the "active" *seme* or "passive" *uke* role in the sex act. Female penis envy is highly abstracted in these texts; the object of envy is rather the phallic positioning inherent in this relationship. Because of this, women can identify with any character in the story. A woman can never assert her own existence in these dramas of phallic desire, but it is precisely because of this inability that she can attempt an identification that is less limited than that of the male. The actual world contains many examples of this freedom women have as sexual subjects.

It is known that men often form homosocial bonds — male unions that lead automatically to homophobia. The resistance heterosexual men generally feel toward homosexual connections is far stronger than the resistance heterosexual women feel toward lesbianism. On the stage of the imagination where desire is played out, men always try to become the agent of that desire, which is why they try to explain desire's origins, and why in turn I am writing this. Put another way, men can feel only the kind of desire that can be described.

To all appearances, the desire of women is constituted much more passively. Women do not like to assert themselves as agents of desire, which is why their desire is so often hard to describe. Can one rationally explain women's taste for jewelry? It is not even fetishism. This resistance to description is directly expressed by the phrase that gives us the word *yaoi*: "No climax, no conclusion, no meaning."

As I mentioned, in these fanciful homosexual relations the thing regarded as most important is who has the *seme* and who the *uke* role. Among *yaoi* readers there are fierce debates about these assignments. This supports our ideas about *yaoi* desire: what matters is the relation between characters and the phase of that relationship.

Consider a slightly different formulation: if we identify *otaku* desire as the desire "to have," *yaoi* desire is the desire "to become." Extending a postulate of psychoanalysis that "a heterosexual is one who loves women," we can say that women are fundamentally heterosexual beings. This is in part the reason why psychoanalysis does not regard lesbianism as an abnormal sexuality (tōsaku) but as an example of "acting out." Yaoi readers are not trying to possess the homosexual relationships in yaoi texts; they are trying to identify with the phallic relationship itself. What permits them to experience jouissance is the form of their desire as a wish "to become."

The moe of male otaku is mainly a fetishistic desire "to have." It is a desire not for reality itself but for reality's shroud or mantle. For that reason the elements of moe tend to multiply. For example, the visual ornamentation of manga and anime characters is increasing. It is easy to speak about the virtual quality of this kind of otaku sexual love, but it is hard to say the same kinds of things about yaoi. It may be because yaoi identification with the object seems to be constituted far more directly than otaku possession, which is, after all, possession of a substitute. In that sense, we might say that yaoi moe is a far more enjoyable experience than otaku moe is.

The Issue of *Shota*

Recently, however, a new genre called shota has blurred many of these distinctions between yaoi fans and otaku. Apparently growing out of yaoi, shota texts feature sexual depictions of prepubescent boys and have a complicated mix of male and female producers and consumers. Shota represents one extreme among current expressions of otaku sexuality.[17]

Shota is an abbreviation for "Shōtarō complex," from Kaneda Shōtarō, the boy who pilots the robot in the manga and anime Tetsujin 28 gō (what became Gigantor in English).[18] Originally an offshoot of yaoi, the origins of this genre are said to begin in the early 1980s.

Yaoi texts naturally feature characters from boys' comics, but shota dote on even younger, obviously prepubescent boys. Except for this, there is almost no difference between yaoi and shota texts, insofar as both depict love or sex between male characters.

Shota has become suddenly popular in recent years, among an audience that uniquely embraces both male otaku and yaoi women. The ratio of men to women is still being investigated, but based on informal observations where dōjinshi are sold, the split between men and women seems to be nearly fifty-fifty. Despite the genre's origins in yaoi, it was reportedly male shota fans who created the Shotaketto, a market specifically for buying and selling dōjinshi in this category.

Naturally, this genre preserves the asymmetry between male and female desire: while shota by male and female authors both depict little boys, *shota* texts by female *yaoi* authors are structurally identical to *yaoi* texts, while *shota* by male *otaku* clearly position these little boys as young girls with penises. Thus the foregoing analysis of *otaku* and *yaoi* fan desire can be applied to *shota* authors and readers with very little modification.

The issue is why this apparent fusion of genres occurred in the first place. Why did the objects of male and female desire become even younger? It is obvious that psychoanalytically, we cannot consider this apart from castration denial and narcissism. But given that, why are the actual pedophiles among these fans so few? I consider *shota* again in my conclusion and return then to some of these unanswered questions. In these days when legal measures restricting child pornography are a constant issue, it is all the more important that we analyze where this desire is directed.

Fictionality and Possession

Being an *otaku* is a matter of possession rather than perversion. To summarize what I have argued in much greater detail in *Sentō bishōjo no seishin bunseki,* it is *otaku* rites of possession that show the *otaku*'s uniqueness most clearly, because the objects of affection (anime, manga, or video-game heroines) are possessed through fictionalization. The proof of this is that the vast majority of the innumerable *dōjinshi* at the Komike are parodies or critiques of existing manga and anime titles. *Otaku* have escaped sexual perversion through this practice of fictionalizing, since the desire to fictionalize a thing is ultimately the desire to own it, and stops there. The desire to possess is the starting point that *otaku* and *yaoi* fans have in common, and it is this that guarantees the heterosexuality of their everyday lives.

Is this fetishism? There is no simple answer to this. *Otaku* and *yaoi* fans are fetishists to the extent that we all are — in the sense that when we desire an object, what we desire is something the object fundamentally lacks. But while the rest of us are usually unaware of this lack, *otaku* are conscious of it to some extent. In other words, they realize that the object of their desire is nothing more than a fiction.

The appearance of perversion is one thing that makes the psychoanalytic study of *otaku* difficult. But a bigger problem is that psychoanalysis lacks the vocabulary needed to analyze possession through fictionalization. Obviously parody and criticism are both creative activities on some scale, and analyzing creative activity itself is extremely difficult.

Clinicians uniformly recognize the need for some separation between an author's private life and his or her work. In other words, human creative processes involve many elements that cannot be reduced to "symptoms," traumas, or other personal factors. In my book *Bunmyakubyō* (1998, Context disease), I posited that the driving force behind creative activity is a concept external to psychoanalysis — the "etiologic drive" *(byōinronteki doraibu)*. I introduced this idea to explain how healthy authors can produce works that one can only regard as diseased.[19] The example I offered was the work of the manga artist Yoshida Sensha, who produced many schizophrenic texts.

Creative works are not always equivalent to disease symptoms. Desire is latent in all creative activity, and it is my own belief that desire falls completely within the realm of psychoanalysis. But perhaps people must overcome desire during creative activity. For example, the three areas of the mind posited by Michael Balint are the oedipal area, the area of the basic fault, and the area of creation.[20] The last is an area in which the object does not exist, one that is dependent only on self relations *(hitorikankei)*. This is where human creative activities have their origin, but Balint writes that this area is unknown, perhaps because objects do not exist there. While Balint's description is not necessarily psychoanalytic, there is something fundamentally true in it.

The *Otaku* as Creator

Calling the *otaku* "creators" will produce objections that most of their work is childish in the extreme: lacking in originality, imagination, expressive skill, and so on. But these criticisms are no more than impressionistic critiques and imagined value judgments. This kind of approach is incompatible with psychoanalysis, but unfortunately even among critics who write from a psychoanalytic perspective we still see a number who are trapped in this kind of narcissistic posture. And from them we hear that tired refrain telling the *otaku* to "grow up and face reality."

One can always counter this kind of impressionistic criticism with more of the same. For example, consider Japanese academic knowledge and its insignificance to the world at large (particularly in the humanities). From one perspective the *otaku*'s knowledge is much more globally relevant than what is taught in our universities. The fact that Japanese anime clubs exist at almost every American university can only bolster this impression.

Japan's greatest cultural export is anime, a commonplace that still bears repeating. Since Sakamoto Kyū's "Sukiyaki Song" topped America's Billboard music chart in 1963, the only Japanese works to repeat this feat in their own category are the anime films *Ghost in the Shell* (1995) and *Poketto monsutaa: Myūtsū no gyakushū* (1995, *Pokemon: Mewtwo's Return*).[21] The supposed "insularity" of *otaku* knowledge is a delusion of academics.

But even if the texts created by *otaku* are regarded as childish, it may be a fortunate thing for us. A brilliant work has an aura that tends to stay the hand of anyone who would analyze it, but this is not a problem when we explore the creative process through the *otaku*. Nakai Hisao famously suggested that a line drawn by a patient and a line drawn by a genius are "philosophically equivalent."[22] In fact, the creative activity of *otaku* may reveal creation in its most primitive form, because the distance between desire and creation is so short.

The Development of *Otaku* Expression

There are several historical milestones in the development of *otaku* culture, but here I limit myself to reviewing the most important points. Some might maintain that the origins of *otaku* culture contain all of its later elements, but the development of *otaku* sexuality over time is something I have verified both in writing on *otaku* and through my own encounters with them. Furthermore, tracing the history of *otaku* culture may hold interesting answers to questions about how the "drawn sexuality" of anime developed and how human desire itself arose through the mediation of visual objects.

In my own view, the "big bang" of *otaku* history is the anime director Miyazaki Hayao's experience watching *Hakujaden (Panda and the Magic Serpent)*.[23] Released in 1958, this was Japan's first color theatrical animation and in 1961 became the first Japanese animated film to be shown in the United States. Miyazaki saw it as a teenager and fell in love with its heroine, then went on to become Japan's master of the animated image. But from one perspective, his work has a quality of Freudian "repetition compulsion" that is sad. Possessed as a boy by an anime beauty, Miyazaki is fated to produce one charming heroine of his own after another, and through them to support *otaku* culture. This compulsion that revolves around beautiful young girls (largely absent in Miyazaki's creative partner Takahata Isao, for example) repeats the initial trauma of Miyazaki's early experience. This is clearly a chain of transference: a transference from receiver to transmitter mediated by the icon of the beautiful girl. Miyazaki's inability to escape it is shown by his countertransferent dislike for adult anime fans *(otaku)*, a scorn he makes no effort to disguise.[24]

The almost forty-year history of the *sentō bishōjo* is proof that this big bang is still echoing today. But while there is continuity in this main current, there has been a great deal of change or "evolution" in the areas that branch off from it. For example, it is only since the 1980s that anime clearly intended as pornography has gained an established place in the market.

The most striking of the changes that occurred in the eighties was the homogenization and diffusion of anime style. Mutual influence and intervention among boys' manga, girls' manga, anime, and some illustrated art established anime not only as a genre or medium but as an iconic visual style. There is a need for more concrete research on this, but one of its most interesting aspects is the enormous influence anime style has had on pornographic comics. Intended primarily to satisfy the sexual appetites of young male readers, this genre is still choosing anime as one of its most important styles. Given this, it is possible to see sexuality as one of the single most important forces driving the evolution of anime illustration.

But these changes were prefigured and fostered by the amateur *dōjin-shi* sold at Komike, specifically the pornographic parodies in the over-eighteen genre. Not only did this genre support Komike itself, it also exerted a strong influence on the circulation and style of major commercial works.

Today there is less and less distinction between manga producers and consumers, or amateurs and professionals. Obviously amateur *dōjinshi* artists who succeed at Komike often go on to professional careers, and it is not uncommon for pros to make some of their work available only at Komike. While it would be unusual if a major prose novelist chose to publish new work in an amateur literary magazine, manga artists often do just that, because Komike is recognized as a valid market. Consumption is probably accelerated by Komike's simple pattern of circulation, in which creators have a close relationship with sellers or act as sellers themselves. There are very few restrictions on content, with no limits placed on sexually explicit material or use of copyrighted material, a situation that has promoted freedom of sexual expression. For all these reasons, it is not uncommon for demand trends at Komike to prompt changes in major commercial titles.

And what changes are taking place in artistic expression? For one thing, if we focus on the works that are deliberate expressions of pedophilia, or on genres like *kemono* (which feature attractive young heroines whose bodies are part human and part animal), then we see the development of expressions that have to be called extremely bizarre. One cannot explain these phenomena simply as transference or changes in taste.

Another point is that we are moving away from that idyllic time when a whole genre could be driven forward by subjects whose artistic expression was privileged. In the case of Miyazaki, that privilege is based on his position as a skilled artisan who will always produce a finely crafted product. But in this (as in other areas beyond anime and manga), creation and expression can no longer be founded on the narcissism of the individual author. More and more today, artistic expression consists of an accumulation of techniques like quotation, editing, arrangement, and compromise. I am certainly not lamenting that. In fact, I am impressed by the new possibilities opened up by these changes in artistic activity.

The Space of the Superflat

The background described above must be considered in any discussion of *otaku* creativity. Let me then summarize my argument up to this point. There are three driving forces behind *otaku* evolution: sexuality, the transference from reader to author, and the comic market. *Otaku* desire (the desire to possess through fictionalization) is supported by all three. We must wait for more concrete research on the comic market and author-directed transference. Here I have focused on the connection between creative activity and sexuality.

The final issue I treat in this chapter is the intersubjectivity of sexuality, or the evolutionary changes in expression that have made that intersubjectivity possible. Naturally, the driving force for sexuality is the "actual reality" of sex. In this sense, *otaku* are trying to face the reality of their own sex constructively. But this kind of reality differs from the search for a sexual partner in the actual world.

In my book focusing on the *sentō bishōjo,* I suggested that this behavior was a survival tactic employed by *otaku* to "resist datafication." As the illusory notion that "everything can be turned into data" becomes more and more widespread, how can one protect sexuality from the same fate? The answer is to spin out a limitless number of illusions from the single source of sexuality.

The *sentō bishōjo,* what I have also called the "phallic girl," is a powerful icon that serves as the medium for these illusions. The most effective strategy against the restricting forces of datafication may be to oppose them with the unrestricted possibilities of illusion, that is, narrative. And I am convinced that an important role served by *otaku* culture is to preserve illusion's unbounded character.

For example, the artist Murakami Takashi's *Second Mission Project Ko²* is a set of figures representing not so much a fighting armored cutie as a *fighter* cutie. The three sculpted figures (Figures 11.1–3) depict a bare-breasted *sentō bishōjo* who transforms into a jet fighter mecha. The most significant figure in the series is the second, intermediate stage, where the figure's bizarre modeling hints nicely at the construction of a "superflat" surface formed from *otaku* illusions.

Superflat (*sūpaafuratto*) is a novel spatial concept proposed by Murakami. As elaborated by the critic Azuma Hiroki, it indicates an imaginary space without depth or thickness, where even the eye of the camera does

Figure 11.1. A *sentō bishōjo* transforms from girl into jet fighter mecha in this series of three sculptures by Superflat artist Murakami Takashi. Here, Murakami Takashi, *Second Mission Project Ko^2* (Human Type), 1999; oil, acrylic, synthetic resins, fiberglass, and iron; 275 x 252 x 140 cm. Courtesy of Blum & Poe, Los Angeles. Copyright 1999 Murakami Takashi/Kaikai Kiki Co., Ltd. All rights

Figure 11.2. Murakami Takashi, *Second Mission Project Ko²*
(Ga-Walk Type), 1999; oil, acrylic, synthetic resins, fiberglass,
and iron; 224.4 x 176.9 x 131.5 cm. Courtesy of Blum & Poe,
Los Angeles. Copyright 1999 Murakami Takashi/Kaikai Kiki
Co., Ltd. All rights reserved.

Figure 11.3. Murakami Takashi, *Second Mission Project Ko²*
(Jet Airplane Type), 1999; oil, acrylic, synthetic resins, fiber-
glass, and iron; 55 x 193 x 186 cm. Courtesy of Blum & Poe,
Los Angeles. Copyright 1999 Murakami Takashi/Kaikai Kiki
Co., Ltd. All rights reserved.

not exist.[25] I would suggest that depth and the camera's eye are replaced
by another regulatory system, namely, the layered "contexts" (of plot, of
authorship, of publication and distribution) discussed in the characterization of *otaku* with which this chapter began. But the form in Figure 11.2
is truly stripped of any context: girl and mecha are arranged together *on
the same plane,* producing a figure with its origins located unmistakably in
otaku creativity.

Sexuality always tends toward a structure; sexuality without structure is impossible. It is interesting that even in seemingly structureless
artistic expression by *otaku,* the asymmetry of male and female desire is
maintained. But the boundaries have been violated recently by the aforementioned genre of *shota,* a genre I would like to return to now briefly before concluding. On their surface, *shota* works look like nothing more or
less than pedophilia. One can construct a psychoanalytic formulation of

pedophilic desire in which subjects are imagining themselves in the position of the mother and choosing the object of their love from that position. The choice is narcissistic, and the castration of the mother is denied. This produces desire directed at children, which is also desire directed at their own younger selves. But *otaku* maintain the separation I have been emphasizing between fantasy and everyday reality: the authors and readers of these texts are not pedophiles in their actual lives.

How or why is it that in *shota*, both male desire and female desire are directed at the same object? The key to this riddle lies in the idea of the superflat — an utterly imagined space with no correspondent in the everyday world, a space of perfect fictionality. Because it escapes the regulation of the camera's eye, this space appears structureless, but in fact the control exerted by various contexts supersedes everything else and establishes an order distinct from structure. Anime and manga are what Edward T. Hall called a "high context" environment.[26] The reader and creator share some context, and this is what initially creates sexual intersubjectivity. If studying and understanding those contexts are what sustain that intersubjectivity, creativity involves stripping them away. So in a superflat space separate from the everyday, imagination is directly connected to creation, "being" is the same as "being possessed," and destruction introduces new forms of regulation.

Figure 11.4 shows a 1999 cover from the *dōjinshi Maidroid,* by the artist called Po-ju. It is exceptional among *dōjinshi* for its original story line and the quality of its illustrations, which are on par with commercial manga. The object of desire in this text is no longer a little boy but a servant robot in the shape of a boy. *Maidroid* belongs to a category spun off or evolved from *shota*, a subgenre called *roboshota*. There are in fact enough of these texts to form their own genre — all directed at adult men whose desire is excited by robotic boys. This is a desire so thoroughly fictionalized that one hesitates even to call it perverse *(tōsaku).* Before one turns away from its strangeness, it worth considering the limitlessness of the imaginative power that is fed by *otaku* sexuality.

Maidroid is the emblem of a sexuality that depends only on these contexts to develop, a sexuality deliberately separated from everyday life. If narrative is possible even after the "end of history," that possibility may reside in emblems like these. But in the way they develop, these high-context expressions are impoverished in the syntagmatic axis, even as they show such richness along the paradigmatic one. We see this in anime, where the almost excessive variation in setting and character combines with a tendency toward cookie-cutter story lines and ideas. It is for this reason that a high-context superflat space needs some stimulus from outside itself,

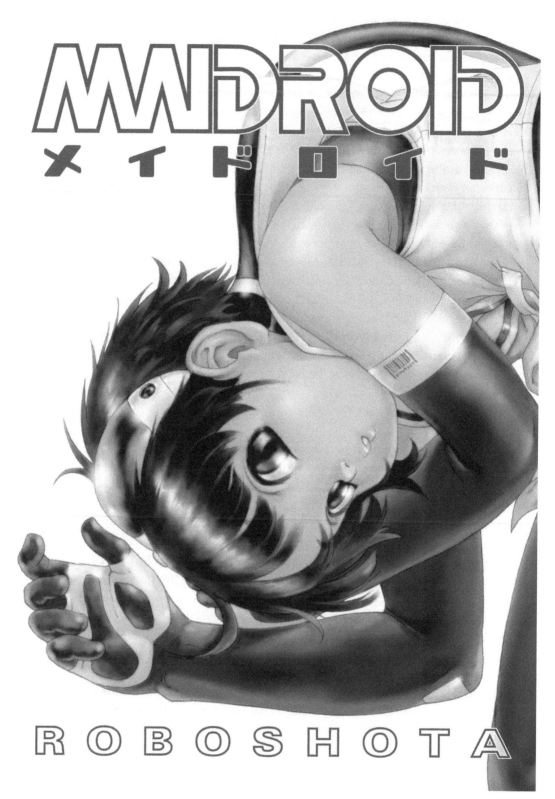

Figure 11.4. Cover illustration from the *roboshota* comic
Maidroid by Po~ju. Copyright Po~Ju. Courtesy of the artist.

to destabilize its internal context. Born at the boundary between modern art and otaku culture, the concept "superflat" itself functions as a point at which to introduce that externality.

If we have a role to play in these processes, it should not be as critics or as opponents of *otaku* culture. We should interact constructively with *otaku*; we should overcome our resistance enough to offer our own interpretations; and we should work from outside to keep stimulating the *otaku* imagination.

Notes

1. Kurimoto Kaoru, *Mayonaka no tenshi* (Midnight angel), 2 vols. (Tokyo: Bungei Shunjū, 1979). Other representative works include Takemiya Keiko, *Kaze to ki no uta* (1977–84, Poetry of wind and trees), 17 vols. (Tokyo: Furawaa Komikkusu, 1977–2000); Hagio Moto, *Tōma no shinzō* (1974, Tōma's heart), 3 vols. (Tokyo: Furawaa Komikkusu, 1975); and Yamagishi Ryōko, *Hi izuru tokoro no tenshi* (1980–86, Prince of the land of the rising sun), vols. 1–9 of *Yamagishi Ryōko zenshū* (Complete works of Yamagishi Ryōko) (Tokyo: Kadokawa Shoten, 1986).

2. Kotani Mari, *Joseijō muishiki* (Techno-gynesis) (Tokyo: Keisō Shobō, 1994).

3. The phrase in Japanese is "josei no shintai o motta dansei dōseiaisha." Sakakibara Shihomi, *Yaoi genron: Yaoi kara mieta mono* (An illusory theory of *yaoi*: What *yaoi* shows) (Tokyo: Natsume Shobō, 1998).

4. Nakajima Azusa, *Komyunikeeshon fuzen shōkōgun* (Incomplete communication syndrome) (Tokyo: Chikuma Bunko, 1995); Nakajima, *Tanatosu no kodomotachi: Kajō tekiō no seitaigaku* (Children of Thanatos: The ecology of hyperconformity) (Tokyo: Chikuma Shobō, 1998); Nakajima, *Bishōnengaku nyūmon* (A bishōnen primer) (Tokyo: Shinshokan, 1984).

5. Joanna Russ, "Pornography by Women for Women, with Love," in *Magic Mommas, Trembling Sisters, Puritans, and Perverts: Feminist Essays* (Trumansburg, N.Y.: Crossing Press, 1985), 79–99.

6. In Japanese, the inserting and receiving roles in *yaoi* sexual relationships are often referred to using the terms *seme* and *uke,* distinct both from the heterosexual roles *dansei* and *josei,* and gay roles like *otokoyaku* or *tachi* and *onnayaku* or *neko.* Nagakubo argues that one thing distinguishing *yaoi* from the gay world is that the sexual organs used in *yaoi* intercourse cannot be characterized as gay or female but seem to be represented very indistinctly, as a kind of "third sexual organ," the "*yaoi* hole." Nagakubo Yōko, *Yaoi shōsetsu ron* (A theory of *yaoi* fiction) (Tokyo: Senshū Daigaku Shuppankyoku, 2005).

7. *DAICON3 Opening Animation* and *DAICON4 Opening Animation,* created by Yamaga Hiroyuki, Anno Hideaki, Akai Takami et al. (1981 and 1983); *Shinseiki evangerion,* dir. Anno Hideaki, TV series, 26 episodes (1995–96); translated as *Neon Genesis Evangelion: Perfect Collection,* 8-DVD box set (ADV Films, 2002).

8. Saitō Tamaki, *Sentō bishōjo no seishin bunseki* (Armored cuties: A psychoanalysis) (Tokyo: Ōta Shuppan, 2000).

9. Saitō Tamaki, *Hakase no kimyō na shishunki* (The doctor's strange adolescence) (Tokyo: Nihon Hyōronsha, 2003).

10. Takahashi's Yōichi soccer manga *Captain Tsubasa* debuted in 1981 and eventually spawned several long-running manga series, an animated TV series,

and multiple films. The supernaturally themed *Yu Yu Hakusho: Ghost Files* has a similarly complex bibliography. For a sample, see Takahashi Yōichi, *Kyaputen Tsubasa* (Captain Tsubasa), bunkobon ed., 21 vols. (Tokyo: Shūeisha Komikku Bunko, 1997–99); *Yū yū hakusho,* TV series (1992–94); translated as *Yu Yu Hakusho: Ghost Files,* 32 DVDs to date (Funimation, 2002–).

11. Here we might also consider the strange eroticism of works by artists said to be virgins or celibate: the poet Ōte Takuji, the fantasy author Miyazawa Kenji, the architect Antoni Gaudí, or the outsider artist Henry Darger. Their work suggests that artistic expressions of sexuality need not always be backed by actual sexual experience.

12. Nobi Nobita, *Sōhyō: Nobi Nobita hihyō zen shigoto* (Complete critical works of Nobi Nobita), self-published *dōjinshi,* 1999; Nobi, "Otona wa wakatte kurenai," in *Otona wa wakatte kurenai: Nobi Nobita hihyō shūsei* (Adults just don't get it: The criticism of Nobi Nobita) (Tokyo: Nihon Hyōronsha, 2003); R. D. Laing, *The Divided Self* (New York: Pantheon, 1969). Anno Hideaki's two *Evangelion* films are *Shin seiki evangelion: Death and Rebirth* (1997); translated as *Neon Genesis Evangelion: Death and Rebirth,* DVD (Manga Video, 2002) and *Shin seiki evangelion: Air/ Magokoro, kimi ni* (1997); translated as *The End of Evangelion,* DVD (Manga Video, 2002). For more on *Evangelion,* see chapters 6 and 9 in this volume.

13. Saitō Tamaki and Nobi Nobita, in Nobi, *Otona wa wakatte kurenai,* 277–303.

14. [Here Saitō uses the verbs *semeru* (aggress) and *ukeru* (receive). While he refers here primarily to the physical roles of the inserting and receiving partner in the physical sex act, his usage resonates with a larger meaning these terms have taken on in *yaoi* fan culture and criticism, a meaning linked to broader gender roles. Although this division often corresponds to traditional gender divisions like male and female, sadistic and masochistic, or active and passive, the translation preserves some distinction (and the right these terms reserve to redefine traditional roles) by using the Japanese critical terms *seme* and *uke.* For more information, see Kotani Mari's discussion of sex roles in her introduction to this chapter. — Trans.]

15. Nakajima, *Tanatosu no kodomotachi.* Nakajima is also a science fiction and fantasy author under the name Kurimoto Kaoru. Kotani Mari discusses Kurimoto's fiction in chapter 3.

16. Yoshida Mayumi, "Inosento e no dasshutsu" (Escape to innocence), afterword to vol. 10 of *Banana Fish,* by Yoshida Akimi, bunkobon ed. (Tokyo: Shōgakukan, 1997), 297; Hashimoto Osamu, *Bokura no sekkusu* (Our sex) (Tokyo: Shūeisha, 1993).

17. The description and theorization of *shota* that follows draws partly on Watanabe Yumiko, "Otaku sekushuaritii (*Otaku* sexuality)," in *Kokusai otaku daigaku: 1998 nen saizensen kara no kenkyū hōkoku* (International otaku university: A report on the latest research, 1998), ed. Okada Toshio (Tokyo: Kōbunsha, 1998).

18. For example, see the 1965 *Tetsujin 28 gō* television series, based in turn on the 1950s manga. *Tetsujin 28 gō,* TV series (1963); translated as *Gigantor,* 2 8-DVD box sets (Wea, 2002–3).

19. Saitō Tamaki, *Bunmyakubyō: Rakan, Beitoson, Maturaana* (Context disease: Lacan, Bateson, Maturana) (Tokyo: Sedosha, 2001).

20. Michael Balint, "The Three Areas of the Mind: Theoretical Considerations," *International Journal of Psychoanalysis* 39, no. 5 (1958): 328–40.

21. *Kōkaku kidōtai: Ghost in the Shell,* dir. Oshii Mamoru (1995); translated as *Ghost in the Shell,* DVD (Manga Video, 1998); *Poketto monsutaa: Myūtsū no gyakushū,* dir. Yuyama Kunihiko (1997); translated as *Pokemon: Mewtwo Returns,* DVD (Warner, 2001).

22. Nakai Hisao, "Seishin bunretsubyōsha no seishin ryōhō ni okeru byōga no shiyō" (Psychopathology of schizophrenics as revealed by various drawing techniques invented for psychotherapy), in vol. 1 of *Nakai Hisao chōsakushū* (The writings of Nakai Hisao) (Tokyo: Iwasaki Gakujutsu Shuppansha, 1984).

23. *Hakujaden* (Legend of the white snake), dir. Yabushita Taiji (1958); translated as *Panda and the Magic Serpent,* DVD (Digiview, 2004).

24. Miyazaki Hayao, *Shuppatsuten 1977–1996* (Starting points 1977–1996) (Tokyo: Tokuma Shoten, 1996), 364, 395.

25. Azuma Hiroki, "Sonzaironteki, hōkokuteki, sūpaafurattoteki" (Existentially, advertisingly, superflatly), *Hōkoku* (January–February 2000). [In English see Azuma's "Super Flat Speculation," in *Super Flat,* ed. Murakami Takeshi (Tokyo: Madra, 2000), 138–51. – Trans.]

26. Edward T. Hall, *Beyond Culture* (Garden City, N.Y.: Anchor, 1976).

Otaku Sexuality

Afterword. A Very Soft Time Machine
From Translation to Transfiguration

Takayuki Tatsumi

The first science fiction writer I met in my life wrote under the name Bien Fu. This was Princess Asaka Fukuko, a member of the Japanese imperial family who published numerous fantasy and science fiction stories throughout the late 1960s. Her work appeared in Japan's inaugural fanzine, Shibano Takumi's *Uchūjin* (Cosmic dust), and she also produced comic strips for a variety of fanzines and semi-prozines.

One beautiful afternoon in Tokyo in the autumn of 1969, Bien Fu, who was then in her late twenties, invited some junior high school students — that is, my classmate and me — to her huge and gorgeous art deco–style residence in Tokyo's Meguro ward, which would be renovated in 1983 as the Tokyo Metropolitan Teien Art Museum. In her ultrachic living room she chatted with us about science fiction and fandom, giving us a sense of what Japanese science fiction writers were like. We were impressed by her deep fascination with cyborgs and Native Americans: among the writings of Bien Fu that attracted us were such stories as "Apukorimitto monogatari" (1969, Apcolimit romance), a psychological cyborg narrative, and the historical romance "Chōja gensōfu" (1968, An Aztec fantasy).[1] At the time, I didn't think she was serious when she told us, "If you are interested in those who want to become cyborgs, I'd be very happy to tell you my own case history." Young, immature, and ignorant, we were puzzled by what she was saying then.

After thirty years, however, I cannot help but consider my close encounter with Bien Fu as highly symbolic. In the very era when the leftist student movement of the sixties was increasingly defining the "imperial" as peripheral, Bien Fu seriously and constructively committed herself to science fiction. Deeply identifying herself with the vanishing Native Americans, she tried to reconstruct herself as a cyborg. This was her own form of resistance. By reconstituting herself in fantasy and science fiction, she in effect became a protocyborg feminist, anticipating Donna Haraway's theory by fifteen years. For Haraway, the cyborg as human–machine interface shares much with the multicultural creole produced by postcolonial heteroglossia. Bien Fu, a granddaughter of Prince Asaka, published in fanzines rather than in Hayakawa's *SF Magajin (SF Magazine)*, the first and then the only popular magazine of the genre. But she was prescient in regarding the writing of science fiction as a way to carry out her own revolution in an age of counterculture.

When I became interested in the cyberpunk movement during the mid-1980s and cotranslated with Kotani Mari the theoretical essays of Haraway, Samuel Delany, and Jessica Amanda Salmonson for *Cyborg Feminism* (1991), I experienced a kind of déjà vu.[2] Cyberpunk writers depict outlaw cyborgs running wild in techno-Japanesque landscapes. But their sympathy with neuromantic antiheroes reminded me of Bien Fu's extreme identification with romantic cyborgs and mythopoeic Native Americans. Japanese culture inspired anglophone cyberpunk writers, but the transaction was not a one-way street. For cyberpunk fiction provided the Japanese with a chance to reinvestigate their own cyborgian identity.

Who Made Science Fiction Invisible?

The heyday of the cyborg and the whole cyberpunk movement in the 1980s, sometimes nicknamed the "Pax Japonica," promoted interest in Japanese science fiction as well as Japanese culture. For the first time, Japanese science fiction was translated into English in such anthologies as *The Best Japanese Science Fiction Stories* (1989) and *Monkey Brain Sushi* (1991), and also in a special "New Japanese Fiction" issue of *Review of Contemporary Fiction* (2002).[3] Although few science fiction novels have been translated, the selection of short stories in translation suggests what Japanese science fiction was, is, and will be. While Japan has always been the empire of excessive importation, the country has begun transforming itself into a republic of reasonable exportation. This paradox in itself suggests the differences between the Japanese backdrop of so much English cyberpunk fiction and Japanese cyborg narratives themselves.

But Japanese science fiction has a history before and beyond the moment when William Gibson and other cyberpunk authors discovered Japan. Let me illustrate the earlier heritage of Japanese science fiction with Hirai Kazumasa's short story called "Hoshi Shin'ichi no naiteki uchū" (1970, Hoshi Shin'ichi's inner space). Hirai is well known for his mythopoeic multimedia novel *Genma taisen* (1967–2005, Armageddon: The great battle with genma), but he has also produced some very intricate short stories. Written in the heyday of New Wave science fiction, this masterpiece "Hoshi Shin'ichi no naiteki uchū" offers the mind-boggling presupposition that the whole heritage of Japanese science fiction literature was simply created within the inner space of Shin'ichi Hoshi, a founding father of Japanese science fiction and the king of the "short short story."

Alone in the president's office of Hoshi Pharmaceuticals (established by his father, passed on to Hoshi in the early 1950s, and now afflicted with financial difficulties), Hoshi tries to escape from reality by creating the imaginary world of Japanese science fiction. To fill a psychological gap, he creates the first SF fanzine *Uchūjin* along with *SF Magajin,* and even fellow writers like Komatsu Sakyō. Hirai vividly describes how the first generation of Japanese science fiction writers gathers at the Hotel New Ōtani in Akasaka with Hoshi as their central figure. Every time Komatsu visits Tokyo from Osaka, these writers are invited to a suite in the hotel, where they all enjoy eating, drinking, mah-jongg, and black humor. Hirai radically reconsiders the happy life of first-generation writers to be an effect of Hoshi's speculative fantasy. And the reason is very simple. Insofar as early Japanese science fiction is concerned, no one ever criticizes Hoshi's short short stories: everyone applauds his art of fiction. Indeed, first-generation Japanese science fiction writers made their debuts believing in this new form of literature: Hoshi wanted to make science fiction a literary instrument for satirizing bureaucratic society. Hirai is part of a new generation, with a new perspective on the old. He was a pioneer in bridging the gap between print and visual media, for example, writing the scripts for the cyborg anime *8 man (Tobor the Eighth Man)* in the 1960s.[4]

Hirai's metafictional dream about (a dream about) Japanese science fiction recalls the dreaming fetus of *Dogura magura,* discussed in chapter 1. It also predicts a new generation of Japanese science fiction, ushered in five years later by an equally radical gesture from Tsutsui Yasutaka. Along with Hoshi and Komatsu, Tsutsui helped forge the conventions of Japanese science fiction in its first generation. But in a 1975 essay titled "Gendai SF no tokushitsu to wa" ("Contemporary SF's defining feature"), he deconstructed the distinction between science fiction and metafiction *(chōkyōkō),* writing that science fiction was part of the tradition of avant-garde metafiction that exposed the novel's inner workings. In fact, if it was not to be

Takayuki Tatsumi

252

subsumed by the avant-garde, science fiction must "circle around behind" the avant-garde and expose its inner workings as well: "If the target is double layered," Tsutsui wrote, "metafictional science fiction must be triple-layered."[5]

Tsutsui followed this up with a series of works that questioned the genre of science fiction from the inside out and prefigured the emergence of the Japanese slipstream in the 1990s. That was when mainstream literary writers such as Murakami Haruki, Murakami Ryū, Shimada Masahiko, Hisama Jūgi, Shōno Yoriko, and Matsuura Rieko all began to incorporate science fiction and magical-realistic elements into their slipstream writings. The Nobel Prize winner Ōe Kenzaburō published in the early 1990s the science fictional diptych *Chiryōtō* (1990, The healing tower) and *Chiryōtō wakusei* (1991, Planet of the healing tower), which clearly was inspired by Arthur C. Clarke, Stanislaw Lem, and Arkady Strugatsky and Boris Strugatsky, and which deconstructed the boundary between serious and popular fiction.[6] During the 1990s, even mainstream writers found it necessary to revitalize their novels through science-fictional devices. And we have already seen the influence of science fiction on anime in this period. During this decade in which Japanese science fiction permeated other genres, media, and cultures, it paradoxically became almost invisible itself. For the more universal science fiction becomes, the less potent seems its own proper genre.

This irony requires us to meditate upon the future of Japanese science fiction in a globalist age. What will happen to traditional print science fiction? What kind of role will the science fiction translator play? Where can we find the multicultural potentiality of science fiction?

Leaving the Empire of Translation

At this point, let me take up for consideration Aramaki Yoshio's famous story "Yawarakai tokei" ("Soft Clocks"), originally published in the April 1968 issue of *Uchūjin* and later revised for the February 1972 issue of *SF Magajin*. I began to read science fiction during the late 1960s, when the New Wave had begun to have a tremendous impact on Japanese science fiction writers, critics, and especially translators. Accordingly, while Komatsu, who made his professional debut in 1962, compares with Clarke, Isaac Asimov, and Robert A. Heinlein, one of the latecomers of the same generation, Aramaki, who first published fiction and criticism in 1970, served as the Japanese equivalent of Philip K. Dick, J. G. Ballard, and Barrington Bayley. While Komatsu, who majored in Italian literature at Kyoto University, showed us science fiction as a new frontier of literature per se, a genre that could clarify the literal frontiers that postwar Japan should explore,

Aramaki, who studied psychology at Waseda University, made a quantum leap into inner space. Deeply influenced by Tsutsui's hyperfiction and metafiction, Aramaki hoped that an emphasis on surreal imagination could reinvigorate even mainstream fiction. In 1969 and 1970, he engaged in a heated controversy with Yamano Kōichi, the young writer-editor of the first commercial science fiction quarterly, *NW-SF* (1970–82). Yamano actually shared the New Wave–oriented perspective of Aramaki, but he could not resist attacking Japanese science fiction writers as mere imitators in a famous essay, "Nihon SF no genten to shikō" (1969, "Japanese SF, its originality and orientation"). Admired by Abe Kōbō and Mishima Yukio, Yamano's essay elicited a number of responses, among which Aramaki's defense of Japanese science fiction stands out most brilliantly. This controversy over the nature of science fiction and prescriptions for its future status had such a strong influence on me that I developed a habit of reading science fiction narratives and science fiction criticism simultaneously.[7]

In 1986 the science fiction writer Lewis Shiner asked me at Armadillo-Con in Austin, Texas, whether I was interested in cotranslating some Japanese science fiction; I immediately thought of Aramaki's "Soft Clocks," the short story that had sparked controversy over the nature of science fiction. Shiner's idea offered me a rare chance to export something to the English-speaking world from the empire of excessive importation. A Japanese New Wave masterpiece, "Soft Clocks" was first roughly translated by my Cornell friend Ms. Kazuko Behrens, then polished by Shiner himself; it was published in *Interzone* in the January–February 1989 issue.[8]

The plot is simple. The story is set on Mars in the near future, where everyone is infected with Martian Disease, a form of low-grade encephalitis. The disease afflicts "Dali of Mars," a surrealist, paranoid millionaire and technophobe whose estate covers "an area of the Lunae Planum about the size of Texas" and who is about to hold in his garden a literally surrealistic party whose theme is "Blackout in Daylight." Modeled on Salvador Dali's famous 1931 painting "The Persistence of Memory," this surrealistic garden is soft and edible, thanks to what is nicknamed "Flabby Engineering." This postnanotech reality is superbly represented by a "soft clock" the size of a dessert plate. If you set it on the edge of the desk, the clock's rim will bend and droop toward the floor. This vivid image drawn from surrealist painting is reminiscent of Ballard's telepathic architecture in "The Thousand Dreams of Stellavista" (1962) and anticipates Gibson's description of the soft clock in Julius Deane's office in the first chapter of *Neuromancer* (1984): "A Dali clock hung on the wall between the bookcases, its distorted face sagging to the bare concrete floor."[9] Aramaki's narrator is a marriage counselor trained in psychiatry who has come from Tokyo at the request of Dali of Mars, who wants him to administer psychological tests to the suitors of his granddaughter Vivi. As the story opens, the two top candidates for Vivi's hand are Mr. Pinkerton, a self-proclaimed artistic descendant of Salvador Dali, and Professor Isherwood, a rheologist (i.e., specialist in the flow of matter) promoting Flabby Engineering.

What complicates the story most is that Vivi is a cyborg who does not know this secret of her body. More than three years earlier, before Vivi began studying art at college, the plane bringing this eighteen-year-old girl from Mars to Tokyo crashed, and only the replacement of her heart, lungs, and stomach with artificial constructs kept her alive. "Knowing the technophobic background, the surgeons had kept the information from her. But her subconscious had evidently at least suspected the truth."[10] This is why Vivi shows the symptoms of anorexia. The narrator, who has fallen in love with her, encourages her to eat a soft clock. Mechanical but edible, the clock should, on consumption, at once cure her of anorexia and technophobia. Dali of Mars has eaten a soft clock and become an imperialist glutton before whom lie worlds not only to conquer but devour. But his granddaughter Vivi obstinately refuses to eat, feeling that the very act of eating is shameful. The narrator describes the battle between grandfather and granddaughter: Dali of Mars devours, while Vivi cannot stop vomiting. Refusal is how the granddaughter triumphs over her grandfather.

Toward the Soft Core of Global Science Fiction

Readers of Sharalyn Orbaugh's "Sex and the Single Cyborg" in this volume will see that her analysis of national identity, permeability, and cyborg gender in anime suggests some provocative approaches to Aramaki's story. Aramaki, who was born in 1933 and came of age in Occupied Japan, could not have completed this seemingly surrealistic fiction without overcoming his own conflict between an imperialist grandfather and himself as a cyborgian grandchild. This opposition is also emphasized in Hirano Kyōko's award-winning study *Mr. Smith Goes to Tokyo: Japanese Cinema under the American Occupation, 1945–1952*, in which the author traces postwar American censorship as organized by the occupation government's Civil Information and Education Section. They repressed the slightest allusion to the emperor, instead promoting the amorous expression of kissing, which until then the Japanese audience had not been familiar with. Hirano concludes:

> The work of filmmakers born during the early to mid-1950s, such as [Morita Yoshimitsu] and [Ishii Sōgo], is not so overtly political. . . . This new generation grew up during the "economic miracle" and takes for granted the freedoms and material comforts for which previous generations had

struggled. . . . Their wholesale adoption of foreign customs and values, radical though it may seem, is yet another example of the same phenomenon that helped the film industry survive the transition to the occupation period, albeit in changed form: the peculiarly Japanese *adaptability* to things new when confronted by a foreign culture.[11]

To sum up, what with the imperative of American democratization and the effect of indigenous adaptability, the postwar Japanese had simultaneously to transform and naturalize themselves as a new tribe of cyborgs.

This context explains why the female science fiction writer Bien Fu hoped to promote her own revolution within the imperial family by writing of cyborgs during the late 1960s. Likewise, the leftist Aramaki projected his obsession with prewar Japanese imperialism onto the imperialist glutton Dali of Mars, envisioning in the portrait of Vivi the cyborgian subjectivity of postwar Japanese made possible by implanting (as in *Blade Runner*) a fake memory of American democracy within a postimperialistic Japanese body-politic. The dynamic between digesting and vomiting acutely symbolizes the dynamic contradiction between prewar imperialism and postwar democracy. As Marilyn Ivy points out, Japanese subjectivity from the beginning has been constructed as cyborgian and creolean: "Although the emperor may be seen as the very epitome of the Japanese 'thing' in that he appears to embody the unbroken transmission of Japanese culture, there is much evidence to show that the line of emperors originated in Korea — Japan's colonized, denigrated national other — and various features of emperorship as an institution lead back to China."[12]

It is remarkable that the late 1980s saw the soft translation, that is, post-cyberpunkish stylization, of "Soft Clocks." Taking a glance at the roughly translated version of the story, Shiner, though admiring this work as "a very, very fine story," decided to reorganize the narrative with three points in mind that were spelled out in a letter of February 5, 1987: theoretical background ("Some things were explained in too much detail"), visual imagination ("The story has very little visual detail"), and character's motivations, which he found "at times . . . hard to understand." Shiner not only translated and stylized but also revised and edited the text of "Soft Clocks." In the last paragraph, Aramaki closes with the following sentence: "If a child is born, we plan to go to Mars again to show Dali of Mars his first great-grandchild." Concluding that Vivi's final victory over her grandfather should have closed with the death of the latter, Shiner replaced the original ending with "Someday, perhaps, we will have children, and one day we may take them to Mars to see the statue of their great-grandfather. But for the moment, we are in no hurry."[13] The author Aramaki completely agreed with Shiner on this revision, as do I, though to tell the truth, I was unfamiliar with the conventions of American creative writing, so at first I was amazed. However, collaboration with him gradually led me to find his translation not simply a plain Americanization of the Japanese short story but a creative dialogue over two decades and two cultures.

In retrospect, the act of translation in a larger sense has always required at once the digestion and vomiting of foreign culture. During the heyday of deconstructive criticism, Paul de Man gave a lecture titled "Conclusions: Walter Benjamin's 'The Task of the Translator,'" which redefines translation not as a recuperation of the lost fundamental unity of language but as a still broken part even after a totality of fragments is brought together. For de Man, translation is not metaphoric but metonymic; for him metaphor is symbolic and totalitarian, whereas metonymy is not. Thus he vividly describes the true image of translation: "We have a metonymic, a successive pattern, in which things follow, rather than a metaphorical unifying pattern in which things become one by resemblance. They do not match each other, they follow each other."[14] This attack on the metaphor's totalitarian nature, which I believe must be read in the context of de Man's shameful involvement with wartime anti-Semitic journalism, sees translation as the fragment of a fragment: the vessel keeps breaking and never reconstitutes itself. At any rate, Aramaki's emphasis on gluttony and anorexia could also be read in de Man's terms as an allegory of translation in the age of postcolonialism. For, as Homi Bhabha has pointed out, any total or "metaphoric" digestion of one culture is essentially impossible; we cannot imitate but only cannibalize or travesty the "other" through the principle of mimicry, omitting or rejecting any puzzling or unpalatable ingredients.[15]

Coming of age in the postwar empire of translation, Aramaki came to synthesize or "digest" surrealism and existentialism as well as Golden Age Anglo-American science fiction; like his heroine Vivi, however, he simultaneously vomited and rejected them as well. This graphic image from physiology also sheds light on the making of culture itself. One culture cannot exist without negotiation between cultures, which requires one people to assimilate or reject (digest or vomit) the culture of the other, ending up with creation of a new culture through mimicry, in Bhabha's term, or through what I designate as "soft translation," completed in soft time and announced by soft clocks.

Aramaki's philosophy of softness is also explored in "The War in the Ponrappe Islands" (1988), a short story reprinted in Shiner's antiwar anthology *When the Music's Over* (1991).[16] The story's pacifist vision inspired Aramaki's "Deep Blue Fleet" series in the 1990s (a later installment in the long line of Pacific texts that Thomas Schnellbächer examines in chapter 2). Aramaki calls them virtual-reality war novels, and they have sold in the millions. In this series, Admiral Yamamoto, the real-life naval commander who planned the 1941 attack on Pearl Harbor, is reincarnated in a parallel world and, looking back on his past life, decides that ultranationalism prevented Japan from managing the war rationally; he prefers healing to winning, giving priority to global peace over national security. The popularity of this type of alternate history during the mid-nineties was probably stimulated by the Gulf war. On March 4, 1995, the *New York Times* featured Aramaki in the sensationally titled "Japanese Novelists Rewrite the War — and Win." Aramaki told the interviewer that "my books stirred interest among young people in World War II, a subject not taught well in schools. This is separate from reality. These are fictions."[17]

Now it is safe to say that while Aramaki digested and cannibalized space-oriented 1950s U.S. science fiction as a Japanese New Wave writer, the American cyberpunk writer Shiner in his turn digested "Soft Clocks," brilliantly reinventing it in English a generation later. Another creative negotiation or form of soft translation invited Aramaki in the 1990s to rewrite (and soften) Pan-Pacific history.

Soft translation was also employed later by Stephen Baxter, who helped translate "Sobakasu no Figyua" (1992, "Freckled Figure"). Written by the award-winning Japanese woman writer Suga Hiroe, it was published in *Interzone* and reprinted in David Hartwell's *Year's Best SF 5 in 2000*.[18] This translated short story has attracted a wide audience, presumably because its description of science fiction fans who construct high-tech action figures coincides with a worldwide interest in one aspect of Japanese *otaku* culture — anime, manga, and action figures modeled after the famous heroines of comics. In this sense, the English version of "Freckled Figure" could also be considered as another type of soft translation between print media and multimedia, including merchandise and media-spanning franchises.

It is true that the more hypercapitalistic society becomes, the softer the act of translation and the less trace of the original. I have little doubt, however, that soft translation will continue to explore and promote the soft power of global science fiction. So let's ride this very slow time machine, and enjoy the fantastic voyage!

Notes

1. Bien Fu, "Apukorimitto monogatari" (Apcolimit romance), *Uchūjin*, January 1969; Bien Fu, "Chōja gensōfu" (An Aztec fantasy), *Uchūjin*, June 1968, reprinted in *"Uchūjin" kessaku sen* (Selected works from the fanzine *Cosmic dust*), ed. Shibano Takumi, vol. 2 (Tokyo: Kōdansha, 1977).

2. Tatsumi Takayuki, ed., *Saibōgu feminizumu* (Cyborg feminism: Donna Haraway, Samuel Delany, Jessica Amanda Salmonson), trans. Tatsumi Takayuki and Kotani Mari (Tokyo: Suiseisha, 2001).

3. John L. Apostolou and Martin H. Greenberg, eds., *The Best Japanese Science Fiction Stories* (New York: Dembner, 1989); Alfred Birnbaum, ed., *Monkey Brain Sushi: New Tastes in Japanese Fiction* (Tokyo: Kodansha International, 1991); "New Japanese Fiction," *Review of Contemporary Fiction* 22, no. 2 (2002).

4. Hirai Kazumasa, "Hoshi Shin'ichi no naiteki uchū" ("Hoshi Shin'ichi's inner space"), *SF Magajin*, May 1970; Hirai Kazumasa, script, *8 man*, TV series, 1963–64, partially translated as *Tobor the Eighth Man*, 4 dubbed VHS tapes (New York: Central Park Media, 1993–96).

5. Tsutsui Yasutaka, "Gendai SF no tokushitsu to wa" ("Contemporary SF's defining feature"), in *Nihon SF ronsōshi* (Science fiction controversies in Japan: 1957–1997), ed. Tatsumi Takayuki (Tokyo: Keisō Shobō, 2000), 251. This volume reprints a number of the twentieth-century critical debates that shaped Japanese science fiction.

6. Ōe Kenzaburō, *Chiryōtō* (The healing tower) (Tokyo: Iwanami, 1990); and Ōe, *Chiryōtō wakusei* (Planet of the healing tower) (Tokyo: Iwanami, 1991).

7. Yamano Kōichi, "Japanese SF: Its Originality and Orientation," trans. Kazuko Behrens, ed. Darko Suvin and Takayuki Tatsumi, *Science Fiction Studies* 21, no. 1 (1994): 67–80. The original Japanese essay and Aramaki's reply both appear in *Nihon SF ronsōshi*, cited in note 5.

8. Aramaki Yoshio, "Yawarakai tokei," *Uchūjin*, April 1968; reprinted in *SF Magajin*, February 1972, and in *Yawarakai tokei* (Tokyo: Tokuma, 1981); translated and revised by Kazuko Behrens and Lewis Shiner as "Soft Clocks," *Interzone* 27 (January–February 1989): 46–53, reprinted in *Review of Contemporary Fiction* 22, no. 2 (2002): 36–52.

9. J. G. Ballard, "The Thousand Dreams of Stellavista," in *Vermillion Sands* (New York: Berkley, 1971); William Gibson, *Neuromancer* (New York: Ace, 1984), 11; I discuss *Neuromancer*'s Japanese reception in my essay "Japanese Reflections of Mirrorshades," in *Storming the Reality Studio*, ed. Larry McCaffery (Durham, N.C.: Duke University Press, 1991), 366–73.

10. Aramaki, "Soft Clocks," 48.

11. Hirano Kyōko, *Mr. Smith Goes to Tokyo: Japanese Cinema under the American Occupation, 1945–1952* (Washington, D.C.: Smithsonian, 1992), 263. The italics are mine.

12. Marilyn Ivy, *Discourses of the Vanishing: Modernity/Phantasm/Japan* (New York: Columbia University Press, 1995), 24.

13. Aramaki, "Yawarakai tokei," page 212 in the Tokuma edition, page 53 in the *Interzone* translation.

14. Paul de Man, "Conclusions: Walter Benjamin's 'The Task of the Translator,'" in *Resistance to Theory* (Minneapolis: University of Minnesota Press, 1986), 90–91.

15. Homi K. Bhabha, *The Location of Culture* (London: Routledge, 1994).

16. Aramaki Yoshio, "War in the Ponrappe Islands," trans. Kazuko Behrens, in *When the Music's Over*, ed. Lewis Shiner (New York: Bantam, 1991), 257–68.

17. Andrew Pollack, "Japanese Novelists Rewrite the War — and Win," *New York Times*, March 4, 1995.

18. Suga Hiroe, "Sobakasu no Figyua," in *Ame no Ori* (Rain cage) (Tokyo: Hayakawa Shobō, 1993); translated by Dana Lewis and Stephen Baxter as "Freckled Figure," *Interzone*, March 1999; reprinted in *Year's Best SF 5*, ed. David G. Hartwell (New York: Eos, 2000), 433–56. The English version was also reprinted in a special "Suga Hiroe" issue of *SF Magajin* in September 2000.

PUBLICATION HISTORY

Chapters 1, 2, 3, 6, 7, 9, and the Afterword were originally published in *Science Fiction Studies* 29, no. 3 (2002).

Chapter 4 is a translation and expansion of "Hamlet to shite no SF: SF to tetsugaku," first published in *SF nyūmon* (Introducing Japanese science fiction), ed. Nihon SF Sakka Kurabu (SFWJ) (Tokyo: Hayakawa Shobō, 2001), 44–47.

Chapter 10 was originally published in *Science Fiction Studies* 31, no. 1 (2004): 97–121.

Chapter 11 is a translation and expansion of "'Otaku' no sekushuaritii" (Otaku sexuality), in *Hakase no kimyō na shishunki*, by Saitō Tamaki (The doctor's strange adolescence) (Tokyo: Nihon Hyōronsha, 2003), chapter 2, 17–56.

CONTRIBUTORS

Christopher Bolton teaches Japanese literature and comparative literature at Williams College.

Hiroko Chiba is associate professor of modern languages at DePauw University.

Naoki Chiba received a PhD in anthropology from the University of Illinois, Urbana–Champaign.

Istvan Csicsery-Ronay Jr. is professor of English and world literature at DePauw University.

William O. Gardner is assistant professor of Japanese language, literature, and culture at Swarthmore College and the author of *Advertising Tower: Japanese Modernism and Modernity in the 1920s.*

Azuma Hiroki is a visiting professor at the Tokyo Institute of Technology Global Communications at the International University of Japan and the author of eight books, including *Sonzaironteki, yūbinteki: Jacques Derrida ni tsuite.*

Kotani Mari is a science fiction and fantasy critic and chair of the Women Writers Committee of the Japan PEN Club. She is the author of

Techno-Gynesis: The Political Unconscious of Feminist Science Fiction and *Evangelion as the Immaculate Virgin.*

Livia Monnet is professor of comparative literature and media studies at the University of Montreal. She is the author of *Critical Readings in Modern Japanese Thought* and the translator of Ishimure Michiko's *Paradise in the Sea of Sorrow: Our Minamata Disease.*

Miri Nakamura is assistant professor of Japanese at Wesleyan University.

Susan J. Napier is professor of Japanese studies at Tufts University and the author of *Escape from the Wasteland: Romanticism and Realism in the Works of Mishima Yukio, Anime from Akira to Howl's Moving Castle: Experiencing Contemporary Japanese Animation,* and *From Impressionism to Anime: Japan as Fantasy and Fan Cult in the Western Imagination.*

Sharalyn Orbaugh teaches Asian studies and women's studies at the University of British Columbia.

Saitō Tamaki works at Sōfukai Sasaki Hospital near Tokyo.

Thomas Schnellbächer teaches modern Japanese literature at Freie Universität Berlin.

Takayuki Tatsumi is professor of English at Keio University in Tokyo and the author of *Full Metal Apache: Transactions between Cyberpunk Japan and Avant Pop America.*

INDEX

Lightning Source UK Ltd.
Milton Keynes UK
UKHW051238270521
384474UK00005B/107